Celtic Myth
and Religion

Celtic Myth and Religion

*A Study of Traditional Belief,
with Newly Translated Prayers,
Poems and Songs*

Sharon Paice MacLeod

McFarland & Company, Inc., Publishers
Jefferson, North Carolina, and London

LIBRARY OF CONGRESS CATALOGUING-IN-PUBLICATION DATA

MacLeod, Sharon Paice, 1960–
Celtic myth and religion : a study of traditional belief, with newly
translated prayers, poems and songs / Sharon Paice MacLeod.
p.   cm.
Includes bibliographical references and index.

ISBN 978-0-7864-6476-0
softcover : 50# alkaline paper ∞

1. Mythology Celtic.   2. Celts — Religion.   3. Religious literature —
Celtic authors — Translations into English.   I. Title.

BL900.M447   2012   299'.16 — dc23   2011033640

BRITISH LIBRARY CATALOGUING DATA ARE AVAILABLE

Front cover: *Celtic Goddess*, 5' × 2½', acrylic on canvas with inserts,
Cynthia von Buhler (www.cynthiavonbuhler.com), commissioned by the
University of St. Michael's College, University of Toronto;
background © 2012 Shutterstock.

Manufactured in the United States of America

*McFarland & Company, Inc., Publishers
Box 611, Jefferson, North Carolina 28640
www.mcfarlandpub.com*

To my ancestors
from Canada, Scotland, Ireland and Wales,
who taught me the power of words,
the joy of song, the inspiration of knowing
where we have come from, and the importance
of knowing where we belong

Table of Contents

Preface

Cha bhi fios air math an tobair gus an tràigh e. (Scottish Gaelic proverb)
Ni wyddys eisiau'r ffynnon onid el yn hesp. (Welsh proverb)
The worth of the well is not known until it dries up.

This book is intended to provide a solid introduction and detailed exploration of many aspects of the indigenous religious traditions of the Celtic-speaking peoples, from the first millennium B.C.E. to the early modern era. Celtic religion is often relegated to the status of "primitive" or "superstitious" pre–Christian belief (along with many other early or indigenous religions). The entire tradition is often handled in a single chapter in books dealing with Celtic history, literature or archaeology, the authors of which are specialists in aspects of Celtic culture (but not necessarily in religion, mythology or folklore). This work is unique in its focus on Celtic religion, mythology, learned traditions, wisdom texts and folklore, and in its comprehensive treatment of many aspects of these traditions.

The ancient Celts inhabited a territory comparable to that of the Roman Empire, and it is their cultural traditions (rather than those of the Classical world) which are now understood as having formed a significant part of the foundations of European culture. The study of Celtic culture and religion is significant in understanding the development of early, medieval and modern Europe and its subsequent influence throughout the world. Additionally, it is extremely important to understand and preserve native wisdom and indigenous religious systems, wherever they are found, for their own beauty and integrity, and for the knowledge they contain. Without careful and respectful understanding and stewardship, many of these traditions are in danger of decline or disappearance.

My study of Celtic culture and religion began over twenty years ago, as I explored my cultural heritage from Scotland, Ireland and Wales. My grandmother, a Highland dancer, was born in Aberdeen, and her father was an artist from Dundee. These family traditions were highly influential during my upbringing in Canada. My maternal great-grandmother was a MacLeod and spoke Gaelic into the twentieth century. I found myself drawn to learn Scottish Gaelic songs, and eventually became involved in Celtic studies.

This book was compiled primarily from teaching materials and academic research undertaken in the last fifteen years. It treats a number of important, foundational aspects of Celtic religious belief, including sacred sites and ritual practices, polytheism in early Ireland and Britain, sacred space and time, and the philosophy and training of druids, poets

1

and other religious practitioners. It also provides information about cosmology and the Celtic Otherworld, sacred plants and animals (including the *ogam* alphabet), ancestral beliefs, wisdom texts, the Arthurian tradition, medieval Welsh legends, fairy traditions, and traditional Irish and Scottish healers and seers.

This book is also unique in that it devotes several chapters to exploring the existence of shamanic practices, beliefs and elements throughout the tradition, including the ritual use of poetry, chant and song. In addition, new translations of poems, texts, prayers, songs and charms have been provided from Old Irish, Middle Welsh and Gaulish sources, as well as Scottish Gaelic, Modern Irish, Modern Welsh, Cornish, Breton and Manx folk traditions.

Excellent studies of aspects of Celtic religion have been produced in the past, most notably by John Carey, Proinsias Mac Cana, Patrick K. Ford, Tomás Ó Cathasaigh, Liam Breatnach, Kim McCone, John Koch, Anne Ross, Liam Mac Mathúna, Joseph Nagy, Elizabeth Gray and Kuno Meyer. Many of these works are out of print, or focus on particular aspects of Celtic religious belief or mythology. It is hoped that the present work will serve as a guide for students of Celtic or world mythology, indigenous cultures, ancient history, medieval literature, anthropology, poetry and many other related topics.

What concepts enable us to speak about Celtic religion, symbolism or beliefs? A religion consists of beliefs, understandings and practices which connect human beings with the world of spirit (whether that is understood as God(s) or goddess(es), Creator, ancestors, spirit teachers or guides, or spirits of place); provide access to multiple levels of spiritual wisdom and understanding; and help manifest personal, cultural, social or environmental change. Religious beliefs are comprised of knowledge and understanding of how the universe is organized, how the gods or spirits manifest themselves in the earthly plane, and how humans are meant to live in relationship with them. Religious symbols are physical representations of spiritual energies, entities, concepts or ideals. As this work will show, Celtic forms of religion and belief have existed for several millennia.

The myths of any culture are not simply the antiquated creation myths of "primitive" or fearful cultures, but sacred stories which have been preserved over many years because they contain knowledge about the world and how people are meant to live within it. Myths help people understand their relationship to the ancestors, the natural world, the gods, and each other. They contain cultural and spiritual knowledge of many kinds, encoded in sacred narratives, symbols and characters.

For many centuries, native religious systems have been judged to be "less than" (or less evolved than) those practiced by modern monotheistic cultures. In more recent years, anthropologists have come to realize that traditional cultures have preserved a vast amount of significant social, cultural, artistic, spiritual and environmental knowledge which deserves recognition and respect. Traditional religions are not empty relics of a superstitious existence, but vibrant, empowered, living repositories of deeply nuanced and sophisticated systems of spiritual and cultural knowledge. It is important that Celtic religious traditions take their place among other world indigenous traditions, and it is in service of that goal that this work has been created.

I am indebted to the Harvard University Department of Celtic Languages and Literatures for their support, and to the Research Librarians at Widener Library. My greatest debt of gratitude is to Professor Tomás Ó Cathasaigh, who heroically fostered my interest in Old Irish language and literature. Many thanks also to Professor Patrick Ford, Professor

Katherine McKenna, Dr. Kathryn Chadbourne, Dr. Dorothy Africa, Dr. Katharine Olson, Dr. Gene Haley, and Margo Granfors for all their support and kindness.

I would also like to thank Dr. Michael Linkletter, Dr. Aled Llion Jones and Dr. Matthieu Boyd for assistance with language materials (Scottish Gaelic, Modern Welsh and Breton, respectively). Many thanks to the staff at Smith College and the University of Massachusetts at Amherst for support during my teaching terms there, and to colleagues at the University of Edinburgh, University College Cork and University College Galway. I am indebted beyond measure to these true friends and colleagues: Dr. Benjamin Bruch, Dr. Charlene Eska, Dr. Joseph Eska and Dr. Michael Newton.

I am grateful for the love and support of family and friends who have encouraged my studies and my journey of exploration: Dr. Carin Roberge, Dr. Michael Verrilli, Debra Uller, Dr. Kevin Gregg, Jorgelina Zeoli, Sharon Gadonniex, Bart Mallio, Walter Lavash, Diane Champigny, Scott Dakota, Laura Wilson, James Mobius, Donna Martinez, Mark Bilokur, Tiana Mirapae, Robbie Callaham, Sharon Manning, Rich Taylor, *Trouz Bras*, and (across the pond) Christine Hurson, Alan O'Domhnaill, Mary McKenna and Jennifer Butler.

A very special thank you to Cynthia von Buhler for allowing me to use her painting of a Celtic goddess (for which I was the model), originally commissioned for the University of Toronto Celtic Studies program, for the cover of the book.

To my students: you have taught me so much. Gratitude to Charlie Maguire, Iain Stewart, John Powell, Diane Gatchell, and so many others, for your faith. Special thanks to Daphne Bishop for helping edit the manuscript and lending her wisdom and grace to its creation. Thanks also to the Omega Institute, Kripalu Center and Rowe Conference Center for allowing me to serve as faculty in Celtic religion and shamanic traditions.

I would also like to thank the indigenous shamans who have given so generously of their time and wisdom, contributing much to my personal path and to the scholarly exploration of shamanic elements in Celtic tradition: Don Martin Pinedo and Marco Nunez (Andean tradition) and Timothy Swallow (Lakota tradition). *Wopila* to the members of the Reading and Rutland lodges—*Mitak' oyas'in.*

Thank You—Buide Dúib—Meur Ras—Diolch yn Fawr—Tapadh Leibh

Introduction:
Journeying to the Well of Wisdom

This volume has been a long time in the making. Celtic myths and legends have been told and retold for centuries, and some are well over a thousand years old. Some Celtic themes and symbols have been in existence for millennia and form part of an ancient cultural and spiritual heritage whose roots run wide and deep. While some stories and traditions were lost over the centuries, other elements have been preserved in Celtic-speaking communities in Ireland and Scotland, Wales and Brittany, Cornwall and the Isle of Man. Some stories and practices survived after crossing the oceans to new homelands in Canada, America, Australia and elsewhere — a testimony to the importance and resonance of these traditions.

The words of these stories, poems, songs and prayers have been spoken aloud in temples and sacred groves, by the shores of lakes and oceans, on hilltops and assembly grounds, and at the sources of rivers and springs. They were recited at sacred sites and the burial grounds of ancestors, to mark the inauguration of kings and the making of poets, at firesides and healing rites, in royal courts and humble dwellings. As with other traditional societies, the Celtic-speaking peoples understood the power of words, songs and stories, as well as the importance of honoring the wisdom of the past.

After more than twenty years of studying the myths, religion and folklore of the Celts, and more than fifteen years of teaching, researching and writing about these traditions, it became clear that a new source of knowledge was needed. The Celtic religions constitute a deep and complex tradition whose constituent parts are spread far and wide in books, journals, manuscripts and other written and oral sources. Many of these sources are difficult for students to access or understand, and this has led to the fabrication of inaccurate or misleading perceptions about Celtic culture and beliefs. These misconceptions do not serve readers or enthusiasts, nor do they serve the people who live in these cultures. This book has been created in order to provide widespread access to the authentic beliefs and traditions of the Celts, and to honor those who have preserved this wisdom over the ages.

The book is divided into three parts — three being a very sacred number in Celtic tradition. The first section focuses on early Celtic religion and mythology, outlining some of the main elements of these belief systems and explaining how we are able to ascertain this knowledge. It discusses sacred practitioners and holy people, gods and goddesses, and the symbolism of the ritual year.

The second section provides information about a variety of Celtic wisdom traditions, including cosmology, sacred lore pertaining to trees, plants and animals, and theological and ethical wisdom for sacred and balanced living. It also explores the theme of shamanism in Celtic religious traditions, including training, initiation, shape shifting, specialized knowledge and languages and the use of ritualized speech and song.

The third section focuses on Celtic legends and folklore traditions, including ancestral traditions, medieval Welsh legends and the Celtic origins of the story of Arthur. Seasonal celebrations are discussed, as well as fairy beliefs, traditional healers and seers, herbal charms, and the importance of poetry, songs and traditional wisdom. At the end of the book are three appendices which outline the rights of women in early Celtic culture, offer examples from the folksong traditions of the six Celtic-speaking nations, and provide information for suggested reading and further study.

The quest for knowledge is one of the most important and enduring themes in the Celtic spiritual tradition. This pursuit is often expressed in terms of the symbolism of a visit to the well of wisdom. Offerings have been made at sacred springs and wells in the Celtic countries since the late Bronze and early Iron Ages.[1] This practice is one of the most ancient and widespread in the entire tradition. It has survived throughout the centuries in spite of political turmoil and religious upheaval and is still practiced to this day. The modern custom of throwing a coin into a fountain is a direct survival of this ancient practice. Rituals, offerings and prayers were offered at wells for healing, assistance, blessings, guidance and protection, as they still are at many locations.[2]

Sacred wells were also associated with the quest for knowledge. Traditional tales abound of kings and queens, heroes and heroines, gods and goddesses, and ordinary men and women who by choice or circumstance find themselves faced with an extraordinary opportunity to visit the well of wisdom. Historical sources tell of druids, poets and seers whose lifelong task was the acquisition of specialized and rarified knowledge, which they expressed ritually through poetry, songs and stories and transmitted to other tradition bearers.

One of the earliest literary representations of the well of wisdom is found in the Irish tale *Echtrae Cormaic*, "The Adventures of Cormac." According to early Irish sources, *Cormac mac Art* was said to have been king of Ireland in the early third century, his reign assigned to the years 227–266 C.E. He was one of the most famous legendary kings of Ireland and frequently depicted as the ideal ruler.[3] In *Echtrae Cormaic*, Cormac is led by an Irish deity to the sacred Otherworld realms where he is shown a vision of a sacred well. Nine hazel trees grew around the well, which symbolized divine knowledge. They dropped their nuts into the well, and the salmon of wisdom that lived inside the well cracked open the nuts. Five streams flowed from the well, representing the five senses through which knowledge is obtained. The deity explains to Cormac that no one will have wisdom who does not drink a draft from the well itself and from the five streams that flow from it. The "Folk of Many Arts" are those who drink from them both.[4]

In other Celtic tales, it is not enough to simply visit the well. One must actually drink its water or consume the sacred salmon or hazelnuts that flourish nearby. In a well-known Middle Irish tale, the legendary hero *Finn mac Cumhall* goes to study poetry with a man named *Finnéces* who lived near the River Boyne. For seven long years Finnéces had been sitting by the river, watching for a supernatural salmon. It had been prophesied that he would catch the salmon, after which nothing would remain unknown to him. The salmon was found, and the poet set young Finn by a fire to cook the salmon for him. Finn was warned not to eat any of it. However, while cooking the fish, Finn burned his thumb and put it into his mouth. As a result, he obtained knowledge and the power of prophecy.[5]

A similar tale was told in Wales during the medieval era. A woman by the name of *Cerridwen* lived near a lake called *Llyn Tegid*. She was said to be a magician, learned in the three arts of magic, enchantment and divination. She decided to use her arts to help her unfortunate son become a great seer and prognosticator. She boiled a number of herbs in a large cauldron, a brew that would eventually produce three magical drops. These drops had the power to confer wisdom and magical powers upon her son. Like Finnéces, Cerridwen set a young boy to tend the fire. She fell asleep, and when the three drops sprang from the cauldron they fell upon the young boy. He too obtained the gifts of poetry and prophecy, as well as the power of shape shifting. He was eventually known by the name *Taliesin*, "Shining Brow."[6]

A version of this tale was still recited by traditional storytellers in Scotland during the twentieth century. The folktale "Saint Fillan and the White Snake" tells of a ninth-century Perthshire saint who was reputed to be a famous healer and renowned for carrying a hazel staff. In the story, upon the advice of a mysterious French "physician," Fillan returns to the place where he had obtained his hazel staff. He built a large fire and placed a pot of honey beside it. Snakes began to appear, drawn by the heat of the fire and the smell of the honey. Eventually a large white snake appeared, as it had been foretold to him. Fillan caught the snake and handed it to the physician.

The physician set a fire under it and told Fillan to guard the snake, but not to touch it. The pot began to boil and one of the bubbles burned Fillan's finger. He put his finger into his mouth, and as he did so, he felt a great change coming over him. From the power of the white snake, Saint Fillan became gifted with the power of healing, as described in the words of the Scottish storyteller Duncan Matheson:

> As I have said he was a wonderful healer and there was a spring over in Kilillan and the spring rose through a birch tree that was hollow inside, you know, an old tree, and the spring came up in the middle of it. And the water from the spring, it had the power of healing.... All anyone had to do was take a drink from it and whatever was the matter with them it was said that it could cure it, and they believed it had that power.... If you believe the tales of the old folk, it did this.[7]

My own quest to drink from the Celtic well of wisdom began as a young person and aspiring musician, as I sought to know more about my Celtic heritage. Starting with medieval history and moving back in time to the ancient sources, I became fascinated with the traditions of my ancestors. From early historical accounts and mythological tales, to the folktales, songs and customs, once I had a taste for the wisdom embodied in these sources of wisdom, there was no turning back.

Eventually I had the opportunity to study some of the Celtic languages, which really "cracked open" the hazelnuts of knowledge, revealing layers of understanding which would have otherwise remained hidden or obscured. I realized that in order to fully understand the sacred stories and beliefs of my ancestors, I needed to not only drink from the five streams, but also from the well itself. I decided to pursue professional academic training in Celtic studies, and this, coupled with my interest in world religions, wove itself together into a path of marvels, mysteries and discovery.

I cannot promise that by reading this book, every person who "drinks from the well" will become endowed with the gifts of poetry, prophecy or healing. However, I have heard remarkable stories from students, who after first hearing an Old Irish or Middle Welsh poem, reading a myth or sacred text, or listening to stories or songs from one of the Celtic nations, found themselves profoundly changed. They report experiences of deep remembering and inner connection. Many are moved to study a Celtic language, work their way through a medieval text, or in some other way support these cultures who, against all odds, have preserved an astonishing amount of their native wisdom.

The best counsel I can provide to those who would visit the well of Celtic wisdom is to sit by the source and listen to it speak. Let the sound of these voices rise up and tell their own stories. It is imperative that we do not project our own ideas and modern culture onto these indigenous traditions. In doing so, we cloud the vision inside the well and cannot hear the true voices of the past.

I hope this book will provide every interested person with a reliable pathway that leads towards the well of wisdom. Whether they are interested in their Celtic heritage, in Celtic history and archaeology, music and poetry, art and literature, mythology and ritual, or folk customs and beliefs, there are many streams flowing from the well. If we first drink from historical sources of knowledge, we can then follow the streams of the senses — the religious, symbolic and artistic expressions of these cultures. In this way, each of us may work towards becoming one of the "Folk of Many Arts," people who seek to respect, preserve and transmit the traditional wisdom and practices of the Celtic-speaking nations.

I will send you on your journey with the work of two poets, the fabled Welsh poet-seer, Taliesin (who received the drops from Cerridwen's cauldron), and the legendary Irish poet and magician, Amairgen. The translations are my own from the Middle Welsh and Old Irish originals, but the meaning and the wisdom do not belong to me. They belong to all who would "weave the web of knowledge," in the words of an anonymous Celtic poet of old.[8]

Excerpts from "Angar Cyfundawt"

Doethur, prif geluyd, dispwyllawt sywedyd...
Gogwn dedyf radeu, awen pan deffreu...
Awen a ganaf, o dwfyn ys dygaf...[9]

A learned one, a poet of excellence, a wise seer provides instruction...
I know the blessings of inspiration at the time it streams forth...
I sing of poetic knowledge, from the deep I wield it...[10]

Excerpts from "The Cauldron of Poesy"

Ar-caun coire ... indber n-ecnai...
Srúaim n-ordan ... srúamannaib suíthi...
Sóerbrud i mberbthar bunad cach sofis...
Búan bríg nád díbdai dín.[11]

I sing of the cauldron ... a river of wisdom...
An estuary of honour ... with streamings of lore...
A noble vessel in which is brewed the source of every great knowledge...
An enduring power whose protection does not perish.[12]

1

The Sacred Elements of the Tradition

One of the first steps to understanding the myths and religions of the Celtic peoples is to identify some of the basic elements of those beliefs and practices. The early Celts lived in an enormous region, stretching from modern Turkey through eastern and central Europe (including much of modern day Switzerland, Austria, Germany and northern Italy), and westwards and northwards into much of Spain, Portugal, France, Belgium, Britain and Ireland.[1] Although there were differences in religion in various regions and in different eras, we can perceive a number of common themes in many of the sources. These common elements include:

- The worship of both male and female deities
- Respect for ancestors and elders
- Appreciation of the natural world
- The interconnection between this world and the Otherworld
- The cyclical nature of time and the immortality of the soul
- Cosmology and the sacred center
- The cauldron, the sword, the well, the head, the number three
- The importance of knowledge and skill
- Respect for truth, honor and courage

Worship of Male and Female Deities

The Celts worshipped a variety of deities, both male and female. Some of these deities were associated with the cosmos (the sun, moon, stars and ocean), while others were connected with more local manifestations of the natural world — hills, rivers, wells, lakes, trees and mountains. Many deities were associated with cultural aspects, such as wisdom and skill, healing and protection, magic and poetry, and fertility and abundance.[2]

Some of these deities or variations on deity archetypes were venerated in many parts of the Celtic world. For example, the early Irish worshipped a god called Lug, while the Celts on the Continent venerated a god known as Lugos. Similarly, the Irish had a deity known as Ogma, while the Gaulish Celts worshipped a god called Ogmios. The British Celts venerated a goddess known as Brigantia, while the Irish honored a goddess called Bríg (later known as Brigid). There were also representations of a horned or antlered god in various Celtic regions. In addition to these widely venerated gods and goddesses, there were other deities who were more localized in nature, connected with certain tribes or associated with features of the local landscape.[3]

One of the most important figures in the various Celtic pantheons was the Sovereignty Goddess. She was a powerful figure associated with the land and its abundance, sovereignty and authority, prophecy and skill, shape shifting and magic, warfare and destruction, and fertility and creation — in short, the many powers of life and death. Her symbols often included the horse and the bird (and in some cases, the raven). She could manifest in both human and animal form, and might appear as a beautiful woman, a warrior or an old hag.[4]

In these forms, she often appeared before a potential king or hero to test him and see if he was worthy of her support. A king could not rule successfully without the blessings of this powerful goddess, and only with her power and cooperation could the king, the land and the people prosper. In Irish tradition, the goddesses known as the Mórrígan and her sister Macha both displayed attributes of the Sovereignty Goddess. The Continental Celts worshipped a horse goddess known as Epona, and in medieval Welsh legend the figure of Rhiannon was also associated with horses and kingship.[5]

Respect for the Ancestors

Throughout the legends and literatures of the Celtic world, we can perceive a tradition of respect for ancestors, as well as for elders and people of wisdom. Classical sources tell us that the druids and poets memorized lengthy genealogies, a practice which is common in many tribal societies.[6] A number of legendary or venerated elder figures, including Cormac mac Art, counseled preserving and following ancient lore, as well as respecting and listening to elders.[7]

In many cases, people were named for their ancestors, as in the names *Finn mac Cumhall* (Finn son of Cumhall, *mac* meaning "son of") or *Conchobor mac Nessa* (in this case, Nessa is a female name). A woman might be named for her ancestors as well, as in the name *Macha ingen Ernmas*, "Macha daughter of Ernmas" (*ingen* meaning "daughter of"). In the modern Goidelic languages (Scottish Gaelic, Modern Irish and Manx), *mac* is still used in surnames. For example, this is seen in the name *Mac an t-Saoir*, anglicized as MacIntyre. In the case of women, *ní* ("daughter of") is used in modern Irish and *nic* in Scottish Gaelic. This was also the practice in Britain, where the word *mab* or earlier *map* (later written *ab* or *ap*) meant "son of" and *merch* (earlier *verch* meant "daughter of") in early British and Welsh, respectively. Even in Christian times, various Irish and British tribes claimed to be descended from certain powerful or venerated figures, including divine and supernatural characters and pagan deities.[8] The wisdom of the past was important and could be used to guide people in the present.

Veneration of the Natural World

Early Irish and Welsh poetry and mythology (as well as modern literary and oral sources) demonstrate that the Celts had a profound appreciation for the natural world.

Nature, the landscape and the environment were respected and honored, as they are in all primal cultures. The natural world was the source of life, and as such was to be venerated and revered. In medieval Ireland, a great body of traditional lore was preserved which contains information about traditional Irish beliefs pertaining to the origins and meaning of the landscape. These were known as the *Dindshenchas* ("The Lore of Places"), and they set forth sacred stories about rivers, lakes, hills, fields, trees and other features of the natural world, including their connection with various Irish deities.[9]

This appreciation of the natural world continued into the Christian era, and Irish monks were noted for writing beautiful poetry in which they worship a new god while still inhabiting the land of their ancestors. One of the most famous of these poems commemorates a single moment of connection and awareness:

> *Int én bec ro léic feit*
> *Do rinn guip glanbuidi;*
> *Fo-ceird faíd ós Loch Láig*
> *Lon do chraíb charnbuidi.*[10]

> The little bird lets go a whistle
> From the tip of its bright yellow beak
> He sends out a cry above Loch Láig
> A blackbird from a heaping-yellow branch.[11]

Throughout the Celtic world, myths and legends, as well as artwork and symbolism, reflect the veneration of an interest in the natural world. Many animals and birds were considered sacred and associated with special properties or characteristics. Horses, deer, boars, hounds, cattle, fish and birds (especially the raven, the eagle, and water birds) formed an important part of the mythological and spiritual tradition. Certain creatures appeared in the myths to guide or entice people into an Otherworld encounter or adventure, particularly deer, boar and birds.[12] Plant life was also venerated, and trees in particular are mentioned quite frequently in myths and poetry. Some of the most sacred trees were oak, hazel, apple, rowan and yew. The apple tree seems to have served as a token of passage between the worlds, while the hazel tree and its nuts symbolized divine wisdom.[13]

Like most indigenous people, the Celts perceived that there were spirits in the land. These included deities associated with hills and mountains, fields and plains, and groves and trees. There were stories of divine ancestresses buried in sacred hills, and since ancient times Celtic goddesses were associated with rivers and other bodies of water. Because the divine was considered to be numinous — inherent in all aspects of the natural or perceived world — the Celts were said to have held rituals out of doors. These took place in sacred groves, on open plains, on top of hills, or near bodies of water. In addition, archaeological evidence shows that they also built temples of wood, stone or earth inside of which they held rituals, ceremonies and tribal gatherings.[14]

The Celtic Otherworld

One of the most pervasive themes seen throughout the Celtic tradition is the belief that the Otherworld — the realms of the divine — exist around us at all times. The Otherworld was a contiguous realm to our own, one that was always connected to our world, existing in a different plane of space and time. In Ireland the Otherworld had a variety of names, including *Tír na nÓg* ("Land of Youth"), *Tír Tairngire* ("Land of Promise or Prophesy"), *Tír na mBán* ("Land of Women") and *Mag Mell* ("Plain of Honey"). In Wales it was known as *Annwfn* (later shortened to *Annwn*) which means "Not-World" or "Un-World." In British tradition, the Otherworld was also called *Avalon* ("Divine Place of Apple Trees" or "Place of Divine Apple Trees"), a name mirrored in the Irish sacred place-name *Emain Ablach*.[15]

The inhabitants of the Otherworld were the gods and goddesses of the Celtic peoples. They were known in Ireland as the *Aes Síde* ("People of the *Síd*" or "Fairy Mounds"), and later as the *Tuatha Dé Danann* (the "Tribes of the Goddess Danu"). In Wales they were known as *Plant Annwn* ("The Children of Annwn") or the Children of *Dôn* (a female figure whose name is likely cognate with that of Danu, in its earlier form *Donu*). In later times, these divine beings were referred to as "the fairies"—as the *Síog* in Ireland, the *Sítheachain* in Scotland, and the *Tylwyth Teg* ("Fair Family") in Wales.[16]

In the early tradition, these Otherworld beings were originally described as fully human sized, often very beautiful or remarkable in appearance. They are frequently described as being very skilled and wise, or having certain powers or attributes. They were fond of things that the Celts also enjoyed: feasting, music, games, poetry—even battle. They were possessed of great power and wisdom, and could confer blessings or destruction. As a result, it was important to respect and honor them at all times.

The Celtic Otherworld itself was described as a realm of great beauty and power, an almost dreamlike place where colors, sounds and experiences were intensified. It was a place where there was little or no grief, sorrow, death or illness—a wondrous and incomparable land. It also seems to have been conceived of as the source of wisdom, skill, abundance and other blessings of life. In one early Irish source, the Otherworld was said to be a beautiful land on which many blossoms dropped, where splendors of every color glistened throughout glorious plains, in which beautiful music was heard.[17]

The inhabitants of the Celtic Otherworld were apparently able to connect with our world whenever they wished. These encounters often took place away from the relative safety of the village or settlement, and occurred in forests or groves, near bodies of water or in the presence of ancient burial mounds. While the most important intersections between the worlds took place at the turning points of the year or the day, interactions between this world and the Otherworld could occur almost anywhere and at any time.[18]

The Cyclical Nature of Existence

Just as the worlds were connected, so too was time perceived of as existing in a circular arrangement (not in a linear pattern, as we have been taught). This is an almost universal belief in indigenous or primal cultures. Life energies are created, die and are reborn. Early written sources state that one of the primary teachings of the druids was that the soul was immortal.[19] The cyclical nature of time was also commemorated in a yearly pattern of seasonal rituals.[20] Each year the cycle of rituals was repeated, but resulted in the creation of a new cycle of existence. The sacrality of the past and the wisdom of the elders were brought forward in this circle of time, while new growth and creation were also honored.

This cyclical pattern also formed part of the Celts' connection with the Otherworld. The inhabitants of the sacred realms were honored and revered, and could thus be prevailed upon to bestow blessings and protection. Sometimes blessings appeared in one's path, and offerings and prayers of gratitude could then be given to acknowledge the gift and strengthen the pattern of friendship and reciprocity. In Old Irish, the name of the "fairy" mounds (which were pre–Celtic burial sites) was *síd* (Welsh *sedd*). This word meant "seat," as in the "seat of kingship" or the "seat of the gods." It also had a secondary meaning of peace, referring to the benefits that resulted from living in right relationship with the *Aes Síde* ("People of the Síd-Realms").[21] In later tradition, this concept seems to have been remembered in the folk practice of referring to the fairies as the "People of Peace" (regardless of the fact that they were not always peaceful). The name seems to have been used to invoke the qualities that people wished to maintain with these supernatural beings, whose presence is still understood to exist in the landscape.

Cosmology and the Sacred Center

Most of our information about Celtic seasonal customs comes from medieval Irish literary and historical sources, early modern ethnographical accounts, and more recent folklore accounts. An Iron Age bronze calendar was unearthed in Coligny, France, which provides some interesting but not entirely decipherable data about the Gaulish calendar.[22] Overall, however, most of our early data has its source in Irish cultural tradition.

The Irish Celts commemorated four sacred festivals: *Samhain, Imbolc, Beltaine* and *Lugnasad.* As some of the Celts appear to have reckoned time by nights rather than days, in these cases festival observances would have begun at sundown rather than sunrise. This reflects a belief in the energies of creation emerging from a point of primal darkness. Originally the holidays would have been observed on the new moon; but after the introduction of the Christian calendar, they were standardized and observed on the first day of a calendar month.[23] In more recent times, these feast days took place on the following dates: *Samhain* on November 1 (but starting on the eve of October 31, the origin of the modern holiday of Halloween), *Imbolc* on February 1, *Beltaine* on May 1 and *Lugnasad* on August 1.

Samhain, which likely comes from an Old Irish phrase meaning "Summer's End," was the most important of the feast days. It marked the end of the old year and the beginning of the new. The crops had to be gathered in by this date and all herds returned from summer pastures. Great tribal assemblies were held, religious rituals were enacted, and feasting, markets and fairs took place. Samhain was considered to be a point outside of time when the boundaries between the worlds were thin. As a potent liminal time, interactions between the worlds could be either beneficial or dangerous.[24]

However, Samhain was not just a dark, fearful holiday (this aspect alone has been preserved in modern Halloween festivities). It was clearly a period of celebration and new beginnings. Samhain was an important time to honor the gods, give thanks, perform divination, and undertake rituals to herald in the new cycle. Samhain seems to have been primarily associated with powerful female deities connected with the energies of life and death, shape shifting and magic, protection and destruction.

Imbolc, whose name may either mean "great belly or womb" or "ewe's milk," marked the end of winter and the beginning of spring. The was the time when animals began to give birth (particularly sheep), providing fresh milk, butter and cheese when winter food stores were running low. It was a time of renewal and rejuvenation, of new birth and the continuation of life. Eventually Imbolc was associated with Saint Bridget, a powerful figure associated with fertility, abundance, and protection. It is believed that she may be a manifestation of *Bríg*, an Irish goddess of healing, smithcraft and poetry.[25]

Beltaine took place on the first of May, and marked the start of the summer season (one of its early Irish epithets meant "First of Summer"). The origin of the word *Beltaine* is unclear, perhaps meaning "bright fires" or the "fires of Bel" (not to be confused or equated with Baal), an otherwise unattested deity who may be similar to the widely worshipped Continental Celtic deity *Belenos*. Beltaine heralded the start of the bright half of the year, as Samhain marked the beginning of the dark half.

Like Samhain, it was also a powerful liminal time when either blessings or danger could prevail. Although the weather was good, it was not yet known whether the crops and herds would survive. Beltaine was therefore associated with magic and the protection of abundance and prosperity. Bonfires were lit on hilltops from various types of sacred wood, and animals were run between the fires to protect them from danger or disease. In Ireland, a large assembly was held at *Uisneach*, the cosmological center of the country. This site was said to be the home of the *Dagda*, a beneficent tribal god associated with the powers of life and death, fertility and abundance, as well as magic and protection.[26]

Lugnasad, the "Assembly of the god Lug," was a harvest festival, among other things. It was instituted by the many-skilled god, Lug, to honor his foster mother, *Tailtiu*, who died from the exertion of clearing many plains (presumably in preparation for agriculture). While the other holidays seem to have been primarily connected with the herds, this holiday was more associated with the growth of crops.

Lugnasad was a time to give thanks for the first harvest of grain. Great gatherings took place on plains or hilltops, and offerings were made. Rituals were held in honor of divine or supernatural women who were associated with the preservation or potential destruction of fertility. There were great tribal assemblies complete with fairs, markets, music, storytelling and horse races, and Lugnasad was a traditional time to visit people and arrange marriages.[27]

In addition to a temporal cosmology in which time was perceived as circular in nature, the Celts may have also been possessed of a spatial cosmology that operated in an analogous way. One early Irish text mentions that each of the four cardinal directions (east, south, west and north) were associated with certain properties or attributes. There is also mention of powerful characteristics associated with the central point or region of the land, which was associated with sovereignty.[28]

Archaeological evidence, as well as information from myths and legends, shows that in a variety of Celtic settings, the center was the most cosmological point. Temples and ritual sites seem to have been focused on a central point or area, and sacred characters are described as ceremonially walking around objects or having encounters in the center of groves or plains. [29] This observance of the sacred center is a very common ritual feature in many primal cultures, including those that practice shamanism. The concept of the center is preserved in an Irish folk saying: "Where is the middle of the world?" The answer: "Here" or "Where you are standing."[30]

The center is known as the location of the sacred World tree, mountain or pillar. In early Ireland, the word *bile* ("sacred or ancient tree; pillar") may attest to a similar belief, and carved pillars or posts may have existed in the center of tribal territories. Certain types of trees (especially oak, ash and yew) were regarded as a *bile*, especially very ancient or venerated trees. There are also Celtic place names which refer to this concept, such as *Mediolanum* ("The Middle of the Sacred Plain," now modern day Milan) and *Medionemeton* ("Sacred Central Place") in early Scotland.[31]

Cauldrons, Wells and Other Symbols

One of the most universal symbols seen in the Celtic tradition is the cauldron or vessel. These appear in the archaeological evidence from the earliest times, and are extremely prominent in myths, legends and folktales. There seem to have been three types of cauldrons or vessels: a cauldron of abundance or nourishment; a cauldron of healing or transformation; and a cauldron of wisdom and inspiration. These symbols likely served as the template for the later legend of the Holy Grail.[32]

Magical weapons, including swords and spears, also figure prominently. Once again, these objects are found in archaeological settings as well as in myths and legends. In the myths, swords were sometimes inscribed with magical words or symbols, and were alleged to be able to communicate or in other ways assist their owners. Swords and other objects were frequently offered into rivers, lakes and other bodies of water (which were often the abode of female divinities), and this may have served as the basis for medieval legends pertaining to Excalibur and the Lady of the Lake.[33]

There is a great deal of evidence for the veneration of bodies of water in Celtic tradition. Since the earliest times, rivers were named for goddess figures. Onomastic tradition, the myths and legends, and the folk tradition all attest to the importance of rivers, lakes, wells and springs.[34] This veneration plays out in early descriptions of wells of wisdom or knowledge which are located in the Otherworld, often associated with sacred trees (primarily the hazel) and other beings, like the salmon.[35]

Another symbol plentiful in both archaeological sources and native legends is the symbol of the head. Human and animal heads abound in Celtic artwork, and in many cases serve to portray or indicate the presence of the entire being. It is believed that the Celts perceived the head to be the seat of the soul, and legends exist in which severed heads can still talk or sing after the demise of the body.[36]

Finally, the number three must be mentioned in any overview of Celtic symbolism. Three appears to have been the most sacred and frequently used number in Celtic artwork and legends, closely followed by nine (three times the sacred three). There were three classes of sacred persons, and in many cases Celtic deities had three names or primary attributes (although they frequently had more than three aspects). The goddess Bríg was said to have two sisters by the same name, and the Irish goddess known as the Mórrigan had two sisters, Macha and Nemain. The number three may have represented the powers of life, death and rebirth, or could have reflected the veneration of three cosmological realms (Upper World, Middle World and Lower World). Rituals and assemblies often took place at locations where two of the three realms come together—on top of hills or mountains, or near the edge of lakes or rivers, for example. Things which are liminal (which are neither this nor that, or which are "betwixt and between") possessed special power and symbolism throughout the Celtic tradition.

Knowledge and Skill

All sources indicate that the Celts had a great respect for knowledge and skill. Classical sources mention the great esteem in which learned members of society were held, and native myths, legends and folktales all attest to the importance of skill and wisdom. Even the deities were known for their wisdom and skillfulness.

In early Celtic society, there were three groups of revered people: druids, bards and seers. The druids presided over rituals, communicated with the gods, made offerings, preserved and taught traditional and sacred wisdom, made prophesies and judgments, and were reputed to perform healing and magic. The bards composed poetry which was recited to the accompaniment of a harp or lyre. Their poems praised or censured leaders and other important members of society, and their words were believed to have almost magical power. Poets were associated with the gift of prophecy, and their work preserved a great deal of traditional lore. The seers engaged in prophecy and divination, which they practiced for the benefit of their community. Some of these divinatory practices were connected with the flight of birds and other omens from the natural world.[37]

In the medieval period, a class of highly regarded poet-seers emerged in Ireland, Scotland and Wales. They preserved a great deal of knowledge and lore from the early period, and were still connected with prophecy well into the Christian era. In fact, in medieval Ireland a poet could not be considered the master of his craft until he had mastered three types of divinatory practices. In many periods of Celtic culture, there existed highly specialized terminology for types of wisdom, knowledge and skill, as well as the people who practiced or transmitted this knowledge.[38]

Truth, Honor and Courage

In addition to honoring the attributes of wisdom and skill, throughout the tradition we can also perceive an enormous respect for the ideals of truth, honor and courage. Many tales demonstrate the importance of being truthful, courageous and acting in an honorable fashion. Irish kings were required to possess a certain kind of "princely truth," without which they could not rule successfully. Heroes and heroines are ultimately judged on their ability to act with honor, courage and integrity, despite whatever adventures or challenges come their way.[39]

In early Ireland and Britain, traditional wisdom was sometimes preserved in groups of threes known as "triads," in order to help students memorize traditional lore.[40] One of my favorite Irish triads runs as follows:

> Three candles that illuminate every darkness:
> Truth, nature and knowledge.[41]

Over a thousand years earlier, the druids of ancient Gaul were said to said to have taught the people this three-fold doctrine:

> Show reverence to the Gods,
> Do no ill deed, and
> Practice valour.[42]

Centuries later, in a Middle Irish tale, Saint Patrick asked the Irish hero *Oisín* what had sustained his people in the pre–Christian era. Oisín answered:

> The truth of our hearts,
> The strength of our arms,
> And the constancy of our tongues.[43]

This famous response reflects some of the most important ideals found in traditional Celtic culture, and its ancient words can still serve us well in these modern times.

2

Sources of Knowledge

In order to fully understand Celtic literature and mythology, we must first learn something about the ancient Celts themselves. Religion cannot be separated from culture, and therefore, taking a look at Celtic culture is crucial when attempting to understand Celtic beliefs and practices. The Greeks referred to the Celts as *Keltoi*; Caesar spoke primarily of the Gauls, but mentioned that some of the Celtic peoples referred to themselves as *Celtae*. Ancient Greek and Roman writers seem to have referred to the Celts fairly indiscriminately as either *Keltoi*, *Celtae* or *Galli*, or *Galatae*, as though the names were interchangeable. Many Celtic peoples would have probably self-identified through tribal designations.[1]

The Celts do not seem to have been centrally organized or governed, but were organized into tribes of various sizes ruled by kings or chieftains. Early maps from the first century BCE show indigenous names for some of these Celtic regions. Ireland was known as *Iweriju*, meaning "Fat or Fertile Land," and the island of Britain seems to have been called *Alba*. Early maps show many Celtic tribes living throughout Europe. Some of these tribes have left their mark on modern place names: the Parisii lived near modern-day Paris, the Boii in Bohemia, the Sequani near the River Seine, the Cornovii north of Cornwall, and the Dumnonii near Devon.[2]

With all of this social decentralization and variation, there would have also been a great deal of local variation in terms of culture and religion. So what makes something "Celtic"? The standard definition of the word *Celtic* refers to both language and culture. The Celtic peoples spoke Celtic languages, which were part of the larger Indo-European family of languages. Several thousand years B.C.E., people living somewhere in the region of the Black Sea began to migrate, bringing their language and elements of their culture with them. Some of these people moved south into the Near East and India, while others spread westwards into Europe (hence the name "Indo-European"). In Indo-European cultures there are a number of parallels in terms of how society was organized, and in the area of religious symbolism (as well as a great deal of diversity and variation).[3]

Over the centuries, the Indo-European languages began to change, but there are similarities between them. Most of the languages of modern Europe are Indo-European, including the Celtic languages (ancient and modern). Linguists can point out connections between these languages. For example, the Latin word *rex* meaning "king" is similar to the Gaulish word *rix* ("king"). The Sanskrit word *raj* which means "king" is likewise similar to Old Irish *rige* meaning "kingship." The word for "bull" is another good example: Old Irish *tarb*, Welsh *tarw*, Gaulish *tarwos* and Latin *taurus*.[4]

In order for something to be "Celtic," it must have historically formed part of the culture or religion of a people who spoke a Celtic language. There are many things labeled "Celtic" nowadays that were never part of any Celtic culture or belief system. It is vitally important to respect other cultures and not project our ideas or values onto them.

The Three Sources of Knowledge

How is it that we know who the Celts were and what they believed? We have three main sources of knowledge about the Celtic peoples: archaeology, Classical accounts and native literature. Each of these sources has its benefits and challenges, and in order to view and utilize this information properly it is important to understand the strengths and weaknesses of each of them.

Our earliest information comes from archaeology. In this discipline, we can see firsthand evidence of where and how the Celts lived, what sorts of objects they made, their artwork, and even evidence of ritual sites and offerings. The upside of archaeological sources is that they provide evidence that is contemporary with the pagan Celts. The downside is that these objects cannot speak to us. It is very difficult to say with accuracy what people believed in based solely on their material objects or dwellings.

Classical accounts constitute the second source. These are early written records, which begin in the first few centuries B.C.E., written down by Classical authors. These were for the most part Greeks and Romans who encountered or had firsthand reports about the ancient Celts. Some of this information is very useful in filling in details that archaeology cannot provide. However, not all Classical writers are completely objective, and some were simply repeating information they obtained secondhand, never having met any Celtic peoples themselves.

The third source is comprised of native writings. After the introduction of Christianity around the fifth and sixth centuries, we begin to see written records produced by the Celtic peoples themselves. These were often produced in monasteries and were not always objective or without influence from Christian ideas or beliefs. In addition, many monks were trained in Classical learning, and were eager to show off what they knew, whether this information came from the Bible, Greek and Roman sources, or Celtic culture. We have to be aware of all of these influences when looking at native literature. In addition, these writings were in many cases produced centuries after paganism began to wane.

Once we train ourselves to have a solid foundation and understanding of what these sources of knowledge actually represent, we can begin to put together the evidence from all three sources to form an idea of who the ancient Celts were and what their religion was like. For now, let's take a look at some of the information provided by the Classical authors in terms of the Celtic peoples, lands and culture.

The Celts

Athenaeus, writing around 200 C.E., provided information about the Gaulish Celts that he said had its source in the earlier writings of Posidonius (first century B.C.E.). He described the feasting habits of the Gauls, saying that they placed dried grass on the ground and ate their meals from tables that were raised just slightly off the ground. They ate roasted, cooked or boiled meat, or if they lived near rivers, fish cooked with salt, vinegar and cumin. Little bread was eaten, and no olive oil (which he says had an unpleasant taste to the Celts). At the feast, the guests sat in a circle ranked around the host or leader, and food was served on wooden, bronze, pottery, silver or woven trays.

Drinks were brought by servers in silver or pottery vessels resembling spouted cups. Most Celts drank a honeyed beer called *corma*. They drank from a common cup, a little at a time, but sipping frequently. Athenaeus mentions that the cup was carried around the circle from right to left, the same direction that they honored their gods (turning to the right). Poets often performed at these gatherings, and sometimes duels broke out amongst warriors vying for the choicest portions.[5]

In the first century B.C.E., Dio Cassius also wrote about the Celtic peoples living in Gaul. He noted the height and strength of the Gaulish women, as well. Dio also wrote about two Celtic tribes, the *Maeatae* and the *Caledonii*, who lived in what is now Scotland, noting that they did not build cities but lived in mountainous areas and marshy plains. He claimed to know that their form of government was mostly democratic, and that they went into battle with chariots and small, swift horses, as well as on foot. Dio noted that these early British tribes were fast runners, able to endure cold, hunger and hardship, and very resolute when they stood their ground.[6]

Around the same time, Diodorus Siculus noted that Britain was inhabited by tribes who were indigenous to the region, who in their lifestyles "preserved the old ways." They lived in simple, wooden houses, and in their land the weather was quite cold. Diodorus also wrote that the people lived a frugal life, different from the luxuries of the Mediterranean. He said the island had a large population and was ruled by kings and chieftains who for the most part lived in peace with one another.[7]

Diodorus also wrote about the Celts in Gaul, describing how they wore gold bracelets on their wrists and arms, gold rings on their fingers, and thick bands of gold around their necks. Apparently the Celts in the interior placed large amounts of gold as dedications to their gods, which was openly displayed in their temples and sanctuaries. It was the tradition that no one dared touch these sacred offerings.

Diodorus stated that the Gauls sat on the skins of wolves or dogs on the ground while eating, and that their feasts were characterized by blazing hearths and cauldrons with roasting spits of meat. Strangers were welcomed to their feasts, and the Gauls only inquired about their identity and business after the meal. The warlike characteristics of the Celts manifested in disputes that sometimes broke out at feasts, as well as the Celtic custom of taking heads in battle.

Diodorus also described in some detail the appearance and language of the Gaulish Celts. He said that their wore "stunning clothing," consisting of shirts which were dyed in various colors, and trousers called *bracae*. They wore striped cloaks with a checkered pattern, fastened with a clasp (thicker cloaks in winter and lighter in summer). Diodorus stated that they were "terrifying in appearance" and spoke with deep, harsh voices. He describes them as boastful, violent and melodramatic, but also very intelligent and quick to learn. They spoke together in few words, using riddles which left much of their meaning to be understood by the listener.[8]

In the late first century B.C.E. to early first century C.E., Strabo described a number of Celtic tribes living in various parts of Gaul. He too mentioned the religious offerings of gold and silver objects, both in temples and bodies of water. Once the Romans had taken control, they sold the lakes at public auctions so that the purchasers could take and melt down the silver hoards found within them. Strabo is somewhat dismissive of the Celts as simple minded and overly warlike, but also stated that they were courageous, frank, not malicious, and able to successfully apply themselves to education and literature if put to the task. He describes them as spirited, sometimes boastful, and intolerable when victorious.

Strabo described in some detail the dress and appearance of the Gaulish Celts. He said they let their hair grow long, and wore tight trousers on top of which were short slit tunics with sleeves. They also wore thick cloaks called *sagi* made from coarse and shaggy wool, and gold ornaments on their arms, wrists and around their necks. They ate meat (especially pork, fresh and salted) and milk, and also raised sheep. They lived in houses made from beams and wicker (probably wattles), with a conical thatched roof.

Although aristocratic in terms of hierarchy, the populace of the tribes apparently used to elect their leaders. During tribal assemblies, if anyone disturbed or interrupted the person speaking, an officer approached them with a drawn sword and ordered them to be silent. If the person did not comply, they were similarly commanded a second and third time. After that, the officer cut off a portion of their cloak as to render it useless.[9]

In the first century C.E., Caesar wrote extensively about the Gaulish and British Celts. He said the interior of Britain was inhabited by people, who, on the strength of their own tradition, claimed to be indigenous to the island. The population was large with many homesteads (which were similar to those in Gaul) and there were many cattle. He said that the Britons dyed themselves with woad, which produced a blue color, and as a result their appearance in battle was all the more daunting.[10]

The men wore their hair long in many cases, or short and daubed with lime to make it stand up on end. Some men had beards or sported long, drooping moustaches. Caesar's descriptions are matched by early Roman statues depicting the Gaulish Celts. Caesar said that the customs of the Gaulish and British Celts were in some aspects quite similar, and their religious beliefs (to his mind) almost the same. He noted similarities in language, the same boldness in courting danger, and the decentralization of government.[11]

Tacitus, writing in the first to second centuries C.E., mentions the red hair and large limbs of the Caledonians (Celts living in what is now Scotland), and similarities in appearance between some of the British and Gaulish Celts. He also noted similarities in language and religious beliefs and practices, and said that the Celts in both regions displayed "the same boldness in courting danger and ... the same panic in avoiding it." He wrote about the long summer days with light well into the nighttime hours in Britain, as well as the frequent rains. Extreme cold was rare, though, he says, and the country produced grain and cattle (the crops being slow to germinate but quick to ripen on account of the "great moisture of earth and sky"). Gold, silver and other metals were produced, as well as ocean pearls which were dark and blue-black in color.[12]

While there would have been variations in language, culture and religion throughout the Celtic regions, there would also have been recognizable similarities. Some of the common elements of early Celtic culture and society that we see in reports about Gaulish, British and other Celtic peoples include the following:

- Tribal organization, ruled by kings, queens or chieftains
- A three-fold division of society: Rulers and Sacred Persons; Warriors and Crafts-people; Farmers and Herders
- The sacred nature of kingship — the prosperity of the land and the people depends on the honor, truth, courage, generosity and worthiness of the ruler
- The ruler's success is also dependant on his union with and blessings from the Goddess of Sovereignty
- Territory, independence, prosperity and life were protected by a warrior class, with a focus on courage, honor and loyalty; some ritualized warfare (including single combat) as well as cattle raiding
- A sophisticated system of kinship which ensured social bonds and ties, and which also encouraged interdependence and community support in times of hardship
- An understanding of the sacredness and importance of the land and the natural world
- A great appreciation for wisdom and skill, learning, ancient traditions and lore, poetry and music, arts and craftsmanship; also a connection between poetry and prophesy
- Fondness for music, storytelling, food and drink, board games and field games, hunting, horses and hounds; beauty of all kinds, cleanliness and adornment [13]

Students who wish to learn more about the ancient Celts will be well rewarded by consulting other reliable books about Celtic archaeology, artwork and society listed in the "Suggested Reading" section at the end of the book. For now, let us proceed and explore what the Classical authors had to say about the religion and beliefs of the Celts.

Early Celtic Religion

The Classical authors had a great interest in the ancient Celts, and recorded quite a bit of information pertaining to their religions and rituals. Writing between the late first century B.C.E. and the first century C.E., Strabo noted that among the Gauls there were three groups of people who were held in special honor: the bards, the seers and the druids. The bards were singers and poets, the seers performed ritual ceremonies and studied natural philosophy, and the druids engaged in both moral and natural philosophy. The druids were also considered to be the most just of men, and for that reason they were entrusted with deciding both private and public disputes. Strabo also mentioned that the Druids and others in Gaul said that the soul, like the universe, was immortal, although at some time both fire and water would overwhelm them.[14]

In the late first century B.C.E., Diodorus Siculus wrote that the Gaulish Celts had composers of songs whom they called Bards. They sang to the accompaniment of instruments similar to lyres either in praise of people or to deride them. Their seers foretold the future by the observation of birds or the sacrifice of animals. The Gauls also had "great philosophers and theologians" called druids, to whom they accorded great honor. It was the Gaulish peoples' custom never to make an offering without a philosopher (druid) present, for they said that thank-offerings should be given to the gods by means of those who were experts in the nature of the divine and in communion with it. They also believed that it was through the druids that blessings should be sought.[15]

In the first century C.E., Pomponius Mela described the tribes of Gaul as both arrogant and superstitious. However, he also pointed out that they had their own type of eloquence, and in the druids, teachers of wisdom. He wrote that the druids professed to know the size and shape of the world, the motion of the stars and the heavens, and the will of the gods. They provided training to the most noble members of their people in "secret locations" (primarily caves or hidden glades), for a period of up to twenty years. One of the things they taught was that the soul was eternal, and that there was an afterlife.[16]

The Gaulish belief in the afterlife and reincarnation was remarked upon by Valerius Maximus. In the Greek trading colony of Massilia in the south of France (modern day Marseilles), he encountered an "ancient usage" of the Gauls, which was the practice of borrowing money to be repaid in the next world. He states the reason for this practice was that the Gauls were convinced the souls of people were immortal. Valerius goes on to say that he would call them stupid were it not for the fact that these "trouser-wearing" folk had the same belief held by the Greek Pythagoras.[17]

In the first century, Pliny recorded a great deal of detail about ancient peoples in his *Natural History*. In this work he writes at some length about Gaulish rituals and beliefs. One of his most famous passages runs as follows:

> Magic undoubtedly had a hold on Gaul, even down to living memory.... Britain today is so mesmerized by it and practices it with so much ceremony that one might think it was she who gave it to the Persians.[18]

Pliny said it was important to mention the respect paid to mistletoe by the Gauls. He claimed that the druids held nothing more sacred than mistletoe and the tree on which it grew (so long as this was oak). He states that the druids even chose groves of oak for their rites for that fact alone and apparently performed no rites without its foliage. They considered anything growing on oaks as sent by heaven, a sign that the tree had been chosen by the god himself. Mistletoe growing on an oak was rare, however, and when it was found it was gathered with great reverence. Pliny said that mistletoe was called "all-healing" in the Gaulish language.

The mistletoe ritual took place primarily on the sixth day of the lunar cycle, for he said it was the moon that marked out for the Gauls the beginning of months and years and cycles of thirty years. The reason for selecting the sixth day of the moon was that on this day the moon was already exercising great influence, even though it was not yet halfway through its course. A priest (i.e., a druid) dressed in a white robe for the ceremony, climbed the tree and reaped the mistletoe with a golden-colored sickle, gathering it into a white blanket.[19]

The connection between druids and trees may even extend to the etymological origins of the name of these religious practitioners. The word *druid* comes from two Indo-European root words: **deru* meaning "firm, solid, steadfast," with extended applications referring to "wood, tree" (giving an early Celtic root word **dru*); and Celtic **wid* from Indo-European **weid* "to see" (with extended meanings related to knowledge). The word *druid* may therefore mean "strong seer" or "strong in knowledge." It is interesting to note that the Indo-European root word *deru* also evolved into the English words *tree, truth* and *trust*, while the word *weid* eventually provided the origins of the English words *wise, wisdom, guide, advise* and *vision*.[20]

In the first century, Caesar wrote extensively about the druids as well. He noted that they officiated at religious ceremonies, supervised public and private offering rituals and expounded on religious questions. Large numbers of young men flocked to them for instruction and regarded them with great respect. The druids also served as judges, handing down decisions on all public and private disputes. If any individual or tribe did not abide by their decision, they were banned from sacrifices (religious rituals in which offerings were made). This was regarded by the people as the heaviest possible penalty.

Druidic students learned a great many verses by heart, and for this reason many remained under instruction for up to twenty years. Caesar claimed that they regarded it as contrary to their religious beliefs to commit their teachings to writing (although this was probably just the custom in an orally based society), and that in other matters, like public or private accounts, they used the Greek alphabet. Caesar suggested that this rule was introduced for two reasons: first, so that their teachings were not disseminated amongst the masses, and second, so that students would not rely on the written word and thus pay less attention to the development of their memories.

He goes on to note that at a particular time of year, the Druids held session at a consecrated spot in the territory of a tribe known as the Carnutes, a site considered the center of all Gaul. Caesar also makes the curious observation that it was thought that the druidic system was invented in Britain and imported into Gaul. He alleged that those who wished to make a more detailed study of druidism generally went to Britain to learn it (although it is unclear if this was a Roman perception or a Gaulish belief).

Caesar also mentions that the Gallic nation was as a whole very much devoted to religion. He says that the Gauls declared that they were all descended from a Celtic deity that Caesar likened to *Dis Pater*, a minor Roman god of the Underworld. Evidently they claimed that this was the tradition of the druids, and that for this reason they measured all periods of time not by the number of days but by the number of nights. He also records that a belief the Druids particularly wished to inculcate was that the soul did not perish, but after death passed from one person to another. This belief was thought by the Gauls to be the greatest incentive to bravery. The druids also engaged in a great deal of discussion about the stars and their motion, the composition of the world, and the strength and power of the immortal gods.[21]

Far from being mysterious, cloaked beings wandering through the mist, we can see that the druids were an educated and highly trained group of teachers, judges and religious leaders who had a profound impact on their culture and guarded the time-honored wisdom and traditions of their people. In the next chapter, we will explore the traditions and beliefs of the druids and other religious practitioners in Celtic culture.

3

Druids, Seers, Poets and Priestesses

In every culture, there are people who are specialists in communicating with and maintaining right relationship with the realms of the divine. As we have seen, in Celtic society there were three special classes of people who were shown great respect for their abilities: druids, bards and seers. The druids were theologians, philosophers, priests, judges, and teachers of wisdom. They presided over rituals, communicated with the sacred realms and were considered experts in the nature of the divine. One of their most important beliefs was that the soul was immortal, inhabiting another body after death.

The druids taught large groups of druidic students in secluded locations over a period of many years. This instruction would have included mythology, theology, genealogy, knowledge of the Otherworld realms and the gods, sacred lore associated with nature, secret languages, healing and magical practices. Caesar mentions that druidic students were sent for training by their parents or relatives, or came of their own free will. They learned many "verses" by heart, which would have included sacred and traditional lore organized in verse form to aid in memorization.[1]

We have seen that the druids ritually collected mistletoe, which was held to be useful in promoting fertility and as an antidote to poison. It was known as "all-heal" in the Gaulish language, from which we might infer that it was used to treat a wide variety of illnesses.[2] Interestingly, folklore accounts from the last century also report the gathering of mistletoe, which was used to treat fevers, heart disease, epilepsy and numerous other ailments. It was also widely held to promote fertility and good luck, and to provide protection against a variety of undesirable influences. Mistletoe was the plant badge of the Hay clan of Errol in Scotland, who regularly gathered it from a huge oak tree at Samhain. Using a new dirk (a type of Scottish blade), it was carried around the tree three times in a sunwise direction while intoning a particular charm or spell.[3]

In addition to the ritual collecting of mistletoe, Classical accounts describes the gathering of another sacred plant in Gaul — club moss. Pliny tells us that the plant was ritually gathered without the use of any iron implement, using the right hand which protruded from the left armhole of the tunic. The person performing the ritual was clad in white with bare feet washed clean, and an offering of bread and wine was made before gathering the plant. Like mistletoe, the club moss was also gathered in a fresh white cloth. The druids of Gaul taught that possession of the plant warded off all harm and that the smoke of it was good for all eye troubles. In the folk tradition, club moss was utilized as a powerful emetic and cathartic; fumigation with club moss was also used to treat eye disease. A Scottish folk charm stated that anyone who carried club moss on their person would be protected from all types of harm or mishap.[4] The Druids in Gaul were also reported to collect *samolus* or brook-weed, which was used to treat diseases in pigs and cattle. It was collected with the left hand by a person fasting, who was not to look at the plant or put it down except in a drinking trough where it was crushed for the animals to drink.[5]

Written sources indicate that the druids in Gaul (and in all likelihood, in Britain as well) officiated at religious ceremonies, supervised offering rituals, and expounded upon religious questions. They served as judges and teachers, and performed prophetic duties on behalf of their community. The druids also preserved a great deal of religious and cultural information, including moral and natural philosophy, beliefs associated with the immortality of the soul, and religious traditions pertaining to the gods and divine ancestors. They were involved in matters of peace and war, either inciting warriors to battle or chanting calming spells over them to induce peace. The druids were renowned for their intellectual capabilities and eloquence, as well as their observations of the natural world, and were involved with astronomy and law. They were said to investigate "questions of a secret and lofty nature" (if we can believe the late fourth century C.E. report of Ammianus Marcellinus). The druids were also reported to perform healing and magic.[6]

The druids of pre–Christian Ireland had high status in early Irish society, where they served as priests, seers, astrologers and teachers of druidic candidates. We know that they also served as judges and historians, and oaths were sworn in their presence. The druids of Ireland seem to also have been held in awe (or perhaps even feared, at least in Christian times) on account of their use of spells and satire.[7]

There are many Irish myths in which the druids play an important role, often serving as advisors to kings and queens, who took their advice very seriously. They were also involved in tribal decisions pertaining to war and peace. There are descriptions of druids standing between armies to encourage them, advise them, or prevent conflict. The druids would have provided counsel regarding practical aspects of life, as well as advice about the sacred or supernatural. In the myths and legends, the druids performed rituals and divination, provided healing, and performed magic (which included power over the elements, shape shifting, and changing the form of other beings or objects). They were also involved with poetry and prophecy, skills that were closely associated in Indo-European tradition.[8]

Another tradition associated with the druids was the practice of expounding their philosophy in riddles or cryptic language. In an early Irish text known as "The Colloquy of the Two Sages," two poets test each other's wisdom in an exchange of poetic questions and answers. At one point, the older poet says to the younger one, "A question, young man of instruction, where did you come from?" to which the young poet replies:

> Not difficult: from the heels of sages, from an assembly of wisdom,
> from the completion of excellence, from the brilliance of the sunrise,
> from the hazel trees of wisdom, from journeys of splendour,
> where truth is measured by excellence,
> in which colours are beheld, in which poems are renewed.[9]

Female Druids

There has often been speculation as to whether there were female druids or not. Although we don't have indisputable historical evidence for this, there are a number of clues that suggest that there were likely to have been female druids. We know that at least some Celtic women served as leaders, physicians, skilled craftspersons, negotiators, healers and poets — traditionally male roles — and so it is not unreasonable to speculate that there may have been some female druids. In addition, we know that some women served as seers and priestesses; therefore it stands to reason that there would also have been druidesses.[10]

Several classical references refer to women described as *dryadas*, a word which likely means a "female druid." Diocletian was once staying at an inn in the region of the Tungri tribe in Gaul. When he went to settle his bill with a druidess, she chided him for being overly acquisitive and stingy with his money. He jokingly replied that he would be more generous when he was emperor. The druidess told him not to joke, adding that he would be emperor after he had slain "The Boar." Aurelian was reported to have once consulted with Gaulish druidesses to ascertain whether his progeny would continue to rule the empire. Apparently they told him that no name would be more famous in the history of Rome than the future descendants of Claudius. The writer, Vopiscus, added that he thought that these descendants would achieve the glory prophesied by the druidesses.[11]

These two reports could be interpreted as stories created after the fact to provide support for the Gaulish campaigns and propaganda validating Roman rule. However, a third account stated that a woman of the druids shouted in the Gaulish language to Alexander Severus as he departed, warning him to hurry onwards, but not to hope for victory or put trust in his soldiers. It is notable that these women are consulted as seers, but no other mention of their druidic roles is mentioned. A druidess working as (or for) an innkeeper in Diocletian's account is also hard to account for, unless the druids' status had declined so dramatically that they took on other work and served as fortune tellers. In this and other scattered historical references to women who may have been female druids, they appear to serve primarily as seers.[12]

Female druids are mentioned in the myths and legends (although this does not necessarily equate with historical fact). Two female druids were said to have raised the Irish legendary hero *Finn mac Cumhaill*. A mythical woman named *Dreco* ("Dragon") is mentioned in the Dindshenchas (the "Lore of Places"), and was said to have been a female druid and a poet-seer. A mythical woman from the same group of texts, the daughter of *Rodub* ("Very Dark"), was also said to have been a druidess, poetess and prophetess (although these two were portrayed as dangerous magicians). However, another woman from Dindshenchas tradition, *Gaine*, was described as a seer (*fáith*) and a chief druid (*prim-drúi*).[13]

There is one other important historical reference to women who may have been druids. This comes from a first-century account by Tacitus in which several Roman legions, who were persecuting the druids in Britain for political reasons, had cornered them in the northwest peninsula of Wales. The British druids had traveled to this area in the hopes of escaping to Ireland, which was free of Roman influence. The account mentions that a group of women accompanied the druids. They were all dressed in black, and are described as brandishing torches and chanting curses at the Romans. The soldiers were so unnerved that they hesitated, and stepped away from the women. Their leaders goaded them into action, telling them not to be afraid of a group of women. The druids and the women were all massacred.[14]

It has been theorized by a number of scholars that these women may have been female druids, as they were traveling with a group of druids and were all dressed alike. It seems unlikely that they would have been wearing similar dress if they were simply the wives of the druids (unless that was a tradition), or if they were attending the male druids in some other formal capacity. It is a tantalizing piece of history, in any case.

Celtic Priestesses

One religious role for which we do have reasonable historical documentation in Celtic tradition is that of the priestess. A Latin inscription from Celtic Spain describes a woman as a *flaminica sacerdos* (a priestess of a particular deity), in this case working on behalf of the goddess *Thucolis*. While the druids, bards and seers operated within the community (or even between communities), early Classical accounts describe isolated communities of men or women who inhabited offshore islands and lived a religious life. Plutarch mentions remote and desolate islands near Britain which were named after gods or heroes. He wrote that one was recorded as having only a few inhabitants, although these were all holy men and held inviolate by the Britons.[15]

In the late first century B.C.E., Strabo wrote about a group of Celtic women who lived on an offshore island, near the mouth of the River Loire (off the coast of Gaul). They did not permit men on the island but traveled to the mainland themselves to have sex. They worshipped a particular deity (who is unnamed in the account) and once a year they replaced the thatched roof of their temple. Strabo claimed that any woman who let part of the new roof touch the ground was torn to pieces. We can reasonably interpret this to mean they were punished or ostracized in some way.[16]

Another Classical account, dating to the early first century C.E., spoke of the holy female inhabitants of *Sena*. This was one of a group of islands probably located off the coast of Gaul or the southwest coast of Britain (possibly l'Île de Sene off the coast of France). On this island there was a Gaulish oracle attended by nine virgin priestesses who were described as being able to predict the future, cure disease and control the elements. (Here we should read the word *virgin* as simply meaning "an unmarried woman."[17])

A group of female magicians or religious practitioners are also mentioned in an ancient Gaulish inscription from Larzac in France. The inscription refers to a group of women, one of whom is referred to as a "seeress." The text mentions the use of "women's magic" and describes the creation and purpose of the magical tablet[18]:

> In this tablet is a magical spell of women, with their special Underworld names/The charm of a seeress, a woman-seer creates this for Adsagsona [a goddess]/Severa, daughter of Tertios, is the writing-magician and spell-weaver/These two manifestations [powers] are maintained below [i.e., in the Underworld]/She [Severa] sends down [or releases] this incantation.[19]

The text lists the names of the women in the group: Banona, Paulla, Aiia, Potita, Severa, Adiega and Abessa. Severa seems to have been the primary magical practitioner, as well as the person who made the magical tablet. The grave in which the inscription was found may even have belonged to her. If so, this would be remarkable physical testimony for the existence of a Celtic seeress and magical practitioner from ancient Gaul who worked with a group of other female religious practitioners, performing divinatory rites and magic.

Although there is some slight confusion in the inscription about the names and gender of the people mentioned, it is possible that there are nine women listed on the tablet. Like the nine priestesses on the island of Sena, the theme of the "nine sacred women" occurs in other Celtic settings as well. Medieval Arthurian legends refer to *Morgan le Fay* living on an Otherworld island with her eight sisters.[20] In the Welsh tale of *Peredur,* the hero encounters a group of nine witches.[21]

A group of nine virgin priestesses or maidens are also mentioned in a poem attributed to the Welsh seer-poet Taliesin.[22] In the poem, Taliesin describes a journey to the Otherworld in search of a magical cauldron:

> My fame is splendid — a song was heard
> in the four quarters of the fortress
> which revolves in the four directions.
> My first word was spoken about the cauldron,
> kindled by the breath of nine maidens
> The cauldron of the Chief of Annwfn
> What is its virtue, with its edge of dark pearls?[23]

In this mystic poem, the offshore island has become an Otherworldly location; this sacred topographical connection is found in a number of other Celtic legends as well.

Bards and Poets

In addition to the druids, a number of Classical accounts refer to another group of highly esteemed people in Celtic society — the bards. They are described as singers and poets who composed poems to praise and support their leaders or patrons, or to criticize, shame or ostracize them.[24] The power of the spoken word was highly revered in Celtic society, and the stinging satire of a poet was believed to have the ability to cause disfigurement or even death. It certainly had the power to cause a person to lose face, which was a powerful incentive to act in a socially acceptable way.[25]

The poets were credited with the gift of prophecy. This connection between poetry and prophecy is a very ancient one, and is seen in other Indo-European societies as well. It may have been understood that if the poets had access to divine inspiration through the power of words, they could also use that connection to see into the future.

In addition to creating poems of praise or satire and performing prophecy, the poets created, memorized and recited poems which preserved a great deal of traditional lore. Some of this poetry was written down during the medieval period, and provides valuable insight into native Irish and Welsh values and beliefs, stories and legends, cultural ideals and constructs, mythological elements and symbolism, sacred and supernatural figures (including pagan deities), and legends connected with sacred places. Here is an example of one of these place-name poems[26]:

> Delightful the descending upon my attention,
> Not only the knowledge of a single place
> My mind illuminates the way forward
> to the mystic places of the world.
>
> Why do none of you seek — at any time
> If you wish to weave the web of knowledge
> from where came the name, of *Carn Máil*
> in the plain of Ulster?[27]

This poem goes on to relate a famous story of the seven sons of Daire (all named *Lugaid*) who pursue an enchanted fawn through the forest. They go to gather water from a well that was guarded by an old hag. The woman said that if they did not sleep with her she would kill them. One of the sons agreed, so that the others might live. The hag then transforms into a beautiful woman whose eyes contained three shafts of sunlight in each. When she reveals herself to be the personification of Sovereignty, the young man who exhibited such courage and selflessness is destined to become king.[28]

Some centuries after the introduction of Christianity, the role and prestige of the druids began to wane. The bards, however, were allowed to continue practicing their craft, and it is possible that they may have taken over or preserved some of the traditional roles and knowledge of the druids. These medieval poet-seers were known as the *filid* (singular *fili*), and like the druids, they underwent rigorous training for many years (seven years, in one source, and twelve in another).[29]

A number of manuscripts have been preserved from the medieval period which record aspects of the training of the *filid*. These texts include treatises on grammar, poetics and language, including various secret or cryptic poetic languages.[30] The poetic training schools continued in Scotland and Ireland until the 1700s, and even after their decline, poets continued to be held in great esteem throughout the Celtic world.[31]

Seers and Prophecy

While the druids and the poets were said to engage in prophetic activities, there was also a third group of respected individuals in Celtic society who specialized in prophecy and foresight.[32] There are also many legendary reports of seers, many of whom were women. The Irish goddesses Macha and her sister the Mórrígan were said to have this ability. In one saga, the mythical martial-arts teacher *Scáthach* was said to have made prophesies to the Irish hero *Cú Chulainn* regarding his destiny.[33]

Prophetic abilities and practices continued well into the medieval period and beyond. A famous account from twelfth-century Wales mentions a special group of seers in Wales known as *awenyddion*. Here is an excerpt from Giraldus Cambrensis' well-known account of these people and their prophetic practice:

> There are certain men among the people of Wales ... called *Awenyddion*, who are led by their innate understanding. When consulted about some uncertainty ... they immediately roar out as if seized from without by some spirit, and, as it were, taken over. They do not set forth coherently that which is requested; rather they speak through many evasions and riddles, and in meaningless and empty words, disjointed rather than cohering — but sounding splendid! The one who listens attentively will have an answer to the information that is sought. In the wake of this ecstasy, they are roused by others as if from a deep sleep, and thus are forced to come to themselves.[34]

The term *awenyddion* derives from the Welsh word *awen*, which means "poetic inspiration." A similar term existed in Old Irish — *aí* — which was sometimes associated with a cauldron of knowledge or inspiration.[35] Many other words formed part of a specialized native vocabulary pertaining to various types of sacred and divine knowledge, divine and poetic inspiration, and mantic or ecstatic practice.

One of the most famous legendary accounts of a female seer comes from the Irish saga *Táin Bó Cuailgne* ("The Cattle Raid of Cooley"). In the tale, queen Medb consults a female seer about an important quest she wishes to undertake. She had already waited for two weeks to set out, having been delayed by druids and sages who were waiting for a favorable sign. Medb then perceives a remarkable looking woman approaching.

She was described as a young adult with golden hair, wearing a red, embroidered hooded tunic and a speckled cloak fastened with a gold pin. Her brow was broad and her jaw narrow, and her dark lashes cast shadows halfway down her cheeks. Her hair was arranged in three tresses, two of which were wound upwards on her head while the third one hung down her back. She held a gold weaving rod in her hands (symbolizing the connection between weaving and spinning, and prophecy). Her eyes had triple irises, and she arrived armed, riding in a chariot drawn by two black horses.

Medb asks the young woman her name. She replies, "I am Fedelm, a woman poet from Connacht." The queen asks her where she has come from, to which she replies, "From learning poetry and vision in Scotland." Medb asks her if she has the power of foresight, and Fedelm says that she does. In response, Medb asks her to use her ability to look and see what will become of her army. Fedelm looks, and three times says, "I see it crimson, I see it red." Medb ignores her counsel, and is later defeated.[36] It is interesting to note that Fedelm's name (like the term *druid*) contains the root word **wid*, "to see."

Poetic Divination

The *filid* were known by several descriptive epithets, including the *Áes Dána* or "People of Skill." The word *dán* means a gift, bestowal or endowment, in both a physical and a spiritual sense. In spiritual terms, *dán* can refer to gifts from the divine to humankind, as well as spiritual offerings. It was particularly used to refer to arts, skills and science, especially the art of poetry.[37] It should be noted that the word *dán* is not related the goddess name Danu or to Celtic river names that contain this root word (such as the Danube). The river names derive from an Indo-European root word that means "river," while Danu's name probably comes from a root meaning "earth" (reflected in its earlier spelling of Donu, and in the cognate British divine name *Dôn*).[38]

The *filid* were associated with various types of specialized or sacred knowledge including *ergnae*, *eólas*, *éicse* and *ecnae*. *Érgna* means discernment, discrimination or understanding. *Eólas* means knowledge gained by experience or practice, especially knowledge of the way or place, as well as guidance, a path or opening, and secret knowledge (prescriptions, spells or charms). *Éicse* refers to divination, wisdom and the profession of the seer. *Ecnae* refers to wisdom, knowledge or enlightenment; wise or enlightened people; or things that are clear, visible or manifest.[39]

In order to become a fully trained *fili*, the medieval Irish poet had to master three types of prophetic or visionary techniques.[40] The first of these was *imbas forosnai*, which literally means "Great Wisdom of Illumination" (frequently translated as the "Wisdom or Illumination of Foresight"). In the ninth century text known as Cormac's Glossary, *imbas forosnai* was said to make known to the poet whatever thing he wished (and whatever it was expedient to reveal). In this ritual, the poet-seer chewed a piece of raw animal flesh and then placed it on a stone behind the door, chanting a spell over it. He offered it to the gods and summoned them to him, staying with them until the following day. He then chanted over his two palms and again summoned the deities. The poet then covered his cheeks with his palms and entered into a trance-like sleep. People sat and watched over the poet during this sacred sleep to make sure that he was not disturbed. When he awoke, whatever he had asked to know was revealed.[41]

This ritual appears be an attempt to obtain revelation or wisdom directly from the gods through an altered state of consciousness. However, scholars are at a loss to explain why the poet would chew a piece of "flesh" prior to his mantic sleep and prophetic vision. The chewing of flesh brings to mind well-known tales in which *Finn mac Cumhaill* chewed his thumb, or put his thumb under his "tooth of wisdom" in order to obtain prophetic wisdom. These scenarios, in which the consumption of special substances results in the acquisition of sacred knowledge, may refer to the ritual consumption of entheogenic substances. These are traditionally used in religious settings in order to produce a heightened state of awareness or an altered state of consciousness during which the participant seeks to connect with the forces of the divine. In particular, the chewing of "sacred flesh" may refer to the consumption of the *amanita muscaria* mushroom used in other cultures to connect the seer with the divine and obtain sacred knowledge.[42]

The second technique that had to be mastered by the *filid* was *teinm laeda*, which means the "breaking open" of a "song," or the "cracking open" of the pith or marrow of something. It involved chanting of some kind (as did *imbas forosnai*). Many Irish legends describe the "cracking open" of hazelnuts in order to obtain divine wisdom. One story tells how Finn utilized this technique, putting his thumb in his mouth and chanting through *teinm laida* to obtain whatever knowledge he required. He was said to chew his thumb "from the bone to the marrow, and from the marrow to the innermost core or sap," apparently alluding to reaching the powerful inner essence of the object and the wisdom it contained.[43]

Saint Patrick outlawed *imbas forosnai* and *teinm laeda* because he felt they involved offerings to pagan deities. However, he permitted the practice of the third kind of poetic divination, because he felt it simply involved spontaneous composition or illumination. This was known as *díchetal di chennaib*, and was a type of inspired and spontaneous incantation or spell ("off the top of one's head"). The phrase is sometimes translated as "spontaneous chanting of foreknowledge."[44] Since this type of divination happened very spontaneously (and was therefore a highly personal experience), we do not have a detailed description of the rituals associated with it.

Both the druids and the poets were said to make use of this method, and in one source it was described as one of the fourteen "streams of knowledge." Rivers and bodies of water were often associated with the pursuit of divine wisdom in Celtic tradition. In addition, sometimes the name of the divinatory method was spelled in a different way —*díchetal do chollaib cenn*. This appears to mean "spontaneous incantation made by way of the 'ends or tips' of the hazel tree." This could be a reference to hazel trees located at the Underworld well of wisdom, and hazelnuts which symbolized divine wisdom.[45]

The concept of a "sacred sleep" or trance state during which the seeker communicates with the gods or spirits is a common element in many religious traditions. It occurs in connection with the Irish divination ritual of *imbas forosnai* as well as with the Welsh *aweny-*

ddion. The concept of mantic sleep or incubation in darkness was associated with illumination or inspiration, and continued as part of Celtic tradition for many centuries. In the seventeenth century, poetic candidates in Scotland were placed in a darkened room where they laid down and wrapped their plaids around their head to block out the light (reminiscent of the darkened environment common in shamanic rituals). They remained like this throughout the day, with a stone on their belly (perhaps to regulate the breath, which would facilitate a trance state). At evening time, the poetic students gathered to recite their creations in front of their teacher. A similar practice also existed in Ireland during the early eighteenth century.[46]

A number of folk rituals associated with prophecy and the acquisition of divine knowledge were still practiced in Scotland in the nineteenth century. In one example — a ritual sometimes known as the *taghairm* — a person was specially selected from the community to undertake the ritual. Ritually wrapped in a bull's hide, they were taken to a secluded place (sometimes near a waterfall), where they were left alone to receive wisdom and guidance from the supernatural world.[47] It is interesting to note that an early form of divination in Ireland also utilized the hide of a bull. In this ritual, known as the *tarb feis* (literally "bull sleep"), a druid or poet was wrapped in a bull's hide and entered into a mantic sleep, during which he would receive a prophetic dream about the future king.[48] It seems that the roots of these druidic or poetic prophetic rituals continued on in many forms throughout the centuries.

4

The Celtic Otherworld

Popular books about Celtic religion and folklore often refer to the Celtic Otherworld almost interchangeably with the terms *fairy* or *faery* realms. In modern times the word *fairy* is applied to many kinds of spiritual beings, including elementals, plant devas, tricksters, household elves, wood sprites and many other types of supernatural entities. In these instances, the term *faery* is used to refer to the nature or powers of these sacred beings, as well as their supernatural realms of existence. Ask about the "fairies" in one of the Celtic countries, however, and you'll get a somewhat different response. There are supernatural entities in these countries who are popularly referred to as "the fairies," but they are generally a very specific type of being. They are often referred to by other names, including "The Good People," "The Good Neighbours" or "The People of Peace," and less obvious labels like "The Others" or even just "Them."[1]

These words, of course, are English terms. The modern English word *fairy* comes from the Old French *fairie* meaning "enchantment or magic." This in turn came from the word *fae* which derived from the Latin *fata,* a word used specifically to refer to the Fates, three goddesses who governed human destiny. The spelling "faerie" is a mock-medieval term introduced by Edmund Spenser in his 1590 work *The Faerie Queene.*[2] "Fay-erie" was originally a state of enchantment, and was only later used to refer to the beings who wielded these powers.[3]

The origin of all of these words can be traced back to an Indo-European root word meaning "to speak," referring to the use of words in magical practices (and reflected in the Latin word *fatum,* meaning "prophetic declaration, fate"). Clearly there is great power in the spoken word. How then should one address these supernatural beings? Folklore sources indicate that the fairies in southern Scotland apparently approved of being called a "seelie wight," an early modern Scots term meaning "blessed being."[4] What about in earlier times? What indigenous names were used to describe the Celtic fairies?

In Celtic tradition, the oldest information we have about the pre–Christian spiritual entities who lived in the unseen worlds comes from tales preserved in early Irish manuscripts. These beings were sometimes referred to as the *síabhra,* the plural of *síabair,* which means "a supernatural being or thing." More often they were referred to as the *Áes Síde,* the "the People of the *Síd.*"[5]

The word *síd* may be more familiar in its later Irish spelling, *sidhe,* popularized by the poet William Butler Yeats and used to describe both the fairy folk and their realms. In Old Irish, the word was spelled *síd* and reflects some of the most important concepts in early

Celtic theology. The word *síd* comes from a root word meaning "seat," as in the "seat or abode of the Gods." It was primarily used to refer to the Celtic Otherworld and the earthly portals that connected that world with our own. These were often associated with "fairy mounds," which are actually pre–Celtic burial sites. When Celtic culture arrived in Ireland, it incorporated some of the earlier sacred sites into its myths and cosmology.[6]

In Celtic tradition, the realms of the *Áes Síde* had a variety of indigenous names. In Ireland the Otherworld consisted of a number of supernatural kingdoms, including *Tír na nÓg* (the "Land of Youth"), *Mag Mell* ("The Plain of Honey"), *Tír Tairngiri* ("The Land of Promise") and *Mag Argatnél* ("The Plain of Silver Clouds"). In Welsh tradition the Otherworld was called *Annwfn*, a word that was later shorted to *Annwn*. This term means either the "Not-World" (i.e., the "Other" World), or the "Very Deep World" (referring more specifically to the Underworld).[7]

In addition to referring to Otherworldly locations, the word *síd* was used to describe the beings who lived in the Celtic Otherworld (the *Áes Síde* or "People of the Otherworld"). These were the old gods and goddesses of Ireland, divine beings who lived in the *síd* mounds and in watery locations like rivers, lakes, oceans, wells and springs. More specifically defined than the fairies of modern tradition (and far from the diminutive teacup fairies of Victorian tradition), the *Áes Síde* were spiritual entities of great wisdom, power and skill. In the medieval period the *Áes Síde* were also called the *Tuatha Dé Danann*, the "Tribes of the Goddess *Danu*" (a many-aspected goddess associated with the land, sovereignty and abundance, among other things).[8]

The inhabitants of the Celtic Otherworld realms were described in early Irish sources as fully human-sized beings, often very beautiful or striking looking, and wearing splendid jewelry and garments. Although their identity was not always immediately recognized by human beings, there was a special quality about them. In the Irish tale "The Wooing of Étain," the king encounters a remarkable woman bathing next to a silver basin engraved with four golden birds.

The story describes the woman combing her golden hair with a comb of silver decorated with gold. She had two braids, each containing a plaiting of four strands. She wore a bright purple cloak beneath which was a mantle with silver borders, and a brooch of gold fastening the garment at her bosom. Her arms were as white as the snow of one night, her cheeks as red as the foxglove of the mountain, and her eyes as blue as the hyacinth. It seemed probable to the king that the woman was from the Otherworld realms.[9]

An early poem in Old Irish describes the inhabitants of the Celtic Otherworld as a remarkable looking and formidable group of beings. The text says that they carry white shields in their hands decorated with emblems of pale silver, with glittering blue-grey swords and mighty horns. A pale-visaged and fair-haired supernatural assembly, they march ahead of their chieftain, scattering their foes. The *Áes Síde* are described as having smooth bodies with bright eyes, pure shining teeth and thin red lips. They are said to possess great strength, and are experts in battle and at playing *fidchell* (a type of early board game). In addition, they are described as being melodious in the mead hall and masterful at making songs. Such was the perception of the early Irish as regards their native pagan deities.[10]

Early archaeological evidence shows that the Celtic peoples venerated many gods and goddesses. The names of some deities suggest that they inhabited the celestial realms, such as *Taranis* ("The Thunderer"), *Loucetius* ("Lightning"), *Sirona* ("Divine Star Goddess") and the later Welsh figure of *Arianrhod* ("Silver Wheel").[11] By the time that the myths and legends were committed to writing, however, the gods seem to primarily inhabit the under-world realms, those located beneath the earth and across or underneath the waters.[12] This may reflect a native belief in three cosmic realms — Upper World, Middle World and Lower World — which is similar to or identical with the three cosmic worlds recognized by shamanic cultures around the globe.[13]

While the Celtic fairy realms were separate from our world in both time and space, it was understood that they existed at all times around (and parallel with) this world. The Otherworld was considered the source of wisdom, skill, truth, healing and power. The Celtic Otherworld realms contained beautiful or desirable elements recognizable from our world, but woven together in an almost dream-like state.[14] Here is an excerpt from a poem in the Irish tale *Serglige Con Culainn* ("The Wasting Sickness of Cú Culainn") detailing the marvels of the worlds that exist inside the *síd* mounds[15]:

> There are, in the doorway to the west, in the place in which the sun sets
> A herd of horses with speckled manes, and another chestnut herd
>
> In the doorway to the east are three sacred trees of bright purple from which
> A gentle, everlasting flock of birds calls to the offspring of the royal fortress.
>
> There is a tree in the doorway of the court, not unseemly the nuts from it
> A tree of silver that shines as the sun with a brightness like that of gold...
>
> There is a vat of intoxicating mead that pours out for the folk there
> It exists yet, enduring is the custom, so that it continues, ever-full.[16]

In the Irish tale "The Voyage of Bran," a woman from the Otherworld appears to the young hero (whose name means "Raven") and describes to him the wonders of her realm. She says that grief, sorrow, sickness and death are unknown in her world, and that wailing and treachery are unknown — the only sound is the sweetness of music. She approaches him bearing an apple branch, which seems to serve as a token of passage, or an invitation to pass between the worlds[17]:

> A branch of the place of apple trees in *Emain*
> I bring, like those that are familiar
> Twigs of white-silver on it
> Brightly fringed with blossoms
>
> There is an island in the distance
> Radiant around the path of sea-horses
> A shining course towards bright-sided waves
> Four feet sustain them
>
> Feet of white bronze underneath
> Gleaming throughout the exquisite worlds
> A fair land throughout the ages of the seas
> On which many blossoms fall
>
> Glistening is the appearance of every colour
> Throughout the gentle winds of the plain...
> From its view, a shining tranquility
> Of no comparison is existence out of the mist.[18]

In the myths, the inhabitants of the Otherworld interact with each other, as well as with the world of mortals. They are frequently beneficent in their interactions with human beings, although they may test or challenge people, or appear in their path to lure or guide them into an Otherworld encounter. If the person is found to be worthy (i.e., to live up to social ideals like truthfulness, courage, loyalty or wisdom), the *Áes Síde* may bless them with Otherworldly gifts such as wisdom, skill, abundance, guidance or protection.

In "Cormac's Adventures in the Land of Promise," King Cormac wanders away from his fortress and becomes separated from his companions, stepping into an archetypal "Otherworld encounter." A great mist descended upon him in the middle of a plain, and he found himself standing alone. In the midst of the plain he saw a large fortress with a wall of bronze around it. Inside the fortress was a house made of white silver, which was thatched with the wings of white birds.

Cormac enters the fortress and sees a shining fountain with five streams flowing from it. The inhabitants of that world took turns drinking the water from the fountain. There were nine hazel trees growing over the well which dropped their nuts into the water. The five salmon in the fountain cracked open the nuts and sent their shells floating down the streams. In a particularly beautiful passage, the text states that the sound of the falling of the streams was more beautiful than any music that humans can create.

A remarkable looking warrior appears to Cormac and takes him on a tour of his realm. Eventually he reveals his identity to the king, saying that he is the god Manannán mac Lir, king of the Land of Promise, and that the reason he brought Cormac to the Otherworld was to see this land. He tells Cormac that the fountain which he saw, with the five streams flowing from it was the Fountain of Knowledge, and the streams were the five senses through which knowledge is obtained. He goes on to tell the king that no one will have knowledge unless they drink from the fountain itself and from the five streams, and that the People of Many Arts are those who drink from them both.[19]

In an early Irish poem that describes the qualities of the Otherworld, a member of the *Áes Síde* invites a human being to visit the Celtic Otherworld realms[20]:

> Blessed friend, will you come with me, to a land in which music is found?
> Hair is like the blooming primrose there, and the colour of snow is every body.
>
> There is neither "mine" nor "yours" here, teeth are bright, and brows are dark
> A delight to the eye is our host, the colour of foxglove is every cheek.
>
> Every neck like the pink field flowers, a delight to the eye are blackbirds' eggs
> Though very beautiful is *Mag Fáil*, it is a desert compared with *Mag Máir*.
>
> Though the ale of *Inis Fáil* is intoxicating, more intoxicating is the ale of *Tír Máir*
> A wondrous land, the land I speak of; youth does not follow the age of elders...
>
> A distinguished people without blemish, conceived without sin, without guilt
> We see everyone on every side and no one sees us.[21]

Many centuries later, in the folklore traditions of the various Celtic countries, the inhabitants of the Otherworld realms were described in similar terms. They were still understood to live in fairy mounds or near bodies of water, and possessed the same dual potential to bless or challenge mortal beings. They were more inclined to assist if their habitations, culture and traditions were respected, and like the gods, could bestow the gifts of wisdom, skill, abundance, protection, fertility or good fortune.[22]

In Ireland, the beings we call the "fairy folk" were known in the Irish language as the *Síogaí* or *Na Daoine Maithe* ("The Good People"). In Scottish Gaelic they were referred to as the *Sìtheachain* or the *Daoine Sìth* ("People of the Síd mounds"). In Wales they were known as the *Tylwyth Teg* (the "Beautiful or Fair Folk") or *Plant Annwn* (the "Children of Annwn").[23]

The Irish and Scottish Gaelic names for the inhabitants of the Otherworld (*Síogaí* in Irish, *Sìthechain* in Scottish Gaelic) derive from the same root as the Old Irish word *síd*. These divine or supernatural beings retained the same name, the same habitations and the same nature as the old gods and goddesses, which is, in Celtic tradition, who they are.

In fact, it is in the Old Irish word *síd* that we may find the key to understanding the deeper significance of the *Áes Síde*. As we saw above, the word *síd* or *síth* referred to the seat or location of the inhabitants of the sacred realms. It was also used to refer to those divine beings themselves and to the magical, supernatural and wondrous qualities of their world. There is another Old Irish word *síd* or *síth* which meant "peace, goodwill, a state of peace," and which may derive from the first word.[24] This word did not refer to the peaceful nature of the *Áes Síde* or the fairies, whose customs and traditions were complex and multi-aspected. What the word does seem to represent is the peace that could result from maintaining a right relationship with the inhabitants of the Otherworld.

In many instances, the Otherworld appears to serve as a model of what our own behavior ought to be. In numerous Celtic tales, the inhabitants of the realms of the *síd* enter this world to guide or test people, and to begin to form alliances with them. These relationships are often instigated by the *Tuatha Dé Danann* or *Plant Annwn* themselves, and the particulars of these Otherworld tests or encounters are determined by them. In the Welsh tale *Pwyll, Prince of Dyfed*, the hero inadvertently gives offense to an Otherworldy king named *Arawn*. Pwyll immediately inquires of Arawn how he can makes things right, and directly asks him, "How shall I gain peace with you?"[25] Similarly, in "Cormac's Adventures in the Land of Promise," Cormac asks Manannán mac Lir if they might form an alliance. Manannán replies that he is well pleased by the prospect, and so, as the story goes, "they became allies."[26]

When humans enter into the presence of these divine beings, part of their task is to recognize their sacred identity. It is also important that they have an awareness of the culture and traditions of the *Áes Síde*, and duly show respect for their wisdom and power. The path to developing right relationship with the inhabitants of the Celtic Otherworld is based upon truth and honor. It is filled with potential blessings and teachings, as well as obstacles and challenges. The boundaries and lessons encountered along the way are set by the *Áes Síde*, who watch, influence and, in some cases, guide the lives of mortals. By respecting the gods, their sacred abodes, and their wisdom, people could aspire to rise above their mortal limitations and gain access to divine wisdom and skill. The potential of those gifts was as boundless as the power of the sacred realms from which they came.

5

The Gods of Britain and Gaul

The ancient Celts were polytheists, worshipping a variety of deities, both male and female. The surviving archaeological evidence has preserved the names or titles of almost four hundred British and Gaulish deities, as well as those from other parts of the ancient Celtic world. These Celtic deities were associated with healing and protection, wisdom and skill, and fertility and abundance. From ancient river goddesses and divine warriors to gods of healing springs and sacred places, the gods of ancient Britain and Gaul exhibited a wide variety of powers and attributes associated with sovereignty and the land, magic and ritual, and the features of the natural world.[1]

Because of the nature of the source materials — primarily place-names and inscriptions from the Romano-Celtic period (roughly first century B.C.E. to fifth century C.E.) — we do not have much in the way of surviving evidence attesting to the myths or stories associated with these deities. However, one Classical writer described the beliefs of the ancient Gauls in relation to a deity by the name of Ogmios, and this can provide us with a glimpse into the rich body of lore which would have been present at this time.

In the mid-first century C.E., the Roman poet Lucan wrote about some of the religious beliefs of the ancient Gauls in a work known as the *Pharsalia*. He described in some detail the tribes of Gaul, and referred to the druids and bards, who constituted their holy people. In the final book of his work, Lucan described a Gaulish sacred grove or *nemeton*, whose trees were cut down by Julius Caesar during a siege against the Celts.

While this poetic creation does contain some of Lucan's own views and opinions about the druids and their practices, it also provides some interesting insights into the religion of the Gaulish Celts. In this passage he addresses the druids and refers to their belief in the immortality of the soul:

> And you, Druids ... to you alone is granted knowledge of the gods and the powers of heaven (or else you alone are ignorant of them). The depths of groves in secluded forests are your sanctuary, your teaching that the shades of the dead do not seek the ... realms of Pluto.... The same soul controls a body in another world, and if what you sing of is true, death is but the midpoint of a long existence.[2]

Lucan also wrote about seeing a depiction of an old man armed with a club, followed by a group of people who were attached by delicate gold and amber chains to his tongue. An educated Gaulish passerby informed Lucan that the Celts did not identify or compare their god of communication and the spoken word with the Greek deity Hermes, but with Heracles (Hercules). This, Lucan was told, was because the power of eloquence is stronger than that of physical strength. The Celtic deity in question was Ogmios, and the power of his speech was so alluring that his followers were more than willing to be led by the sound of his words.[3]

Water Deities

Some of the earliest evidence we have pertaining to Celtic deities are names that are associated with the landscape. The Celts perceived that deities were present in the world around them, and could be communicated with for many different purposes. River goddesses provide us with a fascinating glimpse into the way in which divine beings were woven into everyday life. Many of the river names of modern-day Europe derive from the names of their earlier divine inhabitants. The Severn was named for the British goddess *Sabrina*, the River Wharfe for the goddess *Verbeia*, and the Welsh river Braint in Anglesey as well as the Brent in Middlesex from the goddess *Brigantia*. In Scotland, the river Tay was named after the goddess *Tawa*.[4]

The Gaulish goddess *Sequana* was the goddess of the river Seine. Her sacred springs, located in a valley near Dijon, formed the focus of a religious site where the water welled up from the ground. One image of the goddess shows her standing in a boat whose prow is shaped like a duck (water birds were frequently venerated in the ancient Celtic world). Sequana was offered hundreds of wooden objects, many of which were shaped like particular parts of the body for which supplicants prayed to her for healing.[5]

The connection between female divinities and bodies of water is both ancient and widespread in the Celtic world. Throughout the Celtic territories, there are rivers whose modern name, *Dee*, derives from an early Celtic word *Deva* or *Dewa* meaning "Goddess." A number of rivers named *Don* derive their name from the Celtic word *Devona*, "Divine Goddess." Other rivers exist whose names derive from an Indo-European root word *danu* which means "river." These include the Danube, the Dnieper, and the Dniester.[6]

Place-name evidence from Scotland provides us with insights into the water deities worshipped by the Picts, who were Celtic peoples living in the region of modern Scotland before the arrival of the Gaels. Pictish river goddesses included *Berva* in Aberbervie ("The Boiling or Tempestuous One"), *Boderia* in Aberbothri ("The Noiseless or Silent One"), *Brutaca* in Arbroath ("The Warm or Boiling One"), *Buadhnat* in Arbuthnott ("The Virtuous or Healing One"), *Devona* in Aberdeen ("Divine Goddess"), *Dubrona* in Aberdour ("The Flowing One"), *Gelidia* in Abergeldie ("White or Pure One"), *Labara* in Aberlour ("The Loud One"), *Luathnat* in Aberluthnot ("Little Swift One"), and *Nectona* in Abernethy ("Pure One").[7]

There were also numerous deities associated with springs or wells. At a British site now known as Bath, a British goddess named *Sulis* was venerated at the warm healing springs known as *Aquae Sulis*. The healing waters at Bath gush out of the ground at a rate of a quarter million gallons per day. Sulis received numerous offerings including pins, brooches, rings, shoes, metal vessels, coins and spindle whorls, as well as inscribed lead tablets bearing messages to the goddess (during the Roman era). The goddess' name probably derives from an early Celtic word meaning "sun." The sun seems to have been associated with the powers of warm healing springs, and at Aquae Sulis molds for making amulets were found which resembled a solar wheel.[8]

A divine couple named *Nemetona* and *Leucetius* were also venerated at this site (as well as at shrines and healing sanctuaries in Gaul). Nemetona, whose name means "Goddess of the Sacred Grove or Sacred Site," was a goddess worshipped by the Nemetes and the Treveri. She was also invoked in parts of Germany along with Mars in his capacity as a healer. Leucetius himself was equated with Mars during the Romano-British era as a healing deity, as well as a god of battle or protection. His name may derive from a word meaning "Lightning."[9]

Another local British goddess was *Arnemetiae*, "She Who Dwells Near the Sacred Grove or Sacred Site." A healing spring called *Aquae Arnemetiae* was dedicated to the goddess. Located at the bottom of a valley, the site was actually comprised of two springs that produced two different kinds of water.[10]

In Northumberland, the goddess *Coventina* received many votive offerings, including pins, brooches, coins, pottery, bells, bones, shoes and bronze animals. The offerings of shoes may suggest invocation for protection during a journey, or even the journey to the Otherworld (shoes were also found in Romano-British gravesites). Coventina seems to also have been venerated in northwest Spain and southern Gaul, where in Romano-Celtic inscriptions she was sometimes called *Sancta* ("Holy") or *Augusta* ("Revered"), titles rarely given to any deities other than Roman state goddesses.[11]

Deities of the Natural World

Some Celtic divinities were associated with animals, trees and other elements of the natural world. Inscriptions show that the Gaulish Celts worshipped a deity called *Taranis* ("The Thunderer"). Numerous depictions of a sky god shown with a wheel symbol are thought to perhaps be an image of Taranis or another god associated with the celestial realms. A similar name, *Tarani*, was given to a hero in the medieval Welsh tale *Culhwch and Olwen*, while an Irish place-name legend stated that one of the chief gods of the Britons was called *Etharún* (a name that contains the same root as *Taranis*).[12]

There were also deities associated with trees, groves and forests. *Rigonemetis* was a British god whose name signifies "King of the Sacred Grove." During the Roman period, a British deity was worshipped near Colchester named *Callirius*, "God of the Hazel Wood." A god known as *Cocidius* was in some inscriptions invoked as a god likened to the Roman deity *Silvanus*, a god of greenery and wild things, while elsewhere he was described as a god of soldiers. A native deity worshipped by the Narbonenses was called *Olloudious*, "Great Tree," while the deity *Ialonus* ("God of the Glade") was invoked in Lancaster in Britain where numerous objects were offered to him.[13]

There were also Celtic deities associated with animals. The name of the Continental goddess *Artio* derives from a root word **Art* meaning "Bear" (as does the name of the legendary British king, Arthur, and the Irish legendary king, Art, son of Conn). In Switzerland, Artio was depicted in a seated position, holding a vessel of fruit which she offers to a large bear who stands in front of her. She may have been a goddess or protector of hunters and/or a protectress of wild creatures. Other bear deities included the goddess *Andarta* ("Powerful Bear") and the northern British male god *Matunus*.[14]

The goddess *Arduinna* was associated with the Ardennes Forest in northern Gaul. She was shown riding bareback on a galloping boar with a quiver on her back and a small spear or hunting knife in her hand. The north British god, *Vitiris*, was venerated at more than forty sites and was depicted in single or triple form. He was also associated with the boar, as well as the serpent. Images of deer or stags are also found in connection with deities. A very early cult wagon from Strettweg in Austria shows a goddess presiding over a group of male warriors, some of whom hold stags between them. She holds a large vessel over her head, and may symbolize the abundance of the forest.[15]

Healing Deities

We have quite a bit of evidence for the ancient veneration of gods and goddesses associated with healing. The British deity *Nodons*, whose name has been variously interpreted to mean "He Who Bestows Wealth" or "Cloud-Maker," was a complex deity with many attributes, including that of healing. During the Roman era, a large Romano-Celtic temple was built to honor Nodons on the banks of the Severn river. The temple was situated at the site of an ancient earthwork, and the symbolism inside it — which included the sun, water and dogs — seems to underscore his role as a healer.[16]

Nodons' name is cognate with the Irish god Nuadu, who was considered to be the sacred ancestor or ancestor deity of certain Irish tribes. Nuadu was a divine leader who possessed a magic sword, and who, due to an injury sustained in battle, was given a silver hand by a physician god. Nuadu's name is cognate with the father of the later British divine figure *Gwynn ap Nudd*.[17]

The goddess *Sirona*, whose name means "Divine Star Goddess," was worshipped in Gaul and Austria. She was sometimes worshipped independently, and at other times with Celtic gods like *Grannus* and *Belenus*. She was extremely popular among the Treveria of Gallia Belgica, where her primary center of worship consisted of a healing spring and a sanctuary. Sirona was also worshipped at sanctuaries connected with warm healing waters in the Rhineland, Gaul, and as far east as Brigetio in Hungary. She was often depicted with a snake or a bowl of eggs, suggesting a role as a goddess of renewal and regeneration.[18]

The goddess *Damona* ("Divine Cow or Divine Deer") was also venerated by the Treveri. She was a goddess of healing springs and fertility, and was depicted with a snake and ears of grain. At one Gaulish site, Damona's partner was Borvo, and an inscription there alludes to her association with the healing springs. At this site, pilgrims and supplicants who visited the sanctuary sought a vision or healing dream of the two divine healers during their stay at the temple. A similar practice took place at the temple of Asclepius; the rite as recorded may reflect Roman influence on native Celtic practices.[19]

Other early goddesses were associated with healing shrines throughout the Celtic world. In Celtic Spain, two goddesses associated with bodies of water were *Ataecina* and *Endovellius*. Endovellius also appears to have been a goddess of the Underworld, and she was especially worshipped in Turobriga. *Ianuaria* was a goddess from Burgundy who was invoked at a healing water sanctuary. *Bormana* was a female divinity likewise associated with healing springs. In Gaul she was often linked with male deities like *Bormanus, Borvo* or *Bormo* (whose names suggest warm or boiling waters), although she was also worshipped independently without a consort.[20]

Ancamna was a healing goddess venerated by the Treveri in Gaul. She was associated with the healing god *Lenus* in the Rhineland, where figurines of mother goddesses were offered at her shrine. Small images of a mother goddess have been found at various sites; but as these all date to the Roman period, they may have been influenced by Roman iconography and may not represent native Celtic ideology. The representations of mother goddesses often included images of grain, fruit, bread, animals, cornucopia and children, indicating a connection with fertility and plenty. The mother goddesses appeared in single, double and triple form. Interestingly, they were sometimes depicted along with three small hooded gods, who are thought to represent male fertility.[21]

It should also be noted that the river Marne was named after a British deity called *Matrona* ("Divine Mother"). Her name is cognate with the later Welsh legendary figure *Modron* ("Divine Mother"), who was the mother of Mabon ("Divine Son"). Over time, symbolism associated with Modron may have become associated with the Christian saint *Modrun*. She was a patron saint in certain areas of Wales, and was also venerated in parts of Cornwall and Brittany. In the saint's iconography she is represented as a woman with a small child in her arms.[22]

Gods of Protection

Among the various Celtic tribes, there were numerous deities associated with battle and protection. *Teutates* ("Ruler of the Tribe or People") was venerated in Britain and Gaul where he was invoked as a god of war or protection. *Segomo* ("Victor or Mighty One") was also venerated in Gaul, and perhaps also in Britain and Ireland. The god *Rigisamus* ("Most Kingly") was likewise known in Gaul and Britain. (We should keep in mind that some of these epithets may be titles, rather than primary deity names).[23]

Alator (whose name may be connected with an early British word meaning "to rear or nourish") was also a god of battle. *Belatucadros* was widely worshipped in Britain and was propitiated by soldiers and by non–Roman civilians. His name seems to include a root word meaning "fair or shining." While there are numerous dedications to this deity, very little imagery has survived which could help us understand his attributes.[24]

There were also female divinities associated with war and protection. A statue of a war goddess found in Brittany, and dating to about 100 B.C.E., shows a woman wearing a war helmet. On top of the helmet is a goose with outstretched wings, symbolizing battle or fierceness. The British goddess *Andraste* was invoked by the warrior queen *Boudicca* (whose name comes from a root word meaning "victory") during a divination ritual associated with the outcome of a battle in the first century C.E. Andraste's name may be related to that of a Gaulish goddess named *Andarta*, perhaps meaning "Unconquerable."[25]

The goddess *Brigantia* was the patron goddess of a large tribe known as the Brigantes. Her name comes from the same root as the Irish goddess *Bríg* or Brigid, and means "High or Exalted." The Brigantes were a huge tribal federation in northern Britain both before and during the Roman occupation. Brigantia was therefore a tribal goddess, a protectress and the personification of her tribe. Her iconography included imagery associated with the Roman goddess Victory, as well as the goddess Minerva. Interestingly, Caesar mentioned that the Gaulish Celts worshipped a goddess figure whose attributes he likened to Minerva.[26]

Horned God and Antlered Goddess

There is a great deal of evidence for the worship of horned or antlered deities in Celtic tradition, and this practice may be quite ancient. Images of horned deities occur as far back as the late Bronze Age, where they are sometimes associated with animal imagery. There are also numerous depictions of horned animals, including those which do not normally have horns, like birds. A bronze statue from Maiden Castle in Britain shows a three-horned bull with the busts of three goddesses on his back. This brings to mind the first century C.E. Gaulish depiction of a bull with three cranes on its back and head, aptly inscribed *Tarvos Trigaranus* ("Bull with Three Cranes"). This stone carving was discovered in the church of Nôtre Dame.[27]

One of the earliest depictions of an antlered deity comes from northern Italy and is dated to the mid-fourth century B.C.E. Here the deity is shown with antlers, holding a torc (a twisted neck-ring) in one hand and a serpent in the other. Similar imagery was found a number of centuries later on the silver Gundestrup cauldron. This remarkable object, which was probably created in Thrace for Celtic patrons, was later looted and then lost or deposited in a bog in northern Europe. On the Gundestrup cauldron, an antlered god sits cross-legged, holding a torc in one hand and a ram-headed serpent in the other. He is surrounded by the figures of many animals, including a deer, wolf, lions or bears, and a dolphin, which is ridden by a smaller human figure.[28]

Numerous stone carvings of horned or antlered gods were found in Gaul as well. These include depictions of rams and bulls, which may symbolize fierceness or fertility. There are also symbols associated with the Underworld—the serpent (from Celtic tradition) and the rat (from Roman tradition). One of the most famous of these images shows a horned god, along with symbols of abundance and fertility. Below him is a partial inscription which reads, "*-ernunnos.*" When supplied with the missing initial letter C, it forms the name Cernunnos, "The Horned One." This name has since been used to refer to all horned or antlered deities, although this may be a title or epithet for a variety of similar Celtic deities.[29]

In Britain, the horned god was frequently associated with imagery of war or protection. Symbolism associated with the horned or antlered god is also seen in connection with various Irish legendary heroes, such as *Furbaide Ferbend* and *Conall Cernach*. Furbaide ("the Horned") was said to have three horns coming out of his helmet, two made of silver and one of gold. While Conall's epithet *Cernach* looks as though it could be related linguistically to the name Cernunnos, it either means "angled, having corners," or reflects the attribute of "victory."[30]

Conall Cernach was a legendary warrior and hero, and was considered to be the semi-divine ancestor of the royal house of *Dál nAraide*, a group of people located in northeast and central Ireland. In one Irish tale, a serpent wraps itself around Conall's waist. In some iconographic contexts serpents are shown twined around the waist of some of the horned god figures. There may be a deeper connection between the two than their names would at first suggest. In addition, it has been suggested that the ancestor god of the Gauls, who was likened to the Roman god Dis Pater, may have been a deity similar to Cernunnos due to the Otherworld imagery associated with both figures.[31]

There are also several surviving representations of horned or antlered goddesses. One of these comes from a fairly early Continental context, where it formed part of a metal plaque. In this image, the figure has horns similar to a cow or water buffalo. The other two representations come from Britain, and these depict antlered goddesses. One is a very simplistic image made from clay, while the other is a more complex Romano-Celtic representation of an antlered goddess who holds a bowl or vessel in her hand. Like the realms of healing and abundance, and battle and protection, the archetype of the horned or antlered deity was clearly open to goddesses as well as gods.[32]

Divine Couples

There is also evidence in the ancient Celtic world for widespread and pan-tribal worship of divine couples. One of the most popular consisted of *Rosmerta* (*Ro-smerta*, "Good Provider"?) and a consort often likened to Mercury (a god associated with fertility and commercial success). The couple was widely worshipped in Gaul and the Rhineland, as well as among the *Dobunni* of the British West Country. Rosmerta was often depicted with an offering plate and cornucopia. She was also shown with a rectangular bucket that has been interpreted as being associated with butter or cheese making. However, it has also been suggested that it may be a vessel of regeneration, as the couple was sometimes shown with the Roman goddess *Fortuna*.

In these cases, both of the goddesses are depicted with torches. Fortuna's torch was in an upright position (symbolizing life) while Rosmerta's was in an inverted position (perhaps symbolizing death or regeneration). This possible afterlife or Underworld connection is strengthened by the existence of a depiction of the goddess feeding a snake from her purse. Rosmerta may have been considered more powerful than her unnamed Celtic consort; in one depiction the god offers the contents of his purse to the goddess, who sits on a throne before him. In addition, Rosmerta was also venerated on her own, independently of any male consort. Like many deities, Rosmerta was sometimes associated with healing springs.[33]

Another popular divine couple was *Nantosuelta* ("Meandering Stream") and *Succellus* ("The Good Striker"). The goddess was often depicted with a little house on a pole (a human dwelling, or perhaps a dovecote or birdhouse), as well as with pots and honeycombs. This symbolism suggests domestic abundance and wellbeing. However, a raven was sometimes depicted beneath the couple, suggesting an Underworld aspect. The couple was worshipped in Gaul and the Rhineland, with one additional surviving inscription from Britain. Nantosuelta was also venerated on her own, as was Succellus. In these instances, he was often depicted with a dog (or once, with a partner dressed like a huntress with a bow and quiver). Nantosuelta's high status was indicated by her crown or diadem, and in Britain by the presence of a torc or neck-ring.

Some of the most ardent worshippers of this divine couple were the tribes known as the *Aedui* and the *Lingones*, from the region now known as Burgundy. In this area, the couple was primarily venerated for their associations with wine making. Here the goddess is shown with a cornucopia, offering dish, or fruit; the god is depicted with a pot, wine jar or barrel, and grapes. Succellus is always shown with his hammer (hence the name "The Good Striker"). His name is believed to reflect imagery similar to that associated with an Irish deity known as the *Dagda*. The Dagda possessed a club that wielded life from one end and death from the other. Succellus' name suggests that his followers hoped and wished that he would wield only the good or life-promoting end of his hammer. Another interesting parallel exists between the two deities. Succellus' partner is named for a stream, while in one Irish myth the Dagda was likewise paired with a water goddess — the goddess Boand, tutelary goddess of the river Boyne. [34]

Pan-Tribal Deities

Some Celtic deities were localized in nature, associated with certain tribes or particular landscapes or areas. Others seem to have been more pan-tribal in nature, and were venerated over large regions. One of the most widely worshipped pan–Celtic deities was *Belenus*. Traces of his worship extend from northern Italy, through Gaul and into the British Isles. The root of his name may mean "Bright or Shining," and it is possible that this same root is found in the name of the Irish holiday *Beltaine*.[35]

Another popular deity was *Maponus* ("Divine Son"), who was venerated in the north of Britain, where he was sometimes pictured with a hunter goddess. In later Welsh legend the figure of *Mabon* ("Divine Son") was also associated with the hunt. Maponus was also worshipped in Gaul, where he was venerated in connection with a healing spring. During the Roman era, the Celtic deity Maponus was frequently associated with Apollo, a god who was often pictured as a divine youth (although Maponus himself was not always pictured so).

Dedications to the deity suggest that he may have also been associated with the skills of poetry and music; on one altar from north Britain he was equated with Apollo Cithareodus, "Apollo the Harper." Maponus' name may have been preserved in Scotland in the place-name *Lochmaben* ("The Lake of Mabon"). He was also associated with a megalith in southern Scotland known as *Clochmabenstane* ("the stone of Mabon"). Until fairly recent times, local gatherings were traditionally held at this stone.[36]

Maponus was also mentioned in a magical or religious inscription from ancient Gaul that was discovered in the last century. It was found at Chamalières, retrieved from a sacred spring where it had once been placed. The inscription consists of a prayer asking for the assistance of the god Maponus, who is invoked in his chthonic or Underworld aspect. [37] The inscription provides the names of the individuals who made the prayer, and also includes a specific oath they have taken. The inscription may represent a ceremony in which one group of men is undertaking the religious initiation of another group of male candidates.[38] The following is one possible version of this difficult text:

> I invoke the divine, chthonic Maponus, with vigour
> Come to us [the leaders of the rite] and to them [the candidates]
> through the magic of the Underworld gods,
> and to those who will swear the oath of The Strong One...
>
> A small thing sown, will grow...
> [now] blind, I will see...
> By means of this ritual incantation
> He [the invoker] will persuade him [the god]...
>
> Join [with us] ... I prepare them ... [spoken three times]
> Join with us![39]

Another widely worshipped deity was *Lugos* or *Lugus*, who was venerated in Britain, Gaul, and other parts of Europe. His name is still found in the modern landscape, as the place-name *Luguvalium* ("Strong in the God Lugus") became modern Carlisle in Britain, and *Lugdunum* ("The Fortress of Lug") became associated with both Lyons and Leiden. Lugos' name is cognate with that of the Irish god *Lug*, who was a divine warrior, magician and poet. The Irish festival of Lugnasad was held at the beginning of August, while in Gaul, a festival in honor of Augustus was held at Lugdunum, possibly suggesting some connection.[40]

One of the most widely venerated deities in the ancient Celtic world was the goddess *Epona* ("Divine Horse Goddess"). She was worshipped in numerous Celtic regions, and seems to have been one of the most popular figures in the Celtic pantheons. Epona was most highly venerated in Gaul and the Rhineland, but was also worshipped in Britain and as far east as Bulgaria. Inscriptions to the goddess have also been found in North Africa and Rome, as her veneration was adopted by Roman cavalry and traveled with them to other parts of the ancient world. In fact, Epona was so highly honored that she was given her own official feast day in the Roman calendar (December 18), an honor not bestowed upon any other Celtic deity.

Epona was often depicted seated sidesaddle on a mare, as well as with a foal or other horses. Horses were very important in Celtic society, and may have symbolized beauty, speed, strength, intelligence, bravery, prestige and nobility. Epona was also shown with fruit or loaves of bread, signifying plenty and abundance. She was a goddess of horses and stables, horse breeding and riding, as well as fertility and abundance.

Epona may also have been associated with journeys to the Underworld or the afterlife. In one Romano-Celtic context, she is depicted on a funeral plaque. Another funeral plaque contained the image of several horse heads in silhouette. In another depiction Epona is followed by a human being whom she appears to be leading, possibly to the afterlife. It should be remembered that in various Celtic myths, horses often transport human beings into an Otherworld location or encounter.

Another important aspect of the goddess Epona was her association with the concept of sovereignty. She was sometimes shown with a raven, a bird associated with the Goddess of Sovereignty in Irish contexts. The Irish goddess Macha, who has a pronounced aspect as a goddess of sovereignty, was associated with both ravens and horses. In addition, in one instance Epona was shown as a triple image. This is not uncommon for Celtic deities. In Ireland the three divine sisters known as *na Mórrígna* or "The Great Queens"—*Mórrigan*, *Macha* and *Nemain*—were associated with battles and protection, magic and shape shifting, fertility and abundance, and sovereignty and the Otherworld (to varying degrees). It would not be at all surprising if Epona represented one of the earliest representations of the Sovereignty Goddess in the ancient Celtic world.[41]

As we can see, the ancient Celts living in Britain, Gaul, and elsewhere in Continental Europe worshipped a wide variety of powerful and multi-aspected male and female deities. Their powers covered a wide range of skills and attributes, which often overlapped or were combined in ways that might seem unusual to us. There were many manifestations of the Goddess of Sovereignty throughout the Celtic world, as well as local and pan-tribal deities of abundance, protection, wisdom, skill, healing, nature, crafts and magic. These deities would have been invoked at large tribal gatherings, rituals or assemblies, at local shrines or healing wells, as well as in personal and family devotions. Incorporating almost every aspect of life, death, and rebirth or regeneration into their religious life, early Celtic ritual would have been polytheistic, animistic and devotional, and as complex and sophisticated as any native religion in the ancient world.

6

Irish Gods and Goddesses

Medieval Irish manuscripts have preserved a great deal of information pertaining to the gods and goddesses of the early Irish. Many of these deities were referred to by the collective title *Tuatha Dé Danann*, "The Tribes of the Goddess Danu." A collection of lore pertaining to the Tuatha Dé Danann, composed between 900 and 1100 C.E., stated that among these divinities, their "people of power" (*áes cumhachta*) were considered gods (this would likely refer to sages, magicians, warriors, leaders and divine craftspeople) while their herders and farmers (*áes trebtha*) were non-gods (although this tradition is not repeated elsewhere).[1] The *Tuatha Dé Danann* are a lively, colorful and engaging group of divine figures with an astonishing array of powers, attributes and skills, and their stories formed an important part of the native theology, cosmology and cultural foundations of the early Irish and Scottish.[2]

One of the most important Irish deities was known as the Dagda, "The Good God," as in "good at many things." This seems to have been a title, for he was also called *Eochaid Ollathair*, "Great Father of Many Horses," and *Ruad Rofhessa*, "Red or Noble One of Great Knowledge." He was a king or chief of the Tuatha Dé Danann, associated with abundance and fertility, the weather and the harvest, druidic magic and protection, and the powers of life and death. He owned an inexhaustible cauldron of nourishment, a club that wielded life from one end and death from the other, and a magic harp. In an early Irish source, *De Gabáil in t-Sída*, the Dagda is described as a famous king of the Tuatha Dé Danann. The Gaels of Ireland had to gain his friendship before they could experience prosperity in the land.[3]

In the Battle of Moytura, the Dagda summoned his harp to assist the Tuatha Dé Dannan, which it did by playing the three types of music for which harpers were known: joyful music, sorrowful music, and music for sleeping. The harp killed nine of the Fomorians and then distracted them with its music so that the Dagda and his companions could escape. The Dagda had bound the melodies in the harp so that it would not make a sound until he summoned it, which he did with the following poem[4]:

> Come, Oak of Two Cries!
> Come, Well-Proportioned, Four-Sided One!
> Come summer, Come winter!
> Speech of harps and bagpipes and horns![5]

In one tale, the Dagda unites with the goddess Boand (the spirit of the river Boyne); their son is the god Oengus Mac Óc. He also united with a goddess known as the Mórrigan at Samain, after which she ensured assistance and victory for the gods in an important battle. The Dagda has a number of divine offspring, including *Bodb Derg* ("Red Raven"), *Oengus mac ind Óc* and the goddess *Bríg* (Brigid).[6]

Perhaps the most important of the Irish goddesses was the Mórrígan. Her name either means "Great Queen," reflecting her many powerful attributes, or "Phantom or Nightmare Queen," reflective of her darker or more supernatural side. She had two sisters, Macha and Nemain; all three were referred to by the term *Badb* ("Scaldcrow"). The Mórrígan was associated with fertility, sexuality, magic, shape shifting, prophesy, battle and sovereignty. She could appear on the field of battle, using magic to affect the outcome or affecting armies psychologically through terror or frenzy. She could also help or hinder heroes, as in an Irish tale associated with the great Irish hero *Cú Chulainn*.

The Mórrígan appeared in various shapes: a beautiful woman, a warrior, a hag, or in various animal forms (raven, wolf, heifer or eel). Although popular sources often focus on the dark or threatening aspects of the Mórrígan, she possessed a wide variety of attributes associated with the entire cycle of life and death. One Irish place-name, "The Paps (Breasts) of the Mórrígan," underscore her associations with fertility and the land.[7]

In the Battle of Moytura, she proclaims a poem of victory to the royal heights of Ireland, to its chief waters and river mouths, and to the hosts of the *Áes Síde*[8]:

Peace towards sky, sky towards earth,
Earth beneath sky, strength in each
A flowing vessel, full of honey, mead in abundance
Summer in winter, spear on shield, a shield amongst a company

A fierce, rough host banished, heavy lamentation, spoils...
I prevail over mountains, river, clearings...
Acorns on trees, a branch for rest, repose from it, and growth...
"Do you not have news?" Peace towards the sky — it will be everlasting.[9]

The Mórrígan is one of the most active and present of the Irish goddesses, while the goddess Danu, after whom the god-tribe was named, almost never appears in the written sources. Based on extensive research, I demonstrated that Danu and the Mórrígan were the same figure, and that the name Anu was the original name of this deity (the Mórrígan is more of a title or epithet). The attributes of Anu and Danu, which are known to us from a number of early Irish sources, show that this goddess figure was not just connected with battle and sexuality. Her powers were numerous, including life and death, creation and destruction, fertility and abundance, magic and shape shifting, wisdom and prophecy, and sovereignty and the land. Anu/Danu/The Mórrígan is an example of the widespread Celtic deity archetype known as the Goddess of Sovereignty.[10]

The Mórrígan had two sisters, Macha and Nemain. There are few references to Nemain, who primarily exists in raven form and hovers over the slain on the battlefield. She was said to be the wife of *Nét*, a god of war (although her title, *Bé Néit*, could also mean "Woman of War.") The other sister, Macha, was more well known in Irish tradition. Her name may derive from the Old Irish word *mag*, meaning "plain or field." The early Irish held sacred assemblies and ritual gatherings on open fields, many of which were associated with legendary or divine figures or occurrences. Macha was associated with horses and ravens, as well as sovereignty, prophecy, battle, abundance and shapeshifting.[11]

In Irish tradition, there were three women named Macha. The first was a primordial figure, the wife of Nemed ("Sacred"), who led an early mythical invasion of Ireland. The second Macha appears from the Otherworld and becomes the wife of a wealthy landowner, bringing him good fortune and abundance. However, he boasts at an assembly that although pregnant, his wife can outrun the king's horses. Macha is put to the test and succeeds, but dies after the race (after having given birth to twins). She curses the Ulstermen so that they were as weak as a woman in childbirth in their time of greatest danger, an important element in the saga "The Cattle Raid of Cooley." Cú Chulainn, who figures prominently in the saga, had a horse called "The Grey of Macha."[12]

Macha's race against the king's horses is described in a poem from the Metrical Dindshenchas. In the first stanza below, Macha nobly prepares herself to undertake the ordeal[13]:

> The remarkable, spirited one unbound, loosened the hair on top of her head
> Without a fierce shout driving her, she came to the racing, to the games...
>
> Though swift the horses of the chief, among the tribes strongly apportioned
> The woman was swifter, without effort; the horses of the king were too slow.[14]

The third Macha was *Macha Mongruad* ("Macha of the Red Mane"). She was said to have been an early queen of Ireland, ruling around 350 C.E. Although she had inherited the rulership from her father, her position was disputed by the sons of a rival because she was a woman. In the guise of a hag, she lures the young men into the forest. She cleverly tricks and overcomes them, and forces them to build the rath or circular enclosure at *Emain Macha. Emain* means "twins," referring to the twins of Macha mentioned above. Macha Mongruad then ruled as queen of Ireland, and even shrewdly married one of her rivals as a political move to assure her power and authority.[15]

Another important Irish deity was *Lug Lamfáda* (later spelled *Lugh*). His name may derive from an Indo-European root word meaning "bright or shining," although this is far from certain. One of his epithets was *Samildánach* ("Many Skilled"), for in one tale he proclaims his skill in harping, smithcraft, healing, building, battle, poetry, magic, sagecraft and other arts. In *Baile in Scáil,* Lug appears to *Conn Cétchathach* (Conn of the Hundred Battles) in a vision. In the vision, Conn sees a golden tree on a plain, next to which was a house with a ridgepole of white gold. Inside is a young woman seated on a crystal chair. She is the Sovereignty of Ireland. In front of her is silver vat and a golden cup full of red ale, which is to be given to the rightful king. Lug asks the woman to whom the cup should be given, and she proceeds to name Conn and his descendants.

Lug's name is cognate with that of *Lleu,* a divine figure known from medieval Welsh legendary tradition. Lleu earned the name *Lleu Llaw Gyffes* ("Bright One of the Skillful Hand"), a name which seems to parallel's Lug's names (*Lug Lamfáda,* "Lug of the Long Arm or Hand," or *Lug Samildánach,* "Lug the Many Skilled"). Lleu earns his name after a skillful cast at a bird; Lug kills his grandfather Balor with a skillful cast of a sling. Lug was said to have been the divine father of the great hero *Cú Chulainn.*[16]

Lug was also known for his powers as a magician. In the Battle of Moytura, he chants a spell known as *corrguinecht* (literally "crane-wounding"), which was one of the seven things that constituted a satire. It was believed to have been performed standing on one leg, with one arm outstretched and one eye closed, a position suggestive of the stance of a crane.[17] Here is an excerpt from Lug's spell, as he urges the Tuatha Dé Danann to free themselves from the oppression of the Fomorians[18]:

> Hail! Hail! Woe! Ill-luck! A sharp craft!
> A person of magic behind a cloud of protection
> Through strong crafts of the druid ... with superior power and brightness...
> Towards a partnership with sky and earth, sun and moon...
> This is my host, a mighty, spirited, powerful and hopeful host.[19]

The goddess *Bríg* was a triple goddess of poetry, smithcraft and healing, along with her two sisters of the same name. The early Irish text known as "Cormac's Glossary" states that she was the patron goddess of poets and afforded great honor and affection:

> Brigit ... a female poet, the daughter of the Dagda. This is Brigit the female sage or woman of knowledge, i.e. Brigit the goddess who the poets adored, because very great and very famous was her protecting care. It is for this reason that they call her goddess of poets by this name.[20]

Bríg's name comes from an Indo-European root word meaning "High or Exalted One." She has a son named *Rúadan* with the divine figure Bres, who was the ill-fated son of the Irish goddess Ériu and a Fomorian king. The Fomorians were a legendary race of supernatural beings who imposed hardships upon the Tuatha Dé Dannan. Eventually Bres is deposed as an unworthy king. Ruadán is killed and Bríg laments him; this was said to be the first time that "keening" (ritual lamentation) was heard in Ireland.[21]

It is believed that Bríg served as inspiration for the figure of Saint Brigid. She was associated with fertility, abundance and protection, and was invoked for aid during human and animal birthing rites. The medieval "Life of Saint Brigid" exhibits many interesting pre–Christian elements. Saint Brigid was reported to have grown up in a druid's household where she was fed the milk of magical Otherworld cows. She could provide limitless food without her larder ever dwindling, her cows could provide a lake of milk, and one measure of her malt made enough ale at Easter for seventeen churches.[22]

Another well-known Irish deity was the god *Ogma*. He was the brother of the Dagda, and a skilled warrior and poet. His epithet was *Grian-ainech* ("Sun Face or Countenance"). Ogma was the legendary creator of an early Irish system of writing known as *ogam* (which is described in detail in an upcoming chapter). He may be similar to the Gaulish god *Ogmios* who was also considered to be a "strong man" or hero, his strength derived from the power of eloquence.[23]

The goddess *Boand* ("Bright, White or Blessed Cow") was the wife of Elcmar, an early inhabitant of the sacred site known as *Brug na Boinne*, which is modern day Newgrange. In one tale, the Dagda wished to sleep with Boand, to which she consented. He tricks her husband into leaving for a day, but keeps the sun in the sky for nine months so Boand could bear their son, Oengus that same day. In another tale, Boand visited a well of knowledge guarded by the god Nechtán and walked around it heedlessly three times. The waters rose up and she was drowned, thereafter becoming the spirit of the River Boyne.[24]

Here is an excerpt from the Dindshenchas poem pertaining to Boand in which she approaches the well at the *síd* of Nechtan[25]:

> Nechtan, son of keen Labraid, whose wife was Boand, I assert
> There was a hidden well in his fortress from which flowed every ill mystery...

> Bright Boand came on a journey there, her fiery pride uplifted her
> To the well of no drought, to test its power.

> As she walked around the well three times unwarily
> Three waves burst forth from it, from which came the death of Boand.

> Every way the woman went the bright, cold water followed
> From the *síd* to the open sea, not lacking in power, from this it was called Boand.
>
> Boand from the bosom of our great riverbank, Mother of very fine Oengus,
> The son she bore the Dagda, a clear honour in spite of the man of the *síd*.[26]

Boand's son, *Oengus Mac Óc* ("The Young Son"), was so named because of the circumstances of his birth: "Young is the son who was conceived and born in one day." He was a skilled hunter and warrior, and assisted couples in love, as he does in the stories "The Wooing of Étain" and "The Pursuit of Diarmaid and Grainne." In "The Dream of Oengus," the deity himself falls in love with *Caer Ibormeith*, a woman who existed in human form one year and in the shape of a swan the next. Oengus may have connections with the British deity *Maponus* ("Divine Son"), who in some contexts was portrayed as a hunter. The Welsh figure of *Mabon* ("Divine Son") was also involved in a magical hunt, which was undertaken in order to help a young man win the woman he loved.[27]

As we have seen, there are a number of instances in which deities have three names or are grouped in threes. The three sisters Macha, Mórrígan and the Nemain are one example; Bríg and her two sisters (also named Bríg) are another. The Dagda had three primary names: *An Dagda, Eochaid Ollathair* and *Ruad Rofhessa*.[28]

Another famous trio consisted of the goddesses *Ériu, Banba* and *Fotla*. All three were associated with the land and sovereignty of Ireland. One legend related how when the Gaels arrived in Ireland, they encountered these goddesses and asked their permission to inhabit the land. Each of the divine women requested that the land be named after her. Ériu tells the travelers that their coming has been long prophesied and welcomes them; their chief poet and seer *Amairgen* assures her that her name will be the name of the island forever (*Eire*).[29]

The three sisters Ériu, Banba and Fotla were said to have married three brothers (either sons or grandsons of the Dagda). Eriu married *Mac Greine* ("Son of Sun"), Banba married *Mac Cuill* ("Son of Hazel") and Fodla married *Mac Cecht* ("Son of Plough"). Banba and Fodla were still used as poetic names for Ireland up until the seventeenth century.[30]

Another sacred trio consisted of divine craftsmen, three brothers named *Goibniu, Luchta* and *Credne. Goibniu* was the Divine Smith, *Luchta* the Divine Wright and *Credne* a Divine Metalworker. In the legend "The Second Battle of Moytura" (*Cath Maige Tuired*), these three deities forged magical weapons in order to help the Tuatha Dé Danann vanquish the Fomorians during an important conflict. Goibniu was also the host of the Otherworld feast at which a special ale was served which conferred immortality. His name is cognate with the Welsh figure of *Gofannon* ("Divine Smith") and appears in later Irish tales as the legendary figure of the *Gobban Saor* ("Gobban the Craftsman").[31]

Dian Cecht was the physician god of the Tuatha Dé Danann. He provided healing through knowledge and skill, as well as through magic. He crafted a silver arm for the god *Nuadu* after his was lost in battle. However, Dian Cecht's son *Miach*, who was also a gifted healer, made a new arm for Nuadu out of flesh. In a jealous rage, Dian Cecht killed his son. Dian Cecht's daughter *Airmid* was associated with knowledge of the healing power of plants and herbs. In the Battle of Moytura, Dian Cecht and his children sing incantations over a sacred well. Wounded warriors from the Tuatha Dé Danann were immersed in the well and were healed.[32] Warriors are depicted being immersed in a vat or cauldron by an enormous being (presumably a deity) on a large, highly-ornamented silver vessel known as the *Gundestrup* cauldron which dates to the first century B.C.E.[33] In addition, in the medieval

Welsh tale of *Branwen*, the king of Ireland is presented with a magical cauldron which possessed the magical ability to heal wounded warriors.[34]

Nuadu Argatlám ("Nuadu of the Silver Hand") was an early king of the Tuatha Dé Danann. Due to the blemish of losing his arm, he had to step down from the kingship. He recognized the many divine talents of the god Lug, who reigned after him. Nuadu was said to possess a magical sword that conferred victory in battle. He was also referred to as a seer, as well as a king and champion, and was the ancestor deity of the *Eoganacht* and other population groups in Ireland. It is thought that Nuadu may have some connection with the British deity *Nodons*, as their names are cognate.[35]

The god *Midir* inhabited an Otherworld dwelling at *Brí Léith*. He owned a magic cauldron which was treasured by the Tuatha Dé Danann (but which was stolen by Cú Chulainn). In some tales he is related to the Dagda or Oengus mac Óc. Midir was associated with three cranes that protected his dwelling. He is most well known as the divine lover of the woman Étaín. His name may derive from a word meaning "to judge."[36]

Like Boand, the goddess *Sinann* was associated with water and the pursuit of wisdom. It was said that she possessed all the mystic arts, except for *imbas forosnai*. She has an encounter at the edge of a river, pursuing sacred knowledge, but is swept into the river and drowned or overwhelmed. She became the goddess of the river Shannon.[37]

The following is an excerpt from the Dindshenchas poem about Sinann as she pursues the mystical power of knowledge or poetic inspiration known as *imbas*[38]:

> The well of Connlae, great was its spirit, beneath the summoning edge of the sea
> Six streams, not equal in fame, flow from it; Sinann was the seventh.
>
> The nine hazel trees of Crimall the wise man drop their fruits into the well
> They are by the command of illusion under a dark mist of druidic magic.
>
> At one time, as is not usual, their leaves and their flowers grow
> Remarkable, though a noble attribute this, their being ripe all at once.
>
> When the nuts are ripe they fall into the well below
> They scatter on the bottom so that the salmon eat them.
>
> From the juice of the nuts, no small matter, they form the bubbles of wisdom
> Each hour they come from beyond, over the green flowing streams.
>
> There was a young woman with blonde hair, yonder, from the Tuatha Dé Danann
> Skillful Sinann of the bright countenance, daughter of bright, resplendent Lodan.
>
> One night the young woman thought, the sweet, red-lipped maiden
> That every attribute was at her command, except the power of *imbas*.
>
> One day she went to the stream, the young woman, fair was her form
> Until she saw, it was no small matter, the beautiful bubbles of wisdom.
>
> The woman went, a lamentable journey, after them into the green flowing stream
> She was drowned there from her venture; so that from her Sinann is named.[39]

The goddess *Flidais* was associated with the abundance of animals and the forest, and was said to own herds of wild deer and cattle. She was described as being drawn along in a chariot pulled by deer. A legendary feast associated with Flidais included the milk of wild deer and cattle, and her name may derive from a phrase meaning "deer feast" (*fled*, "feast" plus *os* "deer"). An independent goddess, she lived in her own *síd*-mound, and was associated with fertility, sexuality, healing and abundance, as well as warfare, hunting and protection.[40]

The god *Manannán mac Lir* was the son of the sea-god *Lir*. He was the king of the underwater realms associated with the ocean. As such, appears to rule over a different group of gods than the chiefs of the Tuatha Dé Danann, who primarily inhabited *síd-* or fairy mounds under the earth. Mannanán's realms are beautifully described in the Irish tale "The Voyage of Bran." He was a master of magic, wisdom and illusion, and was said to ride across the waves in a chariot drawn by Otherworld horses.

Manannán owned a number of magical objects, including a boat, a horse, a sword, and magical pigs and cows. He also possessed a "crane bag," made from the skin of a crane (which was in reality a woman transformed into crane form). It held a number of magical objects and talismans. Mannanán mac Lir's name is cognate with that of the Welsh mythic figure of *Manawydan ap Llyr*. In addition, the Isle of Man was named after him. The name of Mannanán's father, Lir, appeared in later times as the namesake of Shakespeare's play *King Lear*.[41]

The Lost Gods of Ireland

The most well-known members of the Tuatha Dé Danann are the deities mentioned above: The Dagda, The Mórrígan, Macha, Lug, Bríg, Ogma, Boand, Oengus mac Óc, Mannanán mac Lir, Nuadu Argatlám, Ériu, Banba and Fodla, Goibniu, Luchta and Credne, Dian Cecht, Miach and Airmid, Midir, Sinann and Flidais. Early Irish sources — myths, legends, annals and place-name tales — also refer to a vast array of other divine figures who played an important role in the Irish religious tradition.[42]

One of these was *Bodb Derg*, whose name means "Red Raven." He was a famous son of the Dagda who was associated with *Brug na Boinne* or Newgrange. Bodb Derg appears in a variety of tales. He had many divine offspring, as well as a noble retinue of one thousand two hundred and ten divinities. His sons included *Artrach*, *Aed Alaind* ("Fair Flame"), also called "Aed of the Poets," *Aengus Ilclessach* (Aengus "Of the Many Feats"), *Ferdoman* and *Derg* ("Red"), whose divine family lived in the *síd* mound of Dorn Buide, associated with the Wave of Cliodna in the south of Ireland.

His daughters included *Findine* and *Scothníam*, who fell in love with Cailte. She was described as wearing a green cloak over a yellow tunic, with a glistening plate of yellow gold at her brow. Bodb Derg's daughters *Mumain* and *Slat* lured and held *Aed*, son of *Eochaid Lethderg*, the king of Leinster, inside a *síd* mound for three years. Another daughter, *Muirenn*, was the foster mother of the warrior *Cáel Cródae Cétguinech*. She helped him by providing him with love poetry with which to woo the fairy woman *Créde* who lived near the Paps of Anu.

Aillenn Fhialchorcra ("Aillenn of the Purple Veil") was also one of Bodb Derg's daughters. She fell in love with *Áed mac Muiredeach*, King of Connaught, but he was forbidden by Saint Patrick to marry anyone other than *Aife Ilchrothach* ("Aife of the Many Shapes"), daughter of the King of Leinster. Later, Patrick allowed the fairy woman to marry the king as a reward for giving up her "false druidical beliefs." The marriage of a divine female with a mortal king was said to be the first marriage Patrick performed in Ireland.

Dairenn was another daughter of Bodb Derg. She desired to be Finn's only wife for one year. When he refused her, she gave him a silver goblet of mead (knowing it was taboo for him to refuse a drink). The mead intoxicated and confused him, and caused him many problems. Dairenn was described as a beautiful woman seated on a stone at the edge of a ford, wearing a dress of red gold with a heavy tunic over it and a green cloak fastened with a gold brooch. She had fifty dark-yellow strands of hair extending from one ear to the other (braids, perhaps) and a diadem of gold on her head as a sign of her Otherworldly queenship.

Sadb was another daughter of Bodb Derg. She was wife to Finn mac Cumall and the mother of Oisín ("Little Deer"). She existed for some time in the shape of a deer after being enchanted by a druid. One of Finn's taboos was that he was not to sleep with her on the shortest night of summer.

In addition to Bodb Derg, the Dagda had other divine children, including *Oengus mac Óg, Bríg, Midir Mongbuide, Aife Fholtfhinn* and *Fergus Foltfhinn. Midir* had a daughter named *Aife.* Oengus had a son *Aed Uchtgel* ("Aed of the White Breast"), who was the father of *Bé Mannair* ("Woman of Destruction"), the slowest of the fairy women in the Hill of Howth, and of *Étain Fholtfinn,* who was the swiftest. *Étain Fholtfinn* was the favorite of her father. She was the lover of Oscar, the son of Oisín, and died of grief upon his death. She was buried under a mound near the Hill of Howth in County Dublin.

Other prominent members of the Tuatha Dé Danann also had divine children. The god Midir had two daughters, *Ailbe* and *Doirenn,* and a son called *Donn.* The god *Nuadu* had a daughter named *Echtga* who was associated with the mountain Slieve Aughty in County Galway. He also had a son by the name of *Tadg Mór,* from the *Síd of Almu* (now known as the Hill of Allen). Tadg had a daughter called *Muirne Muincháem* ("Muirne of the Lovely Neck"), who was said to be the mother of Finn mac Cumhall.

The god *Lir* was primal deity whose name means "Ocean." He ruled over *Síd Finnachad.* Lir was the father of three sons: Mannanán mac Lir, *Eochaid* and *Lódan,* and father of Sinann associated with a mountain and a site called the "Plain of a Great Oak." One of Lir's adversaries was *Ilbrecc,* who was connected with the sacred mound at Assaroe (*Essa Ruadh* in County Donegal).

Bé Binn ("Sweet or Pleasing Woman") was the daughter of *Trén* ("Strong"), King of the Land of the Maidens. She is described as a very tall woman sitting on a mound, wearing a bright purple cloak with a gold pin, a golden breastplate and a diadem of gold on her head. When she took off her helmet she revealed eight score finely-colored tresses which hung loose around her shoulders.

In one tale, she was said to be the daughter of Elcmar of *Bruig na Boinne* (the figure whom the Dagda tricked so that he could sleep with Boand). She was the wife of *Áed Minbrecc* ("Lightly Freckled Flame"), a son of the Dagda, and associated with the *Síd* mound of *Essa Ruad* ("Red Waterfalls"), modern Assaroe. Bé Binn was responsible for guarding the Ale of Immortality (whatever portion was left over from the aforementioned Feast of Goibniu). She used healing herbs to cure the hero *Cailte* in the *síd* mound of Assaroe. She had a son with *Caincinde,* a sage of the Tuatha De Danann. The son's name was *Cas Corach,* and he was a sage and a minstrel.

The ranks of the gods included divine healers and sages. *Libra Primlíaig* was called "The Chief Physician"; he was also Chief Sage to the god Manannán mac Lir. Libra (whose name is not connected with the astrological sign) arose at an early hour of the day to gather healing herbs with the morning dew still on them. He wore a cloak of ram's wool from Otherworld sheep, into which he gathered herbs of healing and curing. *Díangalach* ("Swift

Valiant One") was a noble druid of the Tuatha Dé Danann. His death was said to be one of the three greatest losses ever inflicted upon the Tuatha Dé Danann.

The divine musicians of the gods were also many. *Úaine* was the daughter of *Buide*, from the *Síd* of *Dorn Buide* in the south of Ireland. She was the minstrel of all of *Tír Tairngire* and possessed a flock of Otherworld birds that produced enchanting music. *Fer Tuinne* was a divine musician who played for the people of *Brug na Boinne* as well as the surrounding region. His music could lull to sleep warriors in battle or women in childbed. *Fidach* was a great musician of the Tuatha Dé Danann whose name may mean "Whistle." His daughter *Fethnaid* ("Calming") was also a divine musician. The Tuatha Dé Danann considered her "all their music and all their delight of spirit." Her death was one of the three greatest losses of the gods.

Cnú Deroil was a divine musician and dwarf who served as part of Finn mac Cumhall's retinue. His music was so beautiful that jealous musicians drove him out of Slievenamon (*Sliabh na mBan*, "Mountain of the Women") in County Tipperary. His wife *Blathnait* was a dwarf prophetess from the House of Donn in Munster, whom Finn and his warriors carried off and married to their musician *Cnú Deroil*.

Many members of the Tuatha Dé Danann were skilled in magic. *Aed mac Aed na nAmsach* was a young man of the Tuatha Dé Danann from the Hill of Ardmoll (Rathlin Island). He owned a magic vat that could change spring water to mead and a drinking horn that transformed salt water to wine. *Ben Mebla* ("Woman of Deceit") was a druidess of the Tuatha Dé Danann. She fell in love with Finn mac Cumhall, but when spurned by him she used the power of magical breath to repel one hundred and fifty of his hounds and put them into a fairy mound. *Uaine* was the daughter of *Modarn* and lover of Finn. She was able to change herself into the shape of various animals.

Although in general the gods are considered to be immortal, there are instances in which they suffer illness or die. *Scothníam* was the daughter of *Caissirne*, a supernatural druid from the *síd* of Cruachu. She raided the Fort of Bairnech every Samain Eve, taking the nine best cows to revenge the death of her father and grandfather. She approached the fortress bravely and without fear, with her tunic bound up between her thighs, and two spears in her hand. Scothníam was eventually killed by Cas Corach, the son of Bé Binn.

Cliodna was a queen of *Tír Tairngire*, The Land of Promise. A well-known tale describes how she was drowned by a great wave called *Tonn Cliodna* (The Wave of Cliodna). Fifty of Manannán mac Lir's ships were also destroyed by the great wave. *Teite Brecc* ("Teite the Freckled") was the daughter of *Ragamnach*. Along with a group of one hundred and fifty women, she went to play in the waves. All the women were drowned at a place called "The Wave of the Fort of Téite." These stories are believed to represent elements of native Irish flood myths.

Other members of the Tuatha Dé Danann included *Abairche*, a divine physician and his consort *Tudhcha*; *Uchtdelb*, the wife of the god Manannán mac Lir; *Blái* a daughter of *Derg Díanscothach* of *Síd Ochta Cleitig* (sometimes said to be the mother of Oisín), and *Aed Ruad* ("Red Flame"), king of the *Síd* of Assaroe and in one text the father of the goddess Macha. *Dobrán Dubthaire* was from the *síd* mound of *Liaman Lennchaem* in Leinster. His daughter *Liaman Lenncháem* ("Liaman of the Lovely Cloak") was the owner of that same *síd* mound. The gods were protected by numerous divine warriors, including *Glas, Donn* of *Dumach, Séolbrat* and *Side* from *Sen Gabar* in the south of Ireland, *Donn Ailéin* ("Donn of the Island"), and *Aed Ailéin* ("Aed of the Island"), associated with Rathlin Island off the north coast of Ireland.

Some early divine figures may have survived in a somewhat altered form, as with the figures of *Donn Firinne* and the *Cailleach*. Donn Firinne was a supernatural figure from the southwest of Ireland, where he was associated with weather and storms, as well as a magical white horse. Some people maintained that after death they would be brought into Knock-fierna, a hill associated with Donn Firinne, after their death. This probably reflects his earlier origin as Donn, a son of Mil. He was associated with *Tech Duinn*, "The House of Donn," located off the southwest coast of Ireland. One ninth-century text maintained that it was to Donn, and his house, that people went after their deaths.[43]

Another supernatural figure associated with the southwest of Ireland was the *Cailleach* or "Veiled One." The *Cailleach Bhéara* was connected with the Beare Peninsula in County Cork. Legends associated with her demonstrate her very early connection with the landscape and its primal organization. She was also known in Scotland, where she herded wild deer and guarded wells. A late eighth-century poem attributed to the Cailleach portrays her as an old hag lamenting the day when she was beautiful and powerful, and slept with kings. One theory regarding this poem is that it may reflect the possibility that the Cailleach is a manifestation of the Goddess of Sovereignty.[44]

By exploring Irish myths and legends, and other early written sources, we discover whole worlds beyond our own. These realms are inhabited by vibrant and complex divine beings associated with many aspects of existence, both earthly and Otherworldly, who formed an important part of the religious beliefs of the early Irish.

7

The Ritual Year

Much of what we know about the early Celtic ritual year comes from Irish sources. A yearly cycle of work existed in early Ireland which had a strong seasonal basis and was primarily associated with the movement and herding of livestock. From this cycle, cultural patterns were formed which were associated with a wide variety of social activities including courtship, marriage, raiding, and seasonal festivals. Evidence pertaining to work cycles and gender roles, and folk traditions associated with the seasonal festivals, suggest that one-half of the year may have been regarded as the "male" half and the other the "female" half.[1] These gender associations may have also manifested in the veneration of male or female deities, in accordance with the season of the year.

The yearly cycle seems to have been originally divided into two parts, a warm summer period (*sam*) and a cold winter period (*gam*), a division that reflected patterns associated with livestock. Summer began on May 1 when the herds were moved to their summer pasture, and winter began on November 1 when the animals would have returned from summer grazing. At some point, the year wheel was divided in two once more, resulting in a total of four seasonal festivals: *Beltene* on May 1, *Samain* on November 1, *Imbolc* on February 1, and *Lugnasad* on August 1.[2] An earlier calendar arrangement containing three festivals is also possible, as we have very little evidence pertaining to Imbolc prior to the folklore tradition of the last few centuries. In the folk tradition, the feast of Imbolc was associated with the birth of animals and the return of a fresh supply of milk. Lugnasad, which marked the beginning of autumn, was a harvest festival and a time to honor the ancestors. Let's explore each of these festivals and their connection with social activities, gender roles, and the veneration of divine figures.

Beltene or *Bealtaine* marked the beginning of the summer half of the year. On this day, the herds were moved away from settlement areas to new summer pastures where fresh food would be available. It was necessary to move the herds away from the growing crops so that they would not eat or damage them. For these reasons, the community divided itself into two groups on May 1. Women and children left with the flocks and herds, taking with them any needed equipment for cooking, dairying and spinning. It was important that everyone left simultaneously so that no one's cattle remained near the crops. Due to this cyclical separation of the sexes, May 1 was considered the end of the marriage season and an unlucky day to wed.[3]

During the summer months, the men stayed behind to weed the fields and protect the crops (and in some cases to prepare for warfare or raiding). The summer months were considered the prime season for raiding, but less warfare occurred in August due to the workload of the harvest. *Lugnasad*, which took place on August 1, was a festival that marked the beginning of the harvest. While the reaping of grain was primarily considered men's work, some women would have come down from the hills to help with the flax harvest, as less milking and dairying took place at this point in the summer. Marriageable women would have been present at the Lugnasad assemblies, as temporary marriages were often entered into at this time of year. These marriages could be dissolved by mutual consent of the partners if the union was not considered happy or auspicious.[4]

Samain marked the beginning of the winter season and the start of the new year. It was the end of the raiding season, as well as the end of the main hunting season for deer and wild boar, both being male-oriented activities. All domestic animals had returned to the settlement by this date, and all winter food stores gathered and stored. In addition, all the women would have returned to the community by or before Samain. After Samain, some outdoor work was still required, but the emphasis shifted to indoor or domestic activities. The bounty of food that was generally available at this time of year led to the guesting and feasting season. Nobles and clients met each other at rounds of feasts where relationships might be fostered or tested, and formal marriages arranged (now that the community was reunited). Women were responsible for supervising the use of food stores and providing hospitality at these events.[5]

The beginning of winter was a time of impending darkness and difficulty, with overtones of potential illness, misfortune or death. It is easy to see how imagery associated with death and the supernatural became associated with this time of the year, a liminal period when interactions between the seen and unseen worlds were possible. Rituals of propitiation, thanksgiving and divination likely took place at Samain; these activities are associated with New Year's festivities in many cultures around the world. Cosmogonic legends pertaining to the end of cycles, darkness, rebirth, creation, and the beginning of new cycles may have been ritually recited or enacted at these gatherings.[6]

Imbolc took place on February 1 and was the symbolic beginning of spring. Many animals gave birth around this time, and the return of fresh milk was extremely important. Cow's milk had long since run out and many stores of food had been consumed during the guesting and feasting season, as well as by the family itself during the long winter months. While the origin of the name of Imbolc is uncertain, an association with ewe's milk is possible. Whatever its origin, the emphasis of the season was on female interests and activities, including birth and the renewal of milk. Women were responsible for supervising the use of the remaining food stores for domestic and social consumption, and the birth of lambs and calves, and the subsequent replenishment of food stores, was an occasion for great joy.

For men, this was a season of relative inactivity, as it was not yet time to plow or sow. Weather divination in preparation for these activities was often performed on Imbolc. Men's work with the land and the animals would resume sometime in the following month or so. Spring would also mark the beginning of the raiding season. However, spring warfare was less profitable than summer raiding due to the weakened condition of the cattle, and so spring was often considered a better time for planning and negotiation.[7] The seasonal activities associated with the yearly cycle seem to suggest that the summer half of the year was associated with male energies or activities and the winter half of the year with female concerns.

Folklore and the Ritual Year

Folk customs and beliefs associated with the Quarter Days (Samhain, Imbolc, Beltaine and Lugnasad) formed a strong part of Irish culture even into the present era. Their survival and importance was due in part to their connection with important agricultural practices. Folk traditions recorded in Ireland and Scotland from the sixteenth and seventeenth centuries to the present time also seem to reflect a yearly pattern of male and female symbolism and activities.

Folk Customs at Beltaine

Certain customs associated with Beltaine (such as the gathering of May flowers or the setting up of a May bush) were enacted by the entire community. However, prior to the departure of the herds and half of the community, important social and religious assemblies were held. Great bonfires were lit at these gatherings, and many accounts state that these were created by groups of men who also presided over rituals of propitiation and protection. In Ireland, the male head of household supervised and led a procession at Beltaine around the boundaries of his land, buildings, crops and herds to protect them and encourage fertility and abundance.

In Scotland, groups of men gathered together to ritually create Beltaine cakes or caudles (custards) which were offered in a propitiatory manner to the earth or to certain spirits or animals to protect the flocks from harm. In some cases, after the Beltaine cake was created, it was broken up into pieces, one of which was blackened with ash. Whoever received the blackened piece was called the Hag or Cailleach of Beltaine, a term of derision. This person was sometimes treated as a symbolic victim who was ritually carried "into" the fire. These "victims" may represent male heads of households who were historically excluded from rituals because they had failed to pay their social debts or obligations (their reputations having been "blackened").

The focus on male energies or activities at this time of year may have resulted in certain taboos pertaining to women. Folklore recorded in some Scottish villages suggest that male energies were considered useful or propitious at this time of year. Every May morning a man was sent across the salmon stream to ensure good luck and a good catch. He also prevented any women from performing similar actions in the belief that she would hinder the salmon from coming into the river. In addition, in many May Day processions, men appeared dressed as women, or played the part of any female roles.[8]

Folk Customs at Lugnasad

Great fairs and assemblies were held at Lugnasad, and the presence of women at these gatherings led to the arrangement of marriages at this time of year. The harvesting and presentation of "first fruits" was an important part of the holiday. In many parts of Ireland, festive outdoor gatherings were held on hills or mountain tops, or beside lakes or rivers. Many of these gatherings were associated with a figure known as *Crom Dubh* ("The Bent Dark One"), a legendary druid or pagan chieftain who was said to have opposed Saint Patrick. In Ireland, offerings of fruit or flowers were made at stones or cairns, and horses and cattle were driven into bodies of water to protect them from danger and disease. In Scotland, great fires were lit and charms performed to ensure the continuation of abundance.

In addition, a special cake was toasted on a fire made of sacred wood and distributed by the male head of household to the members of the family.

One notable harvest custom was the ritual cutting of sheaves of grain. In some areas, the first sheaf was referred to as the Harvest Maiden. The privilege of cutting this sheaf was often given to a young woman. She was assisted by a male reaper who held the sheaf while she cut it. The Harvest Maiden was often formed into a female figure that was dressed and decorated, and later honored at the harvest supper. In some cases, the last sheaf was referred as the Hag or *Cailleach*, and was passed along to a farmer who had not yet finished harvesting his crops. Receiving this item was an undesirable event, and whoever had the Hag would be under pressure to finish and pass the sheaf on to another. While the harvest was primarily a male-dominated event, the assistance of women and the arrangement of marriages point to the increasing return or inclusion of female energies and activities. The Cailleach may have symbolized the upcoming shift into the female half of the year, as well as the importance of securing the harvest in a timely fashion to ensure the continuation of life.[9]

Folk Customs at Samhain

In the recent Irish folk tradition, Samhain was regarded by the old people as one of the leading festivals of the year. Offerings of food were left near the door of the house for the fairies in order to ensure their favor in the coming year. Divination was common and was often performed using apples and hazelnuts, the fruits of trees associated with the Otherworld since very early times. At sunset, great fires were lit, usually on heights or hilltops. It is interesting to note the lighting of Samain fires at sunset, in contrast with the Beltaine fires that were often lit at dawn. Various rites of protection and propitiation took place on Samhain Eve or Day. These included the ritual circuiting of fields and herds with torches that had been lit from the Samhain fire.

Feasting often took place at Samhain, even in the poorest households, and apples and hazelnuts were often included in this ritual meal. In Scotland a special Samhain cake was made, and this was created by a group of women who began their work after sundown. A large space in a house was marked out by a circular line and considered consecrated ground. The women sat in a circle and took turns preparing and toasting the sacred cake, working in a sunwise direction. While groups of men ritually created sacred cakes at Beltaine, it was groups of women who performed this task at Samhain.

Guising, processions and pranks often took place at Samhain, and many activities that were not normally acceptable were tolerated or overlooked during this liminal period. One of the most interesting Samhain customs in Ireland was the procession of the *Láir Bhán* or "White Mare." A group of youths were led in procession by a person in a white robe or sheet carrying a decorated horse skull. The youths went from house to house, reciting a long string of verses at the doorway. This custom is reminiscent of the *Mari Lwyd* tradition from Wales, a procession that took place around the Christmas or New Year season. A number of Yuletide or Gregorian New Year's customs may have originally taken place at "old" New Year (Samhain).[10] The focus on a white or grey mare may suggest an association with the Goddess of Sovereignty who was often symbolized by such an animal.

Samhain was often characterized by interactions between this world and the inhabitants of the Otherworld, including deities, spirits, fairies and witches (depending on the age of the account). Just as the Celtic day began at sundown, the Celtic New Year began in darkness, a primal and potent place which led to the re-creation of life and the new cycle.[11] Imagery associated with darkness, mystery and creation suggest that this time of transformation and rebirth was associated with female energies or symbolism.[12]

Folk Customs at Imbolc

The Festival of *Imbolc* had a pronounced female focus. Many folklore traditions focus on the figure of Saint Brigid, who was believed to travel around the countryside on this night, blessing people and livestock. The earlier goddess, *Bríg*, was associated with smithcraft, healing and poetry; Saint Brigid was connected with fertility, abundance and protection. At Imbolc, offerings of cakes or butter were often left out for the saint, and Bridget's crosses made of straw or rushes in the shape of diamonds, lozenges or three- or four-armed crosses were hung in the home and barn.

In Scotland and Ireland a sheaf of straw was made into the shape of a human figure, which was then dressed and decorated. It was carried by groups of girls from house to house, where it was venerated, given offerings, and believed to bestow blessings. In Scotland, after the procession, the girls retired to a nearby house where they feasted on the food received during the procession. Later in the evening, groups of young men waiting outside the house humbly asked permission to enter. After some parleying, the girls allowed them to enter the house to show their respect to Bridget.

Farmers awaited the season of spring plowing, and sometimes symbolically turned a sod or two at Imbolc. Weather divination often took place, and frequently involved the emergence of various animals from their underground lairs (the serpent in Scotland, the hedgehog in Ireland). If the animal stayed out, this indicated the return of good weather, but if it returned to its lair, more bad weather was to come. In Scotland, certain prayers or charms were recited in which a serpent was said to emerge from a hole, or a knoll or mound (reminiscent of the síd-mounds). The serpent was often referred to as a female entity, and was called either the "Daughter of Ivor" or "The Queen."[13]

Deities and the Ritual Year

In addition to male and female-oriented patterns associated with work activities and folk traditions, certain male or female deities were also venerated in connection with the yearly cycles of the seasons. In the seventeenth century, the writer Geoffrey Keating, a clergyman from southern Ireland, wrote a work called *Foras Feasa ar Éirinn* ("Elements of the History of Ireland"). Prompted by negative English accounts of Irish history, he wanted to do justice to the traditions of the indigenous Irish (as well as their Anglo-Norman conquerors), and presented many examples of legendary, mythological and popular traditions.[14]

Geoffrey associated the Beltaine ceremonies with the hill of *Uisnech*, a sacred site located near the traditional center of Ireland. A bonfire was lit at this site in the midst of a large assembly, on whose behalf sacrifices were made. While no other surviving literary evidence corroborates this report, archaeological excavation on the summit of the hill revealed a large area of scorched earth containing the charred bones of many animals.[15]

A supernatural figure was associated with this hill. The Irish myth "The Wooing of Étain" mentions a king of the Tuatha Dé Danann who lived at Uisnech. This was the Dagda, a figure associated with abundance, fertility, magic and the powers of life and death. He is described as a god who "saw to the weather and the harvest."[16] These attributes accord well with the primary concerns and symbolism associated with *Beltaine.*

The Festival of Lugnasad was associated with the god Lug, as well as a number of supernatural female figures. In "The Battle of Moytura" Lug assists the *Tuatha Dé Danann* in obtaining victory and freedom from an oppressive tribute imposed by the kin of Bres, an unfit king. Lug spares Bres' life in exchange for information about plowing, sowing and reaping.[17] Bres was the husband of *Bríg*, whose feast-day takes place on the exact opposite point of the year wheel. Perhaps a lost myth situated Bríg and Bres on opposing points of the calendar, only to have Bres supplanted by the newcomer Lug, a skillful deity who became the patron of the harvest.

Lug was said to have instituted the assembly of Lugnasad to honor his foster mother *Tailtiu* who died from the exertion of clearing many plains (presumably in preparation for agriculture).[18] Other versions of the myth state that he set up the assembly to honor two of his wives (who also died and were buried at sacred sites).[19] Other divine women were associated with the Lugnasad assemblies in other parts of Ireland as well. The Festival of Carmun was held at this time of year to mourn the passing of Carmun, a female warrior and magician who had tried to destroy the sap or essence of the fruits of the land. She was vanquished by four members of the Tuatha Dé Danann, and her grave was dug by Bres. While the reason for mourning Carmun is unclear, it may be that the festival celebrated the victory of the gods over forces which might blight or destroy crops and food. The Festival of Carmun was held over seven days, the third day being devoted to women (following the first two days which were for high kings and saints).[20]

The Assembly of Macha was in all likelihood also held at Lugnasad. The legend of Macha describes her ability to run faster than horses belonging to King Conchobor despite the fact that she is pregnant. She died from the effort and was buried on a plain or in a sacred mound.[21] While the date of the assembly at which she raced the king's horses was not specified, an assembly called *Oenach Macha* ("The Assembly of Macha") was held on the plain around Emain Macha, near Armagh (again, the date not specified).[22] It seems likely that this took place at Lugnasad. Horse races were a prominent feature of the Lugnasad assemblies at numerous locations in Ireland.[23] The swimming of horses at Lugnasad was widespread; there were even horse-swimming races.[24] Interestingly, the Dindsenchas of *Ard Macha* states that Macha was summoned to the assembly from beneath the waters.[25] It is believed that the racing or swimming of horses (particularly mares) helped establish the value of their offspring who were offered for sale at the gatherings.[26]

While the most well-known Lugnasad legend points to a male origin for the holiday, other traditional accounts show that female figures were honored at this time. These women were associated with agriculture, fertility or abundance; and after demonstrating their power to affect the land or the harvest, they "die" or disappear into the hills (after which they are honored *in absentia*). These tales seem to reflect the male focus of energies at the time of the harvest, during which time many women were absent, living on hills or mountaintops. As the harvest season progressed, more and more women began to return from the hills where they had been guarding the flocks and herds. It became increasingly important for women to be present, to assist with the harvest and help prepare the community for the end and beginning of the next cycle.[27] The significance of their presence is commemorated in the great honor shown to sacred and divine women in the traditional accounts of the great Lugnasad assemblies.

A number of mythological events involving supernatural beings took place at Samain. One of the most remarkable was described in a tale known as The Battle of Moytura (*Cath Maige Tuired*). Just before Samain, the Dagda unites with the goddess known as the Mórrigan, as she stands astride a river with one foot to the north of it and one foot to the south. After their union, she provides assistance to the Dagda and the Tuatha Dé Danann in the form of council, prophecy, strategic information and magical assistance. Great efforts are also made by Lug, the Dagda, the physician god Dian Cecht and the "three gods of Danu" (the three craftsmen deities Goibniu, Luchta and Credne).[28]

Near the end of the battle, the Mórrigan chants a magical poem. Immediately afterwards, the battle turned in favor of the gods.[29] Once the Mórrigan had united with the Dagda, she bestowed her blessings upon the god-tribe in a manner reminiscent of the Goddess of Sovereignty (whose symbolic animal, the horse, may have been represented in the Samhain or New Year's rituals associated with the *Láir Bhán* and the *Mari Lwyd*).

Other divine women were also associated with the Feast of Samain in early Irish tradition. An assembly took place at Samain at a site named for a divine female figure known as *Tlachtga*. She was said to be a powerful and independent woman who was well-versed in magic. Her father was the great arch-druid *Mug Roith*, about whom many tales survived in medieval times in the southwest of Ireland. Her sacred site, *Cnoc Tlachtga*, was said to have been the site of Samhain rituals in pagan times.[30]

Another renowned magician associated with Samhain was the woman *Mongfind* ("Bright Mane"), the stepmother of Niall of the Nine Hostages. Concerned about issues of kingship and sovereignty, she arranges for Niall and her own sons to be tested, to see who was worthy of becoming king. This resulted in Niall's famous encounter with the Goddess of Sovereignty and his eventual kingship. One medieval text stated that as long as Mongfind was "in the flesh," had magical powers and was a witch, for these reasons on the Eve of Samhain women and the general populace addressed their petitions to her.[31]

The Mórrigan was also skilled in magic, and her mother Ernmas was described as a witch.[32] These three divine women — the Mórrígan, Tlachtga and Mongfind — were all associated with magic and the feast of Samhain. This type of symbolism was extremely disconcerting to Christian authorities, and it is amazing that these tales have survived. The fear of power associated with independent and powerful female figures associated with magic, authority and ritual may have influenced the later symbolism of Halloween.

As the female half of the year wheel progressed, winter turned to spring. As we have seen, Imbolc was associated with Saint Brigid (and possibly earlier with the goddess Bríg). As spring moved into summer, Brigid's power gives way to that of the Dagda, who was the father of Bríg (and a deity associated with Beltaine and the summer half of the year). The annual cycle of seasonal activities, legends and folk traditions indicate that in Irish tradition (and perhaps elsewhere in the Celtic world) the summer half of the year was associated with male concerns or energies, and the winter half with female concerns, a balanced pattern of complementary powers and authority.

8

Elements of Celtic Shamanism

Over the last few decades, there has been a growing interest in the possible shamanic aspects of Celtic religion and folk practices. The word *shamanism* conjures up many intriguing images, not all of which can rightly be defined as shamanic. In order to explore the possibility that the Celts incorporated shamanic techniques or symbolism in their religious traditions, we need to first define the elements that constitute a shamanic tradition.

Shamans all over the world (by whatever local name they are known) are specialists in fostering, restoring and maintaining a balanced and harmonious relationship between the inhabitants of this world and those of the sacred realms. This is accomplished through a variety of methods, including ritual and ceremony, divination, healing and work with the soul, and interactions with the inhabitants of the sacred realms. This last method may involve the shaman's own spiritual journey to the Otherworld or worlds, or the shaman may call his or her spirit allies into this world for the purposes of assistance, guidance or healing. The shaman is considered to be a specialist in communicating with the divine as well as working with the soul, and can often "see" what others cannot.

A number of specific themes and elements are found in shamanic traditions which distinguishes them from other sorts of religious or mystical practices. One of the most widespread themes is the perception of a three-fold cosmology, which consists of a celestial or Upper World, a Middle World often associated with the earth, and a chthonic or Lower World. In many shamanic cultures, the *axis mundi* or World Tree, Pillar or Mountain connects these three worlds, and may be utilized by the shaman to travel between them. The possibility of two-way travel between the worlds is extremely important. While many other types of spiritual practitioners call upon the gods or spirits for help, the shaman is unique in that he or she is also able to travel back and forth between the sacred realms of their own volition.

Shamanic candidates undergo a lengthy and intensive training period, which is administered by elder shamans or teachers, as well as by spirit guides. This initiation into spiritual power may be preceded by a shamanic illness or a period of divine madness. Once this transformative period and formal training are complete, the candidate's initiation involves a spiritual death and rebirth into a radically altered state of being. Once this new state of existence and ability has been achieved, the shamanic practitioner shows him or herself to be worthy of great respect by performing ceremonies, healing and divination, training new candidates and performing many other functions.

Other frequently occurring shamanic elements include the use of shamanic costumes and secret languages, knowledge of the natural world, spiritual marriages with Otherworld beings, shape shifting, and the use of sound (song, chant, rhythm) in order to facilitate the altered state.[1] As we shall see, there is more than sufficient historical evidence for the majority of these shamanic elements in archaeological sources, Classical accounts, and in the written records of the Celtic peoples themselves.

The Shamanic Cosmos

There is ample evidence to support the assertion that Celtic cosmology involved a three-fold cosmos. The early Irish perception of a three-fold division of the cosmos into *nem* ("sky"), *muir* ("sea") and *talam* ("earth") is referenced in numerous texts.[2] The number three appears to have been particularly sacred to the Celts, and may reflect the veneration of these three sacred realms.

Inscriptions found on altars or shrines dating to the Romano-Celtic period refer to deities who would likely have been associated with the upper world, including *Taranis* ("The Thunderer"), *Loucetius* ("Lightning"), *Nodons* ("Cloud-maker"?) and *Sirona* ("Divine Star Goddess").[3] The Celtiberians believed that the souls of those who died in battle went straight to the Otherworld realms if vultures ate their bodies (birds are associated with the Upper World).[4] When Alexander the Great encountered the ancient Celts in the second century, he asked them what they feared most (hoping that it would be Alexander himself). Their response surprised him, however, for the Celts said that they feared nothing, except perhaps that the sky should fall upon them, underscoring the importance of that sacred realm in maintaining the order of the universe.[5]

Deities associated with the Underworld realms are also present in the archaeological record. In the Gaulish ritual inscription from Chamalières, the god *Maponus* ("Divine Son") is invoked specifically in his chthonic form. The magical tablet from Larzac mentions a group of women practicing some form of women's magic (*bnanom bricton*) which seems to have been associated with the chthonic realms; it refers to a goddess by the name of *Adsagsona*.[6] Irish mythology is replete with descriptions of Otherworld realms that existed under the earth or under the waters. These are particularly well described in "The Adventures of Cormac mac Art," "The Wasting Sickness of Cú Chulainn," and "The Voyage of Bran son of Febal."[7]

Evidence pertaining to the importance of the world tree or sacred center is present in a number of Celtic sources. Archaeological excavations have uncovered numerous offering pits or shafts located at the center of Celtic religious sites (presumably to make offerings to the inhabitants of the Lower World).[8] Stone pillars were also prominently situated in Continental Celtic shrines and sanctuaries.[9]

A possibly related concept is that of the *bile*, an Old Irish word which means a "tree or mast," and especially used to refer to ancient and venerated trees. Sacred assemblies were held beneath these hallowed trees, and it was forbidden to damage them in any way.[10] Sacred places throughout the ancient Celtic world were referred to by the term *nemeton*, "Sacred Place."[11] Some of these sites were associated with sacred groves or trees, and it has been suggested that there may be a connection between these sites and the widespread veneration of the World Tree.

Classical authors referred to an ancient site in Scotland called *Medionemeton* ("The Sacred Central Place"), which was believed to be the cosmological center of the land.[12] In later times, the center of Scotland was described by poets as *Taigh nan Teud* ("The House of the String or Cord"), possibly referring to the strings of a harp. This site was situated near the yew tree of Fortingall, which is the oldest living tree in Europe (and undoubtedly a sacred site in ancient times).[13] Caesar mentioned that the druids of ancient Gaul gathered at a fixed time each year at a consecrated location in the territory of the Carnutes, which was considered to be the center of Gaul.[14] The medieval cathedral at Chartres, with its famous labyrinth, was built near this sacred site. In Ireland, the cosmological center of the land was the hill of *Uisneach*, which in one Irish text is described as the "navel" of Uisneach (thus symbolizing the *omphalos* of the land).[15]

A passage from an eighth-century Irish manuscript may preserve a mythological description of the world tree. In the text, Finn mac Cumhall encounters a man sitting in a top of a tree with a blackbird on his right shoulder. He held a vessel of white bronze in his left hand, in which there was a trout and some water. A stag stood at the foot of the tree. The mysterious figure in the tree was cracking open hazelnuts, symbolic of divine wisdom. He gave half of the nut to the blackbird and ate the other half himself. From inside the bronze vessel he took an apple, symbolizing passages between the worlds, again giving half to the stag and eating the other half himself. He then drank a sip from the vessel so that he, the trout, the stag and the blackbird all drank together.[16]

The blackbird may symbolize the Upper World, the stag the Middle World and the trout the Lower World. This passage is reminiscent of traditional descriptions of the Norse World tree, *Ygdrassil*. In the Norse texts, an eagle and a hawk rested in the uppermost branches of the tree, horned animals (goats and harts) leapt at the sides of the tree, and a serpent lay at the root of the tree. These animals seem to correspond with the three worlds (and with each other): Upper World (blackbird or eagle and hawk); Middle World (stag or deer and goats); and Lower World (salmon or serpent).[17]

Druids and Shamans

It has been suggested that the Celtic equivalent of the shamanic specialist was the druid (and in later eras, the poet). The druids seem to have fulfilled virtually all the same functions as the shaman. Classical authors frequently refer to the high status and respect accorded to the druids (something also shown to shamanic practitioners). Diodorus Siculus mentioned that in Gaul, offerings were made to the gods by the druids, who were considered experts in the nature of the divine and were also in communion with it. It was similarly recorded that it was only through the druids that blessings should be sought.[18] Caesar wrote that the druids engaged in a great deal of discussion about the strength and power of the immortal gods.[19]

Diodorus Siculus referred to the druids as philosophers, soothsayers and theologians.[20] Strabo mentions that they engaged in both moral and natural philosophy.[21] They were described by other Classical authors as religious specialists who performed ceremonies, as well as divination and prophecy, which they enacted through the observation of birds and other natural phenomenon.[22] The druids possessed knowledge about the sacred genealogies of their culture, a practice maintained by the poets well into the early modern period. In the fourth century, Ammianus Marcellinus described the druids as "an intimate fellowship of greater ability" who "rose above the rest by seeking the unseen."[23]

The Gaulish druids were said to perform offering rituals on behalf of people suffering from extreme illnesses.[24] As we have seen, they were recorded as ritually gathering club moss, as well as mistletoe, which was known as "All-Heal" in the Gaulish language. Interestingly, a number of stone statues have been found at Celtic ritual sites that feature humanlike figures, possibly gods, druids or heroes. On top of the heads of the figures are headdresses or symbolic representations of three rounded leaves, whose form is very similar to the lobe-shaped leaves of the mistletoe plant.[25]

Shamans are often the guardians of important traditional lore, including the theology and mythology of their society. They are also often extremely knowledgeable about the local environment and the natural world. Cicero referred to a "eulogist" named Diviticus who practiced divination and possessed "knowledge of nature" (which the Greeks referred to as *physiologia*). He apparently foretold the future partly by means of augury and partly by conjecture.[26]

Sacred animals and plants were frequently associated with Celtic deities, and an intimate knowledge of the sacred properties of animals, birds and trees would have undoubtedly formed part of druidic religious training.[27] A great deal of traditional lore associated with trees was preserved in a variety of native texts, including *Auraceipt na n-Éces* (a medieval primer for poets) and *The Metrical Dindhsenchas*, a compilation of poems recording sacred stores and lore associated with the Irish landscape.[28] The Celts had a great appreciation and respect for the natural world, and Celtic poetry is unique in medieval literature for its vibrant description of the world of nature.

The druids would have also had an intimate knowledge of the Otherworld and its inhabitants. Depictions of these sacred realms and divine beings figure prominently in the literature of Ireland. While early evidence indicates that the Celts venerated gods or spirits in both the upper and lower worlds, by the time the myths of Ireland were set down in written form, the focus seems to have shifted almost entirely to the Lower World. The gods and goddesses of Ireland inhabited the *síd* mounds (under the earth) and also lived near or in bodies of water, as did many deities in Britain and the Continent.[29]

A possibly analogous tradition existed amongst the well-documented shamanic culture of the Yakut in Siberia, who recognized two great classes of gods, those "above" and those "below." As Mircea Eliade, the great scholar of world religions, points out, there was a difference in character among these two classes of spirit beings. The gods and spirits "above" were benevolent, but also relatively passive and therefore of little help in the drama of human existence. The celestial gods inhabited the upper spheres of the sky, from where they rarely mingled in human affairs. They had less influence on the course of life than the "spirits below," who were closer to the earth, potentially more vindictive, and allied to human beings by ties of blood and a much stricter organization into clans.[30]

This description could easily refer to the stories associated with the Irish gods, both in the medieval period and the folk traditions of the early modern era. The inhabitants of the *síd* mounds lived quite close to the earth and often interacted with the world of humans. They could be helpful, as well as vindictive if they were not honored or respected. The *Áes Síde* were organized into family groups whose names were known to the Irish, and in some cases were related or connected to human beings by ties of blood or alliance. Both Celtic and Siberian sources record that Otherworld travelers sometimes had spirit or "fairy wives," and also refer to the prohibition against eating or drinking anything in the Otherworld lest one not return.[31]

Druidic Training

Like their shamanic counterparts worldwide, the druids had great interest in matters pertaining to the soul. Many Classical authors commented on the fact that the druids believed and taught that the soul was eternal and immortal; that it did not perish but passed from one person to another and entered another body after some unspecified period of time.[32] Caesar stated that this was the foremost tenet of the druids' teaching.[33]

Strabo said that the druids taught that the soul, like the universe, was immortal, although at some time fire and water would overwhelm them.[34] Lucan, writing in the mid-first century, poetically wrote about druidic belief in the immortality of the soul, saying: "If what you sing of is true, death is but the mid-point of a long existence."[35]

The training of druidic candidates was discussed by a number of Classical authors. In early times, druidic schools operated in an open and formally organized manner. This would eventually change, however, as a result of the Roman occupation of Gaul and Britain. During the early Romano-Celtic period, written records record that the Gaulish town of Bibracte (near Mount Beuvray), the chief town of the tribe known as the Aedui, was still a notable druidic school. In the year 12 B.C.E., however, the Romans replaced it with the Roman town of Augustodunum. The Aedui and the neighboring Treveri rebelled against the Romans, their chief goal being to take over Augustodunum so that they could gain control of the young people who were being educated there. Celtic rebellion against their Roman oppressors resulted in great difficulties for the druids and their schools, for after the revolt of Sacrovir in 21 C.E., the emperor Tiberius formally suppressed the learned classes of ancient Gaul.[36]

The druids continued to train their initiates in secret locations. Pomponius Mela refers to the training of druidic candidates in "secret locations" (including hidden glades or caves), and Lucan describes this training as taking place in "the depths of the far-off forest."[37] In 54 C.E., Claudius abolished the druidic order as well as its associated religion. His edict was apparently not entirely successful, for Tacitus describes how Gaulish druids used a type of druidic spell known as *canebant* to urge their fellow Celts to rebellion in 69 C.E. There are also records of the druids prophesying the destruction of Roman power in 71 C.E.[38] Even as late as the fourth century, professors and rhetoricians in Roman Gaul were known to have come from druidic families.[39]

Like the shamanic initiate, druidic candidates engaged in lengthy and arduous training administered by druids, who were referred to as "teachers of wisdom." This training could last up to twenty years.[40] After completing this training, the druid (like the shaman) undergoes a radical change of state in terms of social status and ability. Once having been initiated, he or she is able to supervise religious ceremonies, perform divination and healing, communicate with the divine, and perform magic. Druids could also provide information and advice to their community, pass down binding legal decisions, intervene between opposing armies, and teach students and initiates. Their new status was also marked by the fact that they were now exempt from taxation and military service.[41]

Druidic Survivals and Poetic Schools

The druids were considered troublesome to the Roman Empire because of their social and political power, which was more threatening to Imperial order than religious diversity. The Romans also disliked exclusive or secret religions for fear that they might wield a political or magical influence that could weaken their own power. As we have seen, the Roman prohibition against the druids and their traditions was only partially successful; druidic prophecy and druidic-inspired rebellion against the Romans were recorded for some time.[42]

Eventually, however, certain aspects of druidic learning became part of the curriculum taught by professors, rhetoricians and grammarians, as the old druidic order gradually slipped away under Roman rule. One text records how a chief of the Vocontii was found to be in possession of a druidic talisman during a lawsuit in Rome, and put to death as an example. Once the formal institution of druidism had died out in Gaul, some aspects of their traditions may have survived in the practices of village healers and seers.[43]

Elsewhere, druidism as a religious tradition was not permitted to survive in its previous form for both political and spiritual reasons. After the introduction of Christianity, those who had been involved in the druidic order either became Christian clergy or a powerful type of learned poet known as a *fili* (plural *filid*). Interestingly, the druids seem to have had a good reputation in Ireland longer than on the Continent. Irish sources (like earlier Classical sources) associate the powers of healing with druids, and also attribute great importance to them in the earlier era.[44]

In many parts of Ireland the old ways seem to have blended gradually with Christianity. Saint Brigid (who was herself probably a transmuted incarnation of a pre–Christian Irish goddess) was said to have lived with her mother (a Christian) on land owned by a man whose nephew was a druid. As a child she uttered a famous prophecy, which the druid interpreted for his uncle: "You're not going to be happy about this.... She (the saint) is going to own this land until the crack of doom."[45]

When Ireland first steps onto the pages of history through the advent of written records, we see manuscripts that refer to both druids and *filid* (although at this stage the *fili* has a higher social status than the druid). Even in the seventh and eighth centuries when the Irish law tracts were first written down, both the druid and the fili have a well-defined legal status in Irish society. However, it is evident that by this point the fili had acquired some of the functions of the druids, as well as some of their social standing.[46]

Like the druids, the filid underwent formal and lengthy training. Their profession could be hereditary, as was also the case with the druidic vocation. Like their predecessors, the poets performed divination, served in the role of judge or *brithem*, and used secret or obscure languages. The poets could recite an enormous number of tales and thus they preserved a great deal of information associated with the genealogy, mythology and philosophy of their culture, including detailed stories associated with the history of the landscape. In addition to composing complex poetical compositions, the filid were widely credited with the gift of prophecy; and the power of their words, when used in a satire, was believed to have the power to cause illness or death.[47]

Because of their high social standing, independence, and perceived power, the poets were not always on good terms with Irish kings (whom the poets frequently served). As a result, early written sources claim that the *filid* were reported to have actually been "exiled" on three separate occasions. Conflict between kings and poets became so intense that in 575 C.E., at the assembly of Druim Cetta, the high king attempted to abolish the filid altogether. Oddly enough, it was Saint Columba who argued to reform and reorganize the poets rather than disband them. Thus, in a strange turn of events, he helped save a great deal of native pre–Christian culture from obliteration.[48]

One might think that this alliance between the new religion and the poetic order would have severed all connections with the old religion and erased every trace of it from the native literature. Instead it appears that the poets did little more than to obliquely refer to pagan gods as persons possessing supernatural powers.[49] In many cases, they did not even perform this perfunctory task, and overtly mention the divine identity of various gods and goddesses. Numerous Old Irish and Middle Irish manuscripts preserve in written form many tales that outline the names, stories, attributes and genealogies of the pre–Christian gods, the spiritual allies of the early Irish people.[50] It is interesting to reflect upon the fact that at some point these stories must have been dictated by druids, poets or other tradition bearers directly to the filid — or to Christian clerics — who labored long and hard to preserve them in a beautiful visual form on expensive sheepskin vellum.

In many shamanic cultures, shamans perform their rituals and ceremonies in darkened dwellings or under the cover of night. The darkness is believed to help the shaman "see" into the other worlds. The use of darkness to facilitate visionary techniques was also associated with the training of the *filid*. In a text published in 1722, the poetic schools are described for us in some detail. Poetic students were expected to gain a thorough knowledge of the history and land of Ireland, compose in complex meters and on traditional topics, and master an archaic form of poetic language. Only those who were descended from poets, who possessed a good memory, and were "reputed within their tribe," were candidates for the training.

The rooms inside the school were described as being quite plain, but possessed one remarkable feature: they had no windows to let in the day, and no light at all existed within them except that of candles (and these were brought in only at the proper season).

The school term itself even took place during the darkest season of the year, from the first of November until March 25. At night, the students were assigned a subject by their teacher. They worked on their composition alone while laying on their beds during the following day, entirely in the dark. The next evening, lights were brought in and the students' poems were written down and recited for their teachers. The practice of working and composing in the dark was reputed to have been traditional for many historical poetic masters, who did not traditionally compose in broad daylight.

Poetic schools were still active in early eighteenth-century Scotland as well. Here the poets were described as shutting their doors and windows for an entire day, while lying on their beds to compose their works. They wrapped their plaids around their heads, to further block out the light.[51] In addition, the students put a stone upon their belly, presumably to help regulate the breath (and a practice known to help facilitate a meditative state).

At this point we might recall the poetic terms *awen* (in Welsh) and *aí* (Old Irish), which referred to poetic inspiration (and which were both associated with words meaning "breath").[52] Several Irish mythological texts refer to the use of the "druidic breath" (although the specifics of this practice are not always outlined in full).[53] Like their Irish counterparts, Scottish poetic candidates also utilized an archaic type of language, and their compositions were similarly performed for their teachers after the students had emerged from their darkened cells.[54] Once their training was complete, the filid (like the druids) took on a new role and identity, for which they received great honor and respect.

Druidic and Poetic Parallels

As we have seen, all three sources of knowledge support the assertion that shamanic elements and practices formed part of early Celtic religion. Certainly these religions would have had many different forms in different eras and localities. Shamanism would have coexisted along with other forms of native religion (including animism, polytheism, and so forth) as it does in most shamanic cultures. The roles and functions of the druids (and later, of the poet-seers) exhibit an almost direct parallel with the roles and functions of shaman, by whatever indigenous name they are known in various cultures around the world.

Element	Shaman	Druid	Fili
High social status	*	*	*
Communication with Other Worlds	*	*	*
Experts in matters pertaining to Divine	*	*	
Maintain cultural traditions	*	*	*
Conduct ceremonies	*	*	
Guardians of sacred lore	*	*	*
Preserve genealogies	*	*	*
Make offerings	*	*	
Divination	*	*	*
Traditions pertaining to Soul	*	*	
Formal training	*	*	*
Initiation into new life	*	*	*
Knowledge of natural world or land	*	*	*
Use of secret or special languages	*	*	*
Perform healing	*	*	
Special vision or knowledge	*	*	*
Recite and interpret myths or tales	*	*	*
Specialists in theology or philosophy	*	*	*
Teaching and training	*	*	*
Credited with magical abilities	*	*	*
Provide advice or assistance to community	*	*	*
Preserve and interpret traditional or sacred law	*	*	*
Advise on matters of war or peace	*	*	*
Recitation of sacred texts or stories	*	*	*
Inspiration or song or spoken word	*	*	*
Maintain relationship with Sacred	*	*	
High political standing or authority	*	*	*

Other widespread shamanic elements include the use of special costumes, initiatory illness or madness, spiritual marriages with divine beings, shape shifting, the use of sacred songs or words, alliances with spiritual beings, and other specialized techniques (including fasting, ritual postures and sacred dreaming). In the next chapter, we will examine historical and literary evidence for these shamanic elements, which are also prominent in the Celtic spiritual tradition.

9

The Feathered Cloak

In addition to historical evidence for the shamanic functions of druids and poet-seers, the native literature of Ireland and Wales includes many examples of shamanic symbolism. These include the use of shamanic costumes and mantic poetry, shape shifting and other magical abilities, initiatory illnesses, work with spirit allies, and spiritual death and rebirth.

The shaman may work with any type of living creature — plant or animal — as well as with water, stones and other elements of the natural world. In many cultures, the shamanic costume features symbolism associated with animals sacred to the shaman. The most widely occurring shamanic creatures are the bird, deer, horse, snake, and bear (the first three of which figure especially prominently in Celtic mythology and symbolism). Bird symbolism is extremely widespread, and the bird may in fact be the most universal of shamanic creatures.[1]

Bird feathers, wings and bird symbols are often incorporated into shamanic headdresses or capes. Just such a garment is described in an early Irish text known as *Cormac's Glossary*. The text mentions a specialized garment known as a *tuigen,* a "covering of birds" worn by the Irish poets. It was made from white and multicolored birdskins from the waist down and of mallard's necks and crests from the waist up. Only a master poet or *fili* was entitled to wear the tuigen.[2]

A remarkable costume was worn by the legendary Irish druid *Mug Roith*, whose name means "Devotee of the Wheel." In the Middle Irish text *Forbhais Droma Dámhgháire*, the costume and powers of Mug Roith are evocatively described. The hide from a hornless brown bull and a speckled bird mask with billowing wings formed part of Mug Roith's "druidic gear." With these he was reported to fly into the sky along with a magical fire he had created. In the celestial realms, he chanted a magical rhetoric, after which he descended back to earth. Mug Roith then entered his beautifully ornamented chariot that was drawn by oxen with the speed of the March wind and the agility of birds. Its axles were made of rowan wood (a type of tree with many magical associations) and inside the chariot day and night were equally bright.[3]

Mug Roith was reported to have spent the first seven years of his occult training in a fairy mound (*Sí Charn Breachnatan*) under the tutelage of a druidess named *Banbhuana*. He owned a magic spear, shield and stone, as well as a supernatural object known as the *Roth Ramach* or "Rowing Wheel" (from which he apparently took his name). Mug Roith was said to have lived during "the period of the nineteen kings" and was able to invoke or manifest fire and water, alter the landscape, shape shift and perform many feats of magic, although he was blind. Other literary and historical sources refer to the prowess of blind poets or harpers. Prior to performing his supernatural feats, Mug Roith would "place his trust" in his gods, sometimes also invoking them. Mug Roith had numerous students who referred to him as "Beloved Teacher." On one occasion he was assisted by the son of his Otherworldly teacher, a young man who wore a grey-brown mantle hung with talons, bones and horns (a very shamanic garment indeed).[4]

Taliesin: Poet of the Shining Brow

Another magically inspired and supernaturally gifted figure was the Welsh legendary poet-seer *Taliesin*. In the medieval Welsh *Tale of Gwion Bach*, the female magician Cerridwen sets out to brew an elixir of prophetic wisdom for her unfortunately ugly son *Afagddu* ("Utter Darkness"), so that he may prosper in society. Cerridwen was described as being versed in "the three arts" (magic, enchantment and divination). She gathered a number of herbs and boiled them in a cauldron for a year and a day. At the end of that time, three drops containing magical properties would spring from the cauldron.

Cerridwen set a young boy to tend the fire by the name of *Gwion Bach* ("Little Poisonous One"). This is probably a double entendre referring to the magical potion inside the vessel, as well as the poisonous power of the poet's satire (a gift he would eventually obtain). At the moment of truth, Cerridwen is fast asleep, fatigued from her labors. Instead of landing on her son, the three precious drops fell upon Gwion Bach. Cerridwen was outraged and pursued Gwion Bach. The two engage in a shape shifting contest and pursuit during which they transform into various forms. At the end, Gwion Bach changed into a grain of wheat and is eaten by Cerridwen who has taken on the form of a hen. Nine months later, Cerridwen gives birth to the boy in human form, and sets him adrift in a coracle (a traditional Celtic hide-covered boat).[5]

The story continues in a second Welsh narrative, *The Tale of Taliesin*. The coracle is discovered at Samhain by a young man named Elphin. When he sees the forehead of the young child in the boat he exclaims, "Behold the radiant forehead!" (*tal iesin*). This becomes Gwion Bach's new name, and describes the condition of his spiritual rebirth. Taliesin becomes an inspired poet-seer who was able to perform prophecy and compose inspired compositions. In some of the poems attributed to Taliesin, he enumerates the many forms he experienced before being reborn as the inspired poet-seer.[6]

One famous account of Taliesin's shape shifting abilities and his former incarnations appears in a poem called *Cad Goddeu* ("The Battle of the Trees"). This poem involves a long list of trees and their contribution to a supernatural conflict. In this poem Taliesin recounts the unusual circumstances of his rebirth, being created from trees and plants, soil and other elements, and the water of the "ninth wave," a magical boundary between this world and the realms of Spirit.[7]

> I was in numerous forms
> before being released...
> I was a drop in the heavens
> I was the splendour of stars...
> I was a path, I was an eagle,
> I was a coracle in the ocean...

I was a sword in the hand...
I was a harp string
enchanted for nine years
and in water as foam
I was a spark in fire...
Not from a mother or father was I made
My skill was created for me
From nine forms of elements...
From primroses and flowers
From the blossoms of trees and shrubs
From the earth, from soil was I made
From the blossoms of nettles,
From water of the ninth wave...
The incantations of sages invoked me...
A splendid poet of remarkable gifts...
Before I was a seer, I wandered and changed.[8]

Celtic Shapeshifters

Shapeshifting is a highly significant element in many shamanic traditions. It is also frequently found throughout the Celtic mythological and legendary traditions. One well-known Celtic shapeshifter was *Fintan*, an Irish mythological figure who was said to be very wise and extremely ancient. He was reputed to have spent part of his existence in various forms, including an eagle, a hawk and a salmon.[9] In the myths and legends, druids and magicians (both male and female) were credited with the power to transform people into animals or other natural elements, as well as changing objects into different forms.[10] The Classical author Hippolytus specifically mentions that the Druids performed magic; other Classical writers referred to the druids as magicians as well as teachers.[11]

Another figure with shapeshifting abilities was the legendary Irish poet-seer Amairgen. He is mentioned in a number of Irish texts, but figures most prominently in *Lebor Gabála Érenn* ("The Book of the Taking of Ireland"), a text often referred to as "The Book of Invasions." This is a medieval Irish pseudo-historical compilation of Biblical, Classical and native Irish elements that purported to be a history of the Gaels and other inhabitants of Ireland since the time of creation. Although the purpose of the text was to provide the Irish with a Biblical origin in order to fit in with the rest of Christianized Europe, it contains certain fragmented elements of Irish creation myths.[12]

In *Lebor Gabála*, the Gaels have arrived in Ireland and must obtain the permission of the eponymous goddesses of the territory (Ériu, Banba and Fotla) in order to inhabit the land. At one point in the narrative, the druids of the *Tuatha Dé Danann* have conjured up a druidic wind and blown the ships of the Gaels out to sea (out past the ninth wave). Amairgen chants a magical poem in order to enable his people to realize a change of social status by taking possession of the Middle World (the land of Ireland).[13] Like the mantic statements of Taliesin, Amairgen's poetic chant records his ability to "be" or partake of the essence (and presumably the inherent power and wisdom) of various living beings and elements of the natural world.

I am a wind in a sea
I am a wave of fury
I am the sound of an ocean

I am a stag of seven antlers
I am a hawk on a stone
I am the beauty of plants
I am a boar for valour
I am a salmon in a pool
I am a lake in a plain
I am a flame that smokes
I am a word of skill

I am a spear among spoils (pouring out fierceness)
I am a god who shapes commands by spontaneous incantation

Who reveals the stones of the mountain?
Who pursues the ages of the moon?
In what place does the setting sun lie down?
Who brings forth herds from the house of Tethra [the ocean]?
What hero, what god forms sharpness out of the heights?
A poet of keen words — a wise poet.[14]

Spirit Allies

In most shamanic cultures, shamans traditionally form relationships with and work in alliance with spirit helpers. These may include ancestors, spirits of the land, spiritual teachers, and spirits in animal or bird form.[15] There are several ways in which the druids are likely to have worked with Spirit allies. These include working with the *Aes Síde*, the inhabitants of the Otherworld realms; working with spirits associated with the natural world, and working with ancestral spirits.

As we have seen, traditions concerning the Celtic Otherworld and its sacred denizens are a primary feature of early Celtic religious traditions. Historical sources refer to the druids as specialists in communication with the divine. Classical reports maintain that blessings were sought only through the presence and expertise of a druid. The druids would have called upon the gods and goddesses of their tribe, as well as local divinities in the landscape.[16] In *Forbhais Droma Dámhgháire*, Mug Roith and other druidic figures accomplish remarkable feats after invoking, concentrating upon or "placing their confidence" in specific gods and their powers. A specialized "god of the druids" is mentioned in the tale, and this figure (*dé druidechta*) is mentioned in other sources as well. A personal relationship with this druidic deity is suggested by the words of a spell chanted by Mug Roith, in which he invokes this specialized divinity as "my god above every god," and "god of druids."[17] Here we might note that the Dagda is credited as being a god of druidism.[18]

Animals, birds, trees and other living creatures figure prominently in Celtic mythology, and are often associated with particular gods and goddesses.[19] Druids who honored or invoked particular gods may also have worked with the spirit of the animals or plants associated with those deities.[20] Mug Roith's feathered headdress and bull-hide cloak might suggest that he worked with bull and bird spirits. Bulls were featured in an early Irish ritual known as the *tarb feis* ("Bull-Sleep"). In the ritual, the flesh of a consecrated bull was eaten by a priest (or druid) who then entered into a prophetic sleep. During the sleep, the identity of the next king was revealed.[21]

There are numerous stories of animals that were born at the same time as human beings. In many cases the two have a lifelong connection. Two colts were born at the same time as the hero Cú Chulainn. Finn mac Cumhall was connected with a dog, and the Welsh figure of Pryderi with a colt. Twelve half-brothers who transformed into seals were connected with Lug in one legend, while in another the brother of Lleu turned into a fish.[22] Various divine or legendary figures seem to have been connected to certain animals due to the significance of their names: Oisín ("Little Deer"), Branwen ("White Raven"), Cú Chulainn ("the Hound of Culainn") and Boand ("Blessed Cow").

The Celts had great respect for the wisdom and traditions of their ancestors. Therefore, it is reasonable to suppose that the druids worked with various ancestral apirits (whether of their own genealogical lineage, or those associated with their tribe). The importance of ancestral lore and inherited traditions is well documented, and it would be remarkable if the druids did not honor, venerate or otherwise engage in ritual activity focused on their biological or spiritual (druidic) ancestors.[23] The druids of Gaul maintained that the people were descended from a chthonic deity of some kind (who must have been honored in sacred ritual).[24] Even in medieval times, certain Irish tribes still maintained their descent from pagan gods who were considered to be their ancestors.[25] In the second century B.C.E., one Classical account recorded a well-known custom attributed to the Continental Celts. They were reported to spend the night near the tombs of their "famous men" in the hope of receiving a special oracle; in nighttime dreams the dead were said to appear to them.[26]

Shamanic Transformation

One shamanic element present in Celtic literature, but not recorded in the ethnography, is the initiatory death-and-rebirth scenario of historical druids or poets. This is not at all surprising, in that Classical ethnographers were not likely to have been permitted to be present at these ceremonies. As in many other cultures, no one but the druids and the initiates may have been able to witness these rituals. However, themes of magical transformation and rebirth, often associated with shape shifting and the transmigration of the soul, frequently appear in Celtic texts.

In the Irish tale "The Wooing of Étain," the heroine undergoes a number of transfigurations, existing as a woman, a pool of water and a scarlet fly at various times. In this latter form she is swallowed by a warrior's wife and reborn as her daughter (although in this incarnation Étain does not remember her past lives).[27]

Spiritual death-and-rebirth episodes are described in a number of other mythological sources. Some of these tales also record illness, madness or suffering experienced by various figures prior to the new incarnation or rebirth. A remarkably shamanic episode is recorded in the medieval Welsh tale *Math Son of Mathonwy*. The story sets forth the adventures of the young hero *Lleu* (whose name is cognate with the Irish god *Lug*). Under extremely unusual circumstances, Lleu was pierced by a poisoned spear cast by the lover of his supernatural bride. As the head of the spear struck him, he uttered a terrible scream and took flight in the shape of an eagle. Gwydion, a clever magician, searches for Lleu out in the wilderness. He is eventually found sitting in the top of a tree in very serious condition. The eagle's flesh was rotting away and falling off of him (i.e., his old body is dying, in preparation for a new one).

Gwydion sang three magical poems or *englynion*, and as he did so the eagle slowly came down from the tree. The magician transforms Lleu back into human form although he is still in wretched shape, little more than skin and bone. Over a period of time, a group of doctors heal the young hero, who eventually takes revenge on his unfaithful wife and her lover and regains power over his rightful kingdom.[28]

Cú Chulainn, the greatest of Irish heroes, also experiences a spiritual illness. In "The Wasting Sickness of Cú Chulainn," Cú is perplexed because he had missed a cast with his spear (something he had never before done). He went and sat with his back against a stone pillar, for "his spirit was angry within him." Cú fell asleep and in his dream he saw two women, one dressed in a green mantle and one in a purple mantle. The women whip him with horsewhips until he is "all but dead." When his fellow Ulstermen perceive his condition they suggest that he be awakened, but his friend Fergus advises not to move him, "for he is seeing a vision." This element is reminiscent of the medieval Welsh *awenyddion* who were watched over during their mantic state.

Cú eventually regains consciousness but is ill for an entire year. He recalls having had a vision the previous year at *Samhain*, the great liminal point of the year. King Conchobar tells the hero to rise and go to the pillar where he had previously sat. Cú does so, and the woman in the green mantle appears to him. Her name is *Liban* and she tells Cú Chulainn that his assistance is sought in the Otherworld (a scene which illustrates the importance of reciprocity between the worlds, a theme also seen in later folk tales).

After many adventures, Cú Chulainn is successful in providing assistance in the Otherworld. However, while he there he falls in love with a fairy woman named *Fand*, wife of the god *Manannán mac Lir*. Cú Chulainn's mortal wife, *Emer*, becomes jealous and she travels with a group of armed women to the Otherworld to confront him. Cú is torn between the two women, one mortal and one immortal. The two generously discuss which of them should leave, and eventually Fand decides to return to her husband. Upon hearing this Cú Chulainn makes three great leaps until he arrives at Tara Luachra. There he lives for a long time without food and drink, dwelling upon the mountains. Emer seeks the assistance of Conchobar who sends out his druids, learned men and "people of skill" to capture and assist Cú Chulainn. Cú tries to kill them, but through "druidic" and "fairy" spells they are able to bind him and bring him back into society.[29]

Wild Men and Feathered Women

Other examples of spiritual illness or madness are also present in a variety of Celtic narratives. These sources describe men and women who live in a state of near madness, away from society, in the far reaches of the natural world. In Old Irish, they are referred to as *geilt*, a word that refers to a person who goes mad from terror, a panic-stricken fugitive from battle, or a sacred lunatic living in the woods and credited with the power of levitation.[30] One of the earliest of these accounts is the story of *Suibhne*, a prince of the *Dál nAraide* who was said to have gone mad during a battle in the year 637 C.E. After the conflict, he went off to live by himself in the wilderness.[31] A number of remarkable poems exist that are attributed to Suibhne (or "Mad Sweeney"). In these poems he sometimes speaks directly to the inhabitants of the natural world.[32]

Little antlered one, little bellowing one, melodious roaring one
Sweet to us the call you make in the glen.

Longing for my beloved abode came upon my mind
For the herbs in the field, the deer in the mountain.

Oak of many branches and leaves, you are high above every tree
Little hazel tree, branching one, chest of hazelnuts...

Blackthorn, thorny one, you who bear the dark sloes
Watercress, little green-topped one in the belly of a blackbird's nest...

Apple tree, apple-like one, everyone shakes you vigorously
Rowan tree, red-berried one, your blossom is lovely...

Beautiful blessed birch, a shrine of music
Lovely is every joining branch on the top of your head...

Little fawn, of the slender shanks, forbearance for your power
I am riding upon you from peak to peak.[33]

Suibhne describes his journey as lonely, but also says that if he were to search all the mountains of the earth, he would rather have for his dwelling a single hut in the beautiful valley of Glenn Bolcáin. He praises the waters of the glen and the sound of the belling stag; the songs of the birds are music to his soul. In one poem, Suibhne describes how he wanders restlessly from place to place, "without sense or reason." He describes himself as shunning people, racing a red deer over the moor. He runs wildly to the mountains; few have surpassed him in speed. Suibhne sleeps in the woods at night, in the top of a tree, although he has "no feathers."[34]

In this excerpt, Suibhne possesses great speed and agility, but notes that at this point he has "no feathers" on his body. In another passage, however, he says that his body was "shattered" in the fork of a tree (reminiscent of Lleu's suffering and illness). He also declares that he has endured many hardships "since feathers grew on my body" (possibly reflecting a change of spiritual state). Suibhne also announces that his name is not a fit one for him, potentially indicating that he has taken on a new incarnation. He suggests the name "Horn-Head" would be better, perhaps referring to an identification with the stag.[35]

Perhaps the most famous wildman of Celtic tradition is the Welsh figure of *Myrddin* (whose name was later anglicized as Merlin). In Wales he was originally known as *Myrddin Wyllt* (the second element stands for Middle Welsh *gwyllt*, which is cognate with Old Irish *geilt*). Myrddin also goes mad during a battle (purportedly during the Battle of Arfderydd in 573 C.E.) and flees human society to live in the wilderness. Like Sweeney, some of Myrddin's poetic utterances were addressed directly to trees and wild creatures. In the *Black Book of Carmarthen*, a poem attributed to Myrddin mentions the extreme discomfort he endured one night when the snow was up to his thigh, with only wolves for company. Myrddin's possible role as a druidic figure is alluded to in a poem from the *Red Book of Hergest*, where he is described as a wise man and a prophet.[36]

Another *geilt* from early Irish tradition was a woman named Mis, who went mad after seeking the slain body of her father on the battlefield and drinking blood from his wounds. She fled to the mountain known as Sliabh Mis where she stayed for many years, catching and eating the flesh of anything she encountered (animal or human). Like Sweeney, Mis could also run and fly like the wind. In addition, she was described as having grown *clúmh* all over her body — a word that means either "feathers" or "fur."

Because of her ferocity, the king of Munster, Feidhlime Mac Criomthain, issued a proclamation rewarding anyone that could catch Mis and bring her into custody alive. Many people attempted the task but perished in the attempt. Eventually the king's harper, Dubh Ruis ("Dark Wood" or "Dark Knowledge") approaches Mis. She is enticed by his music, and questions the young man about his harp. He places gold and silver on the ground, and as he starts to tell her about where they came from, she begins to regain part of her memory.

Dubh Ruis asks for food, and Mis catches a deer. He encourages her to cook the meat rather than eat it raw; and as she sits quietly and eats, she begins to remember even more about her father and her former life. Eventually the young man is able to place her in a pit of warm water and bathe her. The two spend the night together and the act of sexual union also improves her condition. Dubh Ruis stays with Mis for two months until her senses were recovered, and the fur or feathers that had covered her entire body were gone. Mis married Dubh Ruis and was able to return to society.[37]

The phenomenon of the *geilt* or *gwyllt* incorporate a number of elements, many of which are also seen in accounts of shamanic illness or madness. The wildman or woman experiences an emotional, mental or spiritual illness as the result of a traumatic experience or encounter with the Spirit world. He or she leaves society ("that which is known") and goes to live in the wilderness ("that which is unknown"). The *geilt* is often said to be able to run swiftly, make great leaps, fly or levitate; they are also known to perch in trees (an activity credited to historical Hungarian shamans as well). The *geilt* is often restless and travels great distances. He or she may eat (or avoid) particular foods. The geilt is frequently naked, and is either clothed in rags or has grown fur or feathers on their body. The geilt appears to be in deep connection (and communication) with the natural world. They may be antisocial or even violent, and often experience visions or hallucinations.

Through the completion of certain tasks (or simply by surviving the ordeal), the geilt is able to return to society, profoundly changed after their spiritual and ecstatic experience. These experiences mirror many aspects of the initiatory ordeals of the shaman, after which they formally return to society and utilize their newfound knowledge for the benefit of their community.[38]

10

The Song of the Shaman

A key element of shamanic practice around the world is the use of altered states of consciousness to in order to connect with the sacred realms, to obtain information, perform healing, receive guidance, and many other purposes. As we have seen, the *awenyddion* entered into a trance state in order to attain knowledge from the Otherworld. Irish and Scottish poets were trained in specialized schools where the use of darkness was an important tool for connecting with the powers of inspiration and incubating a poetic vision. Irish poets were expected to know three kinds of poetic or divinatory techniques: *imbas forosnai* ("Great Knowledge of Illumination"), *dichetal di chennaib* ("Incantation or Spell composed Extemporaneously") and *teinm laeda* ("Cracking Open or Reciting of Poems").[1]

The pursuit of *imbas* in particular is mentioned in a number of sources. According to *Cormac's Glossary*, poets were able to discover and manifest whatever they wished through the use of *imbas forosnai*. This power was obtained by calling upon the gods and going into a religious "sleep." This was presumably a trance state, for the text mentions that it might only be a few minutes in length. During the ritual, the person was watched so they would not be disturbed or interrupted, a common feature in shamanic rituals (and mentioned in connection with the Welsh *awenyddion*).[2]

Other traditional shamanic techniques include soul or spirit travel, Otherworld encounters and adventures, ritual fasting, movement and postures, sacred dreaming, the use of special languages, and sacred song, music and chant. We have evidence for all of these techniques in Celtic ethnographic and literary sources.

Shamanic Journeys

One of the signature activities associated with shamanism is soul travel, often referred to as the shamanic journey. This refers to the shamanic practitioner's ability to travel between the worlds, receive information and visions, and communicate with the inhabitants of the sacred realms (primarily in a spiritual or ecstatic capacity). The great druid Mug Roith was reputed to travel into the sky in his winged costume and magical chariot. The men and women of the *geilt/gwyllt* tradition were reported to leap, fly and perch in trees. These same activities are often enacted in shamanic rituals in order to symbolize or facilitate the shaman's spiritual ascent to the Upper World. In fact, the Old Irish word *geilt* was sometimes glossed with the Latin word *volatilis* ("flying").[3]

Druidic training was sometimes held in darkened glades or caves, which may have assisted with lower world (or general Otherworld) travel. As we have seen, in Irish mythological sources, the gods and spirits were perceived as inhabiting the lower world realms.

In Celtic tradition there are numerous accounts of heroes and other adventurers traveling between the worlds. These people step outside of the known world and travel into the unknown realms of the Otherworld. In some instances, druids provide advice about these journeys, assist travelers with information or prophetic guidance, or provide healing or assistance after the experience is over. It would stand to reason that the Druids, who were "experts in communication with the Divine," would have been personally familiar with the Otherworld and its inhabitants. Firsthand knowledge of these realms would seem to be a prerequisite for guiding or assisting others with their journeys.

Celtic mythology abounds with tales of people having encounters with and journeying to the Otherworld realms. Some of these experiences are recounted in a type of tale known as an *echtra*. This word is most often translated as "adventure," but it also means a "journey" or "voyage," or "an expedition in quest of adventure." People also have encounters with the Otherworld in tales known as *immrama*. This term, frequently translated as "journey," literally means a "rowing about" (between Otherworld islands). This word comes from Old Irish *imm-rá*, which means to "travel about" or "navigate."[4] In some cases people from the Otherworld realms appear in the path of the would-be traveler, guiding or enticing them to travel to the world of spirit. In other instances the journeyer sets out in search of their own experience or with a particular goal in mind. Sometimes spirit beings provide the traveler with a token or amulet which helps them accomplish the Otherworld journey. In other cases a word or invitation is sufficient to enable the spiritual travel to occur.

What is not always explicit is exactly how these journeys were accomplished. Native techniques associated with altered states of awareness or perception were undoubtedly utilized. Where the specifics of these techniques are not known, universal shamanic techniques like drumming, rattling and chanting could have been utilized. Let us explore a number of widespread shamanic techniques and their connection with traditional Celtic beliefs and practices.

Ritual Fasting and Sacred Foods

Some shamanic cultures engage in purification and fasting in order to prepare for or facilitate the shamanic experience. In one of the Gaulish ceremonies for gathering healing plants, the person gathering the plant had to have their feet washed clean. In another they were required to fast while performing the ritual.[5] Fasting was also known in medieval Ireland as a legally recognized method of obtaining justice from a person "fasted against."[6] The MacCrimmons, who were the hereditary pipers of my Scottish Clan (Clan MacLeod), were said to have fasted for two days whenever they were faced with a formidable mental or creative task, like the composition of a *pibroch*, a lengthy and highly stylized form of interpretive pipe playing and composition. The MacCrimmons were said to have obtained their gift of music directly from the inhabitants of the Otherworld.[7]

Ingesting special foods, or abstaining from eating particular foods, is another common practice in many shamanic cultures. In early Ireland, the practice of ritually avoiding certain foods, activities or situations was known as a *geis*. In "The Destruction of Da Derga's Hostel," a man known as Conaire is given a lengthy list of *gessa* or taboos, which are laid upon him by the King of the Birds before he is installed as king of Ireland.[8] The Irish hero Cú Chulainn was prohibited from eating dog flesh on account of his name (*cú* means "dog").[9] In early Ireland, there was a taboo against eating the flesh of cranes, and Caesar comments that the early inhabitants of Britain did not eat chickens or geese. Both geese and chickens appear to have been used as offerings, and the goose was associated with combat (and hence also with protection).[10] In other tales, the consumption of certain foods (salmon, hazelnuts, berries or apples) appears to aid or facilitate the Otherworld experience. These foods may symbolize a sacred substance (like the Sanskrit *soma*) which was used to induce an altered or ecstatic state.[11]

Ritual Movement and Postures

Movement is another common ritual element in shamanic contexts. On the banks of the Loire River, across from a Gaulish shrine, a group of bronze figurines were buried at the time of the Roman conquest. These remarkable figurines appear to depict the movements of a sacred dance.[12] Other ritualized postures are depicted in Celtic artwork, such as the cross-legged posture of the horned or antlered god (also seen in connection with other human or possibly divine figures).[13] A type of invoking posture referred to as the *orans* posture is also seen in several contexts. This consists of the divine figure holding their hands upright from bent elbows, palms facing outwards.[14]

The Irish druids were said to have made use of a particular position when performing a type of magic known as *corrguinecht* (literally "crane-wounding"). In this practice, the person performing the magic recited a satire while standing on one leg, with one arm raised and one eye shut (presumably in imitation of the stance of a crane or heron).[15] In "The Battle of Moytura," the god Lug chanted a spell while going around the men of Ireland on one foot with one eye closed.[16] These postures, which focus on one-half of the body, may symbolize an enhanced connection with the sacred realms, rather than connection with worldly reality.

Shamanic Dreams

In many shamanic cultures, information or power may be sought or obtained by the shaman through his or her dreams. In early Ireland, a ritual known as the *tarbfeis* ("bull-sleep") was undertaken in order to decide the identity of the next king. A bull was consecrated and ceremonially offered to the realms of the divine, after which it was cooked for the ritual gathering. The presiding ceremonialist bathed in the broth of the bull. Afterwards the flesh of the bull was eaten by the priest and his assistants. The priest then slept and experienced a divinatory dream during which the identity of the king-elect was made known to him.[17] As we have seen, the Continental Celts slept at gravesites in the hope of receiving an oracular dream from those who were buried there.[18] Dreams formed an important part of the practice of the *awenyddion* in Medieval Wales (as well as the visionary experience of Cú Chulainn).

Musicians and dancers in Gaelic Scotland were reported to have received visions, creative inspiration and gifts through the dream state.[19]

Healing sleep and dreaming rituals were associated with a number of Celtic goddesses. The Gaulish goddess *Damona*, who was venerated at various healing springs, was often depicted with a snake (symbolic of healing, regeneration and transformation) and ears of grain (symbolizing abundance and fertility). An inscription from a shrine associated with Damona and her consort *Borvo* mentioned a healing sleep which was believed to be provided by the divine couple. Pilgrims slept in a special dormitory associated with Damona's temple, where they sought a vision or dream of the deities.[20] This practice was also associated with the sanctuaries of the goddess *Sirona* ("Divine Star Goddess"), whose iconography and veneration was similar to that of Damona. It is believed that supplicants also slept at the temple of the goddess *Sulis* in order to obtain a healing vision. The same practice also took place at the temple of *Sequana* (the goddess of the River Seine) which similarly had a temple dormitory.[21]

Shamanic Songs

As in *most* shamanic contexts around the globe, the use of sacred sound or songs played an immense role in the Celtic spiritual and shamanic tradition. Songs of praise were often performed at Irish assemblies, and bards and poets performed at royal courts and tribal gatherings.[22] A very early Classical account dating to several centuries B.C.E., mentions the prominence of music at the assemblies of Massilia (a Greek trading port in the south of Gaul, now modern Marseilles). This reference is thought to reflect traditional Celtic custom. [23] Music and musicality are referred to frequently in native texts, as are methods of working with the spoken word — poems, spells, charms, incantations, and so forth. These practices would have formed part of the traditional training and practice of the druid or poet.

The use of the human voice in shamanic ritual and ceremony is extremely common around the world. This practice is also present in numerous Celtic contexts. As we have seen, the magician Gwydion recited magical poems in order to facilitate the healing of Lleu, who was in a state of shamanic illness.[24] Dubh Rois played the harp for the divinely mad woman *Mis*, which assisted with her healing and transformation.[25] Druids and other "people of skill" chanted spells to calm and heal Cú Chulainn in "The Wasting Sickness of Cú Chulainn."[26] Historically, the druids sang or chanted spells to pacify armies, perform prophecy, or transmit traditional knowledge.[27]

There is quite a bit of evidence to suggest that some of the earliest Celtic "songs" or vocalizations were associated with the imitation of bird song (something still present in fairly recent Scottish Gaelic folk tradition). Even the Galic practice of "keening" (*caoine*), a type of ritual lament performed by women, has been recorded and shown in some instances to imitate the calls of birds (specifically the redshank). It is also thought that piping may have been associated with the observation and imitation of bird sounds.[28]

The imitation of natural sounds — including animal cries, bird songs, wind, and the sounds of running water — is believed to be the origin of the practice of overtone singing. In this practice, the singer produces a basic or fundamental pitch, as well as a variety of higher or lower "overtones" or "undertones."[29] The magical and inherent sounds of the natural world are mentioned in a number of Celtic texts, including the nature poetry of *Suibhne Geilt*.[30]

In "Cormac's Adventures in the Land of Promise," the hero visits the Otherworld Well of Wisdom. The streams that flowed from the well were reputed to make music more melodious than anything human beings can produce.[31] There was even specialized terminology for types of chanting which may reflect the use of overtone or undertone singing. The Old Irish verb *fo-cain* meant "chant" or "sing under," while the verb *for-cain* meant "sing over," "teach or instruct" or "predict or prophesy."[32]

In the Celtic languages there are numerous words for types of songs and music, each with a very particular meaning. The Old Irish word *ceól*, meaning "music," is also used to refer to the songs of birds. *Amrán* means "singing" or "song," *coicetul* means "singing together" and *dúchann* a "chant, song or melody." There are also special words for other types of sounds, like the term *esnad*. This multilayered term refers to (1) a musical sound, including a roaring, moaning or droning sound (like that of the wind), (2) the singing of certain birds, or (3) a particular kind of human singing or humming. These concepts, like those described by the words *dord* ("buzzing, humming, droning or intoning") and *crónán* ("hum, purr, drone, crooning"), may refer to practices like overtone singing.[33]

In ancient times, what we think of as "singing" may have been more like chanting a simple melody using a few notes (whether short phrases or a lengthy sacred text). This archaic practice was still used in the early twentieth century by tradition bearers in Scotland and Ireland. They sang or recited extremely long stories or songs in the *sean-nós* style, using a traditional kind of chanting or singing technique. The chanting or singing of songs, hymns, prayers, charms, spells and invocations, as well as the recitation of ancient lore and wisdom texts, would undoubtedly have formed part of early Celtic ritual. These spoken and chanted ritual tools made use of the multiple layers of meaning within words, as well as complex rhymes and strings of alliteration, which are especially effective when utilized in a ritual setting.[34]

Shamanic Music

Some of the oldest instruments in Ireland and Scotland consist of a variety of bronze horns. Some of the earliest types are up to three thousand years old and shaped like a cow or bull's horn. Many are still playable. These horns came in two forms, side-blown or end-blown (having a mouthpiece or aperture on the side of the horn, or at the end of the horn). Both types of horns were often buried in combination with each other, and may have been played together in rituals or ceremonies.

The side-blown horns have a range of almost three octaves, and their sound can be augmented by adding the singing voice while playing them. Researchers discovered that the end-blown horns were played in the same way as the Australian didgeridoo. They produce a deep, rich fundamental tone as well as a number of harmonics or overtones. When Australian aborigines from Arnhem Land were given an opportunity to examine these ancient European instruments, they were able to play them without any hesitation.

Other types of Celtic horns were used in the Iron Age and the medieval era. These include the famous boar-headed *carnyx* or war trumpet, as well as other horns which are believed to been used in a religious context. One of the common attributes of these later instruments is that they were played with "circular breathing," a type of technique in which the player never stops blowing and yet never runs out of breath (bringing to mind the powerful associations with the breath connected with poetic traditions).[35]

There is no archaeological or literary evidence for the early Celts having utilized any sort of drum, either for secular or religious purposes. However, the name of the Irish frame drum, known as the *bodhrán*, is attested in what may be an Old Irish spelling (*bodrán, bodarán*). In this form it is translated as "tabor, drum," which could refer to a more widespread form of medieval frame drum, or an indigenous frame drum (whose remnants, made of hide and wood, may not have survived in the archaeological record).[36]

There are examples of ritual rattles, and these were sometimes found in connection with the ritual horns. During the Bronze Age, a type of rattle referred to as a *crotal* was often buried with the horns, and these also seem to have also been associated with bull imagery (being shaped like bull's testicles). These rattles produced a very delicate sound and were created in a variety of pitches.[37]

Another possible candidate for a Celtic shamanic instrument rich in overtones was the *roth ramach* or "rowing wheel" owned by the legendary druid Mug Roith. One text said that his name came from the phrase *mogh roth* (glossed in Latin "magus rotarum"), for it was by "wheel-incantation" that he made his observations. It has been suggested that the object in question might have been similar to the bullroarer used by Australian aborigines. This consisted of a piece of wood attached to a string that was whirled about the head in a wheel or circle. It produced a loud, supernatural sound that was said to be the voice of a god.

Anthropological sources record that the bullroarer should only be seen, heard or touched by certain people. In a medieval Irish text, the dangers of the rowing wheel are similarly enumerated. It would cause blindness to anyone who saw it, deafness to anyone who heard it, and death to anyone who touched it. In another text it was described as an enormous ship that could sail on both sea and land. Interestingly, the bullroarer was sometimes referred to as "the oar."[38] This symbolism may suggest that the sound of the sacred object, the "voice of the gods," could be used to navigate between the worlds, and as such, should only be experienced by initiates or experienced teachers of wisdom. It also brings to mind the type of legendary tale known as the *immrama*.

In Cormac's adventure, an Otherworld being (who later reveals himself as the god *Manannán Mac Lir*) holds a silver "branch" with three golden apples on it. The branch had both magical and musical properties, for when shaken, its music could cure illness or produce sleep. This object, known as the *craeb-síde* or *craeb-sidamail* ("*síd*" or "fairy" branch), is referred to in other texts as well. It consisted of a branched wand or staff from which bells were suspended. After Cormac and Mannanán meet, Cormac suggests that they make an alliance, to which the god agrees. Cormac then asks for the magical branch. It is eventually given to him after he provides Mannanán with three boons, illustrating the important theme of reciprocity between the worlds.[39]

The Power of Words

The power of sound and the spoken word is omnipresent in Celtic tradition. In ancient times, the magical power of words was attested in the Gaulish belief that the god Ogmios had more power than Heracles (Hercules). In the second century C.E., the poet Lucan said he had seen a portrayal of this deity as an old man carrying a club, followed by a group of willing people who were connected to the tongue of this eloquent deity by delicate chains of gold and amber. A Celtic bystander informed the Classical observer that the Celts believed the power of the word to be more potent than physical strength, and that age and experience contributed to the growth of eloquence.[40]

When attempting to understand the spiritual traditions of any given culture, it is important to learn about that culture's history and social organization. In indigenous cultures, there is no boundary between the sacred and the secular (as there is in modern Western culture). The two are inextricably intertwined, and a real understanding of any society's religious beliefs necessitates some knowledge of their culture as well. History also plays a role in how a culture's mythology and theology have changed or evolved over time. The same is true in relation to Celtic religion. For example, the Irish myths are extremely difficult to interpret without knowing how early Irish society worked and what values and ideas were considered important.

Another important key to a spiritual tradition is the native language in which that tradition is encoded and preserved. As we have seen, the power of sound and the spoken word were very important in Celtic tradition. For this reason, any serious and in-depth understanding of the tradition will ultimately require or be substantially deepened by some training in the Celtic languages. This is not to say that those who do not have access to this sort of training cannot engage in a sincere exploration of Celtic religion. But at least some familiarity with one of the modern languages can provide insight into how the languages work as well as the cultural and spiritual information encoded within them.

When using Celtic language songs, texts, prayers and poems in a classroom setting, the student's experiences and understanding are heightened exponentially. Listening to a recitation of an Otherworld poem in Old Irish or a wisdom text in Middle Welsh creates a path between the worlds, bridging the gap between this culture and the culture and traditions of the indigenous Celts.

In shamanic cultures, secret, archaic, or ritual languages are often taught to initiates by spirit teachers or earthly tutors.[41] The Gaulish Celts were said to speak together in few words, using riddles, which left much of the meaning of their conversation to be understood by the listener.[42] The druids were also said to expound their philosophy in riddles, probably alluding to some sort of cryptic or riddling speech.[43] The use of secret language forms, word games and riddles was still used by poets and grammarians in fourth-century Gaul.[44]

In medieval Ireland, the poets utilized a specialized "learned language" (*bérla na mfiled*) which was unintelligible to those outside their profession. A number of these poetic languages are mentioned, including one particularly obscure form with which the poets addressed each other.[45] The medieval Welsh *awenyddion* were also said to provide oracular advice through a type of "riddle" or specialized language which was often difficult to understand.[46]

Caesar reported that the druids trained their initiates through the use of the memory and oral tradition.[47] This would undoubtedly have included the chanting or repetition of sacred texts and lore. Lucan referred to the "singing" of druidic lore associated with the immortality of the soul, while Diodorus Siculus mentioned the chanting of the druids, which was used to intervene between opposing armies.[48] Druidic chanting, spells, recitations and invocations are mentioned with great frequency in both Irish and Welsh native texts.

Highly specialized language and terminology was used to refer to these types of practices, and the poetic use of sound and language may have had their origins in the ritual use of prayers, hymns, invocations and prophecy. These language-based creations, whether a single word or a lengthy ritual text, involved the reciter's awareness of the multiple layers of meaning in words or phrases, as well as their familiarity with traditional knowledge associated with the tribe's history, philosophy, theology and mythology.[49]

Special terminology for various types of divine wisdom and vision is extremely widespread in Celtic tradition, and these native words (*imbas, awen, eolas, dán,* etc.) are important tools for understanding the tradition. Knowledge and language were entwined, and sacred and traditional wisdom was sung, chanted, recited, and proclaimed. It was also prized, remembered, treasured and preserved throughout the centuries. In one Old Irish poem, the poet begins his recitation with the phrase, "I mention this lake each day, as I weave the knowledge of ancient lore."[50] In another, the poet says, "Illuminate for me the ancient wisdom of my tribe; it is sweet for my heart to hear it."[51]

We can see that Celtic ritual or shamanic practice may have included such elements as purification and fasting, ritual movement or postures, breathwork, sacred dreaming, the gathering and use of sacred plants, and the use of darkness to enhance altered states of consciousness. The Otherworld journey or encounter is extremely important in Celtic tradition, and was sometimes associated with knowledge of the natural world and the maintenance of alliances with the inhabitants of the Spirit world. Ritual practices associated with sacred sound were very widespread, and included the use of instruments rich in overtones (horns and rattles), pipes and harps, and a variety of vocal techniques, including chanting, singing, recitation and possibly overtone singing. Whether or not we choose to label or interpret some or all of these beliefs and techniques as "shamanic," they provide fascinating glimpses into the perceptions and practices of the Celtic peoples and their complex religious traditions.[52]

11

Celtic Cosmology

The druids are recorded as having spent up to twenty years in training. Part of their curriculum involved natural philosophy, including the size and shape of the world, and the motion of the stars and the heavens. The druids must therefore have been custodians of traditional lore associated with Celtic cosmology, which included the form, organization and sacred attributes of the earth and the universe.

The Power of Sacred Space

In a Middle Irish text called "The Settling of the Manor of Tara," a supernatural figure appears before the people of Ireland and relates to them — through the questioning of their oldest historian or *seanachie*, Fintan mac Bochra — the sacred divisions of the land and their attributes. Fintan explains how the land has been partitioned in a particular way, with a primary attribute associated with each of the four directions, as well as the sacred center[1]:

Knowledge in the West
Battle in the North
Prosperity in the East
Music in the South
Kingship in the Center

He goes on to provide a more complete list of attributes — about fifteen or twenty for each direction. A sample of the attributes for each direction is provided here[2]:

West: Learning (Fis)
Teaching, foundations, judgment, counsel, stories, eloquence

North: Battle (Cath)
Contention, hardships, strife, pride, rough places, unprofitableness

East: Prosperity (Bláth)
Good customs and manners, abundance, dignity, strength, wealth, hospitality

South: Music (Séis)
Honour, fertility, games, vehemence, fairs, poetic art, minstrels

Center: Kingship (Flaith)
Kings, dignity, stability, ollave-ship, mead, bounty, reknown, fame

The Old Irish word *bláth*, which was associated with the east, means "flower or blossom." It was used to denote things in a flourishing condition (and may therefore be associated with springtime). The "flowering" of prosperity and well being may be a good interpretation of this attribute.[3]

In the south, the primary association was *séis*, which means "sense or meaning," as well as "design or order." This term was associated with subdivisions of the bardic schools, as well as educational commentaries or treatises. In other contexts it was used to refer to melodies or music (the primary attribute of the south).[4]

In the west the main attribute was *fis*, an extremely important concept in early Irish tradition. *Fis* meant "knowledge," in particular "information" or "the act of finding out something." It referred to that which was known, and to knowledge as an intellectual acquisition (as distinct from *ecna*, "wisdom," and *intliucht*, "understanding"). The word also meant "a message or summons" and was used to refer to a learned person or sage.[5]

In the north, the primary attribute was *cath*, which means "battle" or "fight." This may have referred to difficulties or obstacles, or challenges or ordeals, which were often encountered in life (and especially prior to new achievements or states of being).[6]

The Celts were inheritors of certain aspects of what are known as "Indo-European" cultural and religious traditions. The Indo-Europeans are ancient European peoples who probably inhabited the river valleys of the Pontic-Caspian region, in what is now Eastern Europe or Western Russia (near or around the Black and/or Caspian seas), sometime in the fifth millennium B.C.E. and onwards. Archaeology suggests that these people expanded eastwards across the steppe and forest steppe of western Siberia starting in the fourth millennium B.C.E. Over time, these people and their associated languages and culture moved into a number of regions, including the Balkan and Danube regions, south eastern Europe, the Caucaus region, and southwards into Central Asia.[7]

As a result of these expansions, Indo-European languages began to spread and develop throughout much of Europe and beyond. These languages grew to include what we now know as the Celtic, Germanic, Slavic, Baltic, Italic, Illyrian, Greek, Thracian, Iranian, Anatolian, Phrygian, Armenian, Tocharian and Indo-Aryan language branches (including Sanskrit). In addition to sharing common language origins, the Indo-Europeans shared a number of social, cultural and religious ideas, which spread over great distances (and also changed and developed over time). Some of these ideas and practices were preserved most assiduously on the outskirts of the region — in Ireland and India — which is demonstrated by certain parallels in Sanskrit and Old Irish texts, and early Irish and Indian written sources.[8]

A number of scholars have written about what the early or Proto-Indo-Europeans believed — or in their own terminology — to what ideas they "put their hearts" (a concept seen in the Latin verb *credo*, "I believe," the English word "creed" and the Old Irish word *cride*, "heart").[9] Many Indo-European languages, for example, contain words which suggest a belief in a male sky god, thunder and rain deities, gods of the moon and dawn, and a sun god (who was sometimes female). There were also traditions concerning gods of the waters, such as the Indic and Avestan figure of *Apam Napat*, the Latin *Neptunus* and Old Irish *Nechtain* (whose names are cognate). The horse figured prominently in Indo-European myth and ritual, and was sometimes involved in rituals in which the king was involved in a symbolic union with a mare. Divine twins also appear, often associated with or represented by horses.[10] These ancient elements bring to mind the Celtic Goddess of Sovereignty, and the legend of Macha, who outran the king's horses and gave birth to twins.

There are also ancient, shared elements of cosmology in Indo-European traditions. In these religious systems, ritual movement often began in the east and/or moved in a clockwise or sunwise direction. Moving to the right, from an eastern perspective, was considered auspicious and associated with health, strength and propitious attributes. To move from the east towards the north (lefthandwise) was considered unfavorable, weak or unsound. This idea is easily seen in the Latin word *dexter* ("right," as in English "dexterous") and *sinister,* "left." From the ritual orientation of east, the south is propitious and north is dangerous or malevolent.[11] This ritual movement follows the movement of both the sun and the moon, which rise in the east, move southwards and set in the west.

Although the Irish story as we now have it mentions the direction of west first, it does progress in a sunwise direction through the four cardinal directions, ending up at the sacred central point. In certain sources, the Otherworld was associated with the direction of west. In fact, the supernatural figure who converses with Fintan in the story was said to have approached the people of Ireland from the west at sunset. He says his place of origin is from the setting of the sun, and that he was going into the rising of the sun, for it was he that caused both events.[12]

The association of the west with the Otherworld, and with wisdom, may indicate that it was considered especially sacred. This episode probably also represents the Celtic belief that the day began at sunset (and that creation took place in the void, rather than at the point of emerging light). We will explore these concepts in more detail a little further on. For now, we should remember Caesar's famous comment that the Gaulish Celts measured all periods of time not by the number of days, but of nights, and that they observed birthdays and the beginnings of months and years so that day followed night.[13]

If we envisioned the cycle starting in the east and moving in a sunwise or right-hand direction, as seen in many Indo-European traditions, we might perceive or envision a symbolic progression of ideas. First (in the east) are basic concepts associated with life and prosperity, perhaps including health, fertility and abundance. Next (in the south) comes the ordering and expression of internal and cultural life, including sacred lore, music and song, and creative expression. This is followed (in the west) by the acquisition of knowledge and intellectual excellence. The final stage (the north) is associated with conflict, perhaps representing the point of challenges prior to growth, renewal or rebirth. As the place of cosmic darkness, it represents the point between destruction and creation.

In the Celtic "version" of the sacred ordering, however, movement starts in the west, the direction of wisdom. The acquisition, preservation and transmission of knowledge and wisdom were extremely important in Celtic society, and would have been primarily entrusted to the druids (and later, the poet-seers). Armed with this knowledge, movement proceeds into the north, the direction of conflict and battle. It is also the point of cosmic darkness, which contains all energies and life forms, and from which life emerges (in the east). Continuing in a sunwise direction, life is expressed through creativity, poetry and music, which were also considered extremely important in Celtic culture. They were also the methods through which wisdom and knowledge were preserved, maintained and ritually transmitted.[14]

The text also mentions a fifth sacred direction — the center. This was the most sacred point of the Celtic ritual site, reflected in numerous archaeological contexts. It was also incorporated in various place-names, including *Mediolanum*, "The Sacred Central Plain" (now known as Milan) and *Medionemeton* ("Sacred Central Place") in early Scotland.[15]

In this Irish text, the center was associated with a number of attributes, including dignity, stability, support, kingship, warriors, learned elders, mead and ale, renown and fame. Its primary attribute was the all-important concept of sovereignty. This may have referred to the sovereignty of a place or people, as well as sovereignty of the self (mastery, self-knowledge). The sacred center was also the location of the "World Tree," a concept which may have found expression in the Old Irish word *bile* ("sacred or ancient tree, pillar").

The attributes presented in the text were associated with the four provinces of Ireland: Leinter (east), Munster (south), Connacht (west) and Ulster (north), as well as the sacred central province of Meath (from Old Irish *Mide*, which means "Middle"). Not surprisingly, many large cultural and religious assemblies took place at sacred sites located in Meath.[16] It is reasonable to assume that the concept of the four directions and their associated attributes would have been utilized in Celtic religious symbolism or ceremonies.

The Four Talismans

Additional information which may be associated with the four directions comes from another early Irish tale, "The Second Battle of Moytura" (*Cath Maige Tuired*). The text begins by recounting the tradition that the *Tuatha Dé Danann* at some early stage of existence were in the "northern islands of the world." As we have seen, the north represented the cosmic darkness. In a number of mythological contexts, this phrase symbolizes unknown realms which were often associated with magic, knowledge, or supernatural skills or power. In this region, the Irish deities studied druidic knowledge and magic until they had surpassed all the sages of the pagan arts.[17]

The gods pursued their studies in four Otherworldly cities: *Falias, Gorias, Murias* and *Findias*. The name *Falias* appears to be associated with the word *fál* (best known in the phrase *Lia Fáil*, the legendary Irish stone associated with kingship). *Gorias* may contain the word *gor* meaning "heat, fire," and *Murias* the word *muir* or "sea." *Findias* derives from the word *find* (later *finn*) which is used frequently in the Irish mythological tradition. The word means "white, bright, lustrous" or "bright, blessed" (and is cognate with Welsh *gwynn* and *gwen*, the masculine and feminine forms of the word in that language).[18]

A magical object was brought from each of the cities. From Falias was brought the Stone of Fál, which used to cry out beneath the feet of the rightful king. From Gorias was brought the spear of Lug. No battle was ever sustained against it, or against the person who held it in his or her hand. From Findias was brought the sword of Nuadu. No one could resist it, or escape from it once it was drawn from its sheath. From Murias was brought the cauldron of the Dagda from which no company ever went away unsatisfied.[19]

Unfortunately, the text does not specify if the four cities were located in the four cardinal directions, and if so, in which direction each of the cities were located. To compound matters, the list of cities is presented in two different orders in the text. Early on, the list is given as "Falias, Gorias, Murias and Findias," while the list of associated talismans is in this order: Falias, Gorias, Findias and Murias (the sities Murias and Findias switching place).

If we knew the proper order of the cities, as well as their direct association with a particular direction, this would be of great benefit in deepening our understanding of the divisions of the land and the attributes of the four directions.

If we examine the names of the cities and outline the attributes of the talismans, comparing these with other Irish texts, a pattern does begin to emerge. One suggestion of ordering based on the association of these concepts with symbolism in other sources, is as follows:

East: Findias — Sword of Nuadu
South: Gorias — Spear of Lug
West: Murias — Cauldron of Dagda
North: Falias — Stone of Fál

The rationale behind this arrangement comes from information given in "The Settling of the Manor of Tara," as well as other early Irish sources.

East/Findias/Sword of Nuadu/Prosperity

The east was the direction of flowering and prosperity (perhaps associated with springtime). The word *find* suggests a bright or blessed quality, possibly connected with the rising sun. The association of east with the rising sun and springtime occurs in many other traditions. The mythological sword of Nuadu may have transformed over time into the Gaelic folkloric motif of "The Sword of Light." In addition, Nuadu is one of the earlier kings of the Tuatha Dé Danann.

South/Gorias/Spear of Lug/Music

In a number of religious traditions located in the northern hemisphere, the south was geographically associated with warmth (*gor*, "heat, fire"). In later episodes of "The Second Battle of Moytura," Nuadu is succeeded as king by Lug. The god *Lug* was described as a bright and multi-skilled deity of many arts and skills, as well as a poet and harper. The south was also the direction of music.

West/Murias/Cauldron of Dagda/Learning

In "The Settling of the Manor of Tara," the west was the direction of knowledge. While the Dagda was known for his powers of life and death, and his cauldron of abundance, he was also highly venerated as the "god of druidic knowledge." One of his primary epithets was *Ruad Ro-fhessa* ("Noble One of Great Knowledge"). In addition, in Ireland the sea (*muir*) lay to the west.

North/Falias/Stone of Fál/Battle

The Stone of Fál was associated with kingship, which in many cases was only realized or achieved after battles, conflicts, challenges or ordeals.

While this particular patterning of concepts is not certain, it may be the most complete or authentic arrangement possible, based upon the knowledge we currently have. There may have been some confusion or omissions in the written sources, as scribal error was common enough in the medieval era. These errors or omissions may confuse or thwart our attempts to equate the talismans with the directions in a logical manner. For example, one might reasonably be tempted to place the Dagda's cauldron of abundance in the east, the direction of prosperity. However, it is clear that there was at least some degree of symbolic encoding in the story, providing us with intriguing information about the attributes of the four cardinal directions in the Irish tradition.[20]

The Power of Colors

The number three was prominent in numerous Indo-European cultures, and was expressed in both cultural and religious symbolism. It may represent the three cosmic realms; the mysteries of life, death and rebirth; or the concept of sacred duality mediated by a border or center. In Indo-European religious traditions, deities might have three primary names or titles, or display three main attributes. Elements of healing or wisdom might be expressed in "threes" or "triads," as in the Iranian *Avesta* where there are three types of healing: spell-medicine, knife-medicine and herb-medicine.[21] We have already seen the three types of divination required of the *filid* in medieval Ireland (*imbas forosnai*, *dichetal di chennaib* and *teinm laeda*) as well as the three types of venerated persons in Gaulish society (druids, bards and seers). The number three was also conceptually associated with three social classifications or functions[22]:

1. Leaders and Holy Persons
2. Warriors
3. Farmers and Herders

An ancient system of color associations existed in a number of Indo-European cultures which were associated with social groupings and religious symbolism, among other things. While variations would have existed between cultures, the primary color associations were as follows:

White: First Function of Society (Rulers and Holy Persons)
Red: Second Function of Society (Warriors or possibly Craftspersons)
Yellow or Green (or Black or Blue): Third Function (Herders and Farmers)

This set of colors operated in both a three-fold and a four-fold setting, as in some cultures there was a fourth element as well (those who served or supported the first three functions). This might be represented by a class of serfs, or by a goddess figure who incorporated within herself all three of the other functions. In these cases, the fourth element was connected with a color initially associated with the third function.

In Hindu tradition, the threefold system of society was associated with the colors white, red, yellow, and black, while in Roman culture we find white, red, green, and black or blue. In Indo-Iranian, Celtic and Latin ritual, white was associated with holy persons and red with warriors (the other colors display more variation).[23]

Academic studies of color terminology in many cultures shows that in ancient times, the order in which colors were given a name in the earliest stage of verbal or perceptual ordering follows a set pattern. The first and second colors to be named are white and black (representing the duality of light and dark). The third color which is given a name is red. These are the three colors associated with society and religion in numerous cultural contexts. After this, there is more variation. The fourth set of colors to be named includes those associated with the third (or fourth) functions: yellow, green, blue (in varying order). After this are brown, purple, pink and orange (in that order).[24]

These same color groupings appear in various Celtic contexts as well. Early Irish texts appear to have utilized an early system of color preference that involved the colors white, black, red, followed by yellow, green and/or blue. These colors are also given preference in the early Irish text *Saltair na Rann*. The text outlines twelve "winds" that were connected with the various points of the compass. It describes four primary winds in the North, South, East and West, with two additional winds between each of them.[25] The colors associated with the four primary directions in *Saltair na Rann* reflect the ancient primary color groupings seen above:

North: *dub* ("black, dark")
South: *gel* ("white, bright, shining")
East: *corcor* ("crimson or purple")
West: *odar* ("dun," a yellowish-brown)

These four colors — white, black, red and yellow — are frequently the four most commonly used colors in religious symbolism in numerous cultures around the world.

The text provides information about the other winds and their colors, as well. These are as follows (the four primary winds, with the two secondary winds between them, presumably in geographical order as in the text)[26]:

East: corcair ("crimson, purple")
South-East: derg ("red, the colour of blood or flame; orange or tawny like ale, gold"); buide ("yellow")
South: gel ("fair, white, bright, shining")
South-West: uaine ("green, verdant; also used of estuaries or rivers — green or blue"); glas ("various shades of light green and blue, from grass-green to gray," as opposed to uaine, green and gorm, blue); used of growing things, meanings of "fresh, young," colour of wood, metal, frost or ice, shades of grey, a wan complexion
West: odhar/odur ("dun — a dark or dirty yellow-brown or grey-gold in horses; greyish-brown; a sallow complexion")
North-West: liath ("grey; hence aged"); ciar ("dark, murky, black")
North: dub ("black, dark; of ink; melancholy, gloomy")
North-East: teimen ("dark, obscure; hence enigmatic or plain"); alad ("variegated")

In the colors of the winds we can observe a progression from deep crimson or purple in the east (a vibrant life-affirming color), through shades of red and yellow, and then to a shining white color in the south. The winds then shift to greens, blues and blue-greys, and changing to dun (grey-yellow) in the west. From here the colors pass into shades of grey and darkness, arriving at black in the north. From this point, the place of primal darkness, life energies emerge in obscure or mysterious shades of darkness, blossoming forth in variegated hues, and finally arriving back in the east. Perhaps these colors formed part of a more sophisticated system of colors, attributes and ideas which were understood by the early Irish and formed part of their cosmology and ritual system.

Patterns of Sacred Time and Space

We have seen that the four directions were associated with particular attributes in early Irish thought. We also know that there was also a cycle of four sacred holidays. If we visualize an overlay of the attributes associated with sacred time and sacred space, we may begin to perceive a cosmological system which could have formed part of the sacred learning of the druids — and later, the poet-seers — in Ireland.

North — Black
Samain
Battle (Death) or Creation (Rebirth)
Dark Moon or New Moon

West — Yellow   East — Red
Lugnasad   Imbolc
Learning (Harvest)   Prosperity (Growth)
Waning Moon   Waxing Moon

South — White
Beltaine
Music (Blossoming)
Full Moon

Acknowledging that Indo-European ritual traditionally began in the east, in this system the starting point of the ritual year (Samain) may have been symbolically placed towards the north. This sacred point in the year wheel (like the new moon) was a point of death as well as creation. These new life energies might have then more fully manifested in the direction of east (associated with the beginning of springtime).

We know that in the Irish ritual calendar, Samhain and Beltaine were the two most important points of the year. The early Irish text *Lebor Gabála Érenn* alludes to an early division of the land of Ireland that demonstrates a primary spatial demarcation into north and south. The north (at least symbolically) was given precedence over the South. These divisions were associated with Kingship (North) and Music (South).[27]

Black and white (associated here with North/Samhain and South/Beltaine) are the two most basic and important color terms in both a linguistic and symbolic sense. Samhain, and the period of the dark or new moon, both involved symbolism associated with endings (death) and beginnings (rebirth). The color black is a potent symbol of this liminal time, which contains the energies of death as well as creation. This concept is expressed in the figures of various deities who were associated with war and protection and were also protectors and preservers of life.[28]

Saint Brigid was connected with Leinster, which is located in the east of Ireland. She had a marked connection with abundance, prosperity and new life, perhaps reflected in the association with red, a life-promoting color. Red was also the color traditionally associated with the warrior class. While Imbolc was associated with birth and women's concerns, it also marked the peak of the springtime raiding season (which took place from mid–January to mid–March). The spring campaigns which took place around Imbolc served primarily to alleviate or clear away any potential regional strife or difficulties which might affect broader alliances later in the year. Imbolc may also have had associations with rites of purification, preparing and protecting in the year to follow.[29]

The direction of south was associated with music in several sources. The Dagda was said to reside at Uisneach, the site where the early Irish held a major Beltaine assembly. Among his many attributes, the Dagda was said to be a harper. The direction of south was associated with music in several sources. In the north/south division of Ireland outlined in *Lebor Gabála*, a poet was associated with those who resided in the north, and a harper with those in the south.[30]

The color yellow (which may be extrapolated from the dun-colored wind) was in other Indo-European traditions often associated with food producers and fertility. This would certainly be appropriate for the Feast of Lugnasad, which was a harvest festival, among other things. It was also a time for social connection, honoring the ancestors, and the recitation of important cultural and religious lore. A medieval account of a Lugnasad assembly describes the ritualized recitation of native wisdom that traditionally took place at this time. The recitations included myths and legends, riddles and proverbs, place-name stories, "books of lore," "maxims of might" and "the knowledge of every region in Ireland." [31] Perhaps these last recitations included more complete information about the concepts of sacred cosmology in early Ireland.

Sacred Time

Although the Irish calendar includes four holidays (Samhain, Imbolc, Beltaine and Lugnasad), in earlier times there may have only been three holidays. We have almost no information about Imbolc from the early or medieval period, and much of what we know about the holiday comes from more recent folklore sources. Written evidence from a number of Indo-European cultures suggests that during an early period, the ritual year consisted of three seasons: spring, summer and winter. This supposition is supported by the widespread use of three-fold symbolism throughout the Indo-European world. Three divisions were applied to the cosmos (Upper world, Middle world and Lower world), religion (where three-fold symbolism is extremely common in Indo-European cultures), and society (the three functions above).[32]

This division into three may not have resulted in an equal partitioning between the three parts, however. For examples, herders and cultivators would have far outnumbered warriors, who in turn would have been more numerous than priests and rulers. In certain examples of this ideology, this may have actually been reflected in a 1:2:3 ratio. When applied to the human body, for example, the three parts would be unequal in size: (1) the head, (2) the upper body (from neck to waist), and (3) the lower body (below the waist). When this ratio is applied to the ritual year, the annual cycle is divided into three unequal seasons of two, four and six months.[33]

Evidence from various early sources indicate that at least some of the Celts utilized a lunar-based calendar. If the 1:2:3 ratio is applied to the lunar cycle, the dividing points occur on the first, sixth and fifteenth days of the month. The divisions that take place at the first and fifteenth days of the lunar month clearly correspond to the new moon and the full moon. Prior to the start of the Celtic year, there was a liminal period of darkness associated with the symbolism of death and creation. A similar phenomenon also takes place in the lunar cycle.

Just as the year begins at the point of darkness and rebirth, so too does the lunar cycle begin with the appearance of the new moon after a period of darkness (the void or dark moon). The new moon was the symbolic point of the cycle at which major assemblies or rituals would have taken place. The new moon would have corresponded with Samhain in the annual cycle, while the full moon corresponded with Beltaine.[34]

Interestingly, we also have evidence pertaining to the intermediate point of the lunar month. In Pliny's *Natural History*, he refers to a Gaulish ceremony in which druids gathered to harvest mistletoe from an oak tree on the sixth day of the moon. He states that it was gathered with great reverence, above all on the sixth day of the moon. Pliny goes on to say that it was the moon that marked out for the Gaulish Celts the beginning of months and years (as well as larger cycles of thirty years). He also states that on the sixth day of the lunar cycle the moon was already exercising great influence, even though it was not yet halfway through its course.[35]

In later Celtic folk tradition, healing plants were often gathered during the waxing moon in order to preserve their medicinal powers. These effects and properties were believed to be increasing as the moon was waxing, and therefore at their highest potency during that time.[36]

All around the world, there is a parallel between the start of the lunar cycle and the start of the annual cycle. In this system of correspondence, creation takes place out of the darkness, rather than at the point of first light or visibility. The primal darkness is not a void but a place filled with immense power and potential, which has yet to be seen. Caesar wrote that the Gaulish Celts subscribed to this mode of thought, for they defined the divisions of the seasons not by days but by nights, observing the start of months and years in such a way that darkness preceded light.

As the lunar cycle began with the dark moon (which preceded the new moon), so too did the yearly cycle begin with Samhain in Irish tradition. An ancient bronze plaque found in Coligny, France, and dating to the Iron Age provides some interesting parallels between the Irish and Gaulish calendar systems. In the Coligny calendar we find evidence for the use of a lunar-based calendar, as well as clearly defined divisions of lunar months, years, and larger cycles of many years. For example, the Gaulish month name *Samon* appears to be cognate with the Irish word *Samain*. Both are points of creation and rebirth that directly follow a period of sacred darkness associated with death and decline. The three dividing points of the lunar cycle may have corresponded with the three festivals of the early Celtic year for which we have early evidence: Samhain, Beltaine and Lugnasad.[37]

The affirmation of the new moon as the beginning of the Celtic lunar cycle (as well as the ritual year) clarifies another aspect of time measurement seen in the Coligny Calendar. Throughout the calendar, the midpoint of the lunar cycle (the fifteenth day) is labeled by the word *atenux* or "returning night." This term reflects another important archaic cosmological concept. In this mode of thought, temporal movement progressed from a starting point (the new moon) towards a mid-point (the full moon) and then returns back towards the beginning point.[38]

Movement towards the mid-point was often considered positive, while movement back from the mid-point was often considered negative. Later folk tradition once again provides an interesting parallel. In Scottish folklore, the waxing period of the moon was associated with growth and increase (as well as wetness or fertility), while the waning moon was associated with lessening or decrease (and dryness or barrenness). The Coligny calendar provides evidence of an early Celtic system of mapping out sacred time. In this system, the new moon was the sacred starting point, the sixth day of the lunar cycle was the point of increase, and the fifteenth day was the returning point, after which energies returned to the primal darkness to be renewed and reborn.

The Nine Elements

Varied systems of religious and cosmological symbolism exist in ancient and traditional cultures, some of which are associated with the elements of the natural world. Some cultures include elements like earth, air, fire, water and ether or spirit in their sacred cosmology, as well as other elements like wood and stone, sun and moon, and so forth. In Celtic mythology, the two most commonly featured elements were fire and water. The druids taught that the soul, like the universe, was immortal, although at some point fire and water would overwhelm it.[39] In myths and legends, the druids were also said to have magical power over various elements, including fire and water.

We know that the ancient Celts venerated and conducted rituals in connection with bodies of water since earliest times. Offerings were made into lakes, rivers and wells, and ceremonies were held at healing springs. Early maps indicate that throughout the Celtic territories, rivers were associated with goddesses.[40] Water symbolized healing, purification, transformation and wisdom.

Fire was associated with a number of important concepts. It was connected with heroic fury and ardor, poetic knowledge, and the kindling of divine inspiration. The two elements appeared in combination with each other as well. The idea of "fire in water" is a very ancient Indo-European concept, and symbolized the idea that the power of knowledge or flame of inspiration existed in an Otherworldy body of water (usually a well or spring). This power was carefully guarded and transmitted only to those who had undergone sufficient training or who were otherwise worthy of inheriting its potency.[41]

Another very old Indo-European tradition involved a system of nine sacred elements. This system has been documented in numerous cultures for thousands of years. These nine elements included: earth, stones, trees or plants, water or sea, sun, moon, clouds, skies and wind. Each element of the Outer World (macrocosm) was associated with a part of the body (microcosm). The most common form of this system of elemental symbolism was as follows[42]:

Earth — Flesh	Water — Blood	Moon — Mind
Stones — Bones	Wind — Breath	Clouds — Brain
Plants — Hair	Sun — Eyes	Skies — Head

These two elemental systems (the power of fire and water, and the nine elements) may have formed part of early Celtic cultural and religious perceptions. These beliefs and perceptions would have included an understanding of the connection of the inner and outer worlds, as well as the interconnection between human beings and the natural world.

12

Celtic Wisdom Traditions

Early Irish and Welsh manuscripts contain a remarkable amount of information about the cultural knowledge and spiritual traditions of the Celtic-speaking peoples. This information is preserved and encoded in myths and legends, poetry and place-name lore, and sagas and wisdom texts. This chapter presents a few examples from the manuscripts to provide an idea of the complexity, beauty, and sophistication of these traditions.

The Well of Wisdom

One of the most powerful images in the Celtic spiritual tradition is the Underworld Well of Wisdom. This sacred landscape appears in the early Irish tale *Echtrae Chormaic i dTír Tairngire* ("Cormac's Adventure in the Land of Promise"). The tale begins at an important point in the Irish ritual year, daybreak on the first of May. Cormac is approached by an Otherworld figure who carries in his hand a silver branch bearing three golden apples. The sound of the branch puts the king to sleep for a time.

Upon awakening, Cormac asks the magical figure where he comes from. The figure reveals himself as the god Manannán mac Lir, king of the Land of Promise. He tells Cormac that he has brought him to the Otherworld to show him the wonders of this sacred realm. Cormac is given a vision of the Well of Wisdom, where nine purple hazel trees grow and drop their nuts into the fountain. The five salmon that live in the fountain crack open the nuts and send their shells floating down the streams. Manannán mac Lir explains to Cormac that the five streams represent the five senses through which knowledge is obtained.[1]

This famous description of the Well of Wisdom contains a number of important elements: hazel trees, hazelnuts, the sanctity of water, and the salmon of wisdom (*éo fis*). These elements are present in other Irish sources as well, including the *Metrical Dindshenchas*, a collection of traditional lore associated with important and sacred places. The following Dindshenchas poem recounts the story of *Sinann*, a woman from the *Túatha Dé Danann*. It was said that every sort of skill was at her command except a mystical art known as *imbas* (also referred to as *an t-timmus* or *immas sóis*). Sinann approached the edge of a river where she saw some "beautiful bubbles of wisdom" (*bolca áilli immaiss*). She pursued them into the water and was drowned, becoming the spirit of the river Shannon.[2]

> The well of Connlae, great was its spirit, beneath the summoning edge of the sea
> Six streams, not equal in fame, flow from it; Sinann was the seventh.

The nine hazel trees of Crimall the wise man drop their fruits into the well
They are by the command of illusion under a dark mist of druidic magic.

At one time, as is not usual, their leaves and their flowers grow
Remarkable, though a noble attribute this, their being ripe all at once.

When the nuts are ripe they fall into the well below
They scatter on the bottom so that the salmon eat them.

From the juice of the nuts, no small matter, they form the bubbles of wisdom
Each hour they come from beyond, over the green flowing streams.

There was a young woman with blonde hair, yonder, from the Tuatha Dé Danann
Skillful Sinann of the bright countenance, daughter of bright, resplendent Lodan.

One night the young woman thought, the sweet, red-lipped maiden
That every attribute was at her command, except the power of *imbas.*

One day she went to the stream, the young woman, fair was her form
Until she saw, it was no small matter, the beautiful bubbles of wisdom.

The woman went, a lamentable journey, after them into the green flowing stream
She was drowned there from her venture; so that from her Sinann is named.[3]

The objects pursued by Sinann were associated with magical power and the acquisition of divine wisdom. Many sages, seers and poets sought to obtain the power of *imbas.* The word refers to specialized knowledge, poetic talent or inspiration, prophetic ability or magic lore, and particularly to knowledge or foreknowledge obtained through magical or occult means. It was a specialized ability that was part of the required training of the *fili* or poet-seer — *imbas forosnai,* "Illumination of Great Knowledge."[4]

In a prose version of Sinann's story, the bubbles are described as being red in color (*ina mbolcaib corcardaib*). The word *corcair* in Old Irish refers to a range of colors which includes shades between purple and red (hence, the purple hazel trees at Cormac's well). Red hazelnuts were also mentioned in the Metrical Dindshenchas poem about Cnogba (modern day Knowth) and *The Settling of the Manor of Tara.* In the second tale, an ancient figure named *Fintan* is approached by an enormous supernatural hero garbed in a shining crystal veil. The hero carries with him a branch with three fruits upon it (reminiscent of Mannanán mac Lir's branch and its three golden apples). Like the trees at Connla's well, the branch bore nuts, apples and acorns all at the same time.[5]

The name of the supernatural hero was *Trefuilnguid Tre-eochair,* an unwieldy title which could translate as "He Who Supports by means of the Three Keys." The word *eochair* means "key" as well as "clue, solution, guide or means of access." Interestingly, another epithet of the salmon was *eochair-brecc* (perhaps "speckled guide"). The "three keys" are mentioned in other sources as well, where they are connected with the revelation of the "three keys of wisdom" (*éicse*). The gigantic hero explains to Fintan that he is responsible for the rising and setting of the sun, and that the fragrance of his magical branch serves him for both food and drink.[6]

Other tales describe how the five sacred trees of Tortu, Ross, Mugna, Dathe and Uisnech later grew from this magical branch. A Dindshenchas poem on *Éo Rossa* (the Yew of Ross) refers to these sacred trees, and states that the Oak of Mugna bore three crops every year: apples, acorns and "round, blood-red nuts." In the texts we encounter powerful depictions of round red objects, red fruits or red flesh which were associated with the pursuit and acquisition of knowledge or power.[7]

It is possible that these elements (apples, acorns, hazelnuts, salmon) might refer in an encoded way to a type of visionary plant (like the *amanita muscaria* mushroom), a possibility supported by an in-depth exploration of the terminology and texts. However, they may simply symbolize the "fruits of the Tree of Wisdom," the sacred skills and divine wisdom of the Otherworld so frequently mentioned in Celtic wisdom texts.[8]

However they are interpreted, sacred trees and their fruit were perceived as existing both in this world and in the Otherworld. Their powers were transmitted into the waters, and then into the body of a creature associated with the water (the Salmon of Wisdom, the *eó fis*). Those who had access to the Well and Wisdom and partook of these sacred elements obtained wisdom.

The Three Cauldrons

As we have seen, the vocation of the druid and the fili involved years of training, as well as the memorization of complex and esoteric wisdom and lore. In an early Irish manuscript, the legendary figure of Amairgen (who chanted the poem that began "I am a wind in a sea") purports to instruct other poets in a special vein of traditional knowledge.

In this text, three vessels or cauldrons are described, which were envisioned as forming part of a person's spiritual development. There were three cauldrons that existed within each person: *Coire Érma* ("The Cauldron of Movement"), *Coire Goriath* ("The Cauldron of Warming") and *Coire Sois* ("The Cauldron of Great Knowledge"). The cauldrons were associated with poetic inspiration and wisdom and represented the three stages of poetic or spiritual progress.

In a young person, the Cauldron of Warming was born in an upright position, marking the beginning of service. Later, the Cauldron of Movement was born inside a person in a tilted position, marking the next phase of development. Finally, the Cauldron of Knowledge was born inside a person in an inverted position. This symbolized the flowing out or dissemination of knowledge, the stage of full development.

The text states that an event of either great joy or great sorrow moved a person from the first stage (the Cauldron of Warming) to the second stage (the Cauldron of Movement). This sorrow might result from the sadness of leaving one's home to engage in poetic training, on account of people or relationships in one's life, or as a result of disconnection from the divine.

Several types of joyful experience had the power to move a person into the second stage of development. The first type of joy was satisfaction from overcoming an illness or overcoming hardship during one's development. The second type of joy came as a result of qualifying as a poet and experiencing the pleasure derived from applying the rules and principles of poetry. The third kind of joy was delight at the inspiration received from the hazel trees at the Well of Segais (the Otherworld Well of Wisdom located at the source of the River Boyne).[9]

Here are excerpts from the poems associated with the Three Cauldrons, preserved in this unique ancient manuscript (the stanzas below are associated with Coire Goriath):

> My Cauldron, a fitting warming
> A fervent poem in which God has given to me
> the secrets of the elements

The mark of an artificer
which ennobles a bright company
A fortunate language flows forth from it.

I am Amairgen White-Knee, of blue tattooed shin and grey beard
The performing of my inspired heat,
a spontaneous sharing and distribution

Since not the same does God arrange for each person —
on the side, upside-down, or upright —
no knowledge, a portion of knowledge, or a fullness of knowledge

For Éber Donn, creating the form of many great recitations,
in masculine, feminine and neuter, in double consonants, long vowels and short vowels
A meaning that is related, [this is] the manner of service of my cauldron.[10]

The texts go on to enumerate the powers and attributes of the other two cauldrons. The Cauldron of Movement was known for its ability to "sing" and pour forth streams of poetic knowledge and lore. It was renowned for encouraging enlightenment and refreshing the soul. The Cauldron of Movement was activated by poetic inspiration, and was ultimately moved, turned or transformed by joy.

The Cauldron of Great Knowledge was reputed to exalt people of skill through their achievement of a spiritual gift. From the vessel, the laws of every art were set out, which resulted in an increase in prosperity. Divine gifts entered the Cauldron of Great Knowledge, gifts that were associated with both divine and secular poets and seers. The Cauldron of Knowledge was associated with the mastery of language, the use of "dark" or mystical speech, the achievement of understanding, and the refinement of the senses. It was a noble womb in which all poetic knowledge was boiled or brewed, a sacred vessel whose power was steadfast and everlasting.[11]

The Triads of Ireland and Britain

Traditional wisdom associated with Celtic religion, ethics and ideology exist in a number of other early Irish texts. One of these texts is entitled "The Triads of Ireland," and consists of traditional lore arranged in groups of three. This arrangement supported the memorization of knowledge and was one of the methods used to train initiates.

Some of this traditional knowledge was associated with the landscape. For example, the three fairs of Ireland are given as the Fair of Teltown (Tailtiu), the Fair of Croghan, and the Fair of Colman Elo. The three mountains of Ireland are listed as Slieve Gua, Slieve Mis and Slieve Cualann, and the three lakes as Lough Neagh, Lough Ree and Lough Erne. The three rivers of Ireland were the Shannon, the Boyne and the Bann, while the three plains of Ireland were the plains of Meath, Moylinny and Moy-Liffey.

One famous triad listed three things which constituted a king (i.e., which affirmed and demonstrated his authority and power). These three things were abundance during his reign, holding the feast of Tara (*Feis Temro*), and entering into contracts with other kings. Three things that led to the ruination of a tribe were a lying chief, a false judge and a lustful priest. The three glories of an Irish assembly or gathering were a beautiful wife, a good horse and a swift hound. The three preparations of a good man's house included ale, a bath and a large fire (these things were provided for guests, as hospitality was considered a necessity in medieval Ireland).

The triads also contain information about skills and professions. The three types of hands that were best in the world were the hand of a carpenter, a skilled woman and a good smith. The three things that constituted a good physician were the ability to effect a complete cure, leaving no blemishes, and conducting a painless examination. Harpers had to be proficient in three types of music: music that made people cry, music that created laughter, and music that induced sleep. These strains of music were known as *goltraige, gentraige* and *súantraige*, named after three legendary harpers who were sons of the goddess Boand (and who performed this music on a harp belonging to the Dagda). The three things that constituted a poet were *imbas forosnai* ("Illumination of Great Knowledge"), *teinm laeda* ("Cracking Open of Pith or Song") and *díchetal di chennaib* ("Spontaneous Incantation").

Some of the triads included native beliefs pertaining to truth, justice and wisdom. For example, the three things demanded by justice were judgment, measure and conscience. Likewise, the three things demanded by a good judgment were wisdom, investigation and knowledge. Three doors that led to falsehood were an angry pleading in court, an unsteady foundation of knowledge, and giving information without memory.

One triad outlined three types of silence that were better than speech. These were silence during instruction, silence during the performance of music, and silence during religious ceremony. There were three types of speech that were better than silence, however, and these included encouraging a king to undertake a rightful conflict, the dissemination of knowledge, and praise after accomplishment. The three glories of speech were steadiness, wisdom and brevity. Three signs that denoted wisdom were patience, vision, and prophecy. One especially beautiful triad listed three "candles" that illuminated the darkness. These luminaries were truth, nature and knowledge.[12]

The Welsh also preserved traditional knowledge in groups of three. The medieval Welsh text *Trioedd Ynys Prydein* ("The Triads of the Island of Britain") contains a great deal of important cultural and mythological information, including beliefs and lore pertaining to the land and various divine and supernatural beings. The three tribal thrones of the island of Britain were listed in one triad. These included Arthur as Chief Prince in Mynyw, Dewi (Saint David) as Chief Bishop, and Maelgwn Gwynedd as Chief Elder. In another triad, Arthur is listed as Chief Prince in Pen Rhionydd in the North, along with Gerthmwl Wellig as Chief Elder and Cynderyn Garthwys as Chief Bishop. Arthur was also listed as one of the Three "Scurrilous" Bards (i.e., bards who performed satire), along with Cadwallawn son of Cadfan and Rahawd son of Morgant. Additionally, he was one of the Three Red Ravagers of the Island of Britain, with Rhun son of Beli, and Morgant the Wealthy (although another triad gives Lleu of the Skillful Hand as the third "Red Ravager," demonstrating the varying ages of some of the Welsh triads).

The three Battle-Horsemen of the Isle of Britain were Caradawg "Strong-Arm," Menwaedd of Arllechwedd, and Llyr of the Hosts (this is the father of Manawydan ap Llyr, a Welsh legendary figure whose name is cognate with that of the Irish god Mannanán mac Lir). The Three Unfortunate Counsels of the island included making a place for the forefeet of the horses of Julius Caesar and the men of Rome, allowing Horsa and Hengist and Rhonwen on the island (Anglo-Saxon invaders who were reported to have betrayed the Celts), and the dividing of Arthur's forces with his nephew Medrawd (Mordred) at the Battle of Camlann.

Women also figure in the medieval triads of Wales. The three fair "Womb-Burdens" of the land included three sets of three legendary or semidivine offspring. The first set consisted of Urien, Arawn and Lleu, three sons of Cynfarch, who were borne by their mother Nefyn, daughter of Brychan Brycheiniog. The second set involved Owain and Anarun (sons of Urien) and Morfudd (a daughter of Urien) by Modron ("Divine Mother," daughter of Afallach, ("Abounding in Apple Trees"). The third set consisted of Gwrgi and Peredur (sons of Eliffer) and Arddun (a goddess figure) by their mother Efrddyl, daughter of Cynfarch. The three most splendid women in Arthur's court were Dyfyr "Golden-Hair," Enid daughter of Earl Yniwl, and Tegau "Golden-Breast."

Three Skillful Bards who were at Athur's court were Myrddin son of Morfryn, Myrddin Emrys, and Taliesin. The Three Perpetual Harmonies of the island were situated at Bangor, Caer Gardawg, and the Island of Afallach (later known as the Isle of Avalon). At each of these renowned sites were reputed to be 24,000 religious men, 100 of whom prayed ceaselessly during each of the twenty-four hours of the day. It is interesting to note the mention of two Christian sites along with a pre–Christian Otherworld location.[13]

A list of sacred objects is also mentioned in the text. In an appendix to the Triads, the "Thirteen Treasures of the Island of Britain" are described. These included the following traditional legendary talismans and venerated objects:

- Dyrnwyn ("White-Hilt"), the sword of Rhydderch the Genererous
- The Hamper of Gwyddno "Long-Shank" a vessel of supernatural abundance
- The Horn of Bran, which provided whatever drink was wished for
- The Chariot of Morgan the Wealthy, which provided magical transport
- The Halter of Clydno Eiddyn, in which a magical horse manifested at night
- The Knife of Llawfrodedd the Horseman, which served twenty-four at table
- The Cauldron of Dyrnwch the giant, which would only boil food for the brave
- The Whetstone of Tudwal Tudglyd, only sharpened the weapons of the brave
- The Coat of Padarn "Red-Coat," which would only fit a well-born person
- The Dish of Rhygenydd the Cleric, which provided any food that was desired
- The Chessboard of Gwenddolau, on which chessmen played by themselves
- The Mantle of Arthur in Cornwall, which conferred invisibility on the wearer. Anyone who wore it was not seen yet could see everyone else
- The Ring of Eluned the Fortunate, which had a magic stone set in it. This is the thirteenth talisman, and was owned by woman. If the stone set in the ring was hidden, the person who hid it would likewise not be seen.[14]

Celtic Wisdom Texts

Traditional cultural wisdom and spiritual and ethical beliefs were recorded in other manuscripts as well. Some wisdom texts are presented in the form of a teacher or elder advising a student or younger person. The following advice is found in "The Instructions of Cú Chulainn," as presented to Lugaid Réoderg, the newly chosen king of Ireland[15]:

Do not provoke violence or strife
Do not be arrogant or aggressive

Let elders be questioned rightly in your presence
Let those who provide true judgments be located
Let strangers in the land enter the protection of the sanctuary
Do not speak loudly or arrogantly
Do not deride or deceive the elderly
Do not be ill disposed towards others
Be humble when receiving instructions from the wise
Observe the teachings of your forebears
Do not participate in the oppression of others
Do not hoard things which are not needed
Do not sacrifice justice to human passion.[16]

A similar format was used to great effect in another early Irish text, "The Instructions of Cormac mac Art," a figure who was revered as the ideal Irish king. The instructions provided by Cormac included a number of elements that were recognized as part of the rightful behavior of a leader. These elements included exhibiting firmness without anger, showing patience without aggression, and exercising mercy in alignment with traditional law.

A good king was expected to give true judgments, maintain ancient lore, and give truth in exchange for truth. There was even a term for the special type of truth that a leader was expected to have, the *fír flatha*. A righteous leader tended to the sick, provided benefits to the strong, honored poets, fostered arts and science, and consolidated peace whenever possible. A good king's reign resulted in mast (nut-crops) on trees, abundant fish in the river mouths, and a fruitful earth. A rightful leader possessed truth, provided peace to the tribes, and was expected to continually work to improve his soul.

The tribe and the land benefited from the rule of a good leader. A number of themes are described as being good for the tribe as a whole. These included righteous chieftains, good judgments, honoring treaties, and good guardianship of the borders of the land. Tribal or territorial assemblies should be held frequently, according to traditional rules, along with meetings of nobles to discuss tribal business. Other beneficial attributes included the questioning of sages, following ancient lore, having a mind disposed towards inquiry, knowledge of every language, learning of every art, and listening to and heeding the counsel of elders.

Cormac tells his student about his own training and development, as an example for the future king. He describes himself as one who listened in the woods and gazed at the stars, who was silent in the wilderness and mild in the ale house. He was ever watchful and stern in battle, yet he was also a good and gentle friend, and tended to the sick. Although he was wise, he did not display arrogance. Although young, he did not make fun of the elderly. A good fighter, he did not boast of his prowess. He did not criticize others but praised them, did not ask for things but gave generously, and would not speak about anyone in their absence. Cormac counseled his students to be wise and steadfast, generous and righteous, persevering and patient, studious and learned. He instructed them to love their kindred, to be joyous in health, and to be a faithful friend and good counselor. In this cultural and spiritual tradition, "every truth was sweet, every good art and skill resulted in abundance, and knowledge was honoured and preserved."[17]

13

The Knowledge of Trees

Celtic myths and legends frequently mention sacred trees and plants, many of which seem to have functioned in a symbolic as well as a literal sense.[1] Traditional Gaelic poetry and folklore also contains tree and plant lore, much of it quite specialized in nature.[2] In the early Irish material, a number of trees frequently appear in connection with sacred beings and Otherworld encounters. The nine most common trees and plants are hazel, apple, rowan, yew, hawthorn, oak, holly, ash and gorse. Hazel and apple in particular have Otherworld associations. The hazel tree and its nuts symbolized divine wisdom and inspiration, while the apple served as an invitation or token of passage between the worlds.[3]

These trees also appear in connection with a form of writing known as the *ogam* alphabet (later spelled *ogham*). It was developed and utilized in Ireland between about 300 and 600 C.E. and was associated in some cases with the training of poets. The ogam alphabet was written by placing combinations of short lines on either side of (or horizontally or diagonally across) a central vertical line or "spine." These symbols represented the letters of the Irish alphabet, and in order to facilitate memorization of the letters they were associated with various systems of metaphorical meanings or attributes. These systems of attributes included rivers, colors, animals, fortresses and other sets of meanings. The most detailed and well-known was a system of meanings associated with trees and plants.

Ogam was said to have been invented by the god *Ogma mac Elathan,* a brother of the Dagda. He was a divine warrior and hero who was also skilled in poetry and speech. Legends maintain that Ogma created the ogam alphabet to demonstrate his intellectual skill, and that the system was intended to be used by the learned classes alone. The symbolic "father" of the ogam alphabet was Ogma, while its "mother" was the hand or knife. This referred to the carving of ogam into wood or stone, as well as the use of hand gestures to communicate through the use of the ogam symbols. Traditional lore states that the first thing ever written in ogam was a message containing seven Bs on a piece of birch. This was apparently a message of warning to the god Lug that his wife would be carried away from him seven times into the realms of the *síd* unless the birch protected her. Hence, birch was the first letter of the ogam alphabet.

Ogam was carved on early monument stones in Ireland and parts of Britain. In numerous stories, when a famous hero or heroine died, their name was inscribed in ogam on a stone erected above their grave. In other sources ogam was used to create territory markers or inscribe various types of communications on stones. Messages were also written on pieces of wood, although these have not survived in the archaeological record. In one tale a poet was said to have written an incantation on four rods of yew wood, while in other sources poems were written in ogam on staves of wood. Ogam was used to communicate important messages, record incantations or poems, and possibly also to perform divination. One early account referred to symbols carved on pieces of oak or hazel, while another mentioned symbols written on leaves and placed inside a chalice (although it is not clear if ogam symbols were used).[4]

In the tree-based system of associations connected with the ogam letters, the trees were divided into four groups: chieftain trees, peasant trees, herb trees and shrub trees. These groups were arranged as follows[5]:

Chieftain Trees: Oak, Hazel, Holly, Apple, Ash, Yew, Fir
Peasant Trees: Alder, Willow, Birch, Elm, Hawthorn, Aspen, Rowan
Shrub Trees: Blackthorn, Elder, Spindle Tree, Test Tree,
Honeysuckle, Bird Cherry, White Hazel
Herb Trees: Furze (Gorse), Heather, Broom, Bog Myrtle, Rushes

The ogam letters and their associated trees and plants were recorded in various manuscript sources with a great deal of consistency (although a few variations exist). Here is a list of the ogam letters in the traditional order they are given, followed by the Old Irish word for the tree or plant in question. The associations in the right hand column indicate which tree or plant was indicated by the ogam. Some of these words are direct translations, while others are more symbolic in nature. For example, the word *luis* (which features second in the list) does not translate as rowan (which is *caerthann*), but means a "flame" or a "plant or herb." On account of the flame-red berries of the rowan or mountain ash, in this system of associations the letter L (*luis*) was connected with the rowan tree.[6]

B	*Beithe*	Birch
L	*Luis*	Rowan (literally "Flame" or "Plant/Herb")
F/V	*Fern*	Alder
S	*Sail*	Willow
N	*Nin*	Ash (literally "Fork" or "Loft")
H	*hÚath*	Hawthorn (literally "Horror")
D	*Daur*	Oak
T	*Tinne*	Holly (literally "Strong," or "Brilliant")
C/K	*Coll*	Hazel
Q/Kw	*Cert/Quert*	Apple (literally "Bush")
M	*Muin*	Vine (literally "Upper part of back or neck")
G	*Gort*	Ivy (literally "Field or Garden")
GG/NG	*nGétal*	Broom (or Fern) (literally "Wounding or Piercing")
Z	*Straiph*	Blackthorn (literally "Sulphur")
R	*Ruis*	Elder (literally "Red")
A	*Ailm*	Fir or Pine
O	*Onn*	Ash (later also Furze/Gorse)
U	*Úr*	Heather (literally "Earth" or "New")
E	*Edad*	Aspen or Test Tree
I	*Idad*	Yew

In later versions of the tree ogam, a number of vowel combinations were added to the system: EA, OI, UI, IO and AE. These were associated with *Ebad* (EA) Aspen; *Oir* (OI) Spindle Tree or Ivy; *Uilleand* (UI) "Bend" (Honeysuckle); with other variants.

The order of the letters in the ogam alphabet reflected native usage associated with the

Irish alphabet (rather than the order of the Latin alphabet): B L F S N H D T C Q M G GG Z R A O U E I; EA OI UI IO AE. The following list, however, provides an alphabetical guide to the trees and plants of the ogam system according to the Latin alphabet, for the purpose of easy reference:

A	(*ailm*)	Fir/Pine
B	(*beithe*)	Birch
C	(*coll*)	Hazel
D	(*daur*)	Oak
E	(*edad*)	Aspen or Test Tree (or Juniper)
F	(*fern*)	Alder
G	(*gort*)	Ivy or Honeysuckle
GG	(*gétal*)	Broom/Fern
H	(*hÚath*)	Hawthorn
I	(*idad*)	Yew
L	(*luis*)	Rowan
M	(*muin*)	Vine
N	(*nin*)	Ash
O	(*onn*)	Ash or Furze/Gorse
Q/Kw	(*cert*)	Apple
R	(*ruis*)	Elder
S	(*sail*)	Willow
T	(*tinne*)	Holly
U	(*úr*)	Heather
Z	(*straiph*)	Blackthorn

The Language of the Trees

In the manuscripts, the ogam letters were associated with short phrases known as "kennings," which are frequently cryptic or difficult to understand. There were also kennings associated with the Norse system of runes, although the two systems do not seem to be related. Some of the kennings are descriptive, some provide practical information, while others appear to function on a more symbolic level. These phrases were probably utilized in the teaching process, put forth as a clue to test the students' memory and knowledge.

Here is a listing of the Ogam letters and trees, followed by their three primary associated kennings (in italics). Underneath the kennings are phrases (in parentheses) which contain additional information found in ogam sources and other texts, to help students understand more deeply various aspects of the kennings.[7]

There has been a great interest in modern times to ascertain if the ogam alphabet was used for divination, and if so, exactly how it worked. Many systems have been put forth which suggest a wide range of possible divinatory meanings. A great deal of this information is modern in origin, or derives from other cultural systems (including neo- occultism). For the interested student of the ogam system, underneath the second set of associations are provided [in brackets] some suggested divinatory symbolism for the ogam letters. These are based directly upon the actual kennings given in the texts, as well as the symbolism of trees and plants as recorded in other authentic Celtic sources.[8]

B, *Beithe*, Birch

Kennings: Withered foot with fine hair; Greyest of skin; Beauty of the eyebrow

Associations and cultural context: (The pale grey or white bark of the birch tree with its fine small leaves; the first message sent in ogam warning Lug about his wife)

Suggested Divinatory Meanings: [Beauty, gentleness or fragility; first things or beginnings; caretaking; new undertakings]

L, *Luis*, Rowan

Kennings: Lustre of the eye; Friend of cattle; Sustenance of cattle

Associations and cultural context: (The rowan was a "delight of the eye" due to the beauty of its berries; rowan berries were used in folk magic for protecting cattle; in some texts the elm was associated with the third kenning, as cattle supposedly loved its flowers and down)

Suggested Divinatory Meanings: [Bright beauty, protection of livelihood, sustenance]

F, *Fern*, Alder

Kennings: Vanguard of the hunting bands; Protection of the Heart; Milk container

Associations and Cultural Context: (Shields were made from Alder wood, as were milk buckets)

Suggested Divinatory Meanings: [Protection of community or culture; self-protection; nourishment]

S, *Sail*, Willow

Kennings: Pallor of a lifeless one; Sustenance of bees; Beginning of honey

Associations and Cultural Context: (The pale hue of the tree and its leaves; some associations with bees and willow pollen)

Suggested Divinatory Meanings: [Gentle or decreased life energy leading to increased growth later; a sweet reward]

N, *Nin*, *Ash*

Kennings: Establishing of peace; Boast of women; Boast of beauty

Associations and Cultural Context: (Another kenning reads "A check on peace, for spear shafts are made of ash by which the peace is broken"); weaver's beams were also made of ash—in times of peace "weaver's beams are raised"; the legendary prophetess Fedelm held a weaver's beam)

Suggested Divinatory Meanings: [Fostering or maintaining peace; weaving and prophecy; fate and destiny]

H, *hÚath*, Hawthorn

Kennings: Assembly of packs of hounds; Blanching of faces; Most difficult at night

Associations and Cultural Context: (The hawthorn is formidable, like a group of hounds, owing to its thorns; the unpleasant smell of the hawthorn flower causes the blanching of faces; those who attempt to meet secretly at night may prick themselves on the thorns of the hawthorn tree in the darkness)

Suggested Divinatory Meanings: [Fierceness, challenges, secret encounters]

D, *Daur*, Oak

Kennings: Most exalted tree (Higher than bushes is Oak); Handicraft of an artificer (a skilled craftsman); Most carved of craftsmanship

Associations and Cultural Context: (The oak was highly venerated by the Gaulish druids, and perhaps also in Irish tradition; in early times it was associated with celestial deities and with the eagle; oak highly prized in carving and crafts)

Suggested Divinatory Meanings: [The veneration of sacred qualities; connection with the divine; great skill]

T, *Tinne*, Holly

Kennings: One of three parts of a wheel; One of three parts of a Weapon; Marrow of charcoal

Associations and Cultural Context: (A third of a chariot wheel was made from holly; holly wood used in fires)

Suggested Divinatory Meanings: [A third part or portion of a journey; progress or movement forward; igniting or starting an activity]

C, *Coll*, Hazel

Kennings: Fairest tree; Sweetest tree; Friend of nutshells

Associations and Cultural Context: (Another kenning read "A fair wood — Everyone is eating of its nuts"; the beauty of the hazel tree and the association of the tree and its nuts with divine wisdom; the salmon of wisdom removed the shells from the hazel nuts to reveal the wisdom inside)

Suggested Divinatory Meanings: [Seeking knowledge; deciphering mysteries; the acquisition of divine wisdom]

Q, *Quert*, Apple

Kennings: Shelter of a lunatic; Substance of an insignificant person; Dregs of clothing

Associations and Cultural Context: (An additional kenning for the apple tree read "Shelter of a wild doe is the Apple Tree"; there were traditions of holy madmen or women living in the wild with little or no food or clothing — the apple tree may have provided food and comfort; the closeness of holy madmen to the divine or Otherworld)

Suggested Divinatory Meanings: [Difficult spiritual or emotional challenges; initiations; passages to the Otherworld]

M, *Muin*, Vine

Kennings: Strongest in exertion; Proverb of slaughter; Path of the voice

Associations and Cultural Context: (The word referred to the "upper part of the back" of either a person or an ox — hence strength in exertion; another kenning read "Highest of beauty, because it grows aloft"; like the vine, the sound of the voice travels upwards)

Suggested Divinatory Meanings: [Strength or exertion; difficulty before achievement; the power of the spoken word]

G, Gort, Ivy (or Honeysuckle)

Kennings: Sweetest grass; Suitable place for cows; Sating of multitudes
Associations and Cultural Context: (The word *gort* meant a "field" or "field of grain,"
a place full of sweet grass which satisfied herds of cattle)
Suggested Divinatory Meanings: [Abundance; growth and expansiveness; satisfaction]

GG/NG, *nGétal*, Broom (or Fern)

Kennings: Sustenance of a physician; Raiment of physicians; Beginning of slaying
Associations and Cultural Context: (Another kenning read: "A physicians' strength is
broom"; perhaps the plant was used medicinally in cases of severe injury or serious illness;
in folklore the broom had Otherworld and magical associations)
Suggested Divinatory Meaning: [Illness and healing; assistance; the start of a waning
cycle that eventually leads to recovery or rebirth]

Z, *Straiph*, Blackthorn

Kenning: Strongest reddening dye; Increase of secrets; Seeking of clouds
Associations and Cultural Context: (Sulphur is a strong coloring agent and was reported
to make red gold out of white gold; an additional kenning read "The hedge of a stream is
blackthorn"—the smoke of it, i.e., clouds)
Suggested Divinatory Meanings: [Powerful transformation; confusion or obscurity
eventually leading to understanding; a quest to gain knowledge or manifest change]

R, *Ruis*, Elder

Kennings: Most intense blushing; Reddening of faces; Glow of anger
Associations and Cultural Context: (Another kenning read "The redness of shame is
elder"—due to the color of its berries or juice, which can dye things red (including skin,
when handling the berries); the elder was and still is widely used in herbal medicine)
Suggested Divinatory Meanings: [Passions or anger; shame or embarrassment at intense
emotions; healing old wounds]

A, *Ailm*, Fir or Pine

Kennings: Beginning of calling; Beginning of an answer; Loudest groan
Associations and Cultural Context: (The sound "ah" which begins the word *ailm* was
used in calling out or responding; it was also associated with the groan of an ill person, and
the first utterance of an infant at its birth)
Suggested Divinatory Meanings: [Calling out or responding; difficulty leading to a
new cycle; the start of life experiences that may be challenging at first]

O, *Onn*, Ash (or Furze/Gorse)

*Kennings: Sustaining equipment of a warrior or hunting bands; Wounder of horses;
Smoothest of craftsmanship*
Associations and Cultural Context: (Ash was used for weapons and crafts; the spines
of the furze or gorse in the bush could wound passing horses; an additional kenning—
"Helper of horses"—referred to the fact that the rims of a chariot wheel were made of ash,
as was the horsewhip)

Suggested Divinatory Meanings: [Assistance with desired progress or forward movement; motivation or sustenance in one's life path; protection and support]

U, *Úr*, Heather

Kennings: In cold dwellings; Propagation of plants; Shroud of a lifeless one
Associations and Cultural Context: (Heather was used for fuel and bedding; the word *úr* means "earth"—heather grows low upon the ground right next to the earth; the third kenning may refer to white heather)
Suggested Divinatory Meanings: [Comfort; connection with the earth; gentle growth]

E, *Ebad* or *Edad*, Aspen (or Test Tree, or Juniper)

Kennings: Discerning tree; Exchange of friends; Brother of birch
Associations and Cultural Context: (The letter E also stands for *éo* which can signify either "salmon" or "yew"—hence the "exchange of friends"; the salmon was associated with wisdom, and rods of yew were used in divination; another kenning read "Crafty One of the Water," referring to the salmon, as the brother of birch)
Suggested Divinatory Meaning: [Messengers or keepers of wisdom; divination and discernment; exchange of words or ideas]

I, *Idad*, Yew

Kennings: Oldest tree; Fairest of the ancients; Energy of an infirm person
Associations and Cultural Context: (Yew trees can grow to be hundreds or thousands of years old; they were often planted at ancient sacred sites, and later near churchyards)
Suggested Divinatory Meanings: [Age and wisdom; ancient knowledge; the traditional wisdom and lore of the ancestors]

EA, *Ébad*, Aspen (or Honeysuckle)

Kennings: Fair swimming letter; Fairest fish; Admonishing of an infirm person
Associations and Cultural Context: (The first two kennings refer again to the letter E and its connection with the salmon; the third kenning is unclear)
Suggested Divinatory Meanings: [The need to set out on a search for wisdom; challenges encountered during the search; the process of acquiring knowledge]

OI, *Óir*, Spindle Tree (or Ivy)

Kennings: Most venerable substance; Splendor of form
Associations and Cultural Context: (These kennings reflect the similarity between the word *óir* given above and *ór* meaning "gold")
Suggested Divinatory Meanings: [The allure of outward appearance; beauty in form; wealth or unusual quality]

UI, *Uillean*, Honeysuckle (or Juniper, or Spindle Tree)

Kennings: Fragrant tree; Great elbow or cubit
Associations and Cultural Context: (Both kennings appear to refer to the honeysuckle with its fragrant blossoms and bending branches—*uillean* means "bend" or "elbow")
Suggested Divinatory Meanings: [The sweetness and joy of life; a turn in the path for the better; positive change]

IO, *Iphin* or *Pin*, Gooseberry (or Hawthorn, or Pine)

Kennings: Sweetest tree; Most wonderful taste
Associations and Cultural Context: (The kennings allude to the taste of gooseberries)
Suggested Divinatory Meanings: [The sweetness of life's simple pleasures; an appreciation for gifts that have been given]

AE, *Emancholl*, "Twinned C" (CC or Ch)

Kennings: A cry of woe; wasting away or lamenting
Associations and Cultural Context: (The kennings allude to the groan of a sick person, the sound of "*ach*" or "*uch*")
Suggested Divinatory Meanings: [A waning or diminishing cycle; false starts; illness, pain or loss that is necessary for eventual healing or new growth]

While these divinatory meanings are highly speculative, they are derived in a logical manner from the actual kennings in the texts. The "language of the trees" and the knowledge it contains is elusive, but a serious study of the ogam and its traditions may provide interested students with additional insights into its mysteries and its symbolism.

14

Symbolism of Animals and Birds

Animals and birds are among the most frequently occurring representations in Celtic artwork. Early Celtic art was a remarkable blend of inspiration from other ancient art styles, cultural adaptation and unique native innovation.[1] In this wonderfully dramatic art style, depictions of animals were not always fully realistic, but seem to reflect the personality of the artist and the animal itself. They also appear to portray the inner essence or perceived characteristics of the animal or bird in a more symbolic sense. Some of the most commonly depicted animals and birds were the deer, the horse, the bull and the boar, as well as various water birds (swans, geese and cranes).[2] The Picts were known to have made unique representations of many native creatures, including the horse, stag, wolf, bull, boar, eagle, seal, serpent, fish, eel and dolphin.[3]

Animals are also very widespread in the mythological and legendary tradition. Deities were frequently associated with animals or birds, and divine or legendary figures transformed or shapeshifted into animal form.[4] A number of sacred or supernatural figures herded, guarded or cared for various types of animals. Kings, heroes and other supernatural characters often shared a unique connection with certain creatures who were born at the same time as they were. This connection lasted throughout their lifetimes.[5]

We do not have access to one single ancient source which outlines for us a complete or uniform system of symbolic attributes associated with birds and animals. However, by examining Celtic artwork and its context, as well as descriptions of animals in folklore and literature, we can begin to understand how these sacred creatures were perceived and what role they played in Celtic cultural and spiritual traditions. It should be pointed out that the summary given below represents just a brief overview of some of the primary manifestations and attributes of animals, birds and fish in the tradition. Interested readers should consult the footnotes for a more extensive exploration of each creature.

Stag or Deer

In many instances, deer appear in Celtic myths and legends in order to guide, lure or entice people away from the known world and bring them into contact with the realms of the supernatural. The hunting of magical deer also leads people into unexpected Otherworld encounters. Sometimes these deer undergo magical transformation in the tales, and are associated with supernatural women. Deer antlers figure prominently in connection with images of horned or antlered gods or goddesses. The Irish goddess *Flidais* was associated with the abundance and power of the wilderness. Deer or other antlered creatures may have been venerated by a Celtic tribe known as the *Cornovii*.[6]

Horse or Mare

The horse was one of the most important animals in Celtic society. It represented wealth and power and was frequently associated with sovereignty. While the deer led people towards Otherworld encounters, the horse appears to have carried them to or into the Otherworld. Horses were associated with strength, speed, beauty, journeys, fertility and sexuality. Sacred horses were frequently white or grey, red or chestnut, or black in color, while Otherworld horses could appear in almost any color (including blue, yellow and purple).

The white horse in particular seems to have been associated with sovereignty and kingship. Numerous divine figures were associated with horses, especially those goddesses who exhibited a connection with Sovereignty — Macha, Epona and Rhiannon. One of the Dagda's epithets was *Echu Ollathair*, "Great Father of Many Horses." The horse may have been venerated by the early British tribe known as the *Epidii*, who lived in the region now known as Kintyre in Scotland.[7]

Bull and Cow

Cattle were a symbol of wealth and abundance in Celtic culture. The bull represented strength, virility, wealth, fertility and power, while the cow symbolized prosperity, abundance, generosity and fertility. There are several early depictions of divine bulls with three horns, and a number of divine figures were associated with bulls and cows. The goddess *Boand*, whose name means "Blessed Cow," was the tutelary deity of the River Boyne.

Bridget, Flidais and the Mórrígan all owned magical cows. In Celtic legends, some sacred animals appear to have been white with red ears. Cattle of this description were owned by *Manannán mac Lir*. Bulls were also associated with rituals connected with prophecy and kingship, including the *tarb-feis*. The pursuit of cattle was the basis of the early Irish saga *Táin Bó Cuailgne* ("The Cattle Raid of Cooley").[8]

Boar and Sow

The boar is a remarkably tenacious animal, and may have symbolized strength, determination, and the abundance of the wilderness. The preferred food of the boar is the acorn, the fruit of the sacred oak tree. Boar hunting took place before Samhain, and the boar was likely one of the symbolic ritual animals connected with that season. Like the deer, the boar can lead people into an Otherworld encounter. Its association with Samhain also led to its connection with transformation and Otherworld adventures.

Welsh legendary tradition held that pigs came from the Otherworld, and a legendary sow named *Henwen* ("White Ancient One") was connected with tales associated with the origins of farming (including the origins of the cultivation of wheat and barley, and bee-keeping). A magical boar hunt was associated with the Welsh boar *Twrch Trwyth*, who appeared in Irish tales as the *Torc Triath*, a magical king of the boars owned by Brigit. The Continental goddess *Arduinna*, who was associated with the Ardennes Forest, was depicted riding on a boar. The name of the Orkneys (*Orcades*) may suggest that the boar was venerated in that area.[9]

Hound and Wolf

Dogs were depicted in early representations of Continental and British deities, including Succelos, Nehallania, Nodons and Epona. A number of Irish heroes possessed names that included a root word meaning "dog, hound" (such as *Cu Chulainn*, "The Hound of Culann"). Dogs were associated with hunting, guidance, loyalty and healing. The name of the wolf appears to have been taboo, and dog-related words used in personal names in their stead (but understood to represent the wolf). In Scottish Gaelic, the wolf is called "wild dog" or referred to by the phrase *Mac Tíre* ("Son of the Land"). A descendant of King Cormac claimed to be descended from the wolf, as Cormac was reputed to have been raised and suckled by wolves when he was young. The wolf may have symbolized fierceness, courage, cooperation and the power of the wilderness.[10]

Bear

Bears were associated with early Continental deities like the goddess *Artio* and *Artioni* (whose names include the root word *art-* meaning "bear"). Male names, like those of *Art mac Conn* and even that of King *Arthur*, include this root word. The symbolism associated with bear goddesses suggest the abundance of the forest, hunting and protection (these deities may have protected bears and also guided hunters). The Irish name *Math* also means "bear," as seen in the god name *Matunus*.[11]

Ram and Sheep

The most prevalent image of the ram is found in connection with the antlered god, who holds a ram-headed serpent in his hand. Some of the early horned deities were depicted with rams' horns, rather than deer's antlers. Rams may have symbolized fertility, abundance and persistence, while sheep symbolized fertility, abundance and prosperity. The Feast of Imbolc celebrated the birth of sheep and the lactation of ewes. Folk tales tell of magical rams with nine horns, or sheep the size of horses. An early Celtic tribe known as the *Caereni* may have venerated these animals.[12]

Hare

Caesar wrote that the hare was venerated by the British Celts. In one Classical account, the British warrior-queen Boudicca used a hare in a divination ritual to determine the outcome of battle. Early Celtic artwork depicts hunter gods carrying hares, who may have symbolized the abundance of the forest, the hunt, magic and transformation. A number of folk tales depict women (and later, witches) transformed into the shape of hares.[13]

Cat

Cat imagery is not particularly prevalent in Celtic tradition, as domestic cats were not introduced until the medieval period. However, there are some images of deity heads with cat-like ears. The Irish figure of *Cairbre Caitchenn* ("Cairbre Cat-Head") was said to have been the ancestor of a particular Irish tribe. In the folklore and legendary tradition, cats were associated with divination rites and Otherworld encounters or journeys (particularly those connected with the dead). They may have been perceived as mystical, fierce, clever, helpful or difficult creatures. A species of wildcat still lives in Scotland.[14]

Fish

Salmon and trout were particularly revered in Celtic tradition. They were associated with sacred wells of wisdom, and therefore, with wisdom itself. In Irish tradition, the famous *Eó Fis* or "Salmon of Wisdom" was said to live in certain bodies of water or in the Fountain of Knowledge. A number of other sacred salmon lived in the Underworld Well of Wisdom where they cracked open the hazelnuts of wisdom and sent their husks floating down the streams that emanated from the well. In the folk tradition, salmon, trout and eels were connected with holy wells associated with healing, divination or wisdom. The salmon is the most widely mentioned of these aquatic creatures, and was associated with wisdom, divination, prophecy, inspiration and transformation.[15]

Serpent

The earliest depictions of serpents are associated with images of the horned or antlered god, who often holds a serpent in one hand. In the myths, serpents represent healing, regeneration, wisdom and transformation. As underground creatures, they would have also been associated with the Underworld. Saint Patrick was alleged to have banished all the serpents from Ireland. After the last Ice Age, there were no snakes in Ireland, making this a dubious accomplishment at best. Serpent imagery did exist in some Celtic contexts, and they were frequently associated with bodies of water.

Serpents (like dragons) could help or challenge kings or heroes, and were known to guard wells or sacred waters, fortresses or treasure. A charm was recited in Scotland at Imbolc at the burrow of the hibernating adder. The snake was invoked as a form of weather divination in preparation for spring. This ritual was performed in Ireland in connection with the badger, and in North America with the groundhog.[16]

Seal

Seals play a prominent role in the folklore tradition, where they were noted for their remarkable humanlike expressions and actions. In some cases seals were believed to be supernatural creatures, or even human beings transformed into seal form. The *Selkies* are a well-known manifestation of these folklore beliefs. They were connected with transformation, shape shifting and the inhabitants of the watery Underworld realms. In Ireland and Scotland, a number of families were believed to have connections with selkies (or to have been descended from a union between a human being and a seal).[17]

Dolphin

Dolphin imagery appears in several early Celtic contexts, much of it in connection with Romano-Celtic artwork. A young man riding upon a dolphin was depicted on the Gundestrup Cauldron, a silver vessel probably created in Thrace for Celtic patrons (and later found in a bog in northern Europe). In the Welsh tale of Arianrhod, one of her children, a young boy called *Dylan Eil Tonn*, was said to have taken to the sea upon his birth, perhaps a later reflex of the earlier dolphin imagery. Images of dolphins (which were mistakenly interpreted as "swimming elephants") appear in Pictish artwork as well.[18]

Raven

The raven is one of the most commonly depicted birds in Celtic artwork. It was connected with a number of deities whose attributes included battle, fertility, prophecy, and the powers of life and death. One early deity image shows a god with his hands raised in an oratorial gesture. Two birds (raven and/or goose) speak into his ear, and he also appears to be giving them instructions. The raven was widely represented in myths and legends, where it symbolized war, death, omens, divination, magic, wisdom and transformation. Magical ravens prophetically announce the arrival of *Cu Chulainn* in one tale, and the people who hear the announcement were able to understand their speech.

The three divine sisters — The Mórrígan, Macha and Nemain — were all referred to by the epithet *Badb* ("scald-crow"). In the folk tradition, ravens were associated with hags and witches, as well as the figure of the Washer at the Ford, a woman who washes bloody garments at the edge of a body of water. Her appearance symbolized prophecy, fate and death, and in early sources this role was enacted by the Mórrígan.

The Irish god *Midir* owned two white ravens which protected his *síd* mound. Interestingly, Strabo mentioned two crows whose right wings were part white that were said to have been used by the ancient Gauls for divination. Ravens with white feathers were popularly believed to be a good omen in Ireland as well, and were also associated with divination.[19]

Swan

Swans are depicted in early Celtic artwork and were associated with the healing or other beneficial properties of water and the sun. There are early representations of swans pulling sacred ritual wagons, along with deer and bulls. In the myths, deities may appear in swan form, often with chains of gold or silver connecting pairs of swans. Even in the early artwork, some swans were depicted with chains. Swans mate for life, and were therefore associated with tales of lovers.

Otherworldly women were sometimes associated with this bird. The magical song of swans was purported to have healing or sleep inducing properties. The famous Irish myth "The Children of Lir" told of human beings who were transformed into the shape of swans for nine hundred years. They possessed human speech and reason, as well as the gift of producing beautiful music.[20]

Crane

Images of long-legged marsh and water birds, including herons and cranes, also exist in early Celtic artwork. A depiction of a bull with three cranes on its back was found in a Gaulish context; its inscription read *Tarvos Trigaranus* ("Bull with Three Cranes"). Interestingly, in a Gaelic folktale a divine female figure known as the Cailleach was said to own a magical bull; her three sons appeared in crane form.

Imagery connected with cranes shows that they were associated with water and healing, as well as war and fierceness. The god *Midir* owned three cranes, and to see them en route to a battle was a bad omen. The deity *Manannán mac Lir* possessed an object known as a "crane bag," a container made from the skin of a crane. The crane had originally been a woman he admired, who was later turned into the form of a crane. Inside the crane bag were many magical objects and talismans of power.

The god *Lug* and other divine figures were described as performing magic in a crane-like stance. They utilized a ritual posture in which one eye was closed and in which the person stood on one leg (like a crane). In this position they performed a type of dangerous magic known as *corrguinecht* ("crane-wounding"). In the folk tradition, cranes were associated with women or witches who had transformed into crane form, and many accounts tell of priests turning women into cranes or being hostile to these creatures.[21]

Eagle

The eagle is depicted in early Celtic artwork, where it was associated with deities connected with the sky, the sun and the oak tree (a common set of associations in Indo-European religious symbolism). One of these celestial deities may have been *Taranis* ("The Thunderer"), who was pictured with a wheel symbol (perhaps representing the sun). The Welsh figure of *Lleu* transformed into an eagle after being pierced by a spear thrown by the lover of his unfaithful wife *Blodeuwedd*. The eagle was the highest flying bird, and in tales and legends it was associated with age, wisdom, prophecy and power.[22]

Owl

The owl is depicted in some early Celtic art, but rarely appears in the myths and legends. In artwork it most frequently appears in connection with the heads of bulls, rams or human beings. It is most often connected with female figures, rather than male figures. In a Welsh legend, the young man *Lleu Llaw Gyffes* is betrayed by his supernatural bride *Blodeuwedd* who is punished by being turned into an owl, banished into the night and shunned by society. In Welsh the owl is called the "corpse bird" and in Scottish Gaelic it is referred to as the "night hag."[23]

Goose

In early Celtic imagery, the goose was portrayed in a number of instances. Most of these representations occurred in connection with imagery associated with war, courage, protection and strength. Interestingly, the goose was depicted in connection with both male and female war deities. One Continental female war goddess was shown wearing a war helmet topped by the image of a goose with outstretched wings. There is even a small etching of Epona the horse goddess riding upon a goose in flight.[24]

Wren

The wren was associated with divination customs in the folklore tradition, and with ritual processions that took place around Yule (probably originally connected with Samhain). The Welsh figure of Lleu earned his name (*Lleu Llaw Gyffes*—"Bright One of the Skillful Hand")—after a skilful cast at a wren. Some of the names for the wren in Celtic languages were similar to (and possibly related) to words for "druid." In one folktale, the eagle and the wren engaged in a contest of flight. In other folklore contexts the wren was associated with prognostication.[25]

Duck

Water birds figure prominently in early Celtic artwork, especially the duck, swan and crane or heron. Ducks are portrayed on early drinking vessels and feasting gear. The duck's association with water also manifests in its connection with the Gaulish goddess *Sequana* who was associated with the River Seine. She was venerated at a sanctuary near the source of the Seine where numerous offerings were made to her. During the Romano-Celtic era she was portrayed standing in a boat shaped like a duck. There appears to be a connection between ducks and other water birds with solar symbols (sometimes shown being carried in a boat); these images are believed to be associated with healing.[26]

Songbirds

Magical songbirds appear in both Irish and Welsh poetry and legends. The divine figure of Rhiannon owned three magic songbirds whose song had the power of providing healing, sleep, guidance or protection. The Irish divine woman *Cliodna* also owned magical songbirds. Some of her birds were red with green necks, while others had white bodies, purple heads and golden beaks. The eggs of Cliodna's birds were blue or crimson, and the birds sang exceedingly sweet songs for the purposes of guidance or pleasure. It was said that if human beings ate the eggs of Cliodna's songbirds, they would grow feathers on their bodies (although these could be washed off). Otherworld songbirds lulled sick or wounded people to sleep and healed them with their song.[27]

The world of animal symbolism in the Celtic traditions constitutes a rich and fascinating source of knowledge about these cultures. There would have been variations in the animal symbolism associated with different regions, as well as during different eras (in the Iron Age, the medieval period and in more recent folklore contexts, for example). Exploring the complex symbolism associated with animals and birds (of which this chapter is only an introduction) provides an excellent resource for deepening our understanding of Celtic deities and divine figures, myths and legends, and the depth and intricacy of native cultural and religious symbolism.

15

The Wisdom of the Ancestors

The concept of lineage is important in traditional societies, and it is often perceived that the more ancient and more sacred the lineage, the better these ancestral foundations can support the community. The identity of ancestors as well as elders and teachers, often forms part of creation myths. Connection with the past helps members of a community realize their own sacrality and understand that they are part of a greater whole. The ability to walk in the footsteps of the ancestors and follow time-honored traditions guides people in their daily lives and religious activities, which in traditional societies are completely interwoven.

An affiliation with a spiritual tradition located in the historical past provides the community with a basis for the preservation of its time-honored traditions. Awareness of the survival of traditions creates a bridge between the past and future. The past can serve as teacher, inspiration and guide and can help people understand who they are in the present time. Indigenous cultures revere the elders because they represent a link between the wisdom of the past and the practices of the present generation. Ancient myths and traditions are preserved for the same reasons; they are time-honored and time-tested. This wisdom is sacred, and has proven that it serves its intended purposes.

The ancient Celts were extremely interested in the wisdom of the past; both the druids and the poets were repositories of an enormous body of knowledge preserved through oral tradition. Some of this knowledge was eventually written down during the medieval period. These sources preserved information about the historical and legendary past, including detailed genealogies. Court poets could recite the king's genealogy back for many generations. This served as a validation of the king's reign and also connected the tribe with the legacy of the ancestors.[1]

Many of these genealogies involved historical figures, as well as heroic or mythological characters who inhabit the shadowy borderland between legend and fact. In some cases, these lines of descent extend so far back that they include gods and goddesses in their ranks. Identity and ancestry were extremely important to the Celts, as they are in most native cultures, and the ability to trace one's lineage to divine beings provided the community with a profound sense of connection.[2]

Divine Ancestors

In earlier times, certain Celtic tribes were named after their primary or patron deities (as well as animals that appear to have been particularly sacred to that population group).

A large Celtic tribe known as the Brigantes were named after the goddess Brigantia.[3] The Cornovii, who gave their name to modern Cornwall, may have been so titled because they venerated a horned or antlered god, or possibly horned creatures of some kind.[4] A pseudo-mythological group of people known as the *Fir Bolg* took their name from the powerful Celtic tribe known as the Belgae.[5]

Probably the earliest direct evidence we have pertaining to the Celtic practice of tracing the lineage of a population group back to a divine ancestor comes from Julius Caesar's first-century account of the Roman conquest of Gaul. In this account, Caesar lists some of the most widely worshipped gods and goddesses in ancient Gaul. Rather than providing their native names and attributes, however, he loosely equates them with deities that were familiar from his own religious tradition. Caesar wrote that the Gauls maintained that they were all descended from *Dis Pater* ("Father *Dis*"), a minor Roman god of the Underworld. He goes on to say that for this reason, the Gauls measured all periods of time not by the number of days, but of nights.[6] This may represent the belief that creation does not originate at the point of light, but in the primal darkness (which may have been associated with the Lower World or chthonic realms).[7]

There have been numerous attempts to identify the Gaulish deity whom Caesar equated with *Dis Pater*. A likely candidate may be *Cernunnos,* the horned god. The name of the Roman deity (*Dis*) means "wealth," and the horned god was frequently depicted with bags of coins and other symbols of abundance. In addition, several Romano-Celtic depictions of the horned god show him with animals associated with the underworld. These included the serpent (a Celtic Underworld symbol) and the rat (a Roman chthonic motif).[8] It is remarkable to reflect on the ramifications of this account—that the entire population of Gaul believed themselves to be descended from a god. It is even more remarkable if that deity was a horned or antlered god, a widely venerated deity archetype in many parts of the Celtic world since very early times.

A similar tradition existed in early Ireland as well. While images of the horned or antlered god are rare in Ireland, there are a number of supernatural figures who were described as having horns. The Irish legendary hero *Furbaide Ferbend* ("Furbaide the Horned") was said to have either horns of silver and gold on his helmet, or two horns rising directly out of his head. Another Irish hero, *Feradach Fechtnach*, was similarly described as being "a horned one."[9]

The name of the legendary Irish hero *Conall Cernach* has been examined for any possible connection with the name *Cernunnos*. There does not seem to be a direct linguistic connection, however. The Old Irish word *cernach* is often translated as "victorious" (an attribute possessed frequently by Conall Cernach). It also means "angled, or having corners," which could be said (in a roundabout way) to allude to deer's antlers. A more likely connection is found in descriptive representations of the two figures. In one tale, Conall Cernach encounters a serpent, which wraps itself around his waist. In a Gaulish representation of the horned god, the deity is depicted with two ram-headed serpents around his waist. Conall Cernach (perhaps a semi-mortal incarnation of the horned god) was said to be one of the three ancestors of the people of northeastern and central Ireland. The royal house of Dál nAraide traced their ancestry back to him.[10]

We know that another male pagan deity served as a divine ancestor to the Irish. The god *Nuadu Argatlám* ("Nuadu of the Silver Hand") was an early king of the Tuatha Dé

Danann. Through his two sons, *Cú Ois* and *Glas*, most, if not all, of the Irish were said to be descended from the god Nuadu himself.[11]

Female divine figures also served as supernatural ancestresses in ancient Ireland. The goddess *Áine*, whose name means "Brilliance," was a member of the Tuatha Dé Danann. She was reported to live in a fairy mound known as *Cnoc Áine* in County Limerick. As the daughter of *Fer Í*, she was woven into the early genealogies as a sort of hybrid divine-mortal ancestor figure. In Counties Derry and Tyrone she was still remembered until quite recent times. Áine was associated with the O'Corra family, who were believed to be her descendants. Seven miles from Cnoc Áine was another fairy hill, *Cnoc Greine,* which belonged to a divine woman named *Grian* ("Sun"). Grian was also a daughter of Fer Í, and was therefore woven into the same ancestral line as her neighbor and sister Áine.[12]

The Irish goddess Mongfind was said to be the stepmother of the famous Irish king Níall of the Nine Hostages.[13] The legendary king Conchobor mac Nessa was the son of a druid, but named for his mother, Ness. She may be related to the eponymous goddess of the River Ness in Scotland.[14] The god Lug was known by several titles, including *Samildánach* ("Many Skilled") and *Lámfada* ("of the Long Arm or Hand"). However, he was frequently referred to as *Lug mac Ethlenn*, after his divine mother Eithne.[15]

The Ancestry of the Gods

The genealogies of human beings and immortals were recorded with great care in early Irish sources (and in many cases, with remarkable accuracy and consistency). One of these sources was *Lebor Gabála Érenn* (literally, *The Book of the Taking of Ireland*), sometimes referred to as the *Book of Invasions*. It recounts a series of pseudo-historical and legendary invasions of Ireland during earlier eras. While it is tempting to try and read this work as a repository of pagan tradition, the text is actually a medieval Irish creation that combined elements from a number of cultural and spiritual traditions into one great pseudo-historical saga. These elements included native Irish traditions, themes from Classical sources, Christian beliefs, and a wide range of medieval learning of the time.[16]

The medieval concept of "history" is quite a bit more flexible than our own. The *Book of Invasions* was an attempt by the Irish literati to integrate their country into the "modern Europe" of the time by providing them with a Biblical ancestry. Figures from the Book of Genesis were grafted onto early Irish genealogies for this purpose. A number of other themes and characters from biblical and classical sources appear as strange interlopers and unexpected anomalies throughout the text.

There are also confusions associated with language and geography. For example, an early immigrant to Ireland was said to have a wife called Scotta, who was alleged to be the daughter of Pharaoh. However, *Scotta* is just a Latin word meaning "Irishwoman," and is derived from the name of historical invaders from northern Ireland (the *Scotti*) who traveled to what is now Scotland in the sixth century. Likewise, the mortal ancestor of the Irish was named Mil, an Old Irish word that means "soldier." Mil was said to have come from Spain, but this anomaly simply reflects scribal confusion between the Latin name for Ireland (*Hibernia* or *Ibernia*) and that of Spain (*Iberia*).[17]

There are, however, some ancient threads of authentic tradition in the text. One of the early "invaders" was named Cessair, and her story reads like a primal version of episodes seen in other Irish sources. Hers may be one of several authentic Irish "flood stories" which are not believed to have been biblical in origin (a phenomena seen in a number of other cultures as well).[18] Another "invader" was named *Nemed*, a word that means "sacred." This could refer to a sacred place or enclosure, as well as the status of persons within the society. The figure of Donn (or Éber Donn), was one of the sons of Mil (the Gaels). In *Lebor Gabála*, he was said to have drowned off the coast of Ireland. Donn was remembered in Irish folklore until recent times as the supernatural figure Donn Firinne, who lived on *Tech Duinn* ("The House of Donn"), a rocky island off the southwest coast of Ireland. One text reported that after death the Irish would all travel to the House of Donn (ostensibly prior to their rebirth or reincarnation).[19]

We may never be able to confidently reconstruct the processes through which native and learned traditions came together. In any case, one element of the account is likely to be an old one. However they got there, it is the gods who rule Ireland when the Gaels first arrive in the land. When the Sons of Mil arrive, they encounter the eponymous goddesses of Ireland and must gain their blessing before they can inhabit the new land. In much the same way, the king must acquire the blessing of the Goddess of Sovereignty in order to rule justly and successfully, and in order for the land and the people to prosper.[20]

Many people have commented on the apparent lack of a native Irish creation myth. This is not entirely surprising in that the incoming religion had its own myth of origins to promote. It is actually quite remarkable (as well as fortuitous) that any literary evidence concerning the nature of Irish pagan religion has survived at all. The preservation of components of early Irish belief reflects the efforts of the church to blend native and Christian elements into a hybrid system or "tradition" that embodied and consolidated facets of both.[21]

Lebor Gabála speaks of five successive races of "men," recording the names and exploits of these figures and describing their arrival in Ireland in terms of waves of "invasions." The invaders perish over time due to disease, floods, war, or other misfortunes or "destructions," paving the way for the next "age" or "race." The five "invasions" are as follows: Cessair (a flood and origin myth); Partholon (the Irish equivalent of Bartholomew; an era in which the land is formed); Nemed (creation of the land and culture); the Fir Bolg (perhaps early Celtic or "Belgic" immigrants), and the Tuatha Dé Danann. They are followed by the Sons of Mil (the Gaels).[22]

While *Lebor Gabála Érenn* does not represent the survival of an Irish creation myth in its current form, it does concern itself with the origin of things. During various "invasions," lakes, rivers, hills, plains and other features of the landscape are formed. In the era of certain invaders, various skills and activities were first practiced. These included cultivation, grinding, churning, building, trading, horse-racing, arts, crafts, poetry, knowledge, the origin of kingship, the administration of justice and the holding of assemblies.[23]

We do have scattered evidence about aspects of the Celts' beliefs about their origins in a variety of sources. Ammianus Marcellinus stated in the fourth century C.E. that the druids of Gaul maintained that part of the population was indigenous, while others were said to come from remote islands and the region beyond the Rhine.[24] In the early Irish tale *De Gabail in tSída,* it was recorded that the first Gaels in Ireland made peace with the gods of the land in order to successfully raise their crops and herds.[25] We also have tales that recount local flood myths, provide information about the origins of things and the importance of "sacred firsts," and contain traditions pertaining to primal beings who survive throughout the ages in various forms.[26]

These types of traditions may have been originally been preserved by the *filid* or other guardians of native tradition, who steadfastly and conservatively guarded and transmitted a great deal of other traditional lore. This included mythology, philosophy, natural history, theology, genealogy, social customs, place-name traditions and poetry. In later times, some of this knowledge was maintained by professional, local or family storytellers, or by local laypersons who maintained pride and interest in ancient history and traditions (whether local or national).[27]

Lebor Gabála contains a great deal of information about sacred and mortal genealogies. Prehistoric genealogies legitimized the seat or lineage of kingship, preserving the status quo in society and maintaining custom and order. They were often recited at important social or religious events or assemblies. Divine, semidivine (or at least noble or heroic) ancestors provided a foundation upon whose reputation, status (or divinity) one might attain or maintain power and position. They also provided the recipient with a certain supernatural quality or mystique (which in some cases derived its power from the realms of the divine).[28]

In addition to the lines of descent of the Gaels and other "invaders," the genealogies of the Tuatha Dé Danann are woven throughout the text. While the mortal genealogies and mythical history in this manuscript vary in accuracy and consistency, when it came to the old gods, the early Irish were extremely diligent. In tracing the genealogies of the Tuatha Dé Danann back to their very beginnings, I realized that the genealogy of the gods was almost 100 percent accurate (and this in a text ultimately put onto parchment by Christian scribes). Apparently the mythographers of Christian Ireland maintained a fairly keen interest in the pagan deities of their forebears. One early Irish monk refuted the idea that the *Tuatha Dé Danann* were demons because of their obscure origins and their genealogies. He affirmed instead that their divine genealogies were sound, and that arts, crafts, knowledge and poetry derive their origins from the Tuatha Dé Danann. Although Christianity came, he wrote, those arts were not put away, for they were good, and no "demon" ever did good.[29]

After grafting a biblical heritage onto the various groups of invaders, the monks set about the laborious task of writing down a great deal of amount of information about the gods and their genealogies. Prior to the "family tree" of the Irish deities who are most familiar to us is another group of deities and their ancestors. In my research I was able to show that the names of these divine figures appear to reflect elements of a creation myth.

After the three biblical names Noah, Japheth and Magog, are a list of primarily Irish names: *Faithecht, Braimin (d), Esrú, Srú, Sera, Tat* or *Tait, Paimp, Agnoman, Nemed, Iardan* or *Iarbonél, Bethach, Ebath* or *Ibath, Baath, Eno* or *Éna, Tabarn and Tat* or *Tait*. These are said to be the names of early divinities of Ireland. *Faithecht* means "One who is Skilled in the Art of Prophesy" while *Esrú* refers to the bursting forth of water. *Srú* refers to a "stream" or a "sage or ancestor," while *Tat* may be related to a Brythonic word meaning "father." *Nemed* means "Sacred" (or perhaps "Sacred Place"). The name *Iardan (ais)* or *Iarbonél* appears to mean "Dark Skill" or "Skill from the West." This divine figure was a seer, perhaps associated with *iarmbélra*, the obscure language of the *filid*. The druids were also reported to use a sort of obscure or "dark" speech.

The name *Bethach* refers to concepts associated with nourishment or sustenance, while *Ibath* or *Ebath* means "Yew Tree" (in the ogam alphabet the yew was referred to as the

"Oldest Tree." *Baath* means "Ocean," *Eno* or *Éna* means "Water" (or "To Make Known"), *Tabarn* translates as "Sea" and *Tat* or *Tait* means to "Unite or Join." It is at this point of the genealogy that all of the branches of the divine family tree come together. This *Tait* is the common ancestor of all of the Tuatha Dé Danann. The descendants of these primal or cosmogonic Irish deities are the well-known figures of early Irish myth and legend: the Dagda, the Mórrígan, Oengus Mac Óc, Bríg, Ogma, Macha, Lugh, Manannán mac Lir, Goibniu, and so forth.

A number of the names preserved in the text allude to concepts one would expect to encounter in a myth of origins. These include the Ocean, Sacred Waters; Life, Existence, Sustenance, Divine Wisdom or Skill, as well as the primordial sacred site with its central focus on the World Tree. By following the progression of names in this sacred genealogy, we can perceive a flow of mythological ideas or spiritual concepts that may reflect aspects of an Irish creation myth:

> From the Divine Seer came Braimind, and his son Esrú, the Sage who lived at the River which emanates from the Sacred Waterfall. From this ancestral deity, sacred wisdom was said to burst forth. This wisdom passed onto his descendant, a wise man who inhabited the Sacred Stream that encircled the world. His son Sera gave birth to Tait, the ancient Father. Next were Paimp and Agnoman. Their descendant Nemed inhabited the Sacred Place, where the gods communicated with those on earth and received their offerings. Nemed's son was also a seer, associated with the dark skills that have their origin in the west, flowing down the sacred streams from the well of wisdom. From his offspring Bethach, "He who Sustains Life" came Ebad, the Yew, who is the Tree of Life. He exists in the center of the Primal Ocean that surrounds him. His grandson was created from the Waters and gave birth to Tabarn, the Sea. From the Sacred Ocean came the Great Artificer. His descendants are the gods who interact with the people of Ireland.[30]

Druidic Ancestors

Having druidic ancestry was also a source of great pride. The Latin poet Ausonius, who lived and taught in Gaul in the late fourth century C.E., wrote a poem about a fellow professor that commented upon his druidic lineage and divine ancestry. He wrote that if the stories about this teacher were true, he was not only descended from the druids of Bayeux, but also traced his sacred ancestry and renown from the temple of the god Belenus. Ausonius also wrote about an elderly man named Phoebicius who was a priest of Belenus as well. Phoebicius was said to be descended from the druids of Brittany, and with the help of his son he received a scholarship at Bordeaux.[31]

Traditions of druidic ancestry were also recorded in Ireland. A number of tales recount the powerful attributes of the magician and arch-druid *Mug Roith*. He was described as flying through the air in a magic chariot and shooting "druid's arrows" made of fire, but was also considered to be the ancestor of a portion of the Irish population. A group of Mug Roith's descendants lived in the northern part of County Clare near the site of one of his most famous magical battles. This tradition was remembered at least up until the time of the Anglo-Norman invasion. Mug Roith was also said to be the ancestor of the *Fir Maige Féne*, who lived in the Barony of Fermoy in County Cork.[32]

The ancestry of Cormac mac Art, the legendary Irish king, included druids and *filid* or poet-seers. Although it is not certain whether Cormac was a fully historical king, or whether his story was part historical and part legendary (as in the case of King Arthur), he appears in numerous Irish texts as the ideal ruler. In "Cormac's Adventures in the Land of Promise," Cormac is taken to the Otherworld where he is given a magical cup that helps him discern between truth and falsehood. This story was always one of my favorite Irish myths, and so I found it remarkable when I discovered some years ago that through the traditional Irish genealogies, I was apparently a descendant of Cormac (as are thousands of other people, of course).

In one source, Cormac was said to have been a *suí* (a sage or learned master) as well as a *fili*. The office and profession of the *fili* was a hereditary calling or vocation, something that could be passed on to one's descendants. His mother *Achtán* was the daughter of *Olc Aiche* who was a druid-smith, a seer and a magician. His name could translate as "Wolf of Night," although it may derive in part from another legendary figure named *Olc Aí* ("Wolf of Poetic Inspiration"). Cormac was reputed to have been raised by wolves, and wolf terminology figures prominently in his biographical tale.[33]

Divine Ancestry in Ancient Britain

Sacred or divine ancestry was also important in Celtic Britain, and the early Welsh recorded their royal or noble genealogies with as much enthusiasm as the Irish. In these genealogies were families who also traced their ancestry back to legendary or divine figures. The late sixth-century ruler of the North British kingdom of Reget, Urien of Rheged, was said to have had a sexual encounter with a woman at a ford who described herself as the daughter of the king of Annwfn (the Welsh Otherworld). Their mortal-divine union produced two children, a son Owein and a daughter Morfydd. Another source states that the two children were the offspring of the goddess Modron ("Divine Mother"), daughter of Avallach, the king of Annwfn.

In another text, the goddess' name is said to be *Nevyn*, the Welsh equivalent of *Nemhain* (an Irish goddess of war and death who sometimes appeared at a ford). Modron ("Divine Mother") may have been a title or epithet for this goddess figure. An interesting juxtaposition of history and mythology occurred in an ancient Welsh poem. In this text, Modron's divine son Mabon ("Divine Son") appears on a battlefield before the warriors of her half-mortal son Owein.[34]

Some years ago, while researching my family tree, I discovered that my family possessed some interesting Welsh ancestry. Through a Welsh woman named *Nest verch Rhys* (the concubine of an early English king), I could trace my ancestry back to a very ancient British lineage. According to the Welsh genealogists, like thousands of other people, I was apparently descended from the legendary figure of Uther Pendragon, the father of King Arthur. As Arthur did not have any children who survived, this lineage extended through Anna Morgawse, the sister of King Arthur, who was said to have been born around 554 C.E. The Welsh, like the Irish, derived many of their ancestral lines from divine figures. In this case, the lineage included the early British god *Beli Mawr* and the goddess *Dôn* (whose name is cognate with the Irish goddess *Danu*). She was a primal divine ancestress in early British tradition, the mother of *Gwydion* and *Arianrhod*, and grandmother of *Lleu Llaw Gyffes*.[35]

Ancestral fairy connections were also known in medieval Wales. One of the most famous Welsh folktales is the story of the Lady of *Llyn Y Fan Fach*. Near the town of Myddfai, a farmer's son saw a fairy woman rising up from beneath the surface of a lake. He fell in love with her, and wished to win her for his wife. He offered her some of his bread, but it was too dry and she refused him. The next day he offered her some newly made bread, but it was too moist. Finally, on the third day, the fairy woman accepted his offering and agreed to marry him.

Her only condition was that he should not give her "three causeless blows." They lived happily together for many years and had three sons. Over time, her husband forgot that his wife's culture and values were different from his own. He causelessly struck her on three occasions. The first time was when she was reluctant to attend a Christian baptism. The second time was when she cried at a wedding (for she realized that the couple's trials would now begin). The third occasion was when she laughed at a funeral service (for she understood that the departed one's cares were now over). Taking her divine dowry with her, the fairy woman returned back to the Otherworld realms beneath the surface of the lake.

Later, however, she reappeared to her three sons and taught them the virtues of healing plants and herbs. Her eldest son *Rhiwallon* and his descendants became famous physicians to *Rhys Gryg,* Lord of *Dinefwr* in the thirteenth century. They founded a long line of famous healers known as the *Physicians of Myddfai.* The remedies of these physicians were recorded in a medieval manuscript. Even in the nineteenth century, people gathered at the edge of the lake on August the first to see the waters "boiling," a sure sign that the "lady of the lake" was going to appear. Descendants of the fairy woman, this Welsh "Lady of the Lake," are still known in the local area.[36]

Ancestral Gifts from the Otherworld

The belief in divine or supernatural ancestry has continued in the Celtic countries into modern times. In Celtic folk tradition, certain families were believed to have connections with the realms of the *Síd.* The MacCrimmons, who were hereditary pipers to Clan MacLeod, were reported to have received their gift of music from the fairies.[37] The *bean-sidhe,* a supernatural female figure who wailed or "keened" to indicate an impending death, was associated with particular Irish families.[38] Numerous other folktales exist in which certain individuals or families had extremely good (or bad) fortune as a result of their interactions with the inhabitants of the Otherworld.[39]

My Scottish clan, Clan MacLeod (known traditionally as the clan "of fire and music") has long been recorded in Scottish legend to be descended from a mortal-supernatural union. Clan tradition maintains that an early MacLeod king was married to a fairy woman, who gave birth to a son. After the birth, however, the woman was summoned back to the Otherworld. The couple, broken-hearted, parted at the Fairy Bridge (a site that can still be seen on the Isle of Skye).

Despite the fairy woman's departure, a great party was held to celebrate the birth of the MacLeod heir. During the festivities, the child's nurse left the infant unguarded while she attended the party. The child began to cry but his nurse did not hear him. His fairy mother heard his pitiful cry, and she returned to Dunvegan Castle to sing him a fairy lullaby. The nurse returned to the nursery in time to hear the fairy woman singing over her child. She remembered the magical song, and thereafter every nurse of the MacLeod heirs was required to sing this song for the offspring of the clan chiefs. Several versions of the song are still known. Before she left, the fairy woman gave the clan a magical banner known as the "Fairy Flag" that would protect them in times of hardship. It has been used on several occasions with great effectiveness and is still on display in Dunvegan Castle.[40]

When I visited the castle some years ago, I expected that this fairy legend would be treated as little more than superstition. However, the clan and its modern chiefs take their fairy ancestry very seriously. During a video presentation hosted by the most recent chief, Chief John MacLeod of MacLeod stated that although the origins of the Fairy Flag were uncertain, one thing about the flag was clear (and I quote): "It has fairy power." I sat through the video a second time, to make sure I had heard correctly.

Later, on the official castle tour, I read a placard near the sacred object. It stated that the MacLeod chiefs remain firmly committed to the belief that it was their ancestor's connections with the fairies that bequeathed them this banner and its power. This traditional belief is also affirmed in the official guide to Dunvegan Castle in a famous quote by the 27th chief, Sir Reginald MacLeod. After listening to a curator from a British museum expound upon his theories of the historical origins of the Fairy Flag (which are entirely uncertain), Sir Reginald was heard to say, "Mr. Wace, you may believe that, but I *know* that it was given to my ancestors by the fairies."[41]

Now, I mention these stories — some from my familial line, and some from the wider tradition — to underscore the importance and longevity of traditional lines of descent, connection with the ancestors, and honoring the wisdom of the forebears, throughout the tradition. This preservation of ancient lore and sacred genealogies has been part of the culture for a very long time, and reflects a deep reverence for and interest in native traditions of earlier times.

The ancestral wisdom of the pre–Christian Celtic past continued to find expression and adapt to changing circumstances throughout the centuries. Genealogies were still maintained and recorded, with some alterations. Sacred stories and legends were recited for generations, at least until the last vestiges of the poetic schools in Ireland and Scotland. Traditional stories were still told by the fireside until very recent times. Some stories are yet recited by local tradition bearers in the Celtic speaking countries and in regions inhabited by their descendants (in Ontario and Nova Scotia, for example).

The blessings and power of lineage are important in many cultures, providing people with a means of direct connection with the divine and with the wisdom of the past. Aligned with the knowledge of where they come from, people can more successfully navigate where they are going, weaving together the wisdom of past, present and future into a sacred identity and a way of being in the world.

16

The Legend of Arthur

One of the most famous legends associated with the Celtic tradition is the story of King Arthur. The names Arthur, Guinevere, Camelot and Avalon conjure up provocative images that have resonated for more than fifteen hundred years. In the early medieval period, Arthur's story formed an important part of British legendary tradition. In later centuries however, his physical existence came under scrutiny, and many postulated that he was not an historical figure at all. In more recent times, scholars have increasingly come to believe that the figure of Arthur does have some basis in history. There are many stories associated with Arthur, and in order to understand their significance we must examine the earliest references to his story — those written down nearest the time period in which he was believed to have lived.

The island of Britain (or *Prydain*, as it was called in earlier times) was inhabited by British Celts (a culturally Celtic population who spoke a language related to modern Welsh). Their vibrant culture had existed for centuries, but was interrupted by the arrival of the Romans in the first century. Roman domination became a powerful cultural influence in much of southern Britain for four centuries. Some British tribes became allies of the Romans, taking advantage of increased trade and infrastructure, as well as military protection. To others, however, the Romans were unwelcome invaders with whom they often engaged in hostilities, punctuated with uneasy periods of truce.

In the year 410 C.E., the Romans withdrew from the island of Britain in order to respond to revolts and internal unrest in other parts of the Empire. After four hundred years of Roman organization and protection, the south of Britain was left without centralized leadership or military protection. From what we can piece together, the British Celts attempted to organize themselves and protect their borders from potential invaders from the east (Angles, Saxons and so forth). This is the point at which the legend of Arthur begins. There are few surviving records from this early period, and in order to understand the origins of the Arthurian legend, we must follow a trail of clues and references, many of which were written down well after Arthur's lifetime.[1]

The Birth of an Enduring Legend

The earliest surviving references to the events of this tumultuous period were written down by a monk named Gildas around the year 547 C.E. Gildas describes how a "proud tyrant" of Britain, along with his counselors, invited Saxon mercenaries to help them fight against the Irish, Scots and Picts. When the Saxons arrived and realized the British Celts were defenseless, they turned upon their hosts. The Celts were driven into the wild regions of Wales and Cornwall (where their descendants still speak related Celtic languages). Gildas wrote that the surviving Celts rallied under the leadership of a man by the name of Ambrosius Aurelianus. Later writers linked this figure with the story of Arthur, but do not identify Arthur with Ambrosius.[2]

Much of Gildas' story was repeated by Bede in 731 C.E. He described how the downtrodden Celts were saved by a great military leader who was a British Celt, but also a Roman citizen (as were other Celts of the era). According to Bede, the Celts were organized under the leadership of Ambrosius and were victorious against the Saxons on several occasions. The tide turned, however, at the famous Battle of Mount Badon, which took place in the late fifth or early sixth century.[3]

Arthur is first mentioned by name around the year 800 C.E. by a Welshman known as Nennius. Although he wrote in Latin, some elements of Nennius' account may be based on Welsh sources. He stated that Arthur fought against the Saxons, along with the kings of the Britons, and served as their battle leader. All in all, Arthur fought twelve successful battles in a variety of locations, including Wales and southern Scotland (areas where British-speaking Celts are known to have lived). Arthur is credited with performing many great deeds, and Nennius mentions a number of legends that were already associated with Arthur during his time. One of these legends concerned a boar hunt (a theme which recurs in later Arthurian sources). Another said that if a person tried to measure the tomb of Arthur's son, every time the measurement would be different.[4]

The next reference to Arthur appears in the *Annals of Cumbria*, a Welsh text belonging to the tenth century. The *Annals* state that the Battle of Mount Badon took place in 518 C.E., and that Arthur and his nephew Medraut (Morded) both fell at the Battle of Camlann in 539 C.E. In this early reference to Arthur and Mordred, there is no mention of any animosity between the two (who could have actually been fighting together against the Saxon invaders).[5]

Arthur was mentioned in several saints' lives in both Wales and Brittany. One was a Breton saint's life dating to around 1019 C.E. In this account, the Britons (British Celts) fled from the island of Britain across the Channel to northern France at the time of the Saxon invasions, thus founding the Celtic country of Brittany. The "proud tyrant" mentioned by Gildas is provided with a name, Vortigern (a Celtic title meaning "Overlord," rather than a personal name). The saint's life also mentions that Arthur fought on behalf of the Celts in both Britain and Gaul (i.e., Brittany).[6]

Arthur surfaces again in an English source written by William of Malmesbury in 1125. His account stated that Ambrosius worked against the Saxons with the help of Arthur (who is not described as a king, but as a battle leader). William describes Arthur as worthy of being described in "true histories," rather than in the myths of the common people. Apparently, in the twelfth century Arthur was still being "raved about" by the Bretons (a reference which may refer to British Celts or the inhabitants of Brittany).

Two other important Arthurian references appear in the work of William of Malmesbury. One is a reference to another of Arthur's nephews, Walwen (later known as Gawain). He is described here as a brave and very well-known warrior who helped defend Celtic lands, and later ruled over a part of Britain. The second reference consists of the first mention of an ongoing belief that Arthur was not dead, but would one day return to lead his people. William mentions that the location of Arthur's tomb was unknown. This statement could be interpreted as representing the popular belief in Arthur's eventual return, or it could reflect scribal confusion stemming from Nennius' story about the ever-changing size of the tomb of Arthur's son.[7]

Within five hundred years after Arthur's potential historical existence, a number of common elements appear in early written sources. The British Celts were driven by Anglo-Saxon invaders from parts of southern Britain into Wales, Cornwall and Brittany (areas where their descendants still live). A figure by the name of Arthur assisted British leaders in their struggle against the invaders, and was instrumental in securing a number of important victories on their behalf. By inference, then, Arthur was a culture hero, and appears to have been charismatic figure associated with the preservation of Celtic culture, language, and territory. If Arthur lived in the fifth to sixth centuries, he was legendary by the ninth. In the tenth century he was still well known, and legends about his deeds and adventures were extremely popular in Celtic-speaking areas of Britain and France. Since Arthur's son had died, his nephews Gawain and Mordred play an important role in the ongoing struggle. The tomb of Arthur's son was associated with legendary attributes, as was Arthur's own grave, resulting in the ongoing belief that Arthur had not died but would one day return to help his people.

Celtic Origins of Arthurian Tradition

Most of the early references pertaining to Arthur were recorded by people living outside Celtic culture. When did the Welsh — the descendants of the British Celts — first mention his deeds and adventures? The earliest native reference to Arthur comes from a long poem written in an early form of Welsh. The poem is called "The Gododdin," and takes its name from a Celtic tribe known as the Votadini, who occupied part of what is now southern Scotland. The poem recounts the tale of a brave campaign undertaken by Celts from all over Britain, against a much larger English army. The poem celebrates the bravery and valor of these early British Celts, praise which is all the more poignant since all the Celtic warriors perished in the conflict.

The battle took place around the year 600 C.E., not long after the historical era of Arthur himself. While the poem is preserved in a manuscript dating to about the twelfth century, there are many archaic elements in the language and content of the poem. The story outlined in "The Gododdin" is spoken in the voice of the poet Aneirin, who says that he was the sole survivor of the battle. It is especially significant to note that Aneirin would have been born during Arthur's lifetime. In the poem, one of the warriors is actually compared to Arthur. However, although he performed many great deeds, he was "no Arthur." The poem also makes reference to Owain, an early sixth-century ruler of Rheged (a Welsh-speaking region of Britain), who later became known as Yvain or Ywain in medieval romances and legends.[8]

Arthur is also mentioned in the "The Stanzas of the Graves," preserved in *The Black Book of Carmarthen*. The text consists of a series of short poems or stanzas which enumerate the deeds and gravesites of famous heroes from Wales and other parts of Celtic Britain. Although the earliest surviving manuscript dates to about 1200 C.E., the stanzas are believed to have been composed in the ninth or tenth centuries. In these poems we encounter early references to a number of well-known Arthurian figures: Gwalchmai (the Welsh rendering of Gawain), Cei (Sir Kay), Bedwyr (Bedivere) and March (King Mark from the tale of Tristan and Iseult).

The stanzas also include a reference to Arthur's gravesite. In one of the poems, Arthur's grave was described as *anoeth*, a Welsh word meaning "a wonder" or "a thing difficult to find or obtain." If the word was meant to be translated as "a wonder," this may reflect earlier traditions pertaining to Arthur's son's grave. However, if the word means "a thing difficult to find or obtain," this may represent the traditional belief that Arthur's grave did not exist; thus he could return to help the Celts in their time of need.[9]

Arthur, Gawain, and a number of other Arthurian characters are featured in a tenth-century Welsh poem (*Pa Gwyr?*). The poem refers to numerous British divine figures, and similarly mentions Arthur's grave and his possible return. It provides an inventory of Arthur's warriors, which included a variety of historical Welsh figures. Gawain, Cei, Bedwyr and March are also mentioned, as are a number of British divinities, including Manawydan ap Llyr (the Welsh equivalent of Mannanán mac Lir) and Mabon ("Divine Son"). There are actually two references to Mabon in the poem (or perhaps two "Mabons"). One was said to be the son of Modron ("Divine Mother") and the other the son of Mellt ("Lightning").

The poem also refers to the myth about Arthur's grave and his possible return. One interesting passage refers to Arthur's son Llachau, who is mentioned in other Welsh sources as well. Llachau seems to have been an important figure, despite the fact that later Arthurian legends stated that Arthur had no children. If Arthur's son (or sons) did not survive, his sister's sons would be in line to inherit his title and position. The theme of the "sister's son" is common in Celtic sources, and helps explain the importance of Arthur's nephews Gawain and Mordred in the ongoing narrative.[10]

Early Arthurian figures are also found in "The Triads of the Island of Britain." Although contained in manuscripts dating from the thirteenth to fifteenth centuries, quite a bit of the information contained in the triads is believed to be much older. In the Triads, Arthur is listed as a Chief Ruler in Wales, Cornwall and southern Scotland, places were British Celts are known to have lived. The Triads also refer to Gwalchmai (Gawain), who was said to be courteous to guests and strangers (an important Celtic virtue). Arthur's son Llachau is mentioned in the Triads, as are a host of early British divine figures.

In the Triads we also find the first written reference to Guinevere (whose name in Welsh is *Gwenhywfar*). One triad mentions three women all by the name of Gwenhywfar, who were said to be the three wives of Arthur. This group of three women mirrors an Irish tradition in which the goddess Brigid had two sisters, also by the name of Brigid. In some cases, Celtic divine figures had three names, or were part of a group of three siblings. One of the most famous of these divine trios were three Irish goddesses — the Mórrígan, Macha and Nemain — who were collectively known as *na Mórrígna* ("The Great Queens").

The Triads also contain the first mention of any wrong doing on the part of Arthur's nephew Medraut or Medrawd (an earlier spelling of Mordred). In one triad, Medrawd traveled to Arthur's court in Cornwall where he ate and drank everything there, thus diminishing Arthur's capacity to provide abundance and generosity, attributes essential to a Celtic ruler.

Medrawd also pulled Gwenhywfar from her throne, and struck a blow upon her. This represented an affront and challenge to Arthur's power and sovereignty. To retaliate, Arthur went to Medrawd's court and not only ate and drank everything inside the court, but in the entire district as well.

In one triad, Gwenhywfar is described as one of Arthur's three "great queens." This triad is likely to be fairly early in date, and appears to reflect the native tradition of the triune or triple deity figure mentioned above. In another triad (probably dating to a later period), Gwenhywfar is called one of the "Three Faithless Wives of the Island of Britain." She is described as being more faithless than the other two women, since she shamed a better man than any of them. In other native sources, however, Gwenhwyfar was said to have actually been abducted, rather than having run away with a lover. In the hands of later court storytellers, this abduction tale somehow led to the inference that Gwenhwyfar had been unfaithful to Arthur (first with Mordred, and later with Lancelot, who at this stage is not even a glimmer in the eye of a courtly storyteller).[11]

Many of these Arthurian figures also appear in the Welsh tale of *Culhwch and Olwen,* the oldest surviving full Arthurian legend. It is contained in a manuscript dating to the fourteenth century, although its language and content place it in the eleventh century or earlier. One of the main features of the story is a great boar hunt (which was mentioned by Nennius, centuries earlier). In the tale, Arthur helps his kinsman *Culhwch* perform a number of fantastic deeds in order to win the hand of *Olwen* ("White Track"), the daughter of the giant *Ysbaddaden* ("Hawthorn").

Arthur and his company engage in many adventures, including the pursuit of a magic cauldron, battling a witch, meeting and questioning the oldest animals in existence, and trying to free Mabon, the son of Modron. One of the company's tasks was to obtain the magical birds of *Rhiannon,* which had the power to awaken the dead or put the living to sleep. Interestingly, they are described as seeking *anoethau* ("wonders"), the same word used earlier in connection with Arthur's grave.

A number of divine and supernatural figures appear in the tale, including *Morfran,* the son of *Cerridwen,* and the British divinity *Gwyn ap Nudd.* He is listed as one of Arthur's warriors, and was said to have undertaken a magical battle every May Day in order to win the hand of a particular maiden. The company was also assisted in their quest by the deities *Gofannon,* the Divine Smith (whose name is cognate with the Irish *Goibniu*) and *Amaethon,* the Divine Ploughman, son of the goddess *Dôn.*[12]

Finally, Arthur makes an appearance in a famous medieval Welsh poem from *The Book of Taliesin,* known as *Preiddeu Annwfn* ("The Spoils of Annwfn"). In the poem, Arthur and his retinue travel to the Otherworld to rescue a figure named *Gwair.* In other sources, Gwair was described as a figure of some renown, who for undisclosed reasons was being held captive. In *Preiddeu Annwfn,* the prison in which he was held was located in *Caer Siddi,* "the fairy or Otherworld fortress" (the word *siddi* probably influenced by the Irish word *síd*).

The descriptions of the voyage to *Caer Siddi* are cryptic and intriguing. One passage seems to suggest it was a four-sided fortress which revolved to face each of the four directions (or that the men who went there cried out while facing each of the directions). Inside the fortress, the brightness of noon and jet-black co-existed (possibly referring to the all-encompassing Celtic Otherworld qualities of light and dark, beauty and difficulty, and so forth). In *Caer Siddi*, sparkling wine was set before the battalions. The company also visited *Caer Wydr*, the "Glass Fort." Six thousand men stood upon its wall, and it was difficult to communicate with the watchman at this supernatural site.

In the poem, Arthur and his company seek a wondrous cauldron belonging to the Chief of Annfwn. The virtue of the cauldron was that it would not boil the food of a coward, and the fire beneath it was kindled by the breath of nine female attendants. The vessel was described as being dark around its edge and decorated with pearls or precious stones. (Tacitus reported that Britain produced pearls that were dark and blue-black in color.) The journey to Annwfn was so perilous that out of three shiploads of warriors sailing on Arthur's ship *Prydwen*, only seven returned.[13]

> I am renowned for bringing forth fame — a song was cried out
> In the four heights, turning completely in the four directions
> My poetry was spoken concerning the cauldron
> From the breath of nine young women it was kindled
> The cauldron of the Chief of Annwn, what is its virtue?
> Dark-blue with respect to its edge of pearls...
>
> In the four quarters of the fortress...
> Noon and jet-black are mingled...
>
> Three full shiploads of Prydwen, we entered into it
> except for seven, none returned from Caer Siddi.[14]

The idea of a "fortress of glass" appears in a few other instances in both Welsh and Irish sources. The name of this legendary site may have influenced (or even been influenced by) the tradition that Arthur was associated with the town of Glastonbury. In *Culhwch and Olwen*, Arthur assembled warriors from Britain, Brittany, and the "Land of Summer" (Somerset, the region in which Glastonbury is located). Glastonbury became associated with the Isle of Avalon, a legendary Otherworld location whose name means "Place of Divine Apple Trees" or "Divine Place of Apple Trees."

Glastonbury Tor, a majestic natural hill located in Glastonbury, overlooks the entire countryside. During the Iron Age, it was terraced to increase the availability of farmland in this boggy area (an activity that also took place at a comparable site in Scotland). The Tor presents a stunning view from many miles away, and legend had it that the hill was originally an Otherworld island which served as an entrance to Avalon. In fact, in earlier times, the Tor was surrounded by water and bogland. Its magical properties may derive in part from the fact that an ancient sacred spring rises up from it.[15]

The Later Arthurian Legends

The Arthurian legends that are most familiar to people actually reflect medieval adaptations which are much later in date than the early sources we have been exploring. While these well-loved stories do contain threads of native Celtic tradition, for the most part they have been radically transformed from their original form and intention. What precipitated these changes in the Arthurian legends?

In the year 1138, a figure named Geoffrey of Monmouth completed a work in Latin entitled *Historia Regum Britanniae* ("The History of the Kings of Britain"). While Geoffrey's identity is uncertain, he may have been a churchman from Wales (or even Brittany). His work could be described as the first bestseller in Europe, apart from the Bible. Although Geoffrey claimed that its contents were translated from "an ancient British book" (i.e., a book written in the British language), scholars now know that much of what is contained in the work was adapted, enhanced or fabricated by Geoffrey himself. There are elements of native tradition woven into the account, but it is not (as it purports to be) a historical or native history of Britain. Names, characters and episodes taken from Classical legends, Biblical tales, medieval learned sources, and bits of native lore were blended together to create an origin story for the people of Britain. The *Historia* was hugely popular in its day and was translated into a number of languages.

It is at this point in the proceedings that the Arthurian tradition began to change. Most of the later Arthurian writers and storytellers copied Geoffrey's work or used it as their inspiration, adding in their own twists and inventions. The stories continued to change in the works of Wace, Layamon and Chrétien de Troyes, and elements are present in the *Tale of Parzival*, the Lancelot tales, *Le Morte Arthure*, *Sir Gawain and the Green Knight*, and the work of Malory. These stories are great works of medieval literature and examples of the European medieval storytelling tradition. However, none were expressly concerned with preserving native Celtic traditions, and were created for audiences in noble courts (and for wealthy patrons).

Storytellers in a number of European countries freely added new, exciting elements to the stories as they strove to outshine other courtly storytellers, competing for the favor (and rewards) of noble patrons. From their origins as early Welsh legends which preserved numerous native mythological elements, the Arthurian corpus became a medieval storyteller's free-for-all. As a result, these medieval creations cannot be viewed as repositories of pre–Christian Celtic beliefs or windows into Celtic spiritual traditions.

It is in Geoffrey's work that we first encounter a number of well-known Arthurian themes. In the book, Arthur is referred to as a king, rather than a battle leader. The text also sets forth Merlin's prophecies about the Island of Britain (which were created during the medieval era primarily for political reasons). Geoffrey's work describes for the first time a famous episode in which Merlin transforms Uther Pendragon into the shape of the Duke of Cornwall so that he can sleep with the Lady Ygraine. This is also the first time we heard of Guinevere and Morded being involved in an adulterous affair.

There are a number of themes in Geoffrey's work that may reflect native Celtic traditions. In the *Historia*, Arthur is said to have been born in Cornwall. Although this is the first mention of a birthplace, it is possible that Arthur came from this part of Britain. His parents, Uther and Ygraine, had two children: a son, Arthur, and a daughter, Anna (later known as Anna Morgawse). Anna was married to Loth, the ruler of Lothian in southern Scotland. They had two sons, Gawain and Mordred (the two nephews of Arthur). As we have seen, Cornwall and southern Scotland were associated with British-speaking Celts. Later in the tale, Arthur is mortally wounded and carried to the Isle of Avalon for healing (thus leaving open the possibility of his return).[16]

This episode is mentioned in Geoffrey's second book, *The Life of Merlin*, which appeared ten years later. In this work, Geoffrey states that Arthur was ferried to the Isle of Avalon by a supernatural or divine figure known as Morgan le Fay. This is the first mention of this well-known character. He says that Morgan lived with eight of her sisters on the Isle of Avalon. The theme of nine sacred women living in an Otherworld location also appears in the Welsh poem "The Spoils of Annwn." In *The Life of Merlin*, Morgan is noted for her wisdom and learning, her healing powers, and the ability to shapeshift. There are clearly elements in the tale that could be seen to reflect aspects of Celtic tradition. Overall, however, Geoffrey's work appears to be influenced even more heavily by other sources, including his own prodigious creative abilities.[17]

The legends associated with Arthur have changed form over the years, and yet their allure has endured for centuries. The Arthurian mythos and its vibrant characters are still powerful and evocative even in the present day. If we peel away the layers of medieval adaptation and accretion, we can begin to discern those elements that formed the core of the original legend of King Arthur.

Arthur was a tremendously important culture hero for the Celtic-speaking people in Britain (and other parts of the Celtic world). A brave and skillful battle leader, he helped the British Celts fight off invaders and protect their land, their culture and their traditions. Arthur performed numerous famous deeds, many of which were well-known in Britain and Brittany centuries after his death. Some of these stories circulated to other parts of the Celtic world, and were transmitted to medieval courts throughout Europe. Arthur's adventures became associated with legendary figures from the Celtic historical and mythological past, including a number of British deities. His exploits eventually expanded to include adventures in the Celtic Otherworld realms, including his own journey to the famous Island of Avalon. Safeguarded in the realms of the gods, Arthur became timeless and was immortalized. Over the centuries, the Celtic people continued to believe in, and hope for, his eventual return.

One of the most famous examples of this important cultural belief was expressed in the writings of Layamon, a priest from Worcestershire. His *Brut* is a translation of Wace's "History of Britain" from French into Middle English verse, heavily influenced by *Geoffrey of Monmouth*, with some borrowings from Wace and Bede. Unlike other writers of the time, however, Layamon presented his material in a more heroic style, and the characters and episodes are reminiscent of earlier legends and sagas. In addition, living in England, it is possible that Layamon may have had access to sources of British folklore or legends that a French author like Wace did not.[18]

In Geoffrey's work, one of the most powerful scenes occurs after King Arthur is mortally wounded. He is carried from the battlefield to the Isle of Avalon, so his wounds can be healed by Morgan le Fay. In Layamon the scene is laid out dramatically before us, as Arthur begins his journey to Avalon to meet *Argante*, "The Silver One" (possibly an epithet for Morgan le Fay):

> I shall travel to Avalon, to the fairest of maidens,
> To Argante the queen, the most radiant of fays,
> And she shall heal my wounds and make me whole
> by providing me with health-giving potions.
>
> And then I shall come back again into my own kingdom,
> And live among the Britons in joyous delight.
>
> As he spoke, a small boat came gliding in from the ocean
> Moving along lightly, propelled by the tides
> Inside were two women of wonderful appearance
> who raised Arthur up and took him away without delay
> They laid him down gently and off they sailed.

And so it happened, that which Merlin had spoken:
Enormous grief there would be, as Arthur passed forth
The Britons believe he is yet alive
That he lives in Avalon with the fairest of fays,
And still they wait, as always, for when Arthur does return.[19]

17

The Mabinogi

This chapter will provide an outline and explanation of *The Mabinogi*, a group of medieval tales written in Middle Welsh between about 1050 and 1120 C.E. While the setting and dialogue of the stories are very formal and courtly in tone, they also contain elements of Celtic mythology which are likely to be quite old. The word *Mabinogi* means something akin to "stories pertaining to the family of the Divine Maponus," who was an early British deity. The name *Maponus* means "Divine Son," and in *The Mabinogi*, the name appears to refer to a young man called *Pryderi* who has a number of divine or supernatural relatives. There are four main stories or "branches" in *The Mabinogi*, and some characters appear in more than one story or branch. Let us explore each of the four branches, as well as some of the most important thematic elements found in each.[1]

The First Branch: Pwyll Prince of Dyfed

In the first branch of *The Mabinogi*, *Pwyll*, the Prince of Dyfed, goes out hunting and encounters a group of white, red-eared Otherworld hounds that have cornered a stag. Pwyll allows his own hounds to have the stag, and upon doing so, a man on a large grey horse appears. He is *Arawn*, a Lord of *Annwfn*. The stag rightfully belonged to Arawn, and to make amends, Pwyll must go to Annwfn in Arawn's form and vanquish one of his foes. Pwyll travels to the Otherworld, and follows all of Arawn's instructions. He sleeps in the same bed with Arawn's queen, but does not have any sexual contact with her. Pwyll is victorious over Arawn's enemy, an act for which the Otherworld lord is grateful. Pwyll and Arawn exchange gifts and become allies. Thereafter, Arawn refers to Pwyll as a King of Annwfn. Successful in his endeavors, Pwyll returns to his kingdom.

Later, after a great feast, Pwyll goes to the Mound at Arberth. It was said that if a person sat on the mound they would either receive a blow or see a wonder. Pwyll sits on the mound and sees a beautiful woman riding past on a white horse. He tries three times to approach her, but is unable to catch up with her no matter how fast or slow he or his horsemen ride. Finally Pwyll calls out to her, and the lady stops. Her name is Rhiannon, and she tells Pwyll that she has come to his realm to meet him. She also says that she is being given in marriage to a man she does not want to marry, by the name of Gwawl. Pwyll helps Rhiannon trick Gwawl and get out of the arrangement.

Pwyll and Rhiannon are married. After three years, they have no child, and Pwyll's people want him to take another queen. He says he will wait another year, and eventually the couple have a son. However, the nurses who are watching the infant fall asleep, and when they awaken the child has disappeared. In order to avoid blame, they kill some puppies and smear the blood on Rhiannon while she is asleep, claiming that she killed her own son. As a punishment Rhiannon must carry all visitors to Pwyll's court on her back like a horse and relate the story of her disgrace.

In the next episode, we encounter a Welsh lord by the name of Teyrnon (a title which means "Divine Lord"). He owned a beautiful mare that gave birth to a foal every May Day. However, every year the foal disappeared. Teyrnon decides to sit up all night and keep watch. He sees a huge claw come in through the window to snatch the foal. Teyrnon cuts off the monster's arm and saves the foal.

When he steps outside, Teyrnon sees a baby boy, whom he and his wife decide to raise. The boy grows rapidly, and his parents note that the young boy enjoys working with horses. Eventually the foal is given to the child. Sometime later, Teyrnon hears about Rhiannon and Pryderi's loss and he realizes the boy looks like Pwyll. The child is returned to his parents and Rhiannon is vindicated. Rhiannon and Pwyll name the boy *Pryderi* ("care, anxiety"), on account of his mother's worry and concern over his disappearance. The family lives happily together for some time. Eventually, Pwyll passes away and Pryderi becomes Lord of Dyfed.[2]

There are many mythological themes in the first branch. Pwyll and Arawn meet out in the forest, a common setting for Otherworld encounters. Arawn needs Pwyll's help, and through mutual cooperation the two become allies, underscoring the importance of maintaining a reciprocal relationship between this world and the Otherworld. In many traditions, there are tales of women from other cultures (in this case, the Otherworld) who are harshly judged, ostracized or wrongly accused of crimes when they marry into their husband's foreign social setting. There are also many tales of kings or heroes who are born at the same time as a particular animal, their lives thereafter being closely linked.

The figure of Rhiannon ("Divine Queen") is a manifestation of the Goddess of Sovereignty, who often chooses her own mate. Pwyll, whose name means "Wisdom or Good Counsel," must prove himself a worthy consort to the Sovereignty goddess. The name of Rhiannon's suitor, *Gwawl*, is cognate with the Old Irish word *fál*, which is most familiar from the term *Lia Fáil*, a stone associated with kingship.[3]

The Second Branch: The Tale of Branwen

The second branch features a supernatural figure known as *Bendigeidfran* ("Blessed Raven") or *Bran* ("Raven"). One day, Bran was looking out over the sea along with his brother *Manawydan* and two half-brothers named *Nisien* ("Peace") and *Efnisien* ("Enmity"). They see a group of thirteen ships approaching Wales from southern Ireland, a region from which people did historically immigrate to Wales during an early period.

The envoy is headed by an Irish king named *Matholwch*, who wishes to make a marriage of alliance with Bran's sister *Branwen* ("White or Blessed Raven"). After the wedding has taken place, Efnisien arrives. He feels insulted for not having been consulted about the union. In retaliation, he maims Matholwch's horses. Matholwch is outraged and declares that he will leave Wales. To make amends, Bran offers him new horses and treasure. He also offers Matholwch an enormous cauldron that has the power to revive dead warriors, although they will not possess the ability to speak.

Matholwch accepts Bran's offer, but leaves for Ireland soon afterwards, taking Branwen with him. When she arrives, she is honored in her husband's kingdom. Branwen becomes pregnant and has a son. Later, however, the people of Ireland hear about Efnisien's insult to the king and are outraged. Branwen is made to toil in the kitchen, where she is daily struck by the cook. One day, a starling lands near Branwen. She relates her troubles to the bird, and sends it flying off to Bran to request his help.

Bran receives his sister's message, and he and his army set off for Ireland. Bran was said to be so enormous, he merely had to wade across the Irish Sea to reach Wales. Matholwch greets Bran, and offers to crown Branwen's son as the next king in his presence. However, Bran wants half the crown himself. Matholwch offers him hospitality by stating that he will build a house large enough to house Bran.

Just as Branwen's son is about to be crowned king, Efnisien once again steps onto the scene. He becomes offended when Branwen's son won't come to him, and throws the child onto the fire. A huge outcry is raised and a great battle ensues. The Irish use the magic cauldron Matholwch received from Bran to revive their dead warriors. Eventually, however, Efnisien is thrown inside the vessel and it bursts. As a result, the Welsh win the battle. The fighting was so intense, however, that only seven of them escape alive. Bran is mortally wounded and orders the other surviving warriors to cut off his head and take it to the White Hill in London. They return to Wales, bringing the grieving Branwen with them. She dies of a broken heart, knowing so many people perished on her account.

The seven warriors take Bran's head and proceed to Harlech. There they enter a magical Otherworld dwelling that contained the makings of a feast, magical birds and a joyous and blissful experience for all. In the Otherworld dwelling, the head of Bran was as good company to the warriors as it had been when he was alive. Bran warns the warriors not to open the door of the dwelling. After eight years, however, one of the men opens the door. The magic is over, and the company remembers the death of their friends in the great battle. They leave the dwelling, and bury Bran's head in London. His head served as a protective talisman which would thereafter protect the island of Britain.[4]

There are a number of divine figures in the second branch, including Bran, Branwen, and Manawydan. In other Welsh sources, Branwen was described as one of the Chief Ancestresses of the Island of Britain. There are a number of Irish and Welsh tales in which semi-divine women die and are buried at sacred locations. Unlike Rhiannon, however, Branwen does not seem to wield much power or authority, and she perishes as a victim of circumstance. The magical starling parallels a number of other talking birds and animals that appear in Celtic legends. Classical accounts mentioned that the druids were able to understand the speech of birds.

In many Celtic contexts, the head appears to have symbolized the seat of the soul. Skulls have been found in holy wells and other sacred sites, where they were believed to provide healing or protective powers. Magical cauldrons also appear in numerous Celtic tales, and seem to fulfill one of three functions. These included abundance and nourishment, healing and transformation, and wisdom or inspiration.[5]

The Third Branch: Manawydan, Son of Llyr

After Bran's head was duly buried in the White Hill, Manawydan finds himself feeling displaced and at loose ends. Pryderi suggests that Manawydan marry his widowed mother Rhiannon. He states that although the kingdom would remain in his name, Rhiannon and Manawydan may rule it as they wish. After the wedding feast, Manawydan and Rhiannon, along with Pryderi and his wife Cigfa, go to the Mound at Arberth.

A great mist falls upon the two couples, and when it lifts they find everything deserted. The houses, the animals and the people are gone. They wander throughout the land, surviving by hunting, fishing and eating honey. For two years they are content, but grow increasingly unhappy. They decide to go to England and try to support themselves through their skill and ability. They arrive and create beautiful saddles, but the other craftsmen are angered by their superiority. They consider leaving England, but Rhiannon and Pryderi want to stay and fight. Manawydan counsels against it. Instead he suggests they travel on to another location. There they fashion beautiful shields, but the same situation ensues. In a third location they make shoes, and the same thing happens again.

The four of them return to Wales and once more proceed to Arberth. They live by hunting and fishing for another year. One day, Manawydan and Pryderi were out hunting when they saw a shining white boar run out of woods. They follow the boar, and it leads them to a deserted fort. Pryderi wants to enter the fort, but Manawydan advises against it.

Acting against his stepfather's counsel, Pryderi goes inside the fortress. There he finds a beautiful well. Above the well was a golden cauldron suspended on chains that reached up into the sky. Pryderi touches the cauldron and finds that his hands are stuck fast. Rhiannon sees Manawydan and asks about her son. When she hears where he has gone, she enters the fort. Rhiannon touches the cauldron, and becomes stuck to the vessel.

Just then the mist descends once more. When it lifts, the fortress and its occupants are gone. Cigfa is now left alone with Manawydan, and is very upset. They return to England to make a living. Manawydan tries shoemaking once again, but problems ensue. He and Cigfa return to Wales. He brings with him a measure of wheat. In Wales, Manawydan supports Cigfa and himself by fishing and hunting. This time, however, he also sows wheat.

Manawydan plants three fields of wheat, which grow tall. When the grain in one of the fields was ripe, Manawydan went out to reap it. However, he found that all of the ears of grain have disappeared during the night. The same thing happens with the second field of wheat. On the third night he decides to keep watch, and sees hordes of mice descending upon the field.

Manawydan catches one of the mice, which ran more slowly than the others. He decides to hang it as a thief, and Cigfa is convinced he has gone mad. Manawydan creates a little scaffold on top of the Mound at Arberth. He is approached by traveling scholar, and then a priest, who try and talk him out of his intended course of action. Finally a bishop arrives and offers to release Rhiannon and Pryderi in exchange for the mouse.

Before he agrees, Manawydan requests that the bishop also release the spell of enchantment that has been on the land. It is revealed that the mouse is the bishop's wife, and that he created the spell to avenge Rhiannon's old suitor Gwawl. The mice were his magical armies. The bishop agrees to set everything right and all are returned to normal.[6]

The marriage of Manawydan and Rhiannon represents an ancient mythological theme that exists in a number of Indo-European contexts. This consists of a primal union between a goddess associated with the earth and with horses, and a god of the sea.

While Pwyll was Rhiannon's chosen mortal consort, she and Manawydan (two divinities) rule over the realms of earth and ocean. In Irish tradition, the goddess Macha was summoned to a horse race from beneath the ocean waves.

Manawydan is a wise and clever figure, who prefers to solve problems through logical reasoning rather than conflict. He tries new ideas, and is responsible for bringing agriculture to the land. While some elements of the third branch are quite old, others may reflect historical events during the later medieval period. These may have been associated with Welsh resentment concerning English and Norman rule of their land. The loss of honor that resulted from the loss of their former way of life may have seemed like a wasteland, compared to their former autonomy and prosperity.[7]

Fourth Branch: Math, Son of Mathonwy

In the fourth branch, we meet the figure of *Math,* king of North Wales. It was said that except during times of war, Math always had his feet in the lap of a maiden named *Goewin.* One of Math's nephews, *Gilfaethwy,* falls in love with Goewin. His brother *Gwydion,* a magician, offers to magically arrange for Gilfaethwy to sleep with her. He arranges a ruse so that Math will have to leave his kingdom to engage in battle.

Gwydion tells Math about some amazing creatures called pigs, which were given to Pryderi by Arawn, King of Annwn. Gwydion offers to go and visit Pryderi's court in South Wales, disguised as a poet, in order to obtain the animals for Math. The king agrees and Gwydion goes to visit Pryderi. However, Pryderi doesn't want to part with the animals until they've had sufficient time to breed. Gwydion shows Pryderi an array of wonderful treasures he will offer him for the pigs, including horses, hounds and other beautiful and valuable objects.

Pryderi agrees, only to find that the treasure has been conjured by Gwydion out of mushrooms. Pryderi realizes he has been tricked and angrily marches towards Math's kingdom. Math leaves his court to defend the kingdom. While he is away, Gilfaethwy sleeps with Goewin against her will. A great battle takes place between the armies of Math and Pryderi, and many warriors are killed. Finally Pryderi agrees to engage in single combat with Gwydion, since it was he who wronged him. Gwydion uses his magic skill, and Pryderi is killed. The men of South Wales return home dejected.

When Math returns home, Goewin explains to him that she can no longer be his footholder. When he finds out what happened, Math takes his magic wand and turns Gwydion and Gilfaethwy into animals. They exist for one year each in the form of male and female deer, pigs and wolves. With each successive incarnation, they change gender and must mate with each other for three years. When their punishment is over, Math allows them to return to court.

Math realizes he must obtain a new footholder. Gwydion suggests to Math that he consider his niece *Arianrhod.* She comes to court, and her uncle Math asks her if she is a maiden. She replies by telling him "she knows not other than that she is" (i.e., as far as I know, I am). Arianrhod is asked to step over Math's magic wand, and as she does so, she gives birth to two sons, much to her own surprise. The first child is named *Dylan Eil Ton* ("Son of Wave"). He heads immediately for the sea, where he swam as well as any fish.

The other baby is whisked away by Gwydion. He raises the boy, who grows at an astonishing rate. After some time, Gwydion takes the boy to meet his mother. Arianrhod responds angrily, on account of her previous humiliation. She refuses to grant the boy a name, arms or a mortal wife, three things he needed to grow into manhood and assume full adult status.

Gwydion tricks Arianrhod into naming the boy—*Lleu Llaw Gyffes* ("Bright One of the Skillful Hand"). He also tricks her into providing the boy with weapons. Gwydion and Math decide to create a supernatural wife for Lleu out of the flowers of oak, broom and meadowsweet. She is given the name *Blodeuwedd* ("Flower Face"). She proves to be a disloyal creature, and engages in an adulterous affair with another man. Together, they plot Lleu's death.

It was known that Lleu could only be killed under very unusual and liminal circumstances. Blodeuwedd lures him into relating the particulars of those circumstances. She and her lover arrange for everything to occur, and Lleu is pierced by her lover's spear. He flies up into the sky, screeching, in the form of an eagle. Gywdion goes in search of the young man. He follows a magic sow to a huge oak tree. There, in the top branches, is a wounded eagle. Gwydion realizes it is Lleu.

Gwydion sang three magical poems, each one enticing Lleu to come down from the tree. Finally, the eagle rested on Gwydion's knee. He arranged for a team of healers to come and help the seriously wounded Lleu. After a year and a day, Lleu is restored. He turns Blodeuwedd into an owl to punish her. She is exiled to the night, shunned by the other birds. Lleu kills her lover and retakes control of his kingdom, becoming the ruler of North Wales.[8]

Math's virgin footholder may represent the land, which was safeguarded in the lap of the king, sacred, sacrosanct, and not to be violated. It was to be held in a pure or pristine state, except during unavoidable periods of conflict (undertaken in order to protect the land and its people). The pursuit of pigs is explained by their popularity at Celtic feasts. In other sources, pigs were also credited with an Otherworld origin.

The figure of *Lleu Llaw Gyffes*, "Bright One of the Skillful Hand," is reminiscent of the Irish deity *Lug*, whose epithets included the terms *Samildánach* ("Many Skilled") and *Lamfáda* ("Of the Long Arm or Hand"). Both figures were known to have made a skillful cast with a sling (Lleu in relation to a bird, Lug in relation to his monstrous one-eyed grandfather). Lug was a multi-aspected and widely venerated deity, as was the Continental god *Lugos* (whose name is cognate with that of Lleu and Lug).

Lleu's mother, Arianrhod ("Silver Wheel"), may represent a goddess figure associated with the moon. A number of folk tales exist in which woman become pregnant by supernatural lovers, a condition which in some cases is unknown to them. In other instances, the pregnancy is evident, but the women do not know who the father may be. It is sometimes revealed that these supernatural lovers come from the sea, the realm where one of Arianrhod's sons heads for right after his birth.

The story of Arianrhod may reflect an earlier legend in which a goddess associated with the moon gives birth to two children, one associated with the ocean and the other with the sun. The solar powers of the second child may have represented a threat to her nocturnal or lunar authority or power. Indeed, in other Welsh sources Arianrhod is described in very positive terms, alluding to her powers and her connection with the celestial realms.

While it would not be accurate to say that Lleu (or Lug) were "sun gods," they are connected with symbolism that might suggest they were associated with solar attributes. In a number of Indo-European mythologies, the eagle and the oak tree were connected with gods who were associated with the sky realms or with the sun. Lleu's illness and transformation into the form of an eagle have often been described as being shamanic in nature. This healing also demonstrates the power of poetry and the spoken word, which forms an important part of numerous Celtic myths and legends.[9]

The characters in the Mabinogi may be medieval memories or reflections of earlier British deities and divine figures. Many of these figures are mentioned in other Welsh texts as well, including the *Triads of the Island of Britain* and the tale of *Culhwch and Olwen*. They also appear in a Middle Welsh poem called "*Golychaf-I Gulwyd*," attributed to Taliesin. In the poem, Taliesin states that his poetic skill originated in the cauldron of Cerridwen, and describes it as a divine gift created at the same time as the dew, acorns, and fresh milk. He tells how he was in the "Battle of the Trees" with Lleu and Gwydion, and also in Ireland with Bran, where he witnessed the slaying of many strong warriors. Taliesin maintains that his poetic song was harmonious in *Caer Siddi*, an Otherworld location where sickness and old age do not affect those who live there, "as Manawyd and Pryderi know."[10] The inspirational and life-promoting powers of the Otherworld echo throughout the tradition, reflecting the many wondrous qualities accorded to the Celtic Otherworld throughout the ages.

18

Fairies, Healers and Seers

Throughout the Celtic lands, there are plentiful folk tales and traditions associated with "the fairies." These supernatural beings were inhabitants of the Celtic Otherworld, and had the potential to bestow blessings or assistance, or present challenges to human beings ranging from mischief to danger. In Ireland they were known as the *Síoga* (Modern Irish) and in Scotland the *Sitheachain* or the *Daoine Sìth* (Scottish Gaelic).[1] The fairies are recent manifestations of the *Áes Síde*, and their modern names derive from the same root word (*síd*). They still live in the same locations as the *Áes Síde*, and have the same dual nature. These similarities were true in Wales as well, although in this region they are known as the *Plant Annwn* ("The Children of Annwn") or *Tylwyth Teg* ("The Fair Family").[2] The fairies were sometimes given epithets like "The Little Folk" or "The Good Neighbours." These seem to be descriptive or protective terms; if the fairies were referred to by their true names, this might serve as an unintentional invocation. Many people refer to them as the *Sidhe*, a word popularized in the poetry of William Butler Yeats.[3]

Encounters with Otherworld beings could take place at almost any time and in any location. However, it was commonly believed that they could most easily be seen, and their realms most easily accessed, on the four Celtic holidays (Imbolc, Beltaine, Lugnasad and Samain). It was also believed that the fairies could most frequently be seen at the four turning points of the day (dawn, noon, dusk and midnight). Originally the *Áes Sidhe* were fully human sized, and this perception persisted into the folklore tradition. In other folklore accounts, the Sidhe were described as being smaller in stature, usually between one to three feet tall. It may be that as their stature in religious belief declined, they became smaller in physical stature as well.

In the folklore accounts, there were many types of supernatural beings. There were also several varieties of fairies, each with a different signature appearance. In some of the most common descriptions of the Sidhe they wear green gowns or garments, often with a red cap. Other human types of fairies exist as well, with varying types of apparel. The tiny teacup fairy with wings is a creation of the Victorian imagination, perhaps designed to lessen the potential power or perceived danger of the fairies. In Celtic tradition, fairies do not have wings, although they sometimes have the ability to fly or levitate. This was accomplished by reciting a magic password and flying on a bundle of grasses, twigs, or ragwort stems (similar to descriptions of witch's broomsticks in other folk accounts). Some fairies were said to have the power to change form. Others did not possess the ability to shapeshift, or were said to have to study to be able to learn this feat.

The *Sidhe* were fond of music, dancing, hunting, processions and games, and were exceptionally skilled at spinning, weaving, baking, metalwork and crafts. They loved beauty, order, generosity, loyalty, truth, love and fertility. The Sidhe were said to generally be fair and helpful, showing gratitude for kindness shown to them. It was said that even bad fairies did not lie, they only equivocated. Overall, the fairy code of morality was a little different than our own, and this could lead to misunderstandings.

In general, the *Sidhe* appear to keep mainly to themselves. However, there are cases in which they seek out interaction with human beings for assistance with conflicts, breeding and exchanges. Most fairy borrowings consisted of loans of grain, and they often returned more than they borrowed. Barley meal seems to have been their preferred grain, seconded by oats. The Sidhe sometimes baked special cakes for "fairy favourites." They were also known to ask for loan of tools or fire. Mortal midwives were sometimes summoned to the Otherworld to provide assistance, usually with nursing babies. It seems that some amount of interbreeding was considered necessary or beneficial. As we have seen, certain families were known for their blood connections with the Sidhe, including the Physicians of Myddfai in Wales and the MacLeods in Scotland.

The Sidhe were known to assist or bless human beings with aid, abundance, protection, fertility, music, skill or other blessings. These were usually bestowed upon those who respected the *Sidhe*, their dwellings and their customs. The fairies could also be harmful or mischievous, either due to personal character, or more often as a result of human disrespect or misdeeds. A certain amount of homage was paid to the fairies, and in Ireland this was almost considered a necessary "protection payment." The church frowned on people who had dealings with the fairies, but the country folk were more lenient. Certain folk seers and healers said that they worked through the fairies and obtained cures or information from them. These practitioners were sometimes referred to as "white witches" or "fairy doctors."

There were certain dangers inherent in interacting with the Sidhe, and numerous folk accounts describe how people were carried off to the Otherworld. It could be difficult to return to the mortal realms, especially if one had tasted fairy food or drink. Those most in danger of being "carried off" were beautiful children and good-looking young men or women. In some cases, elaborate rituals were required in order to retrieve loved ones from the Otherworld.[4]

Fairy magic took many forms, including shape shifting, flight and invisibility. The word *glamour* was used to refer to a power of illusion that fairies could cast over human beings to avoid being seen or prevent their true location from being ascertained. Glamour was not, as has been suggested in popular sources, a power that people might exercise over the Sidhe. In the Irish language, this fairy power of illusion was known as *pishogue*. Another frequently misunderstood term is "co-walker." In Celtic tradition this was not a "fairy helper," but a human "double," visible only to those with second sight (in Gaelic, *An Dá Shealladh*: literally "The Two Sights"). The particular appearance of a person's co-walker could serve as an omen portending an upcoming visit or the arrival of a spouse, but more often than not it symbolized illness or death.[5]

The Sidhe were said to own or keep a variety of wild or domestic animals, and were frequently associated with certain creatures. Fairy horses were considered somewhat dangerous, while fairy cattle were less so and might provide fertility or abundance if encountered. A number of folktales and legends mention fairy deer, goats, salmon and trout, as well as eagles, ravens, owls, wrens and swans. It is interesting to note that these animals featured prominently in the mythology as well as Celtic artwork. The Sidhe sometimes lived in or near certain trees, most commonly the apple, rowan, hawthorn, hazel, oak, elder, ash, and willow. They were frequently associated with lone hawthorn trees, and people were reluctant to harm or cut down fairy trees (a practice which continued even until fairly recent times).[6]

Celtic communities were aware of a code of "fairy etiquette," which consisted of commonly understood guidelines for maintaining a good relationship with the inhabitants of the Otherworld. It was important to develop and maintain awareness of their culture and traditions, as well as their beliefs as to how human beings should behave or conduct themselves. Both tradition bearers and folktales maintain that the Sidhe liked open, loving people, who were gentle, polite and cheerful. They were extremely fond of music, dancing, good fellowship and true love, and expected all questions to be politely answered. Conversely, the fairies did not like people who were rude, selfish, gloomy, bad mannered or ill-tempered, who engaged in bragging, boasting or wife beating, or who exhibited undue curiosity about fairy activities.

Hospitality was extremely important. The Sidhe were to be made welcome in the houses they visited. They liked neatness and order, a freshly swept hearth, a clear fire, clean water, and offerings of milk, bread or cheese. Traditional fairy foods included barley meal, the milk of red deer or goats, the roots of silverweed, and stalks of heather. In some areas flowers were set on top of known "fairy stones" as an offering. In Scotland milk was poured into cup-and-ring marked stones, or other stones containing natural holes or recessions. This practice continued into the twentieth century.

The Sidhe expected people to honor their privacy and keep any fairy secrets imparted by them. They were fond of solitude and contemplation, and sought to preserve their way of life. Some types of Otherworld beings did not like to be verbally thanked for good deeds or favors, although bowing or curtsying was acceptable. The Sidhe were known to punish those who infringed upon their privacy, stole from them, spied on fairy revels, or boasted of fairy favors. A good rule of thumb was to be open, generous and ready to share with those in need, speak the truth about plans and quests, and be polite, respectful and congenial with the Sidhe (whether their identity was known or suspected).

Seeing or contacting the fairies was a decision best left to them, and overall contact was their prerogative. The Sidhe generally presented themselves to people if they wished to be seen. It was sometimes said they could be observed unaware by using fairy ointment or a four-leafed clover. The fairies could be seen most frequently on the Quarter Days, at the four turning points of the day, or with the assistance of a naturally holed stone. Those with the second sight could sometimes see them, although this ability was not always considered a positive blessing.[7]

There are accounts of spells or rituals that could allegedly be used to call or see the fairies, but these were considered dangerous and unwise. It is also understood to be an extremely bad idea to try and capture or control a member of the *Aes Síde*, take fairy items or treasure, or try to learn their name. If fairy protection was necessary, the most commonly used objects were rowan wood, iron, salt, St. John's wort, and vervain. It was also said that the fairy host could not pursue a person who crossed running water. Physical contact with a Celtic seer could enable a person to see the fairies on a temporary basis. Overall, it was considered best to respect them according to their rules of etiquette.[8]

People showed respect to the Sidhe by leaving out offerings, keeping a tidy house and hearth, and following the above guidelines. Water, milk, and food offerings were set out for the Sidhe, and fairy dwellings, routes and locations were respected. Truthfulness, honesty, generosity, helpfulness and respect, as well as a positive outlook on life, were credited with attracting fairy favors or avoiding fairy mischief. While some aspects of the folk tradition seem to have degenerated into ritualized actions based on fear, overall the people had a healthy respect for (and interest in) the inhabitants of the Otherworld. Like the myths, the folktales are full of stories that describe the interactions between human beings and the *Áes Síde*. They also recognize the importance of mutual benefit and reciprocity that was involved in maintaining a good relationship between the worlds.

Fairy Doctors and Seers in Ireland

Even as late as the nineteenth and early twentieth centuries, there were members of traditional Celtic communities who were known as "Fairy Seers" or "Fairy Doctors." Many of these people were said to have the ability to see the fairies, and knew how to assist others in interacting with them. They could ascertain if a disease had a natural cause, or if it was due to the fairies. If an illness had a natural cause, the healer might prescribe herbs or other natural remedies. If it had a spiritual cause, they would prescribe a charm, ceremony or other remedy. Some traditional healers only dealt with fairy-related issues. If a disease were naturally caused, the healer would indicate that it had nothing to do with "their business," and would refer the patient to a doctor or herbal healer.

Some healers and seers were said to have spent time in the Otherworld, where they received their skills or powers. Others obtained their abilities from interactions with ancestors or dead relations, or through direct contact with a member of the Sidhe. Many fairy doctors were not traditionally paid with money, although they willingly received gifts, food or other forms of assistance. They were extremely careful not to upset or disrespect the Sidhe in their work.[9]

Some fairy doctors did not use herbs, but worked solely with charms. Others used charms when gathering or administering magical or healing herbs. One very interesting charm involved invoking the name of "an old curer or magician," which was spoken or breathed three times into a bit of flax and placed on the person to be cured. Some fairy healers used other objects, including hazel rods, ivy grown on a hawthorn bush, butter, water from holy wells, and sacred stones. Those fairy seers who spent time in the Otherworld reported that there was often a king, a queen and a fool in a fairy troop. While many fairy doctors could cure the touch of the king of the fairies or other members of the Sidhe, they could not cure the touch of the queen or the fool.[10]

One of the most famous Irish healers and seers was Biddy Early, a local woman from County Clare who died in 1874. She owned and used a glass bottle which was either given to her by the *Sióg* or by the spirit of her deceased son or husband (according to different versions of the legends associated with her). When people arrived at her door, Biddy would often know their name, which town they came from, and why they had come. She would look into the bottle with one eye, while keeping the other one open, and could obtain information about illnesses or other difficulties in the present and the future. She prescribed herbs and other healing rituals, as well as magical, propitiatory or protective ceremonies. Some of these activities were to effect healing directly, while others were intended to assist with problems an individual might be having with the inhabitants of the unseen realms. As a mediator between the worlds, Biddy suffered many hardships in life, including arguments with local priests and rough treatment by the fairies themselves.[11]

In the late nineteenth and early twentieth centuries, Lady Gregory gathered and published accounts of Irish folk belief, including reports of fairy doctors and seers. Here are a few examples from her work entitled "Visions and Belief in the West of Ireland":

> I see them in all places — and there's no man mowing a meadow that doesn't see them at some time or other. As to what they look like, they'll change colour and shape and clothes while you look around. Plaid caps they always wear. There is a king and queen and a fool in each house of them, that is true enough — but they would do you no harm. The king and the queen are kind and gentle, and whatever you'll ask them for they'll give it. They'll do you no harm at all if you don't injure them. You might speak to them if you'd meet them on the road, and they'd answer you, if you'd speak civil and quiet and show respect, and not be laughing or humbugging — they wouldn't like that.[12]

> One time I was in the chapel at Labane, and there was a tall man sitting next to me, dressed in grey, and after the Mass I asked him where he was from. "From *Tír na nÓg*," says he. "And where is that?" I asked him. "It's not far from you," he said, "it's near the place where you live." I remember well the look of him and him telling me that. The priest was looking at us while we were talking together.[13]

> Many of *them* I have seen — they are like ourselves only wearing plaid clothes, and their bodies are not so strong or so thick as ours, and their eyes are more shining than our eyes.[14]

> Set a little room for them — with spring water in it always — and wine you might leave — no, not flowers, they wouldn't want so much as that — but just what would show your good will. Now I have told you more than I told my wife.[15]

Folk Healers and Seers in Scotland

Folk healers and seers also existed in Scotland, where they worked with herbs, stones and sacred water. Numerous charms and prayers have been recorded which were recited in order to effect healing. These prayers often supplicated Bridget, Mary or Celtic saints, as well as the elements of the natural world. One traditional prayer invoked the peace of heaven as well as the peace of the fairy dwellings. Another prayer called upon Mary and Jesus, but also granted to the recipient of the prayer the power and assistance of serpent and fire. In some instances, the Christian deity was referred to as *Dé nan dùla*, "God of the Elements." In addition to prayers, folk healers also used songs and chants, and performed healing with the breath and distance healing.[16]

To cure a sprain, Scottish healers used a technique known as *Eólas an Sguchaidh*, "The Knowledge of the Charm of the Sprain." An extract of St. John's wort was rubbed on the affected part of the body while a lengthy invocation was recited. The rubbing and the singing had to be performed simultaneously in order for the charm to work. The recitation of the charm was often punctuated by small emissions of breath released between slightly parted teeth. A flaxen cord called a *tolm* was knotted three times and either passed through or left inside the healer's mouth during the healing. As with all healing charms, it was recognized that the healer was not performing the healing themselves but was effecting a cure through the power and assistance of the Divine (whether this was understood to be God, saints, fairies, ancestors or other beings).[17]

Casgadh fala ("Checking of the Blood") was a practice used to stop the flow of blood in humans or animals. It was performed without physical manipulation or direct contact, and could be effected even at a great distance. The cure had to be undertaken by a person of faith and earnestness, who had a pure heart and lived an upright life. It would not be effective if the healer took food or drink without giving thanks for it. Like many other charms, its power was transmitted from man to woman, and from woman to man.[18]

Distance healing was also common with styes or foreign objects in the eye. In one charm for curing a stye, the healer twirled a glowing splinter of wood around the stye while reciting a counting charm, without pausing to take a breath. At the end of the recitation, the stye had vanished. Motes or foreign objects could be removed without any physical contact by reciting charms and then taking up three successive mouthfuls of water. When the third mouthful was released, the foreign object had been removed from the patient and was expelled with the water. In some cases, the object was seen on the end of the healer's tongue. This method, and others involving sucking or spitting out harmful energies or objects, could be used to remove foreign objects from the eye even at great distances. One woman healer said that she always experienced a bitter, disagreeable taste in her mouth after performing these cures.[19]

There were also numerous charms, prayers and rituals used in Scotland to work with unseen spirits or forces. The removal or counteracting of the evil eye was often performed in the Scottish Highlands. In one prayer, the healer loudly invoked a list of powers they possessed which could counteract malicious intentions or energies. Amongst these were the power of wind, fire, thunder, lightning, storm, moon, sun and stars.[20] One woman healer said that she had inherited the power and the rituals to remove the evil eye from her father. The minute she began her chanting she knew whether the person's condition was due to natural causes or to the evil eye. The healer remarked that the evil eye sent by a man was more difficult to counteract than of a woman. The man's was more powerful, evidently, but the woman's was more venomous. After emerging from the struggle of counteracting the evil eye, the woman reported being mentally exhausted and had to rest for several days. She stated that her powers came from the spiritual realms and that if she ceased communing with the divine, her powers would also cease.[21]

Practitioners in the Scottish Highlands had access to many different methods of obtaining information from the unseen realms. A form of augury known as the *frith* was used to ascertain the location and condition of those who were absent or lost, whether human or animal. The *frith* was performed while fasting, before sunrise on the first Monday of each of the year's quarters. With bare head and feet, and with eyes closed, the seer stood in the doorway, a liminal position between the known world (the house) and the unknown world (outside the house). Placing hands on either side of the doorjamb, silent prayers were made in which the seer asked to be given access to the unseen world and be granted their augury. Afterwards, the seer opened his or her eyes and stared straight ahead with a direct and piercing gaze. From the nature and position of the objects directly within his or her sight, the seer was able to see and interpret the vision.[22]

Certain Scottish folk seers and healers were said to have special knowledge of the Fairy Folk. These practitioners could be called upon to restore good relations between human beings and the spiritual realms, and were considered experts in making offerings or performing rituals to correct or maintain good relationship with the inhabitants of the Otherworld. For example, no one dared enter Glen Liadail without singing a song of propitiation. The only exception were the MacIsaacs, who were known to possess a specialized power and relationship with this place and its spiritual inhabitants.[23]

Healing Plants and Charms

A wide variety of herbs were traditionally utilized in healing and protective magic. Herbal charms and spells were employed to invoke good fortune, health, friendship, joy, love, eloquence, bounty, victory, confidence, safety, and to encourage the milk and young of cattle which were the source of sustenance and abundance. Some plants and trees were associated with rituals that took place on the Quarter Days. Herbal magic was a common method for overcoming or protecting against malice, envy, fear, falsehood, ill luck, fraud, oppression, scarcity, bad news and the evil eye.[24]

Herbal cures and charms were used to provide direct physical healing, or to make use of the magical or spiritual power of the plant. In Ireland, numerous herbs were used by folk healers including apple, bedstraw, black knapweed, bog bine, bog-myrtle, burdock, chamomile, cleavers, clover, dandelion, flax, groundsel, hazel, ivy, juniper, lichen, loose-strife, mugwort, mullein, nettles, oak bark, ox-tongue herb, plantain, quince, rowan, tansy, vervain, water buttercup, watercress and yarrow. There is also a great deal of Irish folklore (including healing charms and remedies) associated with bilberry, bluebell, bracken, bramble, butterbur, buttercup, centaury, charlock, crane's bill, daisy, dock, dog-rose, forget-me-not, foxglove, heather, henbane, honeysuckle, mallow, marsh marigold, mint, mistletoe, ragwort, rushes, scarlet pimpernel, shamrock, St. John's wort, thistle, vetch, violet, water-lily, wood avens and yellow iris.[25]

Healing herbs were often boiled in water and ingested for healing or other benefits. Charming herbs were sometimes burned in a flame or used with sacred water. There were particular times at which herbs were to be gathered or used, and certain methods of culling or administering them. Some herbs had to be taken in three pulls, or were not to be gathered when the wind was shifting. In Ireland, wild chamomile was called the "Father of All Herbs" or "The Father of the Ground," and was cut only with a black-handled knife. Mullein was believed to have the ability to return children who were "away" with the fairies. A small amount of mullein taken daily with a blend of other herbs was believed to bestow long life.[26]

One Irish healer said that when he was looking for a suitable cure, he went down on his knees and said a prayer to the king and the queen of the Sidhe before gathering the plant. If there were overly pale or blackened leaves on the plant, he knew that the illness was "of their business" (i.e., pertaining to the Sidhe). If the plant was fresh, green and clean, then he knew it was not theirs and required a natural or physical remedy. Another healer said that when he made a cure for a male patient, when gathering the necessary herb he called out the name of another man, referring to him as a king (*rí*). If the cure was for a woman, the name of another woman was spoken aloud and she was referred to as a queen (*ban-ríon*). This was explained as calling upon the "king" or "queen" of the plant.[27]

In Irish folk tradition, certain magical or healing practices, including the methods of gathering and utilizing sacred plants, were often attributed to the gifts and influence of the

Fairy Folk. In Lady Gregory's collection of folklore, one elderly woman gave this report about the use of mullein, or *Lus-Mór,* the "Great Herb or Plant":

> As to the *lus-mór,* whatever way the wind is blowing, when you begin to cut it, if it changes while you're cutting it, you'll lose your mind. And if you're paid for cutting it [i.e., for perform-ing a cure], you can do it whenever you like, but if not, *They* [the fairies] might not like it. I knew a woman who was cutting it one time, and a voice, an enchanted voice, called out, "Don't cut that if you're not paid, or you'll be sorry." But if you put a bit of this with every other herb you drink, you'll live forever. My grandmother used to put a bit with everything she took, and she lived to be over a hundred.[28]

A number of plants were used in folk healing in Scotland, including bramble, bog myrtle, bog violet, catkins, club moss, dandelion, fairy wort, figwort, ivy, juniper, mistletoe, passion flower, pearlwort, primrose, purple orchis, red-stalk, reeds, St. John's wort, sham-rock, watercress, and yarrow. In Buchan, healers used vervain, fern seed and orpin (stone crop). On the Isle of Skye, favored herbs and plants included mistletoe, club moss, watercress, ivy, bramble, figwort, St. John's wort and bog violet.

Some plants could only be used if they appeared in one's path "unbidden" or "unsought." Some were gathered during high tide rather than ebb tide, while others were collected or prepared during certain phases of the moon. Many charms refer to traditions or prophecies that specified how the plant could be used or what powers it contained. Magical charms were recited prior to or during the culling of the plant. In some cases the plant was said to be gathered in the same way a holy person did in the past.[29]

In one healing charm for gathering yarrow, the healer says the plant is being gathered so their hand will be more brave, their foot more swift, and their speech like the beams of the sun. The healer prays to be an island in the ocean, a hill on the shore, a star in the waning moon, a rock in the sea, and a staff to the weak. In another charm, the healer states he or she has come to gather the figwort "of a thousand blessings and a thousand virtues, of the nine joys that came with the nine waves." In a charm against urinary infection in cattle from the Highlands, the healer faced the rising sun and intoned a powerful prayer. It invoked the power of the sea, the wave and the ocean, as well as the nine wells of the pagan deity Mannanán mac Lir.[30]

Bog-violet (or pearlwort) was used to promote safe childbirth, provide protection dur-ing travel, promote knowledge, wisdom and eloquence, and overcome oppression and the evil eye. In one traditional charm for gathering bog-violet, the healer refers to it as the most precious plant in the field. Gathering the plant ensured that the healer would possess the eloquence and holiness of "the seven priests," as well as their wisdom and counsel. Bog-violet was also used in love spells. The woman performing the spell gathered nine roots of the plant while resting on her left knee. The roots were knotted together to form a ring and placed in the mouth of a young woman. If the woman kissed a man while the ring was in her mouth, without him being aware, he would fall in love with her forever.[31]

Catkin fiber was used in charms to increase milk and herds, protect against loss of ani-mals or means of survival, bring about success and protect against the loss of friends. Club moss provided protection from all harms or mishaps, and ensured safety during travel, even during the dark. It was said that no harm could befall a person if club moss was in one's path. Fairy wort had the power to overcome every type of oppression, and this power was perceived as emanating from the fairy realms. The plant repelled scandal, hatred, falsehood, fraud, bad luck, ill love or a bad life, for the entire length of one's existence. It was said there was nothing the sun encircled "but is to her [the fairy wort] a sure victory."[32]

Figwort was called the plant of a thousand blessings or virtues. In addition to providing a number of medicinal uses, including cuts, bruises, sores and ensuring a good supply of milk, it had a variety of magical applications. Figwort was gathered during the flowing tide, as it was associated with flowing or releasing of milk, water, produce of land and sea, calves and general bounty. It was believed to bring goodness, joy, love, peace and power. Ivy was associated with the abundance of milk and bringing forth of calves. On the Quarter Days young women pinned three leaves of ivy onto their nightgowns to encourage dreams of their future partners.[33]

Juniper is the plant badge of the Clan MacLeod, and was used to protect against misfortune, fear, danger or fatigue. It was traditionally burned in the house and barn on New Year's morning as a purifying incense for the coming year. In order to invoke its protective powers, the plant had to be pulled up by the roots with its branches formed into four bundles that rested between the five fingers, while a charm was recited.[34]

Purple orchis has two roots, one larger than the other, and this is where its magical properties were believed to reside. The smaller root was said to represent a woman and the larger one a man. The plant had to be pulled up by the roots before sunrise, while facing the south. It was then placed in water, taking care that no part of the sun was above the horizon while doing so. If the plant sank, the person whose love was sought would become the intended partner. The love charm could be made in a more general way as well, for no particular person. In this spell, the roots were taken home and dried, and the powder placed beneath the pillow to invoke dreams of a future partner.[35]

St. John's wort was called "The Noble Yellow Plant," and was used to ward off the malicious use of second sight or enchantment, evil eye or death. It was believed to ensure victory in battle, grant wishes, bring good luck, peace, plenty and prosperity, and encourage abundance and the growth of herds, fields and human beings. It was effective only if found without seeking it, and was gathered with the right hand and preserved with the left. When encountered, the plant was secretly placed in the bodice or vest under the left armpit, while the recipient recited a charm. The herb was believed to bestow spiritual or magical power, and was often used in divination rites.[36]

The shamrock also had to be found without searching, and the four or five-leafed clover was cherished as an invincible talisman. Often referred to as the "Shamrock of Luck or Blessings" or the "Shamrock of Power," it was associated with good omens and "the seven joys" of health, friends, cattle, sheep, sons, daughters, peace and the divine.[37]

Yarrow was prized for its medicinal uses, and was also utilized in love divination on the Quarter Days. It was believed to promote fairness of face, swiftness of foot, and eloquence, effecting lips like the "juice of the strawberry" and speech "like the beams of the sun." It was said to be able to afflict or wound anyone, but no one could harm its bearer.[38]

Combinations of herbs were also used. Protective wreaths were made from ivy, rowan and bramble or honeysuckle. Small wreaths of milkwort, butterwort, dandelion and marigold, about three or four inches in diameter and bound by a triple cord of flax, were placed under milk vessels to prevent the fairies from stealing the essence of the milk. Some herbs were said to deter witches or fairies, although the origin of this belief is probably that the herbs provided general protection from harm, scarcity or unwanted influences. A combination of trefoil, vervain, St. John's wort and dill was said to "hinder witches in their will" (i.e., protect against malicious or non-beneficial influences).[39]

Trees were also used in folk magic, including rowan, elder, hazel, yew, apple, oak and ash.[40] A traditional Scottish rhyme enumerated trees that should be sought out:

> Choose the willow of the stream
> Choose the hazel of the rocks
> Choose the alder of the marshes
> Choose the birch of the waterfalls
>
> Choose the ash of the shade
> Choose the yew of resilience
> Choose the elm of the brae
> Choose the oak of the sun.[41]

The rowan tree is often found growing near cairns, stone circles and other sites of pagan worship. Considered to be a powerful protective charm, it was planted near houses and barns and used to make household and agricultural tools and implements. Sometimes rowan trees were trained to grow in an arch over the barn door or farmyard gate to protect the animals. Highland women twisted red thread around their fingers or wore necklaces of rowan berries as a charm. On the Quarter Days, a wand of rowan was placed above the doorway and a rowan twig carried in pocket for protection.[42]

The elder was second only to rowan for protection and was used in a similar way. If the juice of the inner bark of the elder was applied to the eyelids it was said to give a person the ability to see the fairies on the Quarter Days. Standing under an elder tree located near a fairy hill at Samhain enabled one to see the fairy train pass by.[43]

Hazelnuts were commonly used in love divination rites at Samhain. Children born in the autumn were considered fortunate because they could have the "milk of the nut" as their first food. Hazel rods were used to detect water and underground minerals. Yew trees also figured prominently in the folklore. *Tom na hIubhraich*, "The Knoll of the Yew Wood," was a well-known fairy haunt in Scotland.[44]

Other natural objects were also used in Celtic healing magic. Stones, both large and small, were used to provide healing or blessings. In some cases, offerings of milk, ale, cakes or flowers were left on or near large healing stones. The use of white quartz stones or pebbles was extremely common in the folk tradition. Green stones, rose quartz, and naturally holed stones were also used. In Scotland, smooth spheres or ovals of quartz crystal were guarded and protected by certain families. If someone in the area needed healing, they came to the family's home and asked to use the stone. Many of the quartz spheres were encased in a silver fitting and held on a silver chain. Silver was also used in many healing rites. The healing stone was then dipped into a cup of water, imparting its healing power to the water, which was then drunk by the person in need.[45]

Throughout the Celtic territories, sacred wells and springs were used for healing rites and other religious purposes. This is an ancient custom, which in many cases was so ingrained in traditional practice that it was accepted into the church. Processions were made three times sunwise around a well, making prayers or offerings to the saint or legendary figure associated with that particular well or spring.[46]

Like other traditional cultures, the Celtic peoples had a vast knowledge of the natural world around them, making use of many elements of the landscape in their daily and seasonal practices. From rising up in the morning to smooring the fire at night, all of existence was imbued with awareness and ceremony. Folk beliefs permeated every aspect of life: gathering water, baking bread, planting crops, weaving cloth, singing children to sleep, healing illness, encountering strangers, predicting the weather, choosing a partner, starting out on a journey, divining the future, or encountering fairy sites. A vibrant folk tradition persisted well into the twentieth century, and included customs associated with birth, journeys, work, marriage and death, as well as interactions with people, animals, birds, plants, and the inhabitants of the ever-present Celtic Otherworld.

19

Folklore of Spring and Summer

Folk customs and beliefs are plentiful in all the Celtic countries, although as in other regions, some of these traditions are on the wane. However, even until the middle of the twentieth century folklorists were able to document continuing practices in many areas, and interview tradition bearers who could provide detailed information about folk customs that were still vibrant during their childhood or adult years.

Folk customs have sometimes been relegated to the status of superstition, considered to be meaningless activities undertaken by the simple or the fearful. However, many such customs are still practiced in our culture, including the hiding of Easter eggs, making a wish while blowing out birthday candles, hanging up stockings on Christmas Eve, and so forth. In traditional communities, the term *folklore* refers to traditional beliefs and practices which reflect that community's relationship with the land, with the forces of the divine, and with each other. Seasonal customs reflect all three tiers of interaction (landscape, society and the sacred) and reflect indigenous patterns of life which are in tune with the cycles and flow of life in a particular environment.

This chapter will provide a brief overview of seasonal customs associated with spring and summer in three of the Celtic countries—Scotland, Ireland and Wales. Much more could be written about these traditions, and readers are encouraged to explore the equally intriguing folklore practices of the other three Celtic countries—Brittany, Cornwall and the Isle of Man.

Imbolc: Spring

In Ireland and Scotland, spring began on Imbolc (which took place on February 1) and lasted until Beltaine (May 1). During this quarter of the year, people resumed work with the land and the animals after the relative inactivity of the winter season. The return of animal fertility and life energies indicated the start of the spring season, for this was the time when animals began to give birth. Imbolc was primarily focused on birth and motherhood, both human and animal, as well as the protection of these events. There may also have been ritual elements associated with purification at this time.

The return of fresh milk was hugely significant at this time of year, when food supplies were depleted after the winter season. In many cases, no fresh milk had been available since the end of summer. Women were in charge of food supplies, and when the sheep gave birth and fresh milk began to flow, it was a cause for rejoicing. It was important for the sheep to give birth before the cows, because sheep were better able to graze on the meager grass of late winter to support their milk production. If the cows gave birth too early, there would not be enough vegetation to support the production of milk for their calves. In addition, due to the separation of women from the community that had taken place the previous Beltaine, many children were conceived in late spring (April and May) and born around Imbolc. The nutritious ewe's milk was of great value to breastfeeding human mothers.[1]

Imbolc was associated with Brigid, who is believed to have originally been a pre–Christian goddess, and later manifested as a Christian saint. The goddess Bríg was the daughter of the Dagda, and with her two sisters (also named Bríg), she was a triple goddess of healing, poetry and smithcraft. She also owned two supernatural oxen. The origin of the word *Imbolc* is uncertain. It may derive from Old Irish *imm-* (an intensifying prefix) plus *bolg* (belly, womb), giving a meaning of "great belly or womb," referring to the potential of the pregnant animals. Another possibility is that it reflects an association with milk (*óimelc*, "ewe's milk").[2]

Saint Brigid was one of the three main patron saints of Ireland, along with Patrick and Columba (known in Gaelic as *Colum Cille*). Born sometime in the middle of the fifth century, Brigid was credited with founding a religious house at Kildare (*Cilldara*, "Cell of the Oak"). Near Kildare, there were a number of plains known as "Brigid's pastures." No one dare put a plow to these fields, and even though the animals of the entire province of Leinster ate the grass in these fields right down to the ground, in the morning there would be as much grass as before. From Brigid's time onwards, there was said to be a falcon that frequented the fields and also perched on the church tower. The people referred to this creature as "Brigid's bird" and it was held in respect by all. The bird used to do the bidding of the townspeople or local soldiers. It would not allow a mate to enter the church area, but would leave to find a mate in the mountains and then return.[3]

In the twelfth century, a visitor to Ireland known as Gerald of Wales reported that an eternal flame burned at Kildare that was tended by a group of nineteen nuns. The flame had been lit to honor Brigid, and had been kept burning for over five hundred years at the time of Gerald's visit. In spite of its lengthy existence, the fire produced no ashes. Men were not allowed near the flame, and only women were allowed to "blow the fire," which they did using bellows or winnowing forks, rather than their breath. During Brigid's lifetime, twenty nuns attended the fire, Brigid herself being the twentieth. After her death, nineteen holy women continued to tend the flame. Every night they took turns guarding the fire. On the twentieth night, the nineteenth nun would put the logs beside the fire and say, "Brigid, guard your fire. This is your night." In the morning, the wood was consumed and the fire was still alight. In more recent folklore, prayers to Brigid were often recited while "smooring" the fire — covering over the last embers of the day with ashes to protect them until morning.[4]

Saint Brigid's story is full of mythological imagery, and she was especially associated with symbolism of abundance and fertility. As a young girl, Brigid was fed on the milk of Otherworld cows. She was said to have a limitless larder of food, much like her father's inexhaustible cauldron of nourishment. She was credited with performing numerous miracles, including providing a love spell for a couple whose marriage was troubled, and brewing huge amounts of ale for consumption at Easter time. Brigid was often depicted with cattle, milking pails or sheaves of grain. In the folklore tradition, she was associated with the dandelion, the linnet and a bird known as the oystercatcher.[5]

In Scottish folk tradition, Brigid was said to have been a midwife to Mary and the foster mother of Jesus. When a woman in Scotland was in labor, the midwife went to the door of the house and asked Brigid to come in and give the woman relief. If the birth went well, it meant Brigid was present and amenable to the family. If the birth was difficult, it meant that Brigid was absent and offended.[6]

Brigid was invoked in charms for the protection of the house, and for gathering healing plants. She was especially invoked in connection with the gathering of figwort, a plant associated with the flow of milk. A prayer known as "The Genealogy of Brigid" was invoked for powerful protection and assistance.[7] Here is an excerpt from a version of the prayer:

> *Brighde nam brat, Brighde na bríg*
> *Brighde nan cleachd, Brighde na fríth*
> *Brighde nan gealachos, Brighde na bìth*
> *Brighde nan gealabhos, Brighde na nì...*
>
> *Gach latha agus gach oidhche nì mi*
> *Sloinntearachd na Brighd,*
> *Cha mharbhar mi, Cha ghuinear mi...*
> *Cha loisg teine mi... Cha bhàth uisge mi...*
>
> Brigid of the mantles, Brigid of the peat-heap
> Brigid of the curling tresses, Brigid of the deer forest
> Brigid of the white feet, Brigid of quietness
> Brigid of the bright palms, Brigid of cattle...
>
> Each day and night that I make the Genealogy of Brigid
> I will not be killed, I will not be wounded...
> No fire shall burn me... No water shall drown me...
> Brigid is my beloved companion.[8]

On the eve of Imbolc, a "corn dolly" was created, which was a human-like figure fashioned from stalks of grain. It was placed into a bed or basket, and ritually decorated with stones, shells, flowers and ribbons to honor Brigid. The bed was then taken in a ritual procession from house to house, so that all could pay their respect to her. The women of the house participated in a special ceremony to welcome Brigid into the home. On the morning of Imbolc, the family looked to see if the mark of Brigid's staff was visible in the ashes of the fire. If so, it meant that Brigid had visited the home and was considered a good omen. Bríg's father, the Dagda, also possessed a magical staff.

Brigid's crosses and other traditional woven symbols were created from rushes on Brigid's Day. Saint Brigid was said to have converted a pagan on his deathbed while holding a cross woven from rushes. In Ireland, the cupboards were ritually opened and examined on Imbolc to take stock of the food supplies. In Scotland, fishermen cast lots to determine which fishing areas they would work in the coming year.

Although sowing would not take place until March, men engaged in weather divination to determine when warm weather would arrive. In Scotland, these rites were held near the den of the hibernating adder. A charm was recited which referred to the serpent as the "Daughter of Ivor" or "The Queen." The charm stated that if the serpent came out of its hole, it would not to be harmed, nor would it harm those making the charm. In Ireland, where there are no snakes, a similar ritual took place at a badger's den. These traditions are the source of Groundhog Day customs in America.[9]

In Wales, the transition from winter to spring was marked by the Christian celebration of Candlemas, the Feast of the Virgin Mary. Referred to as *Gwyl Fair y Canhwyllau*, "Mary's Festival of the Candles," the holiday had its origin in a pre–Reformation ceremony of blessing candles. These were distributed to the people who carried them lit in a procession. There is probably no coincidence in relation to the date of Candlemas, which was the second of February (near the Festival of Imbolc). In the seventeenth century, it was referred to as *Gwyl Fair Forwyn ddchre gwanwyn*, "the feast to mark the beginnings of spring."

Candles were lit and set up in every window to provide a beautiful illumination both inside and outside of the house. Candlemas songs or "carols" were sung after dark on Candlemas Eve, with *canu yn drws* ("singing at the door"). When the "carol at the door" was sung, proper poetic or sung responses were expected. If the carolers gained access to the house, they would demand in rhyming words that a chair be placed in the middle of the floor. They also asked for a youthful virgin to sit on the chair, with a young boy on her knee (symbolizing the Madonna and Child). However, the highlight of the festival occurred when the singers were led to the corner of the room to partake of the beer.

In some areas, a form of divination took place at Candlemas. Two candles were lit and placed on a table or high bench. Each member of the family took a turn sitting between the candles. Afterwards, they took a sip from a cup, horn or goblet and then threw the vessel backwards over their head. If the cup fell bottom up, the life of the person who threw the cup would be short. However, the cup landed in an upright position, they would live to a ripe old age.[10]

Beltaine: Summer

At Beltaine, communities separated as the animals and their young were moved away from settlements to summer pastures, which were often located on high hills or mountains. In Ireland and Scotland, it was generally women and children who went with the animals, while men stayed behind to tend and protect the crops and the village. Although the weather was nice, Beltaine was a time of anxiety and potential danger. The crops had been planted and the young animals were born, but it was not yet certain if they would survive until autumn to provide food for the winter. In addition, at this time of year overlords could demand a part of their tribute from the people, often in the form of milk and butter. For this reason, a great deal of magic was performed at Beltaine aimed at the protection of fertility and abundance.

Beltaine was considered the end of the marriage season and was considered particularly unlucky for a wedding (hence, the "June bride"). Temporary marriages, which could ostensibly be set up at anytime, ended on Beltaine, when couples could separate or divorce if they desired. Many of these marriage arrangements took place during large assemblies held the previous year at Lugnasadh.

In Ireland, in earlier times, important assemblies and the inauguration of new chiefs took place at Beltaine. Beltaine ceremonies in Ireland took place on the hill of Uisneach, a site traditionally regarded as the center of Ireland. A bonfire was lit in front of a large assembly on whose behalf rituals and offerings were undertaken. A number of early Irish sources refer to pagan rituals connected with the protection of livestock at this time of year.

In one source, the druids were said to have created two fires "with great incantations," and cattle were driven through the fires for protection against disease.[11]

In more recent times, in the Highlands, cattle were still driven around the fire to protect them from misfortune (possibly as a preventative measure before they went off to summer pasture). Reports from late seventeenth century Scotland stated that all the fires in the community were extinguished on the eve of Beltaine, and a new fire ritually kindled by nine men, or nine groups of nine men. These fires were often created from certain types of sacred wood. This fire was known as the *teine-éiginn,* often translated as "need-fire" (a fire that was necessary to prevent misfortune).

A brand from the new fire was carried to each hearth in the community to relight the domestic fire. The fire was withheld from anyone who had failed to uphold their social or financial obligations, or in some other way failed to support community interests or well-being. In later times, it was thought that anyone asking for a coal or brand on Beltaine must be a witch (i.e., a person who had the potential to harm others). Only those who had not acted in the interest of the community would have been excluded from receiving the Beltaine fire and have a need to ask for it.

In some areas, the bonfire was made by herdsmen from thatch, straw, furze and broom, and was intended to protect against the theft of milk or other disaster. Great fires were created and the herds were driven through (or around) them to protect them from misfortune. People sometimes jumped over the bonfire as well. Fathers might take small children in their arms and leap over the fire for protection.

Other rituals of protection were still being undertaken in the early twentieth century. In the Hebrides, herdsmen lit a fire and cooked a mixture of ingredients together, to which each person contributed a share. Portions of the cooked food were offered in order to propitiate potential enemies of the animals in the summer pastures. In earlier versions of the tradition dating to the eighteenth and nineteenth centuries, the herdsmen lit a fire and sometimes processed three times sunwise around it. They cooked a mixture of eggs, butter, oatmeal and milk over the flame. Some of the cooked mixture was spilled on the ground as a libation. Beef and whiskey were also brought to the feast, and it was important that each person contributed something to the ritual meal.

The herdsmen also cooked a special oatcake with nine knobs or bumps on it. Each raised portion was dedicated to a being who protected the herds and flocks, or to an animal that represented danger to the herds, like the fox, the eagle or the hooded crow. While facing the fire, the herdsman broke off each knob in turn and flung it over his shoulder while saying, "This I give to you, to preserve my flocks."

In other parts of Scotland, a similar rite took place, this time performed by all the men in the village. A Beltaine cake made from oats and eggs, and scalloped around the edges, was cooked over a flame. A small marking of ash was placed on the back of the cake. It was then broken up and distributed among the men. Whoever drew the piece of oatcake blackened with ash was called the "Hag of Beltaine." This was an undesirable condition, and the hag or *cailleach* was symbolically thrown into the fire. These ceremonies included a symbolic "rescue" from the flames as well.

Beltaine cakes were also made for children by their mothers. They were entirely handmade and no metal was allowed to touch them. These cakes were marked with a sign of good fortune on one side and a symbol of misfortune on the other. The cakes were placed in a row and set on their edges, then sent rolling down a hill three times as a form of divination. At Beltaine, young women washed their faces in May dew. Pilgrimages were made to holy wells, and protection rites were undertaken using holy water. Charm stones that were used for healing were especially potent at Beltaine. They were dipped into the water of holy wells and the water was sprinkled on the animals.

On May Eve, rowan branches were brought from the woods and hung inside the home. A wand or cross of rowan tied with red thread was placed over the doorways of the barn, the stable, and other buildings. A circlet of rowan (alone, or with ivy and bramble) was placed underneath dairy equipment and pails. In the Highlands, young girls carried sprigs of rowan for protection. Rowan, elder or juniper were used for protection against fairies, witches or undesirable spirits, and were usually hung above doors or windows. Sheep and lambs were made to pass through a hoop of rowan, and cattle were driven to summer pasture on Beltaine morning with a wand of rowan wood. The wand was then placed above the door where it remained until the animals returned at Samhain.

In Scotland, the Beltaine feast included oatcakes, custard, and sheep's milk cheese. The Beltaine bannock was a special oatcake washed over with a thin batter of whipped egg, milk and cream, and sprinkled with a light dusting of fine oatmeal. It was sometimes round in shape, with a hole in the center through which the cows might be ritually milked. In other cases, they were scalloped or triangular in shape. The Beltaine caudle was a custard made of eggs and milk, with a little oatmeal added to it. It was cooked over the Beltaine bonfire, and a portion of the caudle was poured on the ground as a libation. Sheep's milk cheese was specially prepared at this time of year. It was sliced and placed on the Beltaine bannocks. It had to be eaten before sunset, and any that was left over was preserved until the next feast day.

A traditional Beltaine blessing was recited by the father of the family inside the home, prior to the consumption of the meal. The prayer asked for the blessing and protection of the family, the crops and flocks, and all their possessions. Protection was invoked from "sea to sea, and every river mouth, from wave to wave, and base of waterfall," and a blessing requested for everything and everyone in the household until they saw "the land of joy." The prayer ended by repeating the following phrase: "Accept our Beltaine blessing from us; Accept our Beltaine blessing from us." After consuming their ritual meal, people sang and danced around the fire. The fires were sometimes kept burning for three days, and the sun was ceremonially greeted in the morning by saying, "Good morning, Show us your eye." There are accounts of these traditional festivities until about the mid-nineteenth century.[12]

In Ireland, rents were due at Beltaine and hiring fairs took place. Grazing and meadowlands were also rented out at this time of year. It was a sign of good husbandry if a farmer still had hay at Beltaine, and a source of pride for his wife if she had managed food stores well and had meal for baking bread and porridge. A ritual meal of *stirabout* was made from flour and milk, boiled together until thick. The weather was noted on May Day as an indication of upcoming summer weather. This included the appearance of the sky, the strength and direction of the wind, the amount of rain and the condition of the May moon.

Bonfires were lit on May Day, and these were made from wood, turf, coals, old bones, cow horns, and sometimes even tar. These fires were often held in the cities, as well as in rural areas. There was a great deal of drinking, dancing, singing and debauchery around the Beltaine bonfires. In the southeast of Ireland there are still memories of the cattle being driven through small fires or between pairs of fires, as well as wisps or coals from the fire being used to bless the fields and the herds.

Dew was gathered during the month of May and into June, and kept throughout the year for healing purposes. On May morning, dew was collected before sunrise by striking it off the tops of the plants with the hands into a dish. Another popular method was to take a clean linen cloth and place it on the ground, afterwards wringing the dew from the cloth. While the dew from grass or other herbs was considered good, dew from green growing grain was considered the best. May dew was placed in a glass bottle and set where it would have warm sunshine on it throughout the day. Any dirt settled to the bottom and the clear dew was poured off into another vessel. Women washed their faces in dew for a beautiful complexion, and if they were daring enough they rolled naked in the dew as well. May dew was thought to prevent freckles, sunburn, chapping and wrinkles, cure or prevent headaches, and aid with skin ailments and sore eyes.

In Ireland, children set up a May bush, a green bush (often holly or white thorn) decorated with yellow flowers. It was set by the door of the home to encourage and protect the abundance of milk during the summer. May bushes were also decorated with flowers, ribbons, paper streamers, bright scraps of material, decorated shells of Easter eggs that had been saved, or candles or rush lights (which were lit at dusk). It was considered bad luck to have one's May bush stolen.

At Beltaine, fresh flowers were picked and brought inside the home. These were usually yellow flowers — primroses, cowslips, buttercups, marigolds and furze-blossoms. Flowers were gathered by the children before dusk on May Eve, or collected before dawn. Small bouquets were hung in the house or over the door, or laid on doorsteps or windowsills. Sometimes loose flowers were strewn on thresholds and floors, or on paths near the home. Those who took the first water from the well on May morning left flowers at the well as a token of their achievement. Flowers were tied to horses' bridles, cows' horns or tails, churn dashes or milk-pail handles as a protective measure. Beltaine flowers were also picked for the old or helpless.

In parts of Munster, May boughs were brought in to decorate the home, rather than flowers. These were small branches of recently leafed trees like holly, hazel, elder, rowan or ash. The attributes of "lucky" or "unlucky" trees varied widely from region to region, and might include (in either category) white thorn, blackthorn, elder, broom, woodbine, snowdrops, furze and alder.

Supernatural forces were thought to be at work between sunset on May Eve and dawn on May Day. As at Samhain, spirits were afoot, and were sometimes intent on stealing human children. Dairy produce was especially susceptible to the workings of magic, and many precautions were taken. Any strangers, human or animal, found on the property were unwelcome, as they fell under suspicion of being a supernatural or harmful entity. No fire was given out on May morning. If the May Day fire was lit with dried twigs of rowan, it was free from all bad influence. No cinders, ashes or floor sweepings left the house, and nothing was loaned or given out. Great care was taken with water supplies and milk, as well as barn doors and equipment associated with churning.

The first water drawn from the well on May morning was extremely potent, and could be used for good or ill purposes. Holy water was used in ceremonies to bless the threshold, the hearth, the four corners of the house, the animals, the fields, and family members.

Rowan wood was also used for these purposes. After sunset on Beltaine Eve, farmers and their workers or assistants walked around the boundaries of the farm. They carried with them seeds of grain, implements of husbandry, the first well water, and the herb vervain (or rowan as a substitute). The procession generally stopped at the four cardinal points of the compass, beginning in the east, and rituals were performed in each of the four directions.

It was believed that the fairies changed their residence on May Eve, sometimes snatching children along the way. Supernatural beings of all sorts could be seen at this time of year. People sometimes chose to stay safely at home, or made use of traditional precautions. A sprig of rowan, a spent cinder from the hearth, a piece of iron, or better yet, a black-handled knife, might be carried in the pocket for protection. In some areas, acts of propitiation towards the fairies were noted. People left small offerings of food or drink on the doorstep, or at fairy forts, lone bushes, or other fairy dwelling places. If a person strayed near a fairy location, he or she might see the fairies dancing, hurling or reveling, or traveling to visit with (or do battle with) another fairy group. If a person wanted to see the fairies, a sprig of rowan was twisted into a ring and held up to the eye.

Many encounters between mortals and fairies were recorded at Beltaine. The fairies were sometimes said to cause human beings to lose their way by bringing down a mist or confusing local landmarks. To prevent this, a person could turned their coat inside out, an act which apparently "disguised" them. Infants and marriageable young women were in special danger of abduction by the fairies at this time. Changelings were said to be left in the place of abducted infants. The young and beautiful were considered to be most at risk. Cattle were also susceptible. In some remote areas, cattle were bled for health purposes, and the blood was dried and then burnt. Ritual bleeding often took place at fairy raths or forts. The blood was tasted and then poured on the earth.

The *poc sidhe* or "fairy stroke" could occur at Beltaine, and was characterized by a sudden fall or injury, or unexplained lameness, deafness, loss of speech, fainting or swelling. The evil eye was also more powerful at this time. An illness that began at May Day was considered hopeless. However, May Eve and May Day were among the best days of the year for gathering medicinal herbs. At this time, those skilled in healing were often out of doors, searching for plants. Butter made on May Day was the best when it was used as a base for a traditional salve or ointment. People took blood-purifying medicines at this time of year. These preparations were made from nettles, or the liquid from boiled white thorn blossoms. May Eve was even called "Nettlemas Night," and boys sometimes mischievously stung people with nettles. Young girls might "sting" their lovers as well. The marshmallow was also picked on May Eve, and people stung with the plant for protection against illness and misfortune.

In some areas, particularly in the east and northeast of Ireland, there is evidence for the use of May poles, or May bushes tied to the top of a long stake set in the ground. Dancing and celebrations were held around the poles. However, it should be noted that this custom, like the May Queen and King, Morris Dancing, and Robin Hood Games, were only seen in a few areas. They were introduced into Ireland during medieval times and reflect English or other cultural influences. Another traditional Irish May Day activity was the custom of giving gifts of decorated balls (often hurling balls) and the holding of games and contests to win them. There is evidence for marriage divination rituals that were held on May Eve, even though it was an unlucky time to marry.[13]

While in Ireland a few years ago, I was told by a local informant from County Meath of a May Day custom that took place in the first half of the twentieth century. At that time, children would procure a thorn bush, often with the help of an adult or a gardener. They would place the bush in an open area and decorate it with bunches of primroses. A circle of furze or gorse, with its bright yellow blooms, was made around the thorn bush. The children would dance around the bush, singing a song which began, "All around the May bush...."

In Wales, the first of May was known as *Calan Mai*, the "Calend of May." As in Ireland, hiring fairs took place, and the *twmpath chwarae* or "village green" was officially opened with great ceremony. People gathered on the green for sports and dancing. Many greens were situated on the top of a hill, or on ground that was higher than that which surrounded it. A small mound of earth was raised, on top of which a harper or fiddler sat to perform. Sometimes a large stone was used instead of a mound of earth. The mound was decorated with branches of oak, and people danced in a circle around the musician, the mound, and the branch.

Like the two other *ysbrysdnos* or "spirit-nights" in Welsh tradition, November Eve and Midsummer, it was believed that on May Day supernatural powers were afoot. Bonfires were traditionally lit in many parts of Wales. Nine men would gather, and turn their pockets inside out, making sure that no money or pieces of metal were on their person. They went into the woods and gathered wood from nine types of trees. A circle was cut in the sod, and the men kindled the flame with two pieces of oak wood. Sometimes two fires were lit side by side, known as *coelcerth* ("bonfire"). In some areas, people "made the rounds," or walked in procession around the fire.

Round cakes of oatmeal and brown meal flour were cooked and then broken into four pieces. They were placed in a small bag, and each person picked a piece of oatcake out of the bag. Whoever got a piece of brown meal cake had to leap three times over the flames, and run three times between the two fires. This was believed to ensure a successful harvest. Ashes from the May Day fire were carried home or placed inside the shoes for protection for sorrow or harm. If there was disease among the herds, a young animal was culled and put in the fire to protect the rest of the animals from harm.

Divination also took place on May Eve. In one rite, four women hid themselves in the corners of the room, and the apparition of their sweethearts was said to appear in the room and partake of food, even if they were many miles away. May-pole customs were known in certain parts of Wales. In other areas, people raised the "summer birch" (*y bedwen haf*) or "summer branch" (*y gangen haf*). Morris dancing or *dawns y fedwen* ("the dance of the birch") also took place. Some of these traditions are likely to have been influenced by or imported from England.

People went out on May Eve to gather boughs of white thorn in full blossom, as well as other flowers, to decorate the outside of the house. Unlike Irish tradition, white thorn was considered unlucky inside the house, and was only used for outdoor decoration. In other areas, white thorn trees were "procured" from other parishes and planted near the door of the house. In some regions of Wales, people went out early on May morning, searching the fields and meadows for May flowers. These yellow flowers were used to decorate the inside of the house, the doors, the windows and the gate, and also strewn upon the path. Elsewhere, cowslips or other local flowers, or rowan and birch twigs were gathered and used for decoration.

May songs or carols were also sung, known as *carolan Mai* ("carols of May"), *carolau haf* ("summer carols") or *canu haf* ("summer singing"). They were also referred to by the term *canu dan y pared* ("singing under the wall"). A small group of singers went from house to house early on May morning, accompanied by a harper or fiddle player. They congratulated the people inside on the arrival of summer, expressing expectations for the season, and calling for their gratitude to the giver of all good gifts. The tone of May Day carols was usually serious, and many were even written by clergymen. At the end, they hoped to be invited inside for food and drink.[14] A feast day marked the turn of the seasons, brought the community together in ritual and ceremony, and celebrated the blessings of the land and the people's connection with the realms of the sacred.

20

Folklore of Autumn and Winter

Lugnasad: Autumn

The Festival of Lugnasad was named after the Irish god *Lug*, a many-aspected deity who was a warrior, magician, leader, poet, harper and master of crafts. His name may possibly derive from an Indo-European root word **leuk-*, meaning "light or brightness," although this is not certain.[1] Lug was the son of *Cian*, son of Dian Cecht the physician god and the woman Ethne. Lug was also the foster son of *Tailtiu*, the daughter of *Magmor* ("Great Plain"). Tailtiu was married to a king of the *Fir Bolg*, a group of people who are described as possibly being of supernatural origin.[2] However, the name of the Fir Bolg may well derive from the term *Belgae*, the name of several large historical Celtic tribes.[3]

Lug was said to have instituted Lugnasad—the *nasad* ("feast or funeral games") of Lug—to honor his foster mother. In modern times, Lugnasad was held on the first of August. Written sources indicate that it was quite a lengthy gathering, lasting for up to two weeks on either side of August first. One of the primary aspects of Lugnasad was as a harvest festival. In early Ireland, celebrations were held at a number of locations, including *Carman* in Leinster and probably at *Emain Macha* in Ulster. A medieval poem about Tailtiu begins with the poet inviting listeners to receive a blessing while he recounts for them a legend known by the elders about the origins of Tailtiu's fair.[4]

Tailtiu was said to have cleared a meadowland called *Bregmag* from a great forest, presumably reclaiming the land for agriculture. As a result of her efforts, her heart burst within her. As she lay dying, Tailtiu called the people of Ireland to her and instructed them to hold funeral games to lament her passing. She died on Lugnasad. From that day forth, around her grave was held one of the chief fairs of Ireland. The fair held in her honor was described in great detail in a medieval Irish poem. It was said to involve games, chariot races, and "the adornment of body and soul by way of knowledge and eloquence." Throughout the sacred festival, there was to be a truce that was unbroken for the length of the fair. There were to be no disputes, insults, hostility, theft, fraud, lawsuits, wounding, or other trouble.

It was forbidden to ride through the fair without getting down from one's horse. When leaving the fair to take a meal, it was forbidden to look back at the fair over the left shoulder (the left side being the inauspicious side). The fair was conceived of as a time of peace and fair weather, when there should be grain and milk in every homestead. Poetic tradition maintained that the fair was so important that the Fir Bolg, the Túatha Dé Danann, and the Sons of Mil (the Gaels) all observed this gathering.[5]

169

Another interesting feature associated wtih this time of year was mentioned in other Irish poems associated with sacred sites. During the harvest season, a number of divine or supernatural women were said to have died and been buried near earthen walls at a variety of sacred sites. The lamentation and honoring of these women formed part of the Lugnasad ceremonies. In Leinster, a woman by the name of *Carmun* was also honored at Lugnasad. Great hosts of people assembled for the fair on a level plain often used for horse races. A poem about the Festival of Carmun stated that at harvest time, people came to sacred sites to honor and mourn queens and kings, and to lament the suffering caused by revenges and ill deeds. Twenty-one venerated raths were mentioned, under which lay the honored dead. The ritual site included seven mounds for the keening of the dead, and seven plains on which the funeral games of Carmun were held.

Carmun was described as a fierce female figure and an experienced battle leader. She and her three sons sought to obtain the grain of Ireland, for they were experiencing distress in their own land. Through the use of spells, battle and lawlessness, they tried to destroy the essence or life force of the growing plants. The Túatha Dé Danann perceived their efforts and retaliated against them. A group of gods was sent forth, also comprised of three males and one female (the magician *Bé Chuille*, "Woman of Hazel"). The Tuatha Dé said to Carmun and her sons, "A woman is here to match your mother, and three men to the three brothers." Carmun's sons left Ireland and she was put into a cell in which she eventually perished. For reasons that are not explained, the Túatha Dé Danann raised the first wailing over her, and this was the first true fair of Carmun.

Like the fair of Tailtiu, no hostility, quarrelling, satirizing or misconduct was permitted. At the fair, there were music and streamers, horse races and vendors. Musicians were plentiful and included pipers, fiddlers, drummers and horn players. There was also a lively trade in food and livestock, as well as foreign dealers selling gold and fine clothing. At the festival, tribute and dues were paid, and legal disputes were settled.

It was also a time for listening to traditional tales and lore. Stories recited at the gathering included tales of Finn and his Fiana, chronicles of women, stories from the annals, tales of conflicts, taboos, captures and hostels, and traditional stories and lore about the ritual gatherings held at the Feast of Tara and the fair at Emain Macha. It was also traditional to recite stories and poems pertaining to the origin of places and sacred sites, as well as proverbs, riddles, the teachings of Cairpre and Cormac, other "truthful teachings" and recitations from "books of lore."

The Festival of Carmun was a time characterized by plentiful grain and milk, full nets and abundance from the sea. It was a time of happy ease, when elders and chieftains with their troops gathered together in friendship. Those who did not observe the fair were said to experience weakness, baldness or early greying of the hair, suggesting that the ritual observance of this sacred festival was important to a person's health or life energy. Neglect of the fair resulted in kings without keenness, jollity, hospitality or truth. Anyone who transgressed the laws of the kings at this time would not thrive within their tribe.

Women and men spent time in separate assemblies during the fair, probably to facilitate the ritualized marriage negotiations that often took place at this time. A traditional poem stated that no man was to go into an assembly of women, or women into an assembly of men. Although it was an auspicious time for arranging marriages, it was not considered a good time for elopements or negotiating a second husband or family.

Seven distinct games or assemblies were held during the Festival of Carmun, one each day for a week. The first fair was for holy persons, who had the "strength to hold it and law to direct it." Next was the fair of the high kings. The third day was for the women of Leinster, who were said to be held in high esteem in other parts of Ireland as well. The fourth day was for the dependent tribes of the Laigsi and the Fothairt, while the fifth was for princes. The sixth day was for the other honorable companies of Ireland, and the seventh was for *Clann Condla*. After many days of hospitality, storytelling, music and horse races, it was time for the assembly to draw to a close. A shout was raised by the hosts with spear shafts held high. Next, the king's royal genealogy was recited. Finally, a blessing was given out over Bregmag, which was the sign for ending the fair.[6]

One of the most beautiful stanzas in the poem about the Feast of Carmun describes how a religious ceremony was held during the festival that included the chanting of sacred words. Listening to sacred stories or lore was believed to confer blessings on those who heard them. The blessing bestowed upon the assembly at this event was as follows: "May there be given to them [the blessings of] the earth and her pleasant fruits." In addition, the people of Ireland made a solemn pledge to hold the assembly every third year, swearing by the following sacred elements[7]:

> By heavens and earth, sun, moon and sea
> The fruits of the land and produce of ocean...
> Horses, swords and chariots fair
> Dew, nut-harvest and brightness of elements
> By day and night, by ebb and flow.[8]

Many centuries later, the harvest festival was still widely celebrated in Ireland. "Lugnasad" is the early form of the holiday; it was spelled "Lughnasadh" or "Lughnasa" in later times. It was also called *Lammas* in some regions, although this is an imported English word that comes from the Anglo-Saxon and Christian term *hlaf-mass* ("Loaf Mass"). In Irish folk tradition, it was believed that no crops were to be harvested before Lughnasad. If the grain was still unripe by the time of the festival, a symbolic portion was gathered for the assembly. In many areas, people prepared a ritual meal that consisted of fish, fowl, beef, pork or mutton, as available. It also frequently included cabbage and potatoes (the latter having been introduced in Ireland in the sixteenth century or after). In some parts of Ireland, a festive dish was made from the new grain that had been reaped on the morning of Lugnasad. This dish was reported to be extremely fresh and tasty. Fresh fruit was also an important part of the festive meal, and this included currants or gooseberries from the garden, as well as wild blueberries, strawberries or raspberries.

In many regions, the main event of the holiday was a festive gathering that was held out of doors. It usually took place at a traditional site, frequently on top of a hill or mountain or beside a lake or river. These types of places had traditionally been used as ritual sites since the early Celtic period. Lughnasadh gatherings involved a great deal of feasting, dancing, music, drinking, sports and games. Horse races were also held at some locations. Wild berries were collected, and young people gathered flowers and made them into garlands and bouquets. Sometimes large fires were lit, and people engaged in races around the fire as well as leaping contests over the flames. At Lughnasadh, in some areas people ritually bathed their horses in bodies of water for protection. As in medieval times, this was a traditional time to begin to formally make arrangements for marriages. Divination also took place, much of it associated with weather prognostication.[9]

Harvest fairs also took place in Scotland, complete with music, dancing, bonfires, sports, races and divination. Marriages and handfastings were also organized or performed at this time. As in Ireland, in some areas, people drove their horses down to the beach and swam them in the ocean for cleansing and protection. Festive foods included cheese, curds and butter spread on a special bannock or cake. The harvest cake was often made from grains of barley that had been sun dried on a stone. The grains were then winnowed and ground, and finally were baked over a fire of rowan or other sacred wood. The father of the family broke the cake into pieces and handed them to his wife and children, in order of age. He then recited a prayer for their protection, while walking sunwise around the fire. Afterward, he gathered embers from the fire and placed them, along with pieces of iron, into a pot that was carried sunwise around the house, fields and flocks for blessings and protection.[10]

Later in the autumn season, the full reaping of the grain took place. Reaping was associated with many customs and rituals. The family gathered in the fields and the father laid his hat upon the ground. He then picked up his sickle and while facing the rising sun, ritually cut a handful of grain. He swung the handful of grain around his head three times in a sunwise motion and recited a reaping blessing. The family joined in the blessing, expressing their gratitude for the harvest, food and flocks, wool and clothing, health and strength, and peace and plenty.[11] Here are excerpts from two Scottish reaping blessings:

> At the proper time of the feast-day, at the rising of the sun
> With the back of the ear of grain towards the east
> I go out with my sickle beneath my arm
> And I will reap the stroke, the first turn.

> I will let my sickle down,
> The productive ear in my grasp
> I raise my eyes above
> and turn gracefully on my heel.

> Righthand-wise, just as the sun journeys
> From the direction of east to arrive at the west
> From the direction of north with a level motion
> To the true core of the direction of south.[12]

> God, may you yourself bless my reaping
> Each ridge, plain and field
> Each curved, sturdy, well-formed sickle
> Each ear and plaiting which makes the sheaf
> Each ear and plaiting which makes the sheaf. [13]

At the end of the harvest, it was a matter of pride and good fortune for a farmer to finish reaping before his neighbors. The last sheaf of grain was often called the Hag or *Cailleach* of the harvest, and was passed to those who had not yet finished their reaping. Receiving the "hag" was not an auspicious occurrence, and served as an incentive to finish in a timely manner. In many areas, the last sheaf of grain was actually formed into the shape of a woman. In some cases it was referred to as "the hag" and was considered undesirable. In other areas it was called the "maiden," and was decorated and honored at the harvest dinner.[14]

In Wales, the people engaged in a practice known as *cymhorthau*, which referred to participation in co-operative work groups to help each person or family accomplish their work. This practice was probably at its best during the harvest season. Various tasks were apportioned to the sexes, and usually in a day, the reaping could be completed. At the end, a special supper was served, and afterwards there was dancing and games.

A very widespread custom was the *cased fedi* or "harvest mare." This was an ornament made from the last tuft of grain to be harvested. The people gathered before this last stalk, and the head servant would divide it into three parts and braid or plait them skillfully, securing them beneath the ears of grain. The reapers would stand a certain distance from the "mare" and one by one throw their reaping hooks at it. Whoever cast his hook, cried out a rhyme, which ended with, "I have her!" The others asked, *Beth gest ti*? ("What did you have?") and the winner replied *Gwrach, gwrach, gwrach*, (a hag).

The "hag" was kept dry and hung on a beam in the kitchen or laid on the table. Many games, pranks and contests took place to secure the safety and display of the harvest mare. After the reaping, a special supper was served. The more substantial harvest suppers included beef or mutton, potatoes, wheaten pudding, ale and beer. More modest meals involved potatoes, turnips, oatcakes and whey. No matter what bounty the earth provided, the community celebrated with dancing, games, songs and goodwill.[15]

Samhain: Winter

The greatest of the Celtic festivals was Samhain, which began on the eve of October 31 and into November 1. This was the end of the old year and the beginning of the new, and therefore many important rites and celebrations took place. Samhain was a liminal period of time when interactions between this world and the Otherworld were at their peak. Samhain was the end of the grazing season, and the flocks and herds were brought back to the settlement from their summer pastures. Women and children who had been tending the animals had also returned to their homes.

At this point, the latest grain crop (generally oats) had also been harvested. Even in bad weather, the grain harvest had to be completed by Samhain. The fruits of the orchard and hillside were also gathered in by now, and no previously ungathered fruit was eaten after this point, even if it looked fit. Many sheep and cows were now carrying next spring's young. A few cows were allowed to stay in milk over the winter with their calf, to provide fresh milk. With not much fresh milk available, people availed themselves of cheese made from summer milking and churning, which was storable. At this point in the year, food supplies for the winter season were known and accounted for.

Hunting was permitted primarily between Beltaine and Samhain, when the animals were at their peak of fitness. However, during the fall they were left alone to breed. During the winter, animals (particularly deer) were generally not hunted, in order not to put stress upon the remaining herd members during their most difficult season. Samhain coincided with the breeding season of the wild boar, and was also the end of boar hunting season. It is thought that the boar may have been the preferred sacrificial or festal animal of Samhain, as it was now at its best, having been fattened all autumn on the nuts of oak and beech trees. This may account for various Celtic legends that were concerned with the hunt for sacred or Otherworld boars, an event that was in some cases said to take place before or during Samhain.[16]

At the beginning of winter, a period of rest from outdoor work began. After Samhain, neither the land nor the animals required substantial effort. People stayed indoors performing other appropriate types of work: preserving food, spinning, weaving, and preparing for winter. This was also the beginning of the great winter season of storytelling. Samhain heralded the beginning of the winter period of rest and darkness with which the New Year began. In earlier times, the Celts were said to reckon time by nights rather than days. Feast days also began on the night before. These concepts reflect the perception that darkness was associated with endings, as well as rebirth and regeneration.

Because it was a liminal point of the year, at Samhain communication and other interactions between this world and the Otherworld intensified. In the myths and legends, many important sacred events are said to have taken place at that time. In the folklore tradition, at Samhain the two realms were connected. The world of mortals was influenced by, or could be overrun by, the magical forces of the unseen world. Supernatural beings emerged from fairy mounds and caves. People might enter *síd* mounds, although returning from them was sometimes difficult. Otherworld figures and pagan deities frequently interacted with the human world, and many things that were not possible at any other time occurred at Samhain.[17]

Traditional Samhain rituals would have involved tribal or intertribal gatherings. As at Lugnasad, peace would be declared (at least for the duration of the festival). Kings would transact business, judgments would be made, and bards and warriors engaged in performances and competitions. Food, entertainment and trade would also have taken place. It was also a time for important religious rituals. These would have been associated with prayers of thanksgiving for the bounty of the land, as well as offerings to ensure the renewal and prosperity of the earth and the tribe. It was important to invoke the forces of the Otherworld to ensure good fortune throughout the winter (as well as into the spring and summer), and sacrifices were likely offered to that end.

Samhain was the Celtic New Year, and as such would have been a time for rituals of purification and divination in preparation for the next cycle. In many cultures around the world, creation myths and other sacred texts are chanted, sung or recited at the new year's festival. Deities would have been honored and invoked at Samhain. Possibly all the gods and goddesses would have been mentioned or honored during the festivities, although it seems likely that the Goddess of Sovereignty may have held particular sway at this time of year. Hazelnuts, symbolic of divine wisdom and prophecy, were also frequently connected with Samhain symbolism, and we know that they were used as offerings in very early times. Sacred plants and animals, as well as votive offerings of jewelry, cauldrons and weapons, were also found at many early Celtic sites.[18]

In more recent times, Samhain was celebrated in Ireland with feasting, divination and other festivities. It was sometimes called *púca* night or *oíche na sprideanna* ("spirit night"), as it was believed that both the fairies and the ghosts of the dead were active at this time. It should be pointed out that there is no evidence for ancestor veneration in connection with Samhain in the native Celtic tradition. That practice become associated with this time of year with the Christian institution of All Soul's Day, November 2. Most of the Irish considered All Soul's Day, not Samhain, to be the time when the dead visited the earth.

The festival of All Saint's (November 1) originated in the seventh century, with the conversion of the Pantheon at Rome into a Christian place of worship. At first the event was celebrated on the first of May, but was later changed to the first of November and retained by the Protestant church. The following day, All Soul's Day (November 2) commemorated the departed faithful, souls inhabiting purgatory for whose release prayers were offered and masses performed. This feast, which originated in the ninth century, was discontinued by the Protestant church (but continued to be observed in Catholic countries like Ireland).[19]

November Eve and Day were considered by the old people to be one of the leading festivals of the year. In the folklore tradition, Samhain was considered to be the end of the year's growth cycle. Fairies were believed to visit the plants at this time, and so it was not considered lucky or appropriate to eat any ungathered plant food after this time. Food offerings and vessels of water were left outside near the doors of houses for the fairies, to ensure their favor in the coming year. Holy water was sprinkled on the animals that night to the accompaniment of various charms, prayers and blessings.

Parties and festivities were held at Samhain, and included eating, drinking, games and divination. Apple cakes, blackberry pies, cream pancakes and other special foods were consumed, including *stampy* (cakes made from grated raw potato, flour, cream, caraway seeds and sugar) and *colcannon* (mashed potatoes and cooked cabbage in which small symbolic items were placed as a form of divination). A great deal of Samhain divination was connected with obtaining information about marriages or future events in people's lives. Ducking for apples and the roasting of hazelnuts frequently took place. In some areas, bonfires were lit and guising took place. Pranks and tricks were played on neighbors, and behavior that would otherwise be condemned was overlooked.

Fairy activity was at a peak during Samhain, and interactions between mortals and fairy beings often took place. People could be abducted at Samhain, and those who had been abducted were sometimes seen at fairy raths or in fairy procession at this time of year. If a person encountered the fairies at Samhain, by taking the dust under one's feet and throwing it at them, they would be obliged to surrender any human beings they had taken captive. Carrying a black-handled knife was also good protection. Although the evening was generally merry, people traveling at night preferred to go in the company of others to protect themselves from fairy mischief or misfortune. Fairy activity was so prevalent that anyone throwing water outside on that night would call out to the fairies to beware, enabling them to step aside and avoid being splashed. Many people reported hearing sounds of revelry and merrymaking in ring forts and other fairy locations.

One particularly interesting Samhain custom in Ireland was the procession of the *Láir Bhán* or "White Mare." Groups of young people processed from house to house, blowing on cow's horns. The party was headed by a person dressed in a white robe or sheet who was known as the "White Mare." The *Láir Bhán* led the procession and served as a master of ceremonies. The procession stopped at each house, where a long series of verses was recited. Some of these verses contained overtly pagan material. Those inside the house were expected to donate food, wool, or other gifts; and the more generous the donation, the more abundance they might expect in the coming year. This ritual may have originally had some connection with the Goddess of Sovereignty, who was frequently associated with horses (and in some cases, the white horse in particular).[20]

A similar procession also took place in Wales during the Christmas and New Year's season. It is believed that a number of customs that originally took place at the Old Celtic New Year were later transferred to the Gregorian New Year or Christmas season. In the Welsh procession, a group of people processed from door to door led by a person dressed in a white sheet who carried a decorated horse's skull on a pole. This custom was known as the procession of the *Mari Lwyd* (perhaps "Grey Mare"?). White and light-colored or grey horses often served a similar role in the myths and legends.[21]

At the door of each house, the Mari Lwyd troupe and the people inside the house engaged in an elaborate contest of poetic improvisation. In one of these songs, the people inside the house are referred to as *Y Tylwyth Teg*, the "Fair Folk," which was also a traditional name for the fairies in Wales. An excerpt from one version of the Mari Lwyd song ran as follows[22]:

> Family of fair ancestry,
> Come to the light... to see the Wassail...
> There is not one of its kind in Wales.
>
> It is an orchard of expansive flowers...
> Fine, brilliant multi-coloured ribbons
> Made into rings.
>
> It is a fair (or holy) agile mare,
> Thousands praise her.[23]

In Wales, the old Celtic new year was known as *Nos Galan gaeaf*, "the Eve of the Winter Kalend." Some cattle and pigs were culled to provide food for the winter, and in some areas, portions of this food were distributed to those in need. *Nos Galan gaeaf*, or All-Hallow's Eve, was the most supernatural night of the year. Wandering ghosts might be seen in the form of a white lady or a black sow. Bonfires were prepared during the day and lit at night on top of prominent hills. Fern, gorse, straw and thorn bushes were used to create the fires.

As the fire was lit, horns were blown and other instruments sounded. Apples and potatoes were set on the fire to roast, and there would be shouting, dancing, and leaping over the fire. Some people ran around the fire and cast a stone into the flames. In the morning, they would return to the site and search for their stone. If the stone was found, this indicated good luck during the coming year. If the stone could not be found, this signified misfortune or death.

Parties were held inside the house, including special meals, singing, storytelling, games of skill, and divination. A "mash of nine sorts" was prepared in one part of Wales, involving potatoes, carrots, turnips, peas, parsnips, leeks, pepper and salt, and a small portion of new milk. A wedding ring was hidden inside the mash, and whoever found it would be the first married. In other areas, a punch or "wassail" bowl was served. Boiling ale and whiskey were placed in an elaborate urn, along with biscuits, buns, raisins, spices and sugar, as well as roasted apples.

Apples were a prominent part of the November Eve festivities. Games were played, such as "catching apples with the teeth." They were also used in divination. Apples were peeled without breaking the rind, and the rind thrown over the shoulder. The shape of the rind formed the initial letter of one's future marriage partner. Nuts were thrown into the fire for love divination or more general forms of augury. These and many other types of

Samhain divination practices were recorded in Ireland and Scotland as well. Apples and hazelnuts were especially prominent in games, charms and divination.[24]

Samhain festivities similar to those in Ireland also took place in Scotland. At Samhain, the fairies were said to be "flitting" or moving to new homes, and their procession moved along to the sound of bells and horns. It was believed that people who had been abducted into the fairy realms could be recovered in a year and a day, but the spell used to recover them was potent only when the fairies made their procession on Samhain. Sir Walter Scott said that if anyone went to a fairy mound alone on Samhain and walked around it nine times in a left-handwise direction, the door to the fairy mound would open and admit them. He does not mention how (or if) one might get out again.

At Samhain, bonfires were lit at dusk, in contrast with Beltaine fires which were lit at dawn. In some areas, when the fire had burnt low, the ashes were collected and placed in the form of a circle. A stone was placed around the circumference of the circle to represent each person present. In the morning, if any stone was moved or harmed, it signified that the person was *fey*, and doomed to die before the next Samhain.

In many parts of Scotland, blazing torches were carried around the farms and fields. These brands or torches were lit from the Samhain bonfire or from the hearth fire. Bog fir was frequently used, but stalks of heather could also serve the purpose. Parents stood at the hearth and lit the brands from the peat fire, passing them out to children and other members of the household. The members of the party then spread out at equal distances from each other and walked slowly sunwise around the property with the fire.[25]

In the Isle of Lewis, an offering ceremony was conducted at Samhain to honor the sea. As late as the end of the seventeenth century, a venerated figure named *Seonaigh* was propitiated with an offering of ale. Each family provided a peck of malt for the brewing of this ale. One person waded out into the sea up to his or her waist, carrying a cup of ale, and cried out with a loud voice: "Shony, I give you this cup of ale, hoping you will send us plenty of sea-ware for enriching our ground in the coming year." The ale was then poured into the sea. Seaweed was invaluable as a source of fertilizer in the thin soil of the islands. The origin of the name *Seonaidh* is unclear; it may derive from the Scottish Gaelic term *seonadh*, which refers to augury, divination or druidic magic.[26]

As with the other feast days, a Samhain bannock or cake was made at this time of year. A particularly interesting ritual associated with the creation of the bannock was recorded in the nineteenth century in Strathclyde. In this ceremony, the dough was made from oat flour and water and allowed to slightly ferment. It might then be mixed with a little sugar, anise or cinnamon. The baking was done after sunset and could only be performed by groups of women. In a large area of the house especially chosen for this activity, a circular line was drawn on the ground to delineate consecrated ground. The women sat with their feet facing the central fire.

One of the women was designated "The Queen" and the others were the maidens. They took turns throwing the balls of dough to each other, each one beating or pressing it to make it a little thinner. The dough was passed around sunwise, from east to west, until it reached the queen. It was she who toasted the sacred cakes on the fire. In some cases, the work was accompanied by singing. The Samhain cakes were given away to strangers who attended the Samhain fairs or festivities.[27]

Samhain feasts were common in Scotland, and the food at these festivities included dried mutton, sausages, butter, cheese, and traditional desserts. Guising, singing and dancing also took place. Small lanterns were made from hollowed out turnips for traveling at night from house to house. As in Ireland, numerous pranks took place on Samhain Eve. There was also a great deal of divination, much of it involving apples and hazelnuts, ancient symbols of divine wisdom and connection with the Otherworld.[28]

A wonderful Samhain divination rite from Scotland was referred to as "The Dreaming Stones." In this rite, a person traveled alone to a boundary stream after dark. With eyes closed, three small stones were lifted in succession from the stream using only the middle finger and thumb. As the stones were taken, this charm was recited[29]:

> I myself lift a stone...
> for substance, victory and power
> As long as this stone is in my hand,
> I will reach my journey's end.[30]

An examination of New Year's celebrations in Scotland would not be complete without mentioning Hogmanay. This holiday was situated at the time of the Gregorian New Year, but involved many archaic rites which must be quite ancient in origin. On New Year's day, homes were decorated with rowan, hazel and holly. Doorposts and walls, and the occupants of the house and the barn, were sprinkled with "magic water" taken from a ford crossed by "the living and the dead." All crevices and holes in the home were plugged, and huge bundles of dried juniper were burned for purification, resulting in a thick cloud of purifying smoke.

A number of divinatory rites were performed as well. Omens were taken from the fire, as well as from the shape and form of clouds. A form of augury called the *frith* was performed, in which omens were drawn from whatever was first seen through the window. First-footing was very common, taking omens from the appearance of the first person (other than members of the family) to cross the threshold after midnight.

People gathered at mercat crosses, stone circles, or other traditional sites to welcome in the new year. In some outdoor locations, dancing took place, accompanied only by vocal songs. Hot ale spiced with nutmeg and laced with whisky was sometimes served at gatherings, as well as buns or shortbreads, and oatcakes and cheese. Another traditional drink was *sowans*, made from oats, sweetened with honey and laced with whiskey. Inside the home, outstanding tasks were completed and things were tidied and set in order. It was considered a festival of renewal.

Perhaps the most well-known Hogmanay custom involved a very dramatic ritual procession. A group of young men walked through the village or town at night. One of the men wore the hard hide of a bull which still had the horns and hoofs intact. When the party came to a house, it ascended the thick stone wall and walked around the house sunwise. The man in the bull's hide shook the horns and hooves, and the other men struck the hide with sticks. Then, the revelers descended and recited verses at the door of the house. If admitted inside, they were provided with the best of food and drink. In some areas, the bull hide was singed and the members of the household inhaled the smoke from it for health during the coming year. Here are some excerpts from traditional Hogmanay songs and prayers[31]:

> I have come to your land,
> To renew for you the Hogmanay
> I do not need to tell you about it,
> It has existed since the time of our ancestors.

I ascend by the doorstep...
I sing my song slowly and mindfully...
The Hogmanay skin is in my pocket,
The smoke from it will soon be great.

The man of the house will take it in his hand,
He will place its nose in the fire
He will proceed sunwise around the children,
And seven times around his wife...[32]

Bless the dwelling, each stone, beam and stave,
Bless all food, drink and clothing...
Bless my neighbours... give me a clean heart
Bless to me the new day... may my eye bless all it sees...[33]

21

The Path of the Old Ways

Many of the Classical authors reported upon the traditions, beliefs and way of life of the ancient Celts, commenting on their courage and bravery, feasting and hospitality, colorful dress and high spirits, and their observance of sacred laws and traditional precedents. They characterized the Celts as intelligent and quick to learn, fond of word play, music and poetry, and possessed of a detailed system of cultural and spiritual beliefs. In terms of religion, the Classical writers recorded details of Celtic ceremonies, offering rituals and divinatory rites, as well as information about religious practitioners and training. Their writings noted that the Celts honored the gods, esteemed the learned and skilled members of their society, and preserved their ancestral traditions. These included a belief in the immortality of the soul, and a desire to live a life dedicated to truth, skill and honor.[1]

Much of their traditional knowledge was maintained and passed on through oral teachings, although some of this knowledge was committed to writing beginning in about the fifth and sixth centuries C.E. It has come down to us in various forms; some fragmentary, some altered, but some, no doubt, true to original form and intent. The use of symbolism was prevalent throughout the tradition, and it is through these symbols that we are often able to perceive and follow the core beliefs of the Celtic religious traditions. Concepts like the Goddess of Sovereignty, the sacral kingship and the abundance of the land form part of this tradition, as do themes of poetic wisdom and inspiration, the interconnection between the worlds, and symbolic elements like the hazel tree, the salmon, the apple tree, the sacred cup or cauldron, the horse, boar, raven and so forth.

John Carey has written about the importance of symbolism in early Irish religious thought, pointing out that although we have a "wealth of poetry and legend, radiant with unforgettable imagery" and full of "verbal exuberance," much philosophy, theology and religious belief must be inferred. As he points out, the Celts had no shortage of erudition, intellectual power, imagination or poetic vision, but that vision was communicated through symbolic thought, the natural method of cognition among traditional peoples. Significance cannot be extracted from a symbol by any single interpretation; the symbol participates in the "mystery of existence, the secrets beyond the veil of the phenomenal."[2]

> The literature is ... rich in metaphor and image ... and it is surely here that the key is to be found. The indigenous Irish mentality tends to find expression in *symbolic* rather than in *analytic* terms: concepts are not extracted from phenomena in order to be manipulated on the plane of "pure reason," but are instilled and contemplated in concrete entities.... Such native words for "knowledge" as *fís*, *éicse*, and *senchas* never simply designate a disembodied cognitive faculty,

remaining always inseparable from the contexts of prophetic insight, poetic skill, and the lore of origins. A symbol, unlike an abstract concept, is alive, and therefore *inexhaustible*. It can embrace contraries, point the way into deeper or subtler realms of thought, or be itself transformed and reinterpreted by the unfolding of history.[3]

Professor Carey discusses the impact of indigenous ways of symbolic thought and expression, noting that the Irish preserved their native way of thinking after the introduction of Christianity, even applying it to the new religion. The idea that created things contain the nature of the divine manifested in Ireland in the contemplation of nature (and a remarkable poetic and literary record of that contemplation). This phenomenon had a spiritual significance difficult to parallel elsewhere in Europe. Implicit in the expression of these modes of perception is the belief that sacred meanings are substantial realities; each thing's value depends on its connection with the Divine.[4]

From the earliest recorded glimpses into Celtic ritual, to the storytelling traditions of the twenty-first century, we can perceive the importance of the symbol and its ability to both contain and portray sacred cultural ideals and ideas. The use of language, poetry and song to convey traditional beliefs is extremely widespread, and in some areas these modes of expression are undergoing a small renaissance of their own. However, things have not always been that way, and any resurgence of traditional Celtic cultural expression has come on the heels of oppression, loss and decline.

In the latter part of the medieval era, Celtic poets frequently wrote about the degeneration of their cultural traditions in the face of social and political upheaval and change. They lamented the loss of artistic standards and honorable conduct, and praised those who maintained the old ways and preserved traditional wisdom.[5] In the sixteenth century, the Welsh poet Siôn Tudur wrote a warning to his fellow poets complaining about rampant scandal among their ranks, a general lack of credibility, and a decline in respect for learning. During the following century, the Welsh poet William Philyp wrote a poem of lament upon leaving his home, *Hendre Fechan*[6]:

> Farewell to the fellowship of poetry,
>   to the splendour of right tradition
> Farewell to Hendre Fechan, to books of poems,
> Virtuous, shining craft — to you as well, farewell at last...
>
> Farewell to the forest, fair wood, pure poetry —
>   where melodious birds sang a true song;
> Farewell to each song-encircled grove,
> Every course where songs might dwell.[7]

Centuries later, modern Irish poets also wrote about the importance of traditional learning, as well as their yearning for the land, connection with community, and the customs and ways of the past. In a poem written by Séan Ó Ríordáin in the twentieth century, he implores listeners to fashion their soul into an "ear" in order to receive the words of poets who still write in the Irish language. In another poem, he addresses the Irish flowing from his pen and inquires if it has lost its ancestry. He asks whether any aged words can come to the aid of his "whisperings" in Irish, and if anyone accompanies them as they travel to the well (presumably, the Well of Wisdom).[8]

The twentieth-century Scottish poet Donald Sinclair, who edited a number of anthologies of Gaelic verse from Scotland and Nova Scotia, explored similar themes in a romantic poem that praised and eulogized the wisdom of his people. Here is an excerpt from a wistful and highly romanticized poem of Sinclair's, *Sligh nan Seann Seun* (a title which has been translated as "The Path of the Old Spells").[9]

> Rich is the peace of the fairy music tonight over the Land of Joy
> And gentle the song of learning that surrounds the Isles of Love
> Every wing is nimble in keen obedience to poetic skill
> The path of the old spells is languishing in the west without refuge.
>
> Rich the body of the mountains with remembrance of days gone by
> Blessed the face of the ocean with the dream of a time that has passed
> Shining is each season with the spirit of a wind of tranquility
> O, days of esteem, your nobleness, your affection!
>
> O radiant days of love, with your bright, virtuous customs,
> O times of joy, with your laughter, cheer and music
> O generation of divine fortune, of beams of knowledge and discernment,
> Why have you gone and left no noble light to reflect your honour?[10]

Following centuries of struggle against oppression and upheaval, during the sixteenth and seventeenth centuries, Celtic cultures and languages began to suffer and wane even more intensely as a result of foreign occupation and discrimination. This continued for several hundred years, until during the late eighteenth and nineteenth centuries, people outside Celtic communities began to show an interest in traditional folklore songs, stories and folklore. Well-intentioned in terms of motivation, but not always accurate or objective in their observations, writers, antiquarians and the philanthropically minded began to record the customs and beliefs of the Celtic-speaking peoples.

While these perceptions and portrayals were often highly romanticized, they nonetheless had the desired effect: to retrieve Celtic culture and traditions from the ashcan of existence. During the late nineteenth and early twentieth centuries, the romantic movement in music, art and poetry further elevated Celtic themes and images. However, as a result of generalization, projection and fantasy these romantic creations did not always authentically portray the complex and time-honored traditions of Celtic-speaking communities.[11]

Some of these overly romantic and inauthentic images and portrayals found expression in the work of artists, esotericists and occultists, and many of them still persist to this day. Whether we generalize about another culture in an overly positive or overly negative way, we are still stereotyping that culture. In doing so, we disrespect the complexity and nuances of a way of life, and run the risk of harming that culture through our own projections. Like many native societies, Celtic cultures have suffered from both negative stereotyping and romantic idealizing, neither of which accurately depict their intricate and nuanced (and widely varying) ways of life.

It has been the goal of this work to provide a respectful and authentic overview of many aspects of Celtic religion, mythology and folklore. These beliefs would not have constituted the totality of any Celtic worldview, of course, but would have formed part of a holistic system that included social customs and beliefs, practical and political concerns, and many other aspects of daily life. In traditional societies, religious beliefs and daily life are interwoven into a seamless whole.

It is a regrettable fact today that without exception, popular books about Celtic religion and mythology are between fifty to eighty percent inaccurate. This is the result of the aforementioned romantic projections and misperceptions which have continued unabated for the last several hundred years. These projections not only persist, but continue to change form with each passing generation into even more unrecognizable portrayals of Celtic culture and belief. However, it is also the case that sincere and honest enthusiasm for and interest in Celtic culture, religion and mythology have likewise continued to grow. This open hearted and well-intentioned motivation may ultimately provide the momentum and dedication necessary to restore these traditions to a place of honor and respect.

Our journey has taken us to many places in the ancient world, from sacred sites and timeworn inscriptions, to religious assemblies and druidic training schools. We have passed through the dusty volumes of Greek and Latin writers who were fascinated by the vibrant culture of the Celts, and made our way into the realms of the sacred texts and medieval illuminations of the Celtic-speaking peoples themselves. We have met warrior-queens and hero-kings, bards and poets, druids and priestesses, shamans and wild women, and traditional healers and storytellers. We have learned about Celtic perceptions and beliefs associated with the cosmos and the natural world, encountered the recitations and magical practices of sages and poet-seers, and explored many aspects of the Celtic Otherworld, which was the source of wisdom, skill, healing, blessings and protection.

No one volume can possibly contain every aspect of the religious traditions of the Celts. In the course of my studies, I have read several hundred books and several hundred more academic journal articles in order to create a foundation of knowledge that would eventually serve in the creation of this book. We have access to a prodigious amount of information, some of which has still to be properly collated, translated or interpreted. Due to the restraints of the format, some generalization has by necessity occurred. Still, I stand by it as a solid introduction and exploration of numerous aspects of the tradition, many of which will be explored in more depth in future works.

Prior to publishing this book, teachers of Celtic studies (including myself) have had to advise our students to read numerous academic books on the Celts and their mythological traditions in order to provide them with even a basic sense of who the Celts were, what they believed and practiced, and what their symbols and stories represent. Needless to say, this has been a daunting task for many people who have expressed a sincere interest in the topic in academic settings and at cultural learning centers. It is my honor and privilege to have the opportunity to create this single volume in a spirit of service to the tradition, and hope it will continue to provide guidance and inspiration for many years to come.

Appendix A.
The Rights of Women
in Early Celtic Culture

The Classical authors often mentioned the strength, character and relative independence of Gaulish women as compared with women in Greek and Roman culture.[1] The early Irish law tracts provide us with quite a bit of interesting information about the legal status of women.[2] These may be "laws as recorded," and not reflective of women's status in all cases. Overall, women in Celtic cultures (from what we can see) had more rights than women in other known ancient cultures, although they did not have equal status. This was also the case in our own culture, at least until the twentieth century.

A lack of complete equality does not necessarily mean complete subservience or victimhood, however, and we can certainly envision strong women who "broke the mold" despite whatever the official rules were.[3] We know there were historical female rulers and leaders, for example. Several centuries B.C.E. there is a classical account of a woman named Onomaris from Galatia who bravely led her starving people across the Danube, conquered foes and obstacles, and helped them establish a home in Europe. During the Romano-Celtic period, we know of at least two historical female rulers in Britain, the treacherous Cartimandua and the fierce Boadicea.[4]

Women figure prominently in Old and Middle Irish literature, both mortal and immortal. The figure of the Sovereignty Goddess is one of the most enduring and important in the entire corpus of native literature and legends. Although not necessarily historical in nature, female leaders and warriors are mentioned in a variety of Celtic legends. The female warrior *Scáthach* was reputed to have run a school where she taught the martial arts to men. Queen Medb (later anglicized as Maeve) was a legendary Irish queen made famous in the great Irish saga *Táin Bó Cuailgne* ("The Cattle Raid of Cooley"). The goddesses Mórrigan and Macha displayed martial prowess, and even Saint Brigid was said to have appeared over the battlefield in the eleventh or twelfth century, influencing the outcome of the conflict. The myths and legends also speak of women magicians, seers, prophetesses, poets and druids, although we have less evidence or information about these in an historical sense.[5]

The early Irish law tracts and other medieval Irish sources provide us with interesting documentation of laws and regulations concerning women, including their rights, and men's often conflicting reactions to or perceptions about them. For example, in the Irish triads it stated that the three qualities most admired in a woman were reticence, virtue and industry, and that the three "steadinesses" of good womanhood were a steady tongue, virtue and housewifery. The three types of behavior most censured in a woman were promiscuity, making spells or illegal satires, and thieving.[6] Categories of woman who were considered particularly important to the *túath* or tribe were "the woman who turns back the streams of war" (a druidess, judge, military leader or abbess perhaps) and "the hostage ruler" (perhaps a woman ruler who, like her male counterparts, took hostages in battle). There were also laws concerning queens, women poets and satirists, female wrights, and female physicians. There may also have been female judges.[7] These sources demonstrate some variation in terms of women's rights and roles. While consistency is not one of the most obvious qualities of any medieval literature, early sources do provide us with some idea of the rights and responsibilities of women in early Irish society.

Marriage in Early Ireland

In the early Irish law tracts, there were nine forms of recognized sexual union:

- A union of joint property — in which both the man and the woman bring movable goods to the marriage. In this type of union, the wife is called a "wife of joint authority."
- Union of a woman on man-property: the woman contributes little or nothing
- Union of a man on woman-property: the man contributes little or nothing
- Union of a man visiting: a less formal union in which the man visits the woman at her home with the consent of her kin
- A union in which the woman goes away openly with the man, but is not given by her kin
- A union in which the woman allows herself to be abducted (without consent of kin)
- A union in which the woman is secretly visited (without the consent of her kin)
- Union by rape
- Union of two insane persons

Well into the Christian era, men in early Ireland could have more than one wife. The church opposed this practice, but with limited success. Men could also have a marriage with one woman, but formally visit another. The sons of both types of unions would have rights of inheritance, but the mothers would not have equal status. There were two grades of wife: the *cétmuinter* or chief wife, and the *adaltrach* or concubine, a somewhat looser legal connection. More formal marriages were often arranged by the families. The chief wife was under the rule of her husband unless he failed to carry out his obligations in the marriage. The adaltrach could choose if she wanted to be under the rule of her husband, son or kin. She often had half the status and entitlements of the chief wife.

Unlike other early legal systems, surviving early Irish law-texts do not refer to the legal consequence of non-virginity in a bride (although one triad seems to imply that a chief wife is expected to be). The paternity of a man (especially if he was of royal lineage) was of great importance. Some sources stated that in more formal unions both partners should be of the same social class. One of the reasons for this was that the financial burden of a mixed-class marriage fell more heavily on the family of the lower class partner.[8]

The husband often gave a bride-price to the woman's father. If the marriage broke up due to the fault of the husband, the bride-price was kept by the woman's father. If it was due to the fault of the woman, the bride-price was returned to the husband. There was no term for dowry, but in some cases contributions came from both sides. In others, some or all came from the wife's side of the family. If a child was born of a union forbidden by the man's father, the woman alone was responsible for raising the child (probably at her parent's house). However, if a child was born from a union forbidden by the girls' father (or if the man abducted the woman in defiance of her father or kin), the man alone was responsible for raising the child.

A woman did not totally sever her connection with her own kin when she married (although the more formal the marriage, the greater the potential severance). For a chief wife, one-third of her inheritable assets when she died went to her own kin. The other two-thirds went to her sons. Her kin also received one-third of any fines payable on her behalf, but also had to pay one-third of any fines she or her actions might incur. For a chief wife without any sons, her assets and liabilities were split equally between her own kin and her husband. The maternal kin were entitled to some portion of payments if a son or daughter was killed illegally, and male members of the maternal kin had to join in a blood feud against the culprit if fines were not paid.

Maternal kin were required to intervene if a child's fosterage was not carried out properly. In some cases maternal kin had sole responsibility for the cost and duties of raising children. This was true in cases where the father was an outsider, the mother was a prostitute, or if the father could not carry out normal paternal duties (i.e., if he were a slave, a lunatic or a priest). However, maternal kin had no responsibility for the children of slave women, sick women, or insane women, nor did they have to bear the duty and cost of raising children born against the wishes of the woman's father (or by rape). In these cases, the children were raised by the paternal kin.[9]

Divorce and separation were allowed in early Ireland for many reasons. If the husband repudiated his wife for another woman, she was free to leave him (but also had the right to stay in the house if she wished). A woman could leave her husband if he did not support her, spread a false story about her, or if he tricked her into marriage through the use of sorcery. She could divorce him if he was sterile, impotent ("because an impotent man is not easy for a wife"), too fat to have sex, or practiced homosexuality (although in this last case, she could also stay with him if she chose). A man was forbidden from telling anyone the details of their sexual relationship, and a woman could divorce a man for this. However, if she left him without just cause, she had no rights in society and could not be protected or harbored by anyone.

A husband could divorce his wife for unfaithfulness, persistent thieving, inducing an abortion on herself, bringing shame on his honor, smothering her child, or being without milk through sickness. He could legally strike her to correct her, but could not leave a mark. A couple could choose to separate without fine or penalty. Usually this took the form of the husband leaving—to go on a pilgrimage, to seek a friend across a boundary, to enter a ship, or to take part in a vengeance-slaying. Either party could be brought away from home on sick-maintenance if illegally injured by a third party. If either party was infertile, the other could legally go away "to seek a child." So that a woman didn't have to leave an infertile husband whom she was otherwise pleased with, she could choose to become pregnant by another man and the child was treated as if it were her husband's own offspring.[10]

Women's Legal Rights

In terms of overall legal capacity, officially women did not generally have an enormous amount of independent legal capacity. They could not act as a witness, and usually could not make a contract, sale or purchase without the permission of their husband or father (although there were exceptions to this, as noted below). The tradition was that a father cared for her and was in charge of her when she was a girl; her husband when she was a woman; and her sons when she was widowed. However, as noted above, women with special status or special skills seem to have been able to rise above some of these limitations (see also below).[11]

There were rights and limitations to a woman's legal ability to own property. She had the right to items of her own personal property (including an embroidery needle, workbag and dress) which she could use as a pledge on behalf of another. She was also entitled to a fine and interest if her pledge became forfeit. She could not give pledges of cattle, horses, silver, gold, copper or iron without her husband's permission. However, even in a marriage into which a woman had brought little property, she could "disturb" a disadvantageous contract made by her husband if she was a chief wife. If she was a lower wife, she could only disturb disadvantageous contracts pertaining to food, clothing, cattle and sheep.

Women were entitled to inherit a share of their father's personal valuables upon his death, but not generally his land. However, if her father had no sons, she could become a "female heir" with more legal rights than other women. A woman could inherit a life interest in land when her father had no sons, and there were certain rights inherent in that arrangement. If a woman married a landless man, or stranger from another *túath,* the roles of husband and wife were reversed. In these instances the woman made the decisions and paid fines and debts. In addition, after her death, her property reverted to her own kin (and not to her husband or sons). Women who could count themselves as not dependent on a husband had some independent legal capacity. If she won a case of illegal injury, for example, her award was based upon her own dignity and possessions.

Women were allowed to make gifts in accordance with their rank without their husband's permission. They could make a proper gift to a male superior (a father, husband, a son if she was widowed, a head of kin), or within a close relationship (husband and wife, mother and son, father and daughter, etc.). While women were not usually entitled to transfer property, they could bequeath the produce of their own hands to the church. However, this was not permissible if they left liabilities behind them which had to be met by surviving relatives.[12]

There were special categories of women who seemed to have been awarded higher dignity and respect in the tribe, and potentially, higher legal standing. These included:

- The woman who turns back the streams of war
- The hostage ruler
- The female wright
- The woman-physician of the *túath*

- The woman who is "revered by the *túath*"
- The woman who is "abundant in miracles"

Strangely, a queen had no official or special legal rights independent of her husband. However, the mother of a king or sage had the same honor price as her son (if she was a law-abiding member of the tribe). In addition, the talented embroideress stood to profit by her abilities, as the interest on her needle could be up to an ounce of silver: "The woman who embroiders earns more profit even than queens."[13]

Women, Law and Oaths

If a woman committed an offense, there were numerous rules and regulations concerning her offenses. In cases where a crime was committed by an unmarried woman, the debt was paid by her father (or if he were no longer alive, by her kin). If she was married, the more formal the union the greater the responsibility assumed by her sons. If she had no sons, her husband and kin must each pay half the fine. In a less formal union, the kin paid two-thirds of the fine and her sons paid one-third. If a woman was abducted against the will of her father or kin, all fines had to be paid by her abductor.

In some cases, a woman could injure another woman without liability. Injuries inflicted in a female fight were not actionable. A chief wife could inflict any non-fatal injury on a second wife for a period of three days (probably right after the marriage). A second wife could only scratch, pull hair, speak abusively, or inflict other minor injuries on a chief wife.

If a woman committed murder or arson, she was set adrift. This meant being put into a boat with one paddle and a vessel of gruel. Her judgment was left to the Divine. This punishment was also meted out to men, including people guilty of crimes of negligence or carelessness, or for kin-slaying. If the person washed back into their own territory, if their crime was one of negligence or carelessness, they were taken back into their kin as a lawful person. In cases of kin-slaying, however, they had to serve as a *fuidir* (a criminal with semi-free status, almost a type of slave or worker).

There were seven types of women who were not entitled to any payment or honor price:

- a woman who steals
- a woman who satirizes every class of person
- a "chantress of tales" whose kin pays for her lying stories
- a prostitute of the bushes
- a woman who wounds
- a woman who betrays
- a woman who refuses hospitality to every law-abiding person[14]

Crimes against women were usually regarded as crimes against her guardian (husband, father, son, head of kin), and the transgressor had to pay him his honor price or proportion thereof. There were two kinds of rape: forcible rape, and all other situations where a woman is subjected to sex without her consent. This second type was often associated with drunkenness. Sex with a drunken woman seems to have been as serious an offense as forcible rape.

However, if a drunken married woman went into an alehouse unaccompanied, she had no rights. Rape was widely punished by castration. There was also a twofold punishment of mutilation and death for the killing of a woman.

There were eight categories of women who got no redress if they were raped (either kind of rape). These mostly consisted of promiscuous or adulterous women (such as an unreformed prostitute), women who made "an assignation to bush or bed," or women who committed adultery. A woman had no right to hide the fact that she had been raped. She was legally obligated to call for help if she was near a settlement. This was waived if she was out in the wilderness. Sometimes marriages resulted from rape, but these were usually of the type consented to by the woman, but not by her kin.

Fines had to be paid by a man for shaming a woman by raising her dress, touching a woman, putting his hand inside her girdle or under her dress. Full honor price had to be paid if a woman was kissed against her will.[15]

While a woman's oath was not usually valid in court, in certain cases it was acceptable. This occurred in regards to cases of "female entry into land" or "sick-maintenance" (see below) or regarding the paternity of her child when she was in danger of dying in childbirth. One of the Irish triads stated that the oath of a woman in childbirth was one of the three oaths that could not be countersworn. The evidence of a female witness who accompanied an injured woman on sick-maintenance was accepted if the injured woman was mistreated in any way.

The oral testimony of women was also regarded as conclusive regarding certain sexual matters: If husband claimed he could not consummate the marriage due to a physical defect of the wife which prevented it, she was examined by female witnesses. If what the husband said was true, the bride-price was returned to the husband. However, if it was false, the bride-price stayed with the wife. If a woman complained that husband had not "made her a woman" (i.e., that he has not consummated the marriage), but he claims that he has, the wife was examined by female witnesses and their evidence was accepted in court.[16]

As in most ancient societies, there was an almost invisible lower strata of society which consisted of slaves (often prisoners of war). In Ireland, female slaves worked at the quern, the kneading slab and the trough, and performed other domestic duties. Male slaves performed menial work on farms, herding livestock and chopping wood. A female slave was called a *cumal*, and this term became a unit of value. The honor price of the lowest grade of king was seven cumals or their equivalent, perhaps, in gold and silver. If a man impregnated someone else's female slave he had to arrange for the raising of the child. The son of a slave woman could not become a noble. A man who had sex with his own female slave was encouraged to sell her and perform a year's penance for his deed. If the woman had a child by him, the man should set her free. If a free woman allowed herself to become pregnant by a male slave, she was responsible for rearing the child. Saint Patrick spent time as a slave and was sympathetic to the plight of slave women.[17]

Legal Entry into Disputed Land

In early Irish law, "legal entry" or *tellach* was a legal procedure whereby a person took possession of land to which he or she was entitled, but which was held by another. The person initiated the claim by formally crossing the boundary mound and entering the land, holding two horses and accompanied by witnesses and guarantors. Then they withdrew from the disputed land. The person occupying the land could submit the dispute to arbitration after five days. If they didn't, the claimant entered the land again, ten days later. On this occasion, they were accompanied by two witnesses and four horses. When they withdrew, the occupant once again had the opportunity to submit the case to arbitration after three days. Final entry took place twenty days after first entry, and involved three witnesses and eight horses. If the occupant still didn't submit to arbitration, the claimant obtained legal ownership of the disputed property. To demonstrate ownership, the claimant had to spend the night on the property, kindle a fire and tend to their animals on the land.

There were specific legal provisions for "female entry into disputed land," or *bantellach*. Legend claimed that a judgment had been passed by a legendary judge named *Sencha*, who stated that female entry should happen in same manner as male entry into disputed land. However, blisters appeared on his cheeks as a sign that this was a false judgment. A female judge, *Brig*, cured these blisters by putting forth the correct procedure for female entry. A female claimant to disputed territory first made entry across the burial mounds of the property, accompanied by female witnesses of good character and two ewes. After four days (rather than five), the case could go to arbitration. Second entry took place after eight days, and involved four ewes and twice as many female witnesses. They could submit to arbitration after two days. Final entry could be made sixteen days after first entry. On this occasion, the woman might be accompanied by at least one male witness. To symbolize her rightful possession of the disputed land, the woman brought with her a kneading-trough and a sieve for baking.[18]

Sick-Maintenance

If someone was illegally injured by another person, the victim was brought to his or her own home and cared for by his or her own kin (probably with medical supervision) for nine days. If the person died during the nine days, the culprit had to pay the full penalty. If the patient was still alive after nine days, he or she was examined by a physician. If the person was so well recovered that they no longer needed nursing, the culprit only had to pay for any lasting blemish or disability. If recovery seemed unlikely, the person causing the injury had to pay a heavy fine.

If the patient still needed care after nine days, and the physician believed they would live, the culprit had to take them on "sick-maintenance." This involved bringing the injured person to the house of a third party (probably kin of the culprit), and nursing the patient at the culprit's expense until cured. The injured person was brought there in the presence of three lords. Pledges were exchanged between the culprit and the injured person's kin, and sureties had to guarantee that the culprit's obligations would be fully carried out. The person responsible for the injury had to pay medical expenses, provide suitable food and accommodation for the victim and an accompanying retinue appropriate to injured person's status. The culprit also had to provide a substitute to do the normal work of the victim.

During this time no fools, lunatics or senseless people were allowed in the house where the person was recovering. Likewise no enemies were admitted into the house. No games were played inside the dwelling, no tidings were announced, no children were chastised and neither men nor women could exchange blows. No dogs could fight, no shouts were raised, no pigs squealed, and no brawls were made. In addition, no cries of victory were raised, no shouting while playing games, and no yelling or screaming was permitted. This was all due to the importance of quiet for the person's recovery.

If the victim was married and of reproductive age, the culprit also had to pay an additional fine for the "barring of procreation" (i.e., to compensate for the victim not being able to reproduce during this time). A woman's oath could be accepted during this time; she could swear that she was away on sick-maintenance during suitable times for conception. If an injured man was known to be extremely lustful, he was allowed to bring his wife with him, possibly to protect the women of the house in which he was nursed.

In later times, sometimes fines were substituted for this elaborate system. One text outlined twelve categories of women who received payment rather than sick-maintenance, either because they had special skill or status, or might be a danger or nuisance to those nursing them. Women of special skill or status included women who "turned back the streams of war," hostage rulers, a woman "abundant in miracles," female satirists, female wrights, women revered by the territory and women physicians. This list provides us with evidence that women might have a career or role in medicine, law, negotiations, politics, crafts, poetry and religion. Women who might be a detriment to caretakers included vagrants, lunatics, deranged women, "sharp-tongued viragos" and "werewolves."[19]

Poets and Satirists

In early Irish society, poets had full "sacred" status, known as *nemed*. They created poems of praise or satire, and a person's honor (*enech*, literally "face") could be damaged by satire or increased through praise. For this reason, poets were greatly honored and feared. The poet's supernatural powers could be used for positive purposes as well; for example, to protect the king from sorcery. The poets were also credited with the power of prophecy, similar to that of the druids.

It was believed that satire could not only damage, but also kill. In the year 1024 C.E., the chief poet of Ireland was killed. However, before he died he caused the bodies of his killers to rot within an hour by means of a poet's spell known as *firt feled*. The power of Irish poets to "rhyme to death" people or animals (particularly rats) was referred to in English sources from the sixteenth century onwards.

In addition to criticizing rulers for lack of generosity or hospitality, bad counsel and overall dishonorable conduct or attributes, satire could legally be used to pressure a wrong-doer into obeying the law. However, satirizing someone without just cause was a serious offense. The laws especially looked down on illegal satirizing by women. A woman who "satirized every law-abiding person" could be denied sick-maintenance, and could even lose her honor price altogether. The church particularly treated illegal satirists with hostility, as did the native wisdom texts. But, like the druid, the poets had enough influence in society to achieve some degree of recognition in the law-texts. They are included in a list of important people in Irish society, along with druids, clerics, doctors and harpists.

Female poets are listed in a number of sources. In the Irish saga *Táin Bó Cuailgne*, a legendary woman poet from Connacht by the name of *Fedelm* states that she had just returned from Britain where she learned the arts of poetry and prophesy. Many women who composed verse (at least according to the law-texts) were not legally recognized poets but satirists who used verse for malicious purposes, especially sorcery or witchcraft. However, female satirists were legally recognized to have the right to satirize the head of kin of a person for whom she had given a pledge, if that pledge was allowed to become forfeit.

There are historical records of female poets. Around the year 934 C.E., the Irish annals record the death of *Uallach,* daughter of *Muinechán.* She is described as "the woman poet of Ireland" (*banfili Érenn*). A woman, therefore, could be recognized as a full-fledged poet. Women may have been admitted into poetic training schools when the poet had no sons, or when a daughter exhibited special skill or aptitude. As with other professional women (judges, physicians, wrights, etc.), a woman's status as a poet would likely afford her more legal rights than other women of lesser skill or social standing. This would have also been the case with female rulers, physicians, wrights, judges, military rulers, hostage negotiators, women who brought more wealth into marriages than their partners, and women whose special status of inheritance afforded them power.[20]

Appendix B.
The Celtic Folksong Tradition

Music, songs and poetry form an extremely important part of Celtic culture in the past and in the present time. Songs were sung to lighten the workload, celebrate love and joy, express appreciation for one's family, community or land, lament loss, death or disappointment, or preserve an historical account of important events. Poetry was extremely valued, from earliest times into the modern era.

The ability to compose poetry within traditional meters and guidelines, which was not only useful or remarkable in content but also beautiful to the ear, was a highly prized skill and asset. Some poems were set to music, and over time these lyrics could change slightly through oral transmission. Words might also be set to various tunes in different regions.[1] This chapter presents a variety of song lyrics from the Celtic countries to illustrate the beauty and variety of these art forms.[2] Some of these songs were written down in collections and anthologies, while others were passed along orally and either notated or recorded in the last century.[3]

An Fhideag Airgid

This popular Jacobite song commemorates the arrival of Bonnie Prince Charlie and the hopes of the people in eighteenth-century Scotland that he would restore the glory of traditional Gaelic culture.

Có sheinneas an fhideag airgid?
Ho ro hu-a hu ill o, I rill u hill o ho

Mac na rìgh 's air tighinn a dh'Alba
Air luing mhóir air bharr na fairgeadh
Air long rìomhach nam ball airgid
Tearlach Óg nam gormshuil meallach
Fàilte fàilte mùirn 's cliù dhut
Fidhleireachd is ragha ciùil dhut
Có sheinneas an fhideag airgid?
Có chanadh nach seinnin fhìn i?

Who will sound the silver whistle?
The son of the king has come to Scotland
On a great ship across the top of the ocean

194

On a fine ship with silver rigging
O Charles of the beautiful blue eyes
Welcome, welcome, joy and renown to you!
Fiddle tunes and choicest of music for you!
Who will sound the silver whistle?
Who is to say that I will not sound it myself?

Irish Beltaine Song

This Irish folksong commemorates a traditional Beltaine custom in which groups of girls processed from door to door with a corn dolly known as the Beltaine maiden.[4]

Bábóg na Bealtaine maighdean a' tsamhraidh
Suas gach cnoc is síos gach gleann
Cailiní maiseacha bángheala gléigeal
Thugamar féin an samradh linn.

Chorus: Samradh buí ó luí na gréine
Thugamar féin an samradh linn
Ó bhaile go baile 's na bhaile 'na dhiadh sin
Thugamar féin an samradh linn

Tá nead ag an ghiorra ar imeall na haille
Is nead ag an chorr éisc i ngéagaibh an chrainn
Tá 'n chuach 's na héanlaith a' seinm le pléisiúr
Thugamar féin an samradh linn

Tá an fhuiseog a' seinm 's a' luascadh sna spéartha
Beacha is cuileoga 's bláth ar na crainn
Tá mil ar na cuiseoga 's coilm a' biceadh
Thugamar féin an samradh linn

The dolly of Beltaine, maiden of summer
Up every hill and down every glen
Beautiful young girls, brilliant, bright women
We bring the summer with us.

Chorus: Yellow summer from where the sun sets
We bring the summer with us
From town to town, and the town after that
We bring the summer with us

There is a nest nearby on the edge of the cliff
It is a grey heron's nest on the branches of the tree
Cuckoos and a flock of birds are singing with pleasure
We bring the summer with us

A lark is singing and swaying in the heavens
Bees and flies and blossoms on the branches
There is honey on the grass and the doves are calling
We bring the summer with us.

Mari Lwyd Song

This Welsh song is part of a tradition that took place during the Christmas and New Year's season. A traditional ceremony took place that was headed by the "Mari Lwyd" (perhaps

"Grey Mare"?). The "mare" was a person dressed in a white sheet carrying a decorated horse's skull on a pole. The horse led a procession from house to house in which the troupe engaged in a contest of poetic skill with those inside the house. If the troupe was deemed more skillful than the people inside, the Mari Lwyd came in and whirled about in a frightening display.[5]

Wel, dyma ni'n dwad, Gyfeillion diniwad
I 'mofyn am gennad—i ganu.

Rhowch glywed wyr doethion, Pa faint ych o ddynion
A pheth yn wych union—yw'ch enwau?

Cwech o wyr hawddgar, Rhai gorau ar y ddaear
I ganu mewn gwir-air—am gwrw.

Rhowch glywed, wyr difrad, O ble r'ych chwi'n dwad
A phaeth yw'ch gofyniad—gaf enwi?

Cenwch eich gorau, Felly gwnaf finnau
A'r sawl a fo orau—gaiff gwrw.

'Dyw wiw i chwi'n scwto, A chwnnu'r latch heno
Waith prydydd diguro—wyf, gwiriaf.

Mae Mari Lwyd lawen, Am ddod i'ch ty'n rhonden
A chanu yw ei diben—mi dybiaf.

Mari Lwyd: Behold, here we come, simple friends
To ask for permission to sing.

People: Let us hear, wise men, how many of you there are,
And what exactly are your names?

Mari Lywd: Six fine men, the best in the world
To sing truly for ale.

People: Let us hear, honest men, where you come from
And what is your request, if I may ask?

Mari Lwyd: Sing your best, and I shall do so as well,
And whoever is the best shall have ale.

People: It is no use your pushing us or to lift the latch tonight,
Since I am an unbeatable rhymer.

Mari Lwyd: Merry Mari Lwyd wants to come to your house,
And to sing is her purpose, I believe.

Delyow Sevi

Although there are no surviving traditional Cornish language songs, this folk song about the dangers of love was borrowed from England and translated and sung in Cornish.[6] The girl's "black head and yellow hair" probably refers to a traditional formula associated with female beauty, in which the hair is fair but the brow is dark.[7]

Ple'th esowgh hwi ow mos, mowes fethus teg,
Gans agas penn du ha'gas blew melyn?

Ow mos dhe'n fenten, syrra hweg
Rag delyow sevi a wra mowesi teg.

A wrav vy mos genowgh hwi,
Gwrewgh, mar mynnowgh hwi

Fatell a kwrav vy agas, gorra hwi y'n dor
My a vynn sevel arta

Fatell a kwrav vy agas dri hwi gans flogh
My a vynn y dhoen

Piw a vynnowgh hiw kavoes rag, sira rag 'gas flogh
Hwi a wra bos y sira

Pandr'a vynnowgh hwi gu-ul rag, lennow rag' gas flogh
Y sira vydh tregher

Where are you going, pretty fair maid, with your black head and your yellow hair?
I am going to the fountain, sweet sir, For strawberry leaves make maidens fair.

Shall I go with you, pretty fair maid, etc.
Yes, if you want to sweet sir, For strawberry leaves...

What if I put you on the ground, etc.
I will rise again, sweet sir, For strawberry leaves...

What if I bring you with child, etc.
I will bear it, sweet sir, For strawberry leaves...

Who will you get for a father for your child, etc.
You will be his father, sweet sir, For strawberry leaves...

What will you do for clothes for your child, pretty fair maid,
With your black head and your yellow hair?

His father will be a tailor, sweet sir
For strawberry leaves make maidens fair.

Merlin the Diviner

This is a Breton song connected with the Arthurian legend probably collected in the nineteenth century. It seems to reflect an aspect of the medieval legend of Arthur as recounted by Geoffrey of Monmouth's work concerning the prophecies of Merlin. In Geoffrey's recounting, the young Merlin revealed two dragons — one red (symbolizing Wales) and one white (symbolizing England) — which battled beneath the foundations of Vortigern's tower.[8]

Merlin! Merlin! Where are you going,
So early in the day, with your black dog?

I have come here to search the way,
To find the red egg,
The red egg of the marine serpent,
By the seaside, in the hollow of the stone.

I am going to seek, in the valley
The green watercress, and the golden grass
And top branch of the oak,
In the wood by the side of the fountain.

Merlin! Merlin! Retrace your footsteps;
Leave the branch on the oak,
And the green watercress in the valley.

Leave as well the golden grass
And the red egg of the marine serpent
In the foam by the hollow of the stone.

Merlin! Merlin! Retrace your steps;
There is no diviner but God.

Fear a' Bhata

In this well-known Scottish Gaelic song, a young woman laments the absence of her beloved, who has gone to sea and never returned to her.

Fhir a' bhàta, na ho ro eile
Mo shoraidh slàn leat s' gach àit an téid thu

'S tric mi sealltain on chnoc is àirde
Dh'fheuch am faic mi fear a' bhàta
An tig thu 'n diugh, no 'n tig thu màireach?
'S mur tig thu idir, gur truagh a tha mi.

Tha mo chridh-sa briste bruite
'S tric na deòir a' ruith mo shùilean
An tig thu nochd no 'm bi mo dhùil ruit
No 'n dùin mi n' doras le osna thùrsaich?

'S tric mi faighneachd de luchd nam bàta
Am fac' iad thu, no 'm bheil thu sàbhailt
(Ach) s'ann a tha gach aon diubh 'g ràitinn
Gur górach mise ma thug mi gràdh dhuit.

O Boatman, my blessing for success and health to you
In every place you may go

Often I watch from the high hill
To try and see the boatman
Will you come today, or come tomorrow?
Unless you come at all, I will be wretched.

My heart is crushed and broken
And often tears run from my eyes
Will you come tonight or will I be hoping for you
Closing the door with a sad sigh?

Often I ask the boat people
If they have seen you or if you are safe
But every one of them says
I am foolish to give my love to you.

Cha Bhi Mi Buan

Boat imagery is also featured in this Scottish Gaelic work song, known as a "waulking" song. Waulking or "fulling" cloth was a complicated process used to finish tweed cloth. Women performed the waulking, sitting around a long table pounding and passing the cloth. The rhythm of the songs helped them make light of the work, which was both time-consuming and strenuous.[9]

Cha bhi mi buan, 's tu bhi bhuaim
Thug mi luaidh óg dhut
Cha bhi mi buan, 's tu bhi bhuaim

Chi mi 'm bàta dol seachad 'm muir a' sgapadh ma bòrdan
Mura deachaidh mi mearachd, bha mo leanan ga seòladh
Bha mo leanan ga stiùreadh, óigear ùr a' chùl bhòidheach
Òigear ùr a' chùl bhuidhe, O, b'aithne dhomh òg thu
'Se do bhòidheachean fada, 's ghaol, a Lachlainn, a leòn mi

O, nam faicinn thu tighinn, 's mi gu ruitheadh 'nad chòmhdhail
'S mi gu ruitheadh 'na do choinneamh, air mo bhonnan gun bhrògan
Ged tha reothadh glè chruaidh ann, 's sneachda fuar air a' mhòine.

I will not last long while you are away from me
I gave my young love to you.

I see the boat going by, the sea dispersing about her sides
If I'm not mistaken, it was my sweetheart who was sailing her
My sweetheart was sailing her, the fair young man of beautiful hair
The fair young man of beautiful hair, I have known you since I was young
It is your lasting vows and your love, Lachlann, that have afflicted me
If I saw you coming, I would run to meet you
I would run to meet you on the soles of my bare feet
Though there was a very hard frost and cold snow on the peat.

Tra Bo Dau

Another take on love is expressed in a Welsh folksong in which a young man has not yet gained the heart of his beloved, but still believes in the power of love.

Mae'r hon a gar fy nghalon i, Ymhell oddi yma 'n byw
A hiraeth am ei gweled hi, A'm gwna yn ddrwg fy lliw

Cyfoeth nid yw ond oferedd, Glendid nid yw yn parhau
Ond cariad pur sydd fel y dur, Yn para tra bo dau

O'r dewis hardd ddewisais i, Oidd dewis lodes lan
A chyn bydd hithau gennyf fi, A rhewi wnaiff y tan

She who my heart loves lives far from here
And it is longing for her that has made me pale

I choose in a choice of beauties a young woman of pureness
But before she will be mine, fire will freeze over

Wealth is but vanity, beauty is not everlasting
But love is as sure as steel when two are true.

Hymn to Bridget

In addition to songs about history, work and love, there were also songs that were sung at particular seasons, such as this traditional Irish hymn to Brighid.[10]

Gabhaim molta Bríde, Ionmhain í le hEirinn
Ionmhain le gach tír í, Molaimis go léir í.

Lóchran geal na Laighneach, A' soilsiu feadh na tíre
Ceann ar óghaibh Eireann, Ceann na mban ar míne.

Tíg an geimhreadh dian dubh, A' gearradh lena ghéire
Ach ar Lá 'le Bríde, Gar dúinn earrach Eireann.

I praise Brighid, Beloved is she in Ireland
Beloved is she in every country, Great praise to her.

Bright light of Leinster, shining through the land
Chief for purity in Ireland, Chief among women for gentleness.

The dark, swift winter comes, sharp with its keenness
But on Brighid's Day, the Irish spring is near us.

Eilean Fraoich

Songs of longing for one's land, community and traditions are common. In this Scottish Gaelic song, a woman expresses her longing and affection for the land of her youth, the Isle of Lewis.

Eilean Fraoich, Eilean Fraoich,
Eilean Fraoich nam beann àrd
Far an d'fhuair mi m'àrach òg,
Eilean Leòdhais mo ghràidh.

Far an robh mi 'n làithean m'òig
Ruigh gun bhròig dol don tràig
'S mi ri streap gu nead an eòin
Anns gach còs sam bi àl.

Thug mi greis de làithean m'òig
Air a' mhòintich 'nam phàisd
'S mi ri tional nan laogh òg
Is nam bò aig an tràth.

'S ged a bheirte dhomh an tír-s'
Eadar chraobhan is bhàrr
B'àill leam a bhith measg an fhraoich
Anns an tìr nam beann àrd.

Island of heather, Island of heather
Island of heather of the high mountains
Where I was raised when I was young
Island of Lewis, my love.

Where I spent the days of my youth
Running without shoes down to the shore
And climbing up to the bird's nest
In each hollow there was a brood.

I spent part of my younger days
On the moorland as a child
Gathering in the young calves
And the cows at feeding time.

And though I were given this land
Between the trees and the point
I would rather be amongst the heather
In the land of the high mountains.

Ailean Duinn

This exceedingly poignant and powerful song of grief was sung by a woman lamenting the death of her beloved. She is so angry with the men who killed her husband that she expresses her rage by drinking the blood of her dead husband.

Gura mise tha fo éislean
Moch 's a' mhadainn is mi'g éirigh
Ò hi shiùbhlainn leat,
Hi ri bhò hò ru bhi, Hi ri bhò hò rionn o ho,
Aileann duinn, ò hi shiùbhlainn leat.

Ma 's e cluasag dhut a' gheanneamh
Ma 's e leabaidh dhut an fheamainn

Ma 's e'n t-iasg do choinnlean geala
Ma 's e na ròin do luchd-faire

Dh'òlainn deoch ge boil le càch e
De dh'fhuil do choim 's tu 'n déidh do bhathadh

I am sitting alone under a shroud
Early in the morning I am rising
O dark Alan, death's journeys be with you.

If the wood is your pillow
If the seaweed is your bed

If the fish are your bright candles
If the seals are your watchmen

Drinking a draught through rage with each one
From the blood of your bosom, and you dead.

An Drouiz

In the nineteenth century, a collection of Breton songs was published known as the *Barzhaz Breizh* ("Bard-craft of Brittany").[11] This is a song from that collection which appears to consist of a dialogue between a teacher (possibly a druid, *an Drouiz*) and a child or student (*an Bugel*). It takes the form of a counting song or riddle, a few verses of which are given here.

An Drouiz: *Daig, mab gwenn Drouiz, ore, Petra 'ganin-me dit-te?*
An Bugel: *Kan din eus a ur rann, Ken e' oufen breman.*
An Drouiz: *Hep rann ar Ret hepken:*
Ankou, tad an Anken, Netra kent, netra ken.
An Bugel: *Kan din eus a dri ann, Ken e oufen breman.*
An Drouiz: *Tri rann er bed-man a vez, Tri derou ha tri diwezh,*
D'an den ha d'an derv ivez, Teir rouantelezh Varzhin.
An Bugel: *Kan din eus a eizh rann, Ken e oufen breman.*
An Drouiz: *Eizh avel o c'hwibanat, Eizh tan gant an Tadtad*
E miz Mae e menez kad, eizh onner wenn-kann-eon
O peurin en enez don, Eizh onner wenn d'an Itron.
An Bugel: *Ken din eus a nav rann, Ken e oufen breman.*
An Drouiz: *Nav dornig gwenn war daol 'lleur, E-kichen tour Lezarmeur*
Ha nav mamm o keinaft meur. E koroll, nav c'horrigan
Bleunvek o blev, gwisket gloan, Kelc'h ar feunteun, d'al loargann.

Druid: Well, holy son of a Druid, hey! What shall I sing for you?
Boy: Sing to me of one part, so that I may know now.
Druid: Without parts, only Necessity: Death, the father of Sorrow,
Nothing before, nothing after.
Boy: Sing to me of three parts, so that I may know now.
Druid: There are three parts of this world, Three beginnings and three ends,

To the man and to the oak tree as well, Three kingdoms of Merlin...
Boy: Sing to me of eight parts, so that I may know now.
Druid: Eight winds whistling, Eight fires with the Bonfire
In the month of May, on the mountains of battle, eight foam-bright white heifers
Grazing on the deep island, Eight white heifers for the Lady.
Boy: Sing to me of nine parts, so that I may know now.
Druid: Nine little white hands on the table of the area near the tower of Lezarmeur
And nine mothers wailing greatly. Nine korrigans [fairies] dancing,
Flowers in their hair, dressed in wool, around the fountain by the full moon.

Arrane Ny Sheeaghyn Troailtagh

The fairies and elements of the natural world are also featured in this Manx folksong, "The Song of the Traveling Fairies."

V'ad oie ayns y Glion dy Ballacomish
Jannoo yn lhondoo ayns shen e hedd
Chaddil oo lhianoo, hig sheeaghyn traoiltagh orrin
Bee dty host nish, ta mee g'eamagh er'n ushag.

V'ad oie ayns Glion Rushen dy reagh ny sleityn
Jannoo yn shirragh ayns shen e hedd

V'ad oie er ny creggyn Kione ny Spainagh
Jannoo y foillan ayns shen e hedd

Hig ad gys Gordon, agh ayns shen, cooie
Jannoo yn dreean veg y hedd.

One night in the glen, in the Glen of Ball'comish
The blackbird will come to build her own nest.
Sleep, little child, the fairies will come to us
Hush now, my baby, the bird I will call.

One night in Glen Rushen, high in the mountains
The falcon will come to build her own nest.

Sleep, little child, etc.

One night on the rocks of the Spanish headland
The seagull will come to build her own nest.

Sleep, little child, etc.

They'll come to Gordon, but there so conveniently
There will the little wren build her own nest.

Sleep, little child, the fairies will come to us
Hush now, my baby, the bird I will call.

Craobn nan Ubhal

This is a beautiful Scottish Gaelic prayer in song form, venerating the beauty of the apple tree and wishing it many blessings.

O Craobh nan Ubhal, O, Craobh nan ubhal,
Geug nan Abhall, O Chraobh nan ubhal, ho.

Aithnich fhein a' chraobh tha leamsa, o

Chraobh as mutha 's a mils' ubhlan, o
Chraobh nan ubhal, gu robh Dé leat, o
Gu robh n' aird an ear 's an iar leat, o
Gu robh gach gealach agus grian leat, o
Gu robh gach sion a thainig riamh leat, o.

O Apple Tree, Branch of the Apple Tree
Know that the tree is mine
The tallest tree with the sweetest apples
O Apple Tree, May God be with you
May the direction of East and West be with you
May every moon and sun be with you
May everything that comes before me be yours.

This chapter has provided just a brief glimpse into the extremely rich folksong tradition of the six Celtic countries — Ireland, Scotland and the Isle of Man (whose languages are related), and Wales, Brittany and Cornwall (whose related languages constitute another branch of the modern Celtic languages). In addition to the songs given above (which were selected to some extent for their imagery and lyrics pertaining to folk religion, nature and other topics pertinent to this book), there were also many songs associated with work, love, family life, the local landscape and community, and political and social realities. Many vocal songs were traditionally sung a capella, without any instrumental accompaniment. Aspects of these traditions are still current in many areas where Celtic languages are spoken, and sound archives and folksong recordings can provide important insights into the depths of this remarkable and vibrant tradition.

Appendix C.
Suggested Reading and Further Study

This book is intended to provide a reliable introduction and overview of many of the most important themes in Celtic religion, mythology and folklore. It also includes a great deal of rare and in-depth material pertaining to many aspects of these topics, much of which can be found only in academic source materials. These academic materials can be difficult for the general reader to access or interpret, a situation that does not help students or seekers, teachers or tradition bearers, or the tradition itself. Weaving together information from these many sources into one volume is a good first step in bringing the veracities of the tradition to light, helping to preserve, protect and transmit this knowledge for future generations of poets, teachers and tradition bearers.

Every aspect of religion, myth and folklore discussed in this book could benefit from additional study. Scholars have worked diligently over the last number of decades to collect, translate and interpret the source materials, and their work can provide students with a point of entry into deeper levels of knowledge and understanding concerning these complex and fascinating traditions. The following books are recommended to students who would like to further develop their understanding of Celtic mythology, religion and folklore, and are available through public libraries, used bookstores or on-line sources.

Celtic History, Culture and Art

The Celtic World— Barry Cunliffe
The Celtic Realms— Myles Dillon and Nora Chadwick
The Celtic World— Miranda Green, ed.
Ireland in Prehistory— Michael Herity and George Eogan
Roman Britain: A Sourcebook— Stanley Ireland
The Celts— Venceslas Kruta, ed.
The Picts and the Scots— Lloyd and Jenny Laing
Celtic Art— Ruth and Vincent Megaw
Warriors of the Word: The World of the Scottish Highlanders— Michael Newton
Newgrange— Michael O'Kelly
Cattle Lords and Clansmen— Nerys Patterson

The Celts—T. G. E. Powell
Celts and the Classical World—David Rankin
Scotland: Archaeology and Early History—Graham and Anna Ritchie
The Illustrated Archaeology of Ireland—Michael Ryan, ed.
Celtic Britain—Charles Thomas

Celtic Religion and Mythology

Ancient Irish Tales—Tom Cross and Clark Slover
The Mabinogion—Sioned Davies
The Mabinogi—Patrick K. Ford
Early Irish Myths and Sagas—Jeffrey Gantz
The Táin—Thomas Kinsella
Celtic Mythology—Proinsius Mac Cana
The Druids—Stuart Piggott
Celtic Heritage—Alwyn and Brinley Rees
Tales of the Elders of Ireland—Ann Dooley and Harry Roe
Pagan Celtic Britain—Anne Ross

Celtic Poetry and Literature

The Irish Literary Tradition—J. E. Caerwyn Williams and Patrick Ford
The Cycles of the Kings—Myles Dillon
Early Irish Literature—Myles Dillon
The Irish Tradition—Robin Flower
A Guide to Welsh Literature—A. O. H. Jarman and Gwilym Rees Hughes
The Celtic Heroic Age—John Koch and John Carey
The Mabinogi—Proinsias Mac Cana

The Arthurian Tradition

The Arthur of the Welsh—Rachel Bromwich, A. O. H. Jarman, and Brynley F. Roberts
Arthur in Medieval Welsh Literature—Oliver J. Padel
The Romance of Arthur—James Wilhelm

Celtic Folklore

The Gaelic Otherworld—Ronald Black
An Encyclopedia of Fairies—Katherine Briggs
The Year in Ireland—Kevin Danaher
The Fairy Faith in Celtic Countries—W. Y. Evans-Wentz (pages 23–225 only)

Visions and Belief in the West of Ireland— Lady Gregory
The Holy Wells of Ireland— Patrick Logan
The Silver Bough— F. Marion McNeill
Welsh Folk Customs— Trefor Owen
The Folklore of the Scottish Highlands— Anne Ross

Shamanism and World Indigenous Religions

Shamans of the World— Nancy Connor
The Myth of the Eternal Return— Mircea Eliade
Rites and Symbols of Initiation— Mircea Eliade
The Sacred and the Profane: The Nature of Religion— Mircea Eliade
Shamanism: Archaic Techniques of Ecstasy— Mircea Eliade
The Fruitful Darkness— Joan Halifax
Shamanic Voices— Joan Halifax
Dreamtime and Inner Space— Holger Kalweit
Shamans, Healers and Medicine Men— Holger Kalweit
A Joseph Campbell Companion— Diane K. Osbon, ed.

Students are encouraged to read through the bibliography to familiarize themselves with advanced sources that can provide possibilities for further study and exploration. It is also recommended that whenever possible, students devote some time to learning one of the modern Celtic languages in order to familiarize themselves with how those languages operate and how ideas and traditions are preserved within them.

Chapter Notes

Introduction

1. Jane Webster, "Sanctuaries and Sacred Places," in *The Celtic World* (London: Routledge, 1995), 449–452; Anne Ross, *Pagan Celtic Britain* (Chicago: Academy, 1996), 46–59; Barry Cunliffe, *The Oxford Illustrated History of Prehistoric Europe* (Oxford: Oxford University Press, 2001), 259; Timothy Darvill, *Prehistoric Britain* (London: Routledge, 1996), 122, 127.

2. Patrick Logan, *The Holy Wells of Ireland* (Gerrards Cross: Colin Smythe, 1992); Anne Ross, *The Folklore of the Scottish Highlands* (New York: Barnes and Noble, 1993), 16, 79–81; Anne Ross, *Folklore of Wales* (Stroud: Tempus, 2001), 78–86.

3. Tomás Ó Cathasaigh, *The Heroic Biography of Cormac mac Airt* (Dublin: Dublin Institute for Advanced Studies, 1977), 24–26.

4. Tom P. Cross and Clark H. Slover, *Ancient Irish Tales* (New York: Barnes and Noble, 1996), 503–507.

5. Ibid., 365.

6. Patrick K. Ford, *The Mabinogi and Other Medieval Welsh Tales* (Berkeley: University of California Press, 1977), 162–165.

7. A. J. Bruford and D. A. MacDonald, eds., *Scottish Traditional Tales* (Edinburgh: Polygon, 1994), 288–291.

8. Edward Gwynn, *Metrical Dindshenchas*, pt. IV (Dublin: Dublin Institute for Advanced Studies, 1991), 135.

9. Marged Haycock, *Legendary Poems from the Book of Taliesin* (Aberystwyth: CMCS, 2007), 113–114, 119.

10. Liam Breatnach, "The Cauldron of Poesy," *Ériu* XXXII (1981): 68–71; P. L. Henry, "The Caldron of Poesy," *Studia Celtica* 14–15 (1979–1980): 126.

Chapter 1

1. Barry Cunliffe, *The Ancient Celts* (Oxford: Oxford University Press, 1997), 28–67; Barry Cunliffe, *The Celtic World* (New York: McGraw-Hill, 1979), 16–19; Venceslas Kruta, ed., *The Celts* (New York: Rizzoli, 1997), see chapters spanning 206–422; T. G. E. Powell, *The Celts* (London: Thames and Hudson, 1980), 18–23.

2. Venceslas Kruta, "Celtic Religion," in *The Celts* (New York: Rizzoli, 1997), 533–541; Miranda Green, "The Gods and the Supernatural," in *The Celtic World* (London: Routledge, 1996), 465–488.

3. Kruta, *The Celts*, 533–541; Green, "The Gods and the Supernatural," 465–488; Powell, 150–157, 160, 168; Proinsias Mac Cana, *Celtic Mythology* (New York: Peter Bedrick, 1987), 22–53; Ross, *Pagan Celtic Britain*, 172–220; also see index under "*Lugh*," "*Lugos*," "*Ogma*," "*Ogmios*," "*Brigantia*."

4. Proinsias Mac Cana, "Celtic Goddesses of Sovereignty," in *Goddesses Who Rule* (Oxford: Oxford University Press, 2000), 85–99; Anne Ross, "The Divine Hag of the Pagan Celts," in *The Witch in History* (New York: Barnes and Noble, 1996), 139–164.

5. Mac Cana, "Celtic Goddesses," 85–99; Proinsias Mac Cana, "Aspects of the Theme of King and Goddess in Irish Literature," *Études Celtiques* VII (1995): 76–90; Maire Herbert, "Goddess and King: The Sacred Marriage in Early Ireland," *Cosmos* 7 (1992): 265–275; Jean Gricourt, "Epona-Rhiannon-Macha," *Ogam* VI (1954).

6. Stanley Ireland, *Roman Britain* (London: Routledge, 1992), 187, 182; David Rankin, *Celts and the Classical World* (London: Routledge, 1996), 278; J. E. Caerwyn Williams and Patrick K. Ford, *The Irish Literary Tradition* (Cardiff: University of Wales Press, 1992), 22–26, 42, 46–47; Eleanor Knott and Gerard Murphy, *Early Irish Literature* (New York: Barnes and Noble, 1966), 13, 21–22; A. O. H. Jarman and Gwilym Rees Hughes, *A Guide to Welsh Literature, Volume 1* (Cardiff: University of Wales Press, 1992), 17–18, 142.

7. Kuno Meyer, ed., *Tecosca Cormaic mac Airt* (Dublin: Todd Lecture Series 15, 1909); Fergus Kelly, ed., *Audacht Morainn* (Dublin: Dublin Institute for Advanced Studies, 1976); J. Pokorny, ed., "On the Briatharthecosc Conculaind," *Zeitschrift für Celtische Philologie* XV (1925).

8. Ross, *Pagan Celtic Britain,* 184, 194–196, 200; M. A. O'Brien, ed., *Corpus Genealogiarum Hiberniae* (Dublin: Dublin Institute for Advanced Studies, 1976); Thomas F. O'Rahilly, *Early Irish History and Mythology* (Dublin: Dublin Institute for Advanced Studies, 1984), 288–289, 466–467, 490–492, 519–521, 528.

9. Edward Gwynn, Pts. I–V.

10. Gerard Murphy, ed., *Early Irish Lyrics* (Oxford: Oxford University Press, 1956), 6.

11. Old Irish translation by author.

12. Miranda Green, *Animals in Celtic Life and Myth* (London: Routledge, 1992), 92–127, 128–161, 162–195, 196–238; Ruth Megaw and Vincent Megaw, *Celtic Art* (New York: Thames and Hudson, 1989), 27–35, 82–87, 143–145, 160–163, 174–180; Ross, *Pagan Celtic Britain,* 302–377, 378–446.

13. Ross, *Pagan Celtic Britain,* 59–66; Mac Cana, *Celtic Mythology,* 48–50; Michael Newton, *Warriors of the Word* (Edinburgh: Birlinn, 2009), 125–134, 237–242, 288–292, 350–353.

14. Green, *Animals in Celtic Life and Myth*, 1–5; Mac Cana, *Celtic Mythology,* 48; Powell, 161–175; Cunliffe, *The*

Celtic World, 88–95; Proinsias Mac Cana, "Placenames and Mythology in Irish Tradition: Places, Pilgrimages and Things," *Proceedings of the First North American Congress of Celtic Studies*, 1986, 319–341.

15. John Carey, "The Location of the Otherworld in Irish Tradition," *Éigse* XIX (1982), 36–43; Patrick Sims-Williams, "Some Celtic Otherworld Terms," in *Celtic Language, Celtic Culture* (Van Nuys: Ford and Bailie, 1990), 57–81; Kathryn Chadbourne, "The Celtic Otherworld," *Cosmos* 14, no. 2 (1988), 157–177.

16. John Carey, "The Name 'Tuatha Dé Danann,'" *Éigse* XVIII, 291–294; Ross, *Folklore of Wales*, 133–135; Sharon Paice MacLeod, "*Mater Deorum Hibernensium*: Identity and Cross-Correlation in Early Irish Mythology," *Proceedings of the Harvard Celtic Colloquium*, Vol. XIX, 1999, 340–384.

17. Murphy, *Early Irish Lyrics*, 92–111.

18. John Carey, "Time, Space and the Otherworld," *Proceedings of the Harvard Celtic Colloquium*, Vol. VII, 1987, 1–27.

19. Ireland, 182, 184–186.

20. Powell, 144–150.

21. Tomas Ó Cathasaigh, "The Semantics of *Síd*," *Éigse* XVIII, pt. II: 137–155.

22. Eóin MacNeill, "On the Notation and Chronography of the Calendar of Coligny," *Ériu* X (1926–1928): 1–67; Powell, 145.

23. Ireland, 183; Sharynne MacLeod NicMhacha, *Queen of the Night* (Boston: Weiser, 2005), 137–145.

24. Nerys Patterson, *Cattle Lords and Clansmen* (Notre Dame: University of Notre Dame Press, 1994), 119–129.

25. Ibid., 129–135.

26. Ibid., 135–140.

27. Ibid., 141–147.

28. Alwyn Rees and Brinley Rees, *Celtic Heritage* (New York: Thames and Hudson, 1961), 118–145.

29. Ibid., 146–172.

30. Ibid., 187.

31. Ross, *Pagan Celtic Britain,* 61–64.

32. Megaw and Megaw, 42–3, 52, 107, 142, 174–6, 218, 282–6; Ross, *Pagan Celtic Britain*; see index under "Cauldron"; John Carey, *Ireland and the Grail* (Aberystwyth: Celtic Studies Publications, 2007).

33. Darvill, 121–122, 128–130, 136; Ross, *Pagan Celtic Britain,* 70, 239, 241, 260.

34. Miranda Green, *Celtic Goddesses* (New York: George Braziller, 1996), 89–104; Ross, *Pagan Celtic Britain*, 274–275, 279–281, 293–296.

35. Sharon Paice MacLeod, "A Confluence of Wisdom: The Symbolism of Wells, Whirlpools, Waterfalls and Rivers in Early Celtic Sources," *Proceedings of the Harvard Celtic Colloquium*, Vol. XXVII, 2007, 337–355.

36. Ross, *Pagan Celtic Britain*, 94–171.

37. Ireland, 181–187; Rankin, 259–294.

38. Caerwyn Williams and Ford, 21–49, 85–98, 119–125, 155–179; J. E. Caerwyn Williams, "The Celtic Bard," *A Celtic Florigelium* (Lawrence: Celtic Studies Publications, 1996), 216–226; E. I. Rowlands, "Bardic Lore and Education," *Bulletin of the Board of Celtic Studies*, Vol. XXXII (1985): 143–155.

39. Fergus Kelly, *A Guide to Early Irish Law* (Dublin: Dublin Institute for Advanced Studies, 1998), 18, 191, 197, 240; Robin Chapman Stacey, *The Road to Judgment: From Custom to Court in Medieval Ireland and Wales* (Philadelphia: University of Pennsylvania Press, 1994), 199–221; Thomas Charles-Edwards, *The Early Medieval Gaelic Lawyer* (Cambridge: University of Cambridge Press, 1999), 23–27; Robin Chapman Stacey, *Dark Speech: The Performance of Law in Early Ireland* (Philadelphia: University of Pennsylvania Press, 2007), 82–85, 200–206; Meyer, *Tecosca Cormaic*; Fergus Kelly, *Audacht Morainn*.

40. Kuno Meyer, ed., *The Triads of Ireland* (Dublin: Todd Lecture Series 13, 1906), 1–35; Rachel Bromwich, *Trioedd Ynys Prydain* (Cardiff: University of Wales Press, 2007).

41. Meyer, *The Triads of Ireland*, 26–27.

42. Ireland, 187.

43. Ann Dooley and Harry Roe, *Tales of the Elders of Ireland: A new translation of Accalam na Senórach* (Oxford: Oxford University Press, 1999), 6.

Chapter 2

1. Timothy P. Bridgman, "Names and Naming Conventions Concerning Celtic Peoples in Some Early Ancient Greek Authors," *CSANA Yearbook* 7, 113–127; Ireland, 1–23; S. A. Handford, ed., *Caesar: The Conquest of Gaul* (London: Penguin, 1982), 28; Timothy P. Bridgman, "Keltoi, Galatai, Galli: Were They All One People?" *Proceedings of the Harvard Celtic Colloquium,* Vol. XXV, 2005, 155–162; Kim McCone, *The Celtic Question: Modern Constructs and Ancient Realities* (Dublin: Myles Dillon Memorial Lecture, 2008), 1–56.

2. Cunliffe, *The Celtic World*, 18–19; Powell, 18–24; John T. Koch, "New Thoughts on Albion, Ierne, and the Pretanic Isles (Part 1)," *Proceedings of the Harvard Celtic Colloquium*, Vol. VI, 1986, 1–28.

3. J. P. Mallory, *In Search of the Indo-Europeans* (London: Thames and Hudson, 1999), 94–142; Ireland, 28–32.

4. Mallory, *In Search of the Indo-Europeans*, 9–23; Calvert Watkins, *Dictionary of Indo-European Roots* (Boston: Houghton-Mifflin, 2000), 9, 70.

5. John T. Koch and John Carey, eds., *The Celtic Heroic Age* (Oakville: Celtic Studies Publications, 2000), 10–11.

6. Ireland, 23–24.

7. Ibid., 15–16.

8. Koch and Carey, 12–13

9. Ibid., 15–19.

10. Handford, 110–111.

11. Ireland, 19, 22; Cunliffe, *The Celtic World*, 46–47, 109, 127; Powell, 60, 66, 131.

12. Ireland, 21–23.

13. Mallory, *In Search of the Indo-Europeans*, 107–109, 122–127, 128–142; Myles Dillon, "The Archaism of the Irish Tradition," *Proceedings of the British Academy*, Vol. XXXIII, 1947, 1–21; Powell, 76–86, 184–186; Timothy Champion, "Power, Politics and Status," in *The Celtic World* (London: Routledge, 1995), 85–94; Glenys Lloyd-Morgan, "Appearance, Life and Leisure," in *The Celtic World* (London: Routledge, 1995), 95–120; Martin Bell, "People and Nature in the Celtic World," in *The Celtic World* (London: Routledge, 1995), 145–158; Mac Cana, "Theme of King and Goddess," 76–90. See also Patterson, *Cattle Lords and Clansmen*; Rankin, *Celts and the Classical World*; and Caerwyn Williams and Ford, *The Irish Literary Tradition*.

14. Ireland, 184.

15. Ibid., 185.

16. Ibid., 186.

17. Ibid.

18. Ibid., 190.

19. Ibid., 188.

20. Watkins, *Dictionary of Indo-European Roots*, 16–17, 96–96.

21. Handford, 139–143.

Chapter 3

1. Handford, 188–189.
2. Ireland, 188–189
3. Tess Darwin, *The Scots Herbal: The Plant Lore of Scotland* (Edinburgh: Mercat Press, 1996), 175–176; Niall Mac Coitir, *Irish Wild Plants: Myths, Legends and Folklore* (Wilton: Collins Press, 2008), 21–26.
4. Ireland, 189; Darwin, 56–57.
5. Ireland, 189.
6. Ibid., 181–190.
7. Fergus Kelly, *A Guide to Early Irish Law*, 60.
8. Rankin, 272, 274, 279, 292–293; Stuart Piggott, *The Druids* (New York: Thames and Hudson, 1975), 96–119. See also Elizabeth A. Gray, *Cath Maige Tuired* (Naas: Irish Texts Society, 1982), and Cross and Slover. A bronze figurine believed to represent a druid or Celtic priest was found at Neuvy-en-Sulias and dates to the second or third century C.E. A representation of this remarkable find from the Romano-Celtic period (as well as two other figurines representing a musician and a dancer) can be found in Cunliffe, *The Celtic World*, 26–27.
9. Old Irish translation by the author. See also Whitley Stokes, "Immacallam in Dá Thuarad," *Revue Celtique* 26 (1905): 8–53.
10. Rankin, 247–249, 251, 253, 258; Fergus Kelly, *A Guide to Early Irish Law*, 77; Koch and Carey, 40–46.
11. Rankin, 292; Koch and Carey, 34–35.
12. Koch and Carey, 34.
13. Edward Gwynn, pt. IV, 14–15; pt. III, 94–95; pt. II, 44–45.
14. Ireland, 58–59.
15. Phillip Freeman, *War, Women and Druids* (Austin: University of Texas Press, 2002), 36; A. L. F. Rivet and Colin Smith, *The Place-Names of Roman Britain* (London: Batsford, 1981), 42, 81; Ireland, 83. A bronze figurine believed to represent a priestess holding a *patera* (offering-plate) comes from a Romano-British context. A photograph may be found in Green, *Celtic Goddesses*, 144.
16. Koch and Carey, 19.
17. F. E. Romer, *Pomponius Mela's Description of the World* (Ann Arbor: University of Michigan Press, 1998), 115.
18. Koch and Carey, 3–4.
19. Translation from Gaulish by the author.
20. Rees and Rees, 193.
21. Gwyn Jones and Thomas Jones, *The Mabinogion* (London: John Dent, 1993), 164–165.
22. Haycock, *Legendary Poems*, 433–451.
23. Translation from Middle Welsh by the author.
24. Ireland, 181, 184–185.
25. Roisin McLaughlin, *Early Irish Satire* (Dublin: Dublin Institute for Advanced Studies, 2008).
26. Edward Gwynn, pt. IV, 134–135.
27. Old Irish translation by the author.
28. Edward Gwynn, pt. IV, 134–143.
29. Caerwyn Williams and Ford, 21–25.
30. George Calder, *Auraicept na n-Éces* (Dublin: Four Courts Press, 1995); Lambert McKenna, ed., *Bardic Syntactical Tracts* (Dublin: Dublin Institute for Advanced Studies, 1979).
31. Caerwyn Williams and Ford, 159–164, 191–203.
32. Ireland, 184–185.
33. Paice MacLeod, "*Mater Deorum Hibernensium*," 343–344, 369, 371, 376–377, 379 n86 and n88, 380.
34. Lewis Thorpe, trans., *Gerald of Wales: The Journey Through Wales and the Description of Wales* (London: Penguin, 1978), 246–247.
35. Patrick K. Ford, *The Celtic Poets* (Belmont: Ford and Bailie, 1999), xxvii.
36. Thomas Kinsella, trans., *The Tain* (Oxford: Oxford University Press, 1979), 60–63.
37. E. G. Quin, ed., *Dictionary of the Irish Language: Based Mainly on Old and Middle Irish Materials (DIL)* (Dublin: Royal Irish Academy, 1983), s.v. "*dán.*"
38. Paice MacLeod, "*Mater Deorum Hibernensium*," 364–369.
39. *DIL*, s.vv. "*érgna*," "*éolas*," "*éicse*," "*ecnae.*"
40. John Carey, "The Three Things Required of a Poet," *Ériu* XLVIII (1997), 41–58.
41. Whitley Stokes, ed., *Sanas Chormaic* (Calcutta: Irish Archaeological and Celtic Society, 1868), 94–95.
42. Sharon Paice MacLeod, *The Hazel of Immortality*, Lecture notes (unpublished) for GSAS Research Lecture, Harvard University, Department of Celtic Languages and Literatures, December 2000.
43. Carey, "The Three Things Required of a Poet," 41–58.
44. Ibid., 41–58.
45. Paice MacLeod, "A Confluence of Wisdom," 337–355.
46. Caerwyn Williams and Ford, 159–163.
47. Paice MacLeod, "A Confluence of Wisdom," 352–354.
48. Cross and Slover, 97.

Chapter 4

1. Lady Gregory, *Visions and Beliefs in the West of Ireland* (Gerard's Cross: Colin Smythe, 1902); W. B. Yeats, *Writings on Irish Folklore, Legend and Myth*, ed. Robert Welch (London: Penguin, 1993), 1–49.; Lizanne Henderson and Edward J. Cowan, *Scottish Fairy Belief* (London: Tuckwell Press, 2001).
2. John Ayto, *Dictionary of Word Origins* (New York: Little, Brown and Co., 1990), 217.
3. Katherine Briggs, *An Encyclopedia of Fairies* (New York: Pantheon, 1976), 131.
4. Watkins, *Dictionary of Indo-European Roots*, 7; Carl D. Buck, *A Dictionary of Selected Synonyms in the Principal Indo-European Languages* (Chicago: University of Chicago Press), 1, 497; Briggs, *Encyclopedia of Fairies*, 434.
5. *DIL*, s.vv. "*síabhra*," "*síd.*"
6. Ó Cathasaigh, "The Semantics of *Síd*," 137–155; Peter Harbison, *Pre-Christian Ireland* (London: Thames and Hudson, 1988), 56–84, 138, 155–172; Michael J. O'Kelly, *Newgrange: Archaeology, Art and Legend* (London: Thames and Hudson, 1982), 25, 35, 43–8, 116, 123, 127; Ross, *Pagan Celtic Britain*, 65, 85, 299 n.62, 325, 328, 401, 413.
7. Sims-Williams, "Some Celtic Otherworld Terms," 57–81; Chadbourne, "The Celtic Otherworld," 157–177.
8. Paice MacLeod, "*Mater Deorum Hibernensium*," 340–384; Carey, "Tuatha Dé Danann," 291–294.
9. Cross and Slover, 83; and many other references describing the *Áes Síde* throughout the other tales.
10. Kuno Meyer, *Selections from Ancient Irish Poetry* (London, 1911), 19.
11. Ross, *Pagan Celtic Britain*; see references to *Taranis*, wheels, and *Loucetius*; Green, *Celtic Goddesses*, 59–60, 102–104, 125, 134–135, 169–170, 178; On *Arianrhod* see NicMhacha, *Queen of the Night*, 167–192.
12. Vernum Hull, "De Gabáil in t-Sída," in *Zeitschrift fur Celtische Philologie* XIX (1933): 53–58; Sims-Williams, "Some Celtic Otherworld Terms," 57–81.
13. Carey, "Location of the Otherworld," 36–43; Liam Mac Mathúna, "Irish Perceptions of the Cosmos," *Celtica* XXIII (1999): 174–186; Mircea Eliade, *Shamanism: Archaic*

Techniques of Ecstasy (Princeton: Princeton University Press, 1974), 184–189, 259–273.

14. John Carey, "Time, Space and the Otherworld," *Proceedings of the Harvard Celtic Colloquium* VII, 1987, 1–27; Séamus Mac Mathúna, *Immram Brain: Bran's Journey to the Land of the Women* (Tubingen: Niemeyer, 1985), 32–59.

15. Myles Dillon, ed., *Serglige Con Culainn* (Dublin: Dublin Institute for Advanced Studies, 1975), 16–19.

16. Old Irish translation by the author.

17. Séamus Mac Mathúna, 33–38.

18. Old Irish translation by the author.

19. Cross and Slover, 503–507.

20. Murphy, *Early Irish Lyrics*, 104–107.

21. Old Irish translation by the author.

22. Gregory; Henderson and Cowan; W. Y. Evans-Wentz, *The Fairy Faith in Celtic Countries* (New York: Citadel, 1990): only pages 23–225 should be considered reliable information. The rest of the work contains outdated perceptions and theories.

23. Niall Ó Dónaill, *Foclóir Gaeilge-Béarla* (Athchló: An Gúm, 1992), *síogaí, duine*; Edward Dwelly, *Faclair Gaidhlig gu Bearla* (Glasgow: Gairm, 1994), *sìth, sìtheach*; Ross, *Folklore of Wales*, 133–135; Robin Gwyndaf, "Fairylore: Memorates and Legends from Welsh Oral Tradition," in *The Good People: New Fairylore Essays* (Lexington: University of Kentucky Press, 1997), 155–196.

24. *DIL*, s.vv. 1 "*síd/síth*," and 2 "*síd/síth*"; Ó Cathasaigh, "The Semantics of *Síd*."

25. Ford, *The Mabinogi*, 37–38.

26. Cross and Slover, 503.

Chapter 5

1. Cunliffe, *The Celtic World*, 68–81; Powell, 150–165; Ross, *Pagan Celtic Britain*, passim.

2. Ireland, 185.

3. Rankin, 283–285.

4. Rivet and Smith, 45, 450–451, 493, 278–280, 470.

5. Green, *Celtic Goddesses*, 91–93.

6. Rivet and Smith, 336–337, 329.

7. W. F. H. Nicolaisen, *The Picts and Their Place-Names* (Rosemarkie: Groam House Museum Trust, 1996), 3–36.

8. Green, *Celtic Goddesses*, 93–99.

9. Ibid., 98, 133; Ross, *Pagan Celtic Britain*, 57, 62, 126, 207, 228–229, 237, 246, 257, 271, 421.

10. Ross, *Pagan Celtic Britain*, 62, 280.

11. Green, *Celtic Goddesses*, 99–102, 105.

12. Ross, *Pagan Celtic Britain*, 80, 99, 132, 181, 252, 260, 344, 347, 349, 421, 476, 481.

13. Ross, *Pagan Celtic Britain*, 64, 75–78, 203–208, 222–226, 229, 236, 240, 249–252, 257, 418, 463–467, 471–472, 481–483.

14. Green, *Celtic Goddesses*, 32, 165–167; Ross, *Pagan Celtic Britain*, 433–435, 471, 481.

15. Green, *Celtic Goddesses*, 3, 33, 161–163, 165–167; Ross, *Pagan Celtic Britain*, 203, 211, 213, 368, 468–471, 481.

16. Ross, *Pagan Celtic Britain*, 48, 50, 57, 230–233, 246, 249, 254, 258, 269, 277, 423–427, 437, 440, 458; John Carey, "Nodons in Britain and Ireland," *Zeitschrift fur Celtische Philologie* 40 (1984): 1–22.

17. Ross, *Pagan Celtic Britain*, 224–225, 230–232, 257–258, 421; Carey, "Nodons in Britain and Ireland," 1–22.

18. Green, *Celtic Goddesses*, 102–104, 125, 134–135, 169–170, 178.

19. Ibid., 103–104, 134–136, 170, 182.

20. Rankin, 263; Green, *Celtic Goddesses*, 104, 135.

21. Green, *Celtic Goddesses*, 103–104, 105–116, 134–136; Ross, *Pagan Celtic Britain*, 242–243, 249, 279, 294, 382, 421, 428, 470, 476–477, 479–481.

22. Ross, *Pagan Celtic Britain*, 46–47, 270, 277, 290, 293; Daphne Brooke, *Saints and Goddesses: The Interface with Celtic Paganism* (Mansefield: Whithorn Trust, 1999).

23. Ross, *Pagan Celtic Britain*, 76, 80, 224–226, 229, 237, 257, 405, 413.

24. Ibid., 77–78, 203, 213, 224, 227–228, 235–237, 251, 253, 257–258, 463, 466–467, 472–473, 476.

25. Green, *Celtic Goddesses*, 31–34; Rankin, 222, 269.

26. Ross, *Pagan Celtic Britain*, 47, 251–253, 277–280, 289–291, 295, 447, 452–456, 461, 470.

27. Ibid., 69, 175, 277–278, 351, 362–363, 380, 385.

28. Ibid., 174–177, 181–182.

29. Ibid., 180–182.

30. Ibid., 194–195.

31. J. P. Mallory "The Career of Conall Cernach," *Emania* 6 (1989): 22–28; Ross, *Pagan Celtic Britain*, 195–199 201, 431, 433, 440 n.3.

32. Ross, *Pagan Celtic Britain*, 190, 192; Green, *Celtic Goddesses*, 167–168.

33. Green, *Celtic Goddesses*, 125–128, 130, 134, 182.

34. Ibid., 125, 128–131, 172; Ross, *Pagan Celtic Britain*, 47, 213–214, 221, 224–225, 233, 237, 257, 273–274, 279–282, 284, 295, 313–317, 389, 422–423.

35. Ross, *Pagan Celtic Britain*, 83, 472; Powell, 148, 168; Jacques Gourvest, "Le Culte de Belenos," *Ogam* VI (1954): 257–262; Watkins, *Dictionary of Indo-European Roots*, 9, "*bhel*-1".

36. Ross, *Pagan Celtic Britain*, 106, 114, 117, 193, 270, 276–278, 290, 293, 350, 370 n7, 453, 458, 463–466, 471, 477–478.

37. Koch and Carey, 1–3.

38. Joseph F. Eska, "Remarks on Linguistic Structures in a Gaulish Ritual Text," in "Indo-European Perspectives," R. V. South. ed., *Journal of Indo-European Studies* Monograph 43 (2002): 33–59.

39. Gaulish transliteration by the author. I am indebted to the work of Joseph Eska regarding the possible interpretation of the socio-religious setting of this inscription. However, I take full responsibility for the suggested translation presented here.

40. Ross, *Pagan Celtic Britain*, 80, 319–325, 346, 349, 367, 457, 462.

41. Ross, *Pagan Celtic Britain*, 131, 189, 255, 267–269, 281–290, 293, 296, 300 n79, 313, 316, 337–338, 340, 344, 405–407, 410, 415–416, 419, 423, 439, 449, 457; Green, *Celtic Goddesses*, 36, 48, 50–51, 112, 166, 172, 184–187.

Chapter 6

1. Carey, "Tuatha Dé Danann," 291–294; John Carey, "A *Tuath Dé* Miscellany," *Bulletin of the Board of Celtic Studies* 39 (1992): 24–45.

2. The members of the *Tuatha Dé Danann* are referenced in a number of early Irish sources. They are prominent in the following books, to which readers may refer for additional information: Gray, *Cath Maige Tuired*; Edward Gwynn, *The Metrical Dindshenchas*; Cross and Slover, *Ancient Irish Tales*; R. A. S. MacAlister, *Lebor Gabala Érenn*, Vol. IV (London: Irish Texts Society, 1997); Dooley and Roe, *Accalam na Senórach*; Koch and Carey, *The Celtic Heroic Age*.

3. Ross, *Pagan Celtic Britain*, 48, 65, 213–214, 221, 224, 233, 237, 257, 284, 289, 305, 313–314, 317, 399; Gray, 121; Hull, 53–58.

4. Gray, 70–71.

5. Old Irish translation by the author.

6. Edward Gwynn, pt. II, 10–25; Gray, 44–45; Ross, *Pagan Celtic Britain*, 54–55, 289, 305, 399, 454.

7. Ross, *Pagan Celtic Britain*, 48, 131, 199, 265–293, 313–314, 317, 389, 431; Gray, 44–47, 52–53, 64–65, 70–73, 129–130.

8. Gray, 70–71.

9. Old Irish translation by the author.

10. Paice MacLeod, "*Mater Deorum Hibernensium*," 340–384; Mac Cana, "Celtic Goddesses," 85–99; Ross, "The Divine Hag," 139–164.

11. Ross, *Pagan Celtic Britain*, 131, 267, 281–290, 293, 313, 316, 406–407, 416, 439, 449; John Carey, "Notes on the Irish War-Goddess," *Éigse* XIV, pt. II (1983): 263–275; Gricourt, 25–40.

12. Edward Gwynn, 124–131; 308–311; Carey, "Irish War-Goddess," 263–275; Gray, 128.

13. Edward Gwynn, pt. IV, 128–129.

14. Old Irish translation by the author.

15. Edward Gwynn, pt. IV, 308–311; Carey, "Irish War-Goddess," 263–275.

16. Ross, *Pagan Celtic Britain*, 31, 200, 289, 319–325, 346, 367, 410, 425, 427; Gray, 38–43, 126–127; Kevin Murray, ed., *Baile in Scáil* (London: Irish Texts Society, 2004), Vol. 58, 33–71; Watkins, *Dictionary of Indo-European Roots*, 49, "*leuk-*"; Ford, *The Mabinogi*, 100–101.

17. Fergus Kelly, *A Guide to Early Irish Law*, 43–44, 137–138; McLaughlin, 36.

18. Gray, 58–59.

19. Old Irish translation by the author.

20. Stokes, *Sanas Chormaic*, 23.

21. Ross, *Pagan Celtic Britain*, 267, 279, 289, 295, 399, 454–455; Gray, 119.

22. Donncha Ó hAodha, ed., *Bethu Brigte* (Dublin: Dublin Institute for Advanced Studies, 1978); Seamas Ó Catháin, "Hearth-Prayers and other Traditions of Brigit: Celtic Goddess and Holy Woman," *JRSAI* 22 (1982): 12–34.

23. Ross, *Pagan Celtic Britain*, 477–478; Gray, 131; Damian McManus, *A Guide to Ogam* (Maynooth: An Sagart, 1997), 19–20, 138–140, 150–152.

24. Ross, *Pagan Celtic Britain*, 47, 279–291, 295, 389; Edward Gwynn, pt. III, 26–39.

25. Edward Gwynn, pt. III, 28–31.

26. Old Irish translation by the author.

27. Edward Gwynn, pt. III, 26–39, pt. II, 10–25; Ross, *Pagan Celtic Britain*, 65, 270, 276–290, 293, 350, 400, 453, 465; Cross and Slover, 82–92, 370–421; Gray, 127–128.

28. Ross, *Pagan Celtic Britain*, 131, 213–214, 257, 267–268, 273, 279, 281, 285, 289, 290, 293.

29. Koch and Carey, 264–266.

30. Koch and Carey, 258; Mac Cana, *Celtic Mythology*, 62–63; Caerwyn Williams and Ford, 217–218.

31. Gray, 44–45, 50–53, 120, 125–126; Ross, *Pagan Celtic Britain*, 252, 476.

32. Gray, 24–25, 32–33, 40–41, 50–51, 56–57, 122–123; Ross, *Pagan Celtic Britain*, 199, 431.

33. Megaw and Megaw, 174–177; Cunliffe, *The Celtic World*, 109; Ross, *Pagan Celtic Britain*, 50, 181; Ralph M. Rowlett, "North Gaulish Forms on the Gundestrup Cauldron," *Proceedings of the Harvard Celtic Colloquium*, Vol. XIII, 1993, 166–177.

34. Ford, *The Mabinogi*, 63.

35. Gray, 24–25, 32–33, 38–43, 130–131; Ross, *Pagan Celtic Britain*, 224–224, 230–232, 257–258, 421.

36. Ross, *Pagan Celtic Britain*, 160, 288, 308–309, 325, 332, 337, 352, 356, 361–365, 407, 414.

37. Edward Gwynn, pt. III, 286–297.

38. Ibid., 292–295.

39. Old Irish translation by the author.

40. Ross, *Pagan Celtic Britain*, 66, 277, 286, 295, 303, 389, 410, 420.

41. Ibid., 357–358, 364–365, 389, 309–310, 401–402, 412, 415–416; Cross and Slover, 588–595.

42. The information presented below was taken from Dooley and Roe, *Accalam na Senórach*, 3–223. Other references to these individuals appear in Edward Gwynn, *The Metrical Dindshenchas*; Gray, *Cath Maige Tuired*; MacAlister, *Lebor Gabala Érenn*; Cross and Slover, *Ancient Irish Tales*; Stokes, *Sanas Chormaic*; Sharon Arbuthnot, ed., *Cóir Anmann*, Part 1 (Dublin: Irish Texts Society, 2005), 1–153; and isolated references in other early Irish sources. Additional information may be found in Ross, *Pagan Celtic Britain*, as well as in a number of Middle Irish tales associated with *Finn mac Cumhall*, such as Gerard Murphy, ed., *Duanaire Finn* (Dublin: Irish Texts Society, 1953).

43. Kate Miller-Lisowski, "Donn Firinne, *Tech Duin, An Tarbh*," *Études Celtiques* (1953–1954): 21–29. See also "Contributions to a Study in Irish Folklore: Traditions about Donn," *Béaloideas* 18 (1945) by the same scholar, 142–199.

44. Gearóid Ó Crualaoich, "Continuity and Adaptation in Legends of the Cailleach Bhéarra," *Béaloideas* 56 (1988): 153–178; Gearóid Ó Crualaoich, "Non-Sovereignty Queen Aspects of the Otherworld Female in Irish Hag Legends: The Case of Cailleach Bhéarra," *Béaloideas* 62–63 (1994–1995): 147–162; Gearóid Ó Crualaoich, *The Book of the Cailleach* (Cork: Cork University Press, 2003), *passim.*

Chapter 7

1. Patterson, 118–121.

2. Ibid., 119–120.

3. Ibid., 135–140.

4. Ibid., 141–146.

5. Ibid., 121–129.

6. Mircea Eliade, *The Myth of the Eternal Return* (Princeton: Princeton University Press, 1971), 51–79.

7. Patterson, 129–135.

8. Kevin Danaher, *The Year in Ireland* (Cork: Mercier Press, 1972), 86–127; F. Marian McNeill, *The Silver Bough*, Vol. 2 (Glasgow: Maclellan, 1959), 55–74.

9. Danaher, 167–177; McNeill, Vol. 2, 94–101. See also Máire MacNeill, *The Festival of Lughnasa* (Dublin: University College Dublin, 2008).

10. Danaher, 200–227; F. McNeill, *The Silver Bough*, Vol. 3, 11–42; Trefor M. Owen, *Welsh Folk Customs* (Llandysul: Gomer Press, 1987), 121–141.

11. Eliade, *The Myth of the Eternal Return*, 57, 62–63, 78, 81, 86–88.

12. These concepts are discussed at length in *The Myth of the Eternal Return*, *The Sacred and the Profane*, and *Rites and Symbols of Initiation* by Mircea Eliade. See also NicMhacha, *Queen of the Night*, 15–16, 23–25.

13. Danaher, 13–37; McNeill, Vol. 2, 19–34; Ó Catháin, 12–34.

14. P. S. Dinneen, ed., *The History of Ireland: Forus Feasa ar Eirenn, by Geoffrey Keating*, Vols. II–IV (London: 1908–1914).

15. Dinneen, Vol. II, 246; Patterson, 139.

16. Jeffrey Gantz, *Early Irish Myths and Sagas* (London and New York: Penguin, 1981), 39.

17. Gray, 67–69, 119, 126–127, 133–134. When Lug asks Bres how the people of Ireland should plow, sow,

and reap their crops, Bres tells him that each activity should take place on *mairt*, a word that has been usually translated "on Tuesday." While the Old Irish word *mart* could be used to indicate "Tuesday" (or by connection with the god Mars, the month of March), in Scottish Gaelic (*màrt*) it also means "a suitable time for agricultural work" (deriving from the concept that March was the suitable time for sowing seed).

18. Edward Gwynn, pt. IV, 146–163; Máire MacNeill, 311–338.

19. Edward Gwynn, pt. III, 40–47, 48–53.

20. Ibid., 1–25; Máire MacNeill, 339–344.

21. Edward Gwynn, 124–131, 308–311.

22. Máire MacNeill, 348–349.

23. Ibid., 143, 254, 305, 319, 326–9, 338, 341, 344–345, 619, 624.

24. Ibid., 243–248, 251–252, 258–259, 262, 337, 426–427, 626.

25. Edward Gwynn, pt. IV, 126–127.

26. Patterson, 144.

27. Ibid., 121–123.

28. Gray, 44–45, 50–57.

29. Gray, 64–65.

30. Edward Gwynn, pt. IV, 186–191; Kathryn Chadbourne, "Giant Women and Flying Machines," *Proceedings of the Harvard Celtic Colloquium*, Vol. XIV, 1994, 106–114.

31. Standish H. O'Grady, ed. and trans., *Silva Gadelica* (New York: Lemma, 1970), Vol. 2, 368–375.

32. Paice MacLeod, "*Mater Deorum Hibernensium*," 377, 380 n90.

Chapter 8

1. Eliade, *Shamanism*, 3–145.

2. Liam Mac Mathúna, "Irish Perceptions of the Cosmos," 174–187; Liam Mac Mathúna, "The Christianization of the Early Irish Cosmos?" 532–547; John Carey, "The Irish Otherworld: Hiberno-Latin Perspectives," *Éigse* XXV (1991): 154–159.

3. Ross, *Pagan Celtic Britain*, 228–233, 246, 249, 252, 260; Green, *Celtic Goddesses*, 102–104, 135.

4. Rankin, 169.

5. Ibid., 59.

6. Koch and Carey, 1–4.

7. Cross and Slover, 188–190, 503–507, 588–595.

8. Powell, 171–175; Barry Raftery, *Pagan Celtic Ireland* (London: Thames and Hudson, 1994), 64–83.

9. Powell, 162–165; Raftery, 180–182.

10. *DIL*, s.v. "*bile*"; Ross, *Pagan Celtic Britain*, 59–66, 85, 144–145, 461, 467; Powell, 164–166; Rankin, 281.

11. Rankin, 280–281; Powell, 166–170.

12. Rankin, 281.

13. Michael Newton, *Handbook of the Scottish Gaelic World* (Dublin: Four Courts Press, 2000), 211.

14. Ireland, 181.

15. Rees and Rees, 159.

16. Ross, *Pagan Celtic Britain*, 421.

17. Hilda Ellis Davidson, *Gods and Myths of Northern Europe* (London: Penguin, 1990), 26–27.

18. Ireland, 185.

19. Ibid., 182, 185.

20. Ibid., 185.

21. Ibid., 184.

22. Ibid., 181–190.

23. Ibid., 187; Rankin, 278; Caerwyn Williams and Ford, 34, 46–48.

24. Ireland, 182, 188.

25. Powell, 162–163; Ross, *Pagan Celtic Britain*, 61,

96, 349; Megaw and Megaw, 74–75; Stephen Allen, *Lords of Battle* (Oxford: Osprey, 2007), 20; Mac Coitir, 21–27.

26. Ireland, 183.

27. Ross, *Pagan Celtic Britain*, 59–66, 85, 144–145, 302–446, 461, 467; Green, *Animals in Celtic Life*, 162–195, 196–238; Caerwyn Williams and Ford, 65–66; Alden Watson, "The King, the Poet and the Sacred Tree," *Études Celtiques* XVIII (1981): 165–180. See also Mac Coitir and McManus.

28. Calder; Edward Gwynn.

29. Carey, "The Location of the Otherworld," 36–43; Chadbourne, "The Celtic Otherworld," 157–177.

30. Eliade, *Shamanism*, 185–186, 189. Note the occurrence in Altaic shamanism of "white shamans" (who undertake soul journeys to the sky realm or Upper World), and "black shamans" (those who travel exclusively to the lower world realms). The two types of shamans wear white or black colored costumes, according to their role. This potentially brings to mind the white colored garb of the Gaulish druids (as described in the ritual gathering of mistletoe) and the women dressed in black who either were (or accompanied) British druids during the attack in Anglesey. It is interesting to note that in the Altaic context, female shamans always undertake the lower world journey.

31. For examples of these themes in Celtic fairy lore, see Gregory, *Visions and Beliefs in the West of Ireland*; Henderson and Cowan; and Evans-Wentz, 17–225 only. For examples in various shamanic contexts, see Eliade, *Shamanism*, 76–79, 133, 168, 189, 361, 381, 421.

32. Ireland, 181–186.

33. Koch and Carey, 22.

34. Ireland, 184.

35. Ibid., 185.

36. Rankin, 290.

37. Ireland, 185–186.

38. Rankin, 290.

39. Ibid., 233, 243.

40. Ireland, 181–182, 186.

41. Ibid., 181–190. See also Piggott, 25–90, on the druids in Classical and vernacular texts.

42. Rankin, 288–291.

43. Ibid., 291.

44. Ibid., 270, 274, 280, 283; Caerwyn Williams and Ford, 21–49; Fergus Kelly, *A Guide to Early Irish Law*, 59–61; Caerwyn Williams, "The Celtic Bard," 216–226; William Gillies, "The Classical Irish Poetic Tradition," *Proceedings of the Seventh International Congress of Celtic Studies*, Oxford, July 1983, 108–120.

45. Rankin, 270; Caerwyn Williams and Ford, 27, 42, 66, 95.

46. Fergus Kelly, *A Guide to Early Irish Law*, 59–61; Caerwyn Williams and Ford, 21–29, 42; J. E. Caerwyn Williams, "The Court Poet in Medieval Ireland," (Lecture, British Academy, 1972), 1–51.

47. Caerwyn Williams and Ford, 21–49; Caerwyn Williams, "The Court Poet," 1–51; Gillies, 108–120; Caerwyn Williams, "The Celtic Bard," 216–226.

48. Caerwyn Williams and Ford, 26–27, 66.

49. Ibid., 27, 34, 42, 66, 95.

50. For good examples, refer to *Ancient Irish Tales* (Cross and Slover); *The Metrical Dindshenchas* (Edward Gwynn); "*Lebor Gabála Érenn*," in *The Celtic Heroic Age* (Koch and Carey).

51. Caerwyn Williams and Ford, 158–162; Rowlands, 143–155.

52. Calvert Watkins, "Indo-European Metrics and Archaic Irish Verse," *Celtica* 6 (1963): 215–217; Caerwyn Williams, "The Court Poet," 22–23; Ford, *The Celtic*

Poet, xxvii; E. J. Gwynn, "An Old-Irish Tract on the Privileges and Responsibilities of Poets," *Ériu* 13, pt. 1 (1940): 37–40

53. Several examples may be found in Séan Ó Duinn, *Forbhais Droma Dámhgháire* (Dublin: Mercier Press, 1992): 29, 31, 37, 75, 79, 91, 101.

54. Caerwyn Williams and Ford, 162–163.

Chapter 9

1. Eliade, *Shamanism*, 145–158.
2. Stokes, *Sanas Chormaic*, 160.
3. Ó Duinn, 103.
4. Ibid., 53, 59, 63, 73, 77, 79. Here we might also mention a stone carving from northern Scotland which features two bird-headed figures — or humans wearing bird head masks (Ross, *Pagan Celtic Britain*, 316).
5. Ford, *The Mabinogi*, 162–164.
6. Ibid., 164–181.
7. Haycock, *Legendary Poems*, 167–239.
8. Middle Welsh translation by the author.
9. Ross, *Pagan Celtic Britain*, 348, 440; R. I. Best, "The Settling of the Manor of Tara," *Ériu* IV (1910): 159, 127, 133.
10. Ross, *Pagan Celtic Britain*, 55–56, 79–80, 83, 87, 191, 438; Rees and Rees, 17, 42, 221, 236, 272, 305, 310, 337.
11. Koch and Carey, 35; Ireland, 188–190.
12. John Carey, *A New Introduction to Lebor Gabála Érenn* (London: Irish Texts Society, 1993), 1–21; R. Mark Scowcroft, "*Leabhar Gabhála* — Part I: The Growth of the Text," *Ériu* 38 (1987), 81–140; R. Mark Scowcroft, "*Leabhar Gabhála* — Part II: The Growth of the Text," *Ériu* 39 (1988), 1–66.
13. Koch and Carey, 264–271.
14. Old Irish translation by the author.
15. Eliade, *Shamanism*, 88–95.
16. Ireland, 182, 183, 185, 186, 187; Rankin, 260–262, 265–269.
17. Ó Duinn, 45, 73, 85, 87, 99, 105, 109; Rankin, 276.
18. Gray, 121.
19. Green, *Animals in Celtic Life*, 162–195, 196–238; Ross, *Pagan Celtic Britain*, 38, 59–66, 85, 144–145, 302–377, 378–446, 461, 467.
20. Rankin, 260–262, 265, 267–268, 272, 276–278, 281; Green, *Animals in Celtic Life*, 196–238.
21. Cross and Slover, 97; Caerwyn Williams and Ford, 30.
22. Green, *Animals in Celtic Life*, 162–195.
23. Rankin, 265, 270, 276, 278, 283; Ireland, 183, 186–187; Caerwyn Williams and Ford, 20–28. On the importance of honoring elders, ancestors, and ancestral wisdom, see Meyer, *Tecosca Cormaic*; Fergus Kelly, *Audacht Morainn*; Myles Dillon, "Wasting Sickness of Cú Chulainn," *Scottish Gaelic Studies* 7, 57–58.
24. Ireland, 183; Rankin, 265–266.
25. Refer to chapter 15 for references on this subject.
26. Koch and Carey, 10.
27. Gantz, 39–59.
28. Ford, *The Mabinogi*, 105–109.
29. Cross and Slover, 176–198.
30. *DIL*, s.v. "*geilt*."
31. Joseph Falaky Nagy, "The Wisdom of the Geilt," *Éigse* XIX (1982): 44–60; John Carey, "Suibne Geilt and Tuán mac Cairill," 93–105; Nora Chadwick, "Geilt," *Scottish Gaelic Studies* V, pt. 1 (1942): 106–153.
32. Murphy, *Early Irish Lyrics*, 122–127.
33. Old Irish translation by the author.

34. Murphy, *Early Irish Lyrics*, 115, 117, 127–129, 131, 133, 135, 139, 141.
35. Ibid., 121, 131, 137, 139, 141.
36. A. O. H. Jarman, "The Welsh Myrddin Poems," in *Arthurian Literature in the Middle Ages* (Oxford: Oxford University Press, 2001), 20–30. See also Basil Clarke, *Life of Merlin: Vita Merlini by Geoffrey of Monmouth* (Cardiff, University of Wales Press, 1973), 22–23, and Nora Chadwick, "Geilt."
37. Brian Ó Cuív, "The Romance of Mis and Dubh Ruis," *Celtica* 2, pt. 2 (1954): 325–333; Angela Partridge, "Wild Men and Wailing Women," *Éigse* XVIII, pt. 1, 25–37.
38. For a more in-depth discussion of *geilt* figures and traditions, including comparisons with shamanic cultures, see Pádraig Ó Riain, "A Study of the Irish Legend of the Wild Man," *Éigse* XIV (1972): 179–206; Nagy, "The Wisdom of the Geilt"; Susan Shaw Sailer, "Leaps, Curses and Flight: Suibne Geilt and The Roots of Early Irish Culture," *Études Celtiques* XXIII (1997): 191–208, Carey, "Suibne Geilt"; and Daniel F. Melia, "Law and the Shaman Saint," in *Celtic Folklore and Christianity*, 120–121.

Chapter 10

1. Carey, "The Three Things Required of a Poet," 41–58; Joseph Falaky Nagy, "Liminality and Knowledge in Irish Tradition," *Studia Celtica* XVI–XVII (1981–1982): 135–143.
2. Stokes, *Sanas Chormaic*, 94–95. See also Nora Chadwick, "Imbas Forosnai," *Scottish Gaelic Studies* IV, pt. II (1935): 97–135.
3. Nora Chadwick, "Geilt," 118–119.
4. *DIL*, s.vv. "*echtra*," "*immrama*." Some interesting points are made in David M. Dumville, "*Echtrae* and *Immram*: Some Problems of Definition," *Ériu* XXVII (1976), 73–93.
5. Ireland, 188–189.
6. Fergus Kelly, *A Guide to Early Irish Law*, 182–183.
7. Otta F. Swire, *Skye: The Island and Its Legends* (London: Blackie and Sons, 1961), 134–137; Newton, *Warriors of the Word*, 254–272; Barbara Hillers, "Music from the Otherworld: Modern Gaelic Legends about Fairy Music," *Proceedings of the Harvard Celtic Colloquium*, Vol. XIV, 1994, 58–75.
8. *DIL*, s.v. "*geis*"; Fergus Kelly, *A Guide to Early Irish Law*, 20–21.
9. Green, *Animals in Celtic Life*, 186.
10. Ibid., 23–24, 87–88, 178.
11. Paice MacLeod, *The Hazel of Immortality*.
12. Cunliffe, *The Celtic World*, 100–101; Megaw and Megaw, 173.
13. Ross, *Pagan Celtic Britain*, 181–182, 184–185, 195; Cunliffe, *The Celtic World*, 73, 76; Megaw and Megaw, 156, 169, 175.
14. Ross, *Pagan Celtic Britain*, 75, 179, 181, 316, 391, 418.
15. Fergus Kelly, *A Guide to Early Irish Law*, 60.
16. Gray, 58–59.
17. Cross and Slover, 97; Caerwyn Williams and Ford, 30.
18. Koch and Carey, 10.
19. Nora Chadwick, "Dreams in early European literature," in *Celtic Studies Essays in Memory of Angus Matheson* (New York: Barnes and Noble, 1968), 33–50; Newton, *Warriors of the Word*, 243–283; Hillers, 58–75.
20. Green, *Celtic Goddesses*, 103–104, 134–136, 170, 182.
21. Ibid., 102–104, 125, 134–135, 169–170, 178.

22. Caerwyn Williams, "The Celtic Bard," 216–226; Gillies, 108–120.

23. Rankin, 43.

24. Ford, *The Mabinogi*, 106–107.

25. Ó Cuív, 325–333; Partridge, 25–37.

26. Cross and Slover, 197–198.

27. Ireland, 181–187.

28. John Purser, *Scotland's Music* (Edinburgh: Mainstream Publications, 1992), 23–25.

29. Theodore Levin, *Where Rivers and Mountains Sing: Sound, Music and Nomadism in Tuva and Beyond* (Bloomington: Indiana University Press, 1996), 75–103, 117–119, 134–140.

30. Murphy, *Early Irish Lyrics*, 112–137.

31. Cross and Slover, 505.

32. *DIL*, s.vv. "*fo-cain,*" "*for-cain.*"

33. *DIL*, s.vv. "*ceól,*" "*amrán,*" "*coicetul,*" "*dúchann,*" "*esnad.*"

34. Breandán Ó Madagáin, "Echoes of Magic in the Gaelic Song Tradition," *Proceedings of the Second North American Congress of Celtic Studies*, Halifax, 1989, 125–140; Alan Bruford, "Song and Recitation in Early Ireland," *Celtica* 21 (1990): 61–74.

35. Simon O'Dwyer, *Prehistoric Music of Ireland* (Stroud: Tempus, 2004), 27–83.

36. *DIL*, s.v. "*bodrán.*"

37. O'Dwyer, 54–55.

38. Chadbourne, "Giant Women and Flying Machines," 106–114.

39. Cross and Slover, 503–507; *DIL*, s.v. "*cráeb.*"

40. Rankin, 283–285.

41. Eliade, *Shamanism*, 96–99.

42. Koch and Carey, 13.

43. Ireland, 187.

44. Caerwyn Williams and Ford, 67–69, 72–74; Caerwyn Williams, "The Celtic Bard," 216–226.

45. Lisi Oliver, ed., *Watkins, Calvert: Selected Writings*, Vol. II (Innsbruck: 1994), 674–690; See also Gerard Murphy, *Early Irish Metrics* (Dublin: Royal Irish Academy, 1961); and Liam Breatnach, ed., *Uraicecht na Ríar* (Dublin: Dublin Institute for Advanced Studies, 1987).

46. Ford, *The Celtic Poets*, xxvi–xxvii.

47. Ireland, 182.

48. Ibid., 184–185.

49. Watkins, "Indo-European Metrics and Archaic Irish Verse," 194–249; Oliver, 456–472; Stacey, *Dark Speech*, 105–117.

50. Edward Gwynn, pt. III, 338–339; Old Irish translation by the author.

51. Edward Gwynn, pt. III, 810–811; Old Irish translation by the author.

52. For an exploration of shamanic themes in Celtic poetic contexts, see Nora Chadwick, *Poetry and Prophecy* (Cambridge: Cambridge University Press, 1952).

Chapter 11

1. Best, "The Settling of the Manor of Tara," 147.

2. Ibid., 147–151.

3. *DIL*, s.v. "*bláth.*"

4. Ibid., s.v. "*séis*"; Murphy, *Early Irish Metrics*; Breatnach, *Uraicecht na Ríar.*

5. *DIL*, s.v. "*fis.*"

6. Ibid., s.v. "*cath.*"

7. Mallory, *In Search of the Indo-Europeans* (London: Thames and Hudson, 1999), 262–265. There are a number of competing theories concerning the exact location of the Indo-European homeland, as well as the dates and progression of their movements.

8. Mallory, *In Search of the Indo-Europeans*, 23–109; Dillon, "The Archaism of Irish Tradition," 1–21.

9. Mallory, *In Search of the Indo-Europeans*, 128.

10. Ibid., 129–130, 135–136

11. Ibid., 140.

12. Best, "The Settling of the Manor of Tara," 138–141.

13. Koch and Carey, 23.

14. On the oral transmission of knowledge see Powell, *The Celts*, 184–185. See also Rees and Rees, *Celtic Heritage*, 124, for a discussion of stories associated with thinking in the west, willing in the north, and feeling in the south.

15. Jean Louis Brunaux, *The Celtic Gauls: Gods, Rites and Sanctuaries* (London: Seaby, 1987), 7–11, 26–41; Cunliffe, *The Celtic World*, 92–95; Powell, 166–174; Webster, "Sanctuaries and Sacred Places," 459–460.

16. Rees and Rees, 146–172.

17. Francoise M. Le Roux, "Les Îles au Nord du Monde," in *Hommages à Albert Grenier* (Brussels: Latomus, 1962), 1051–1062; Rees and Rees, 95–103, 124–125; Gray, 24–25, 74.

18. *DIL*, s.vv. "*fál,*" "*gor,*" "*muir,*" "*find*"; Gray, 74–75. See also Tomás Ó Broin, "*Lia Fáil*: Fact and Fiction in the Tradition," *Celtica* XXI (1990), 393–401.

19. Gray, 24–25, 74–75.

20. To complicate matters, the text also states that four druids were in the four cities: Morfessa ("Great Knowledge") was in Falias, Esras ("Passage, Way, Opportunity") was in Gorias, Uiscias (a name associated with *uisce* "water") was in Findias, and Semias ("Slender; Rarified — of air, transparent, bright") was in Murias. I would suggest that the names of the druids have became disassociated with their original positions, which may have been as follows: Uiscias in the West (Murias), Morfessa in the North (Falias), Semias in the East (Findias) and Esras in the South (Gorias). The patterning is not perfect, however; one could certainly make an argument for Morfessa ("Great Knowledge") being associated with the west, for example.

21. Mallory, *In Search of the Indo-Europeans*, 130–133.

22. Ibid., 132. See also *Archaic Cosmos* by Emily Lyle (Edinburgh: Polygon Cosmos, 1991), particularly chapter 2. Those skilled in certain crafts were sometimes included in the second or third function.

23. Mallory, *In Search of the Indo-Europeans*, 133. Emily Lyle discusses these associations at some length throughout *Archaic Cosmos*.

24. Bent Berlin and Paul Kay, *Basic Color Terms: Their Universality and Evolution* (Berkeley: University of California Press, 1969).

25. Heidi A. Lazar-Meyn, "Colour Terms in Táin Bó Cuailgne," *Ulidia* (1994): 201–205.

25. John Carey, "A Tract on the Creation," *Éigse* XXI (1986), 1–9; John Carey, "Cosmology in Saltair na Rann," *Celtica* XVII (1985): 33–52. In the *Celtica* article Carey discusses the aspects of the color-winds scheme, which may be common to other medieval traditions, and which appear to be native Irish concepts or variations; he especially discusses the concept of the four directions on pages 37–38.

26. Carey, "A Tract on the Creation," 3, 7.

27. Rees and Rees, 100–103.

28. Patterson, 119–129; Rees and Rees, 156–157, 163–166.

29. Patterson, 129–135.

30. Ibid., 135–140; Rees and Rees, 100–103.

31. Patterson, 141–146; Edward Gwynn, pt. III, 20–21.

32. Mallory, *In Search of the Indo-Europeans*, 130–133; Bruce Lincoln, *Myth, Cosmos and Society* (Cambridge: Harvard University Press, 1986), 100–102, 141–169.

33. Lincoln, 142–162. An excellent discussion of these concepts may also be found in *Archaic Cosmos* by Emily Lyle, particularly pages 58–60.

34. NicMhacha, *Queen of the Night*, 135–145.

35. Ireland, 188.

36. Alexander Carmichael, *Carmina Gadelica* (Hudson: Lindisfarne, 1992), 283; McNeill, [volume number needed], 57–58.

37. Eóin Mac Neill, 1–67.

38. Ibid., 11–14. I am indebted to Emily Lyle's work in *Archaic Cosmos* for information on the points of the lunar cycle, and the significance of the term *atenux*.

39. Ireland, 184; Rankin, 260–261, 273, 275, 278–279, 291, 293.

40. Powell, 176–179; Webster, "Sanctuaries and Sacred Places," 449–452; Cunliffe, *The Celtic World*, 88–91.

41. Georges Dumézil, "*Le Puits de Nechtan,*" *Celtica* VI (1963): 50–61; Patrick K. Ford, "The Well of Nechtan and '*La Gloire Lumineuse,*'" in *Myth in Indo-European Antiquity* (Los Angeles: University of California Press, 1974), 67–74.

42. Lincoln, 1–40.

Chapter 12

1. Cross and Slover, 503–507.

2. Edward Gwynn, pt. III, 286–295.

3. Old Irish translation by the author.

4. Carey, "The Three Things Required of a Poet," 41–58; Nora Chadwick, "Imbas Forosnai," 97–135.

5. *DIL*, s.v. "*corcor*"; Edward Gwynn, pt. III, 42–43; Best, "The Settling of the Manor of Tara."

6. *DIL*, s.vv. "*fuilngid,*" "*eochair,*" "*éicse.*"

7. Edward Gwynn, pt. III, 144–149.

8. Paice MacLeod, *The Hazel of Immortality*.

9. Breatnach, "The Caldron of Poesy," 45–93; Henry, 114–127.

10. Old Irish translation by the author.

11. Breatnach, "The Caldron of Poesy"; Henry.

12. Meyer, *The Triads of Ireland*, 1–55.

13. Bromwich, *Trioedd Ynys Prydain*.

14. Ibid., Appendix One.

15. Pokorny, 187–191.

16. Old Irish translation by the author.

17. Meyer, *Tecosca Cormaic*, 2–56.

Chapter 13

1. Ross, *Pagan Celtic Britain*, 38, 59–66, 85, 144–145, 461, 467.

2. Newton, *Warriors of the Word*, 118, 125, 127, 132, 134, 173, 178, 199, 223, 237–242, 288–292, 326, 350–353.

3. Useful information about trees in Irish traditions may be found in Mac Coitir, *Irish Wild Plants: Myths, Legends and Folklore*.

4. McManus, 1–33, 147–166.

5. Calder, 88–91.

6. Ibid., 90–93; McManus, 1–3, 36–39.

7. McManus, 36–39, 42–43.

8. Fergus Kelly, "The Old Irish Tree List," *Celtica* XI (1976): 107–124; John Carey, "Vernacular Irish Learning: Three Notes," in *Éigse* XXIV (1990): 37–44; R. A. S. MacAlister, *The Secret Languages of Ireland* (Cambridge: Cambridge University Press, 1937), 34–60; Bell, 145–158; Rankin, 207, 275, 280–281, 284–285; Edward

Gwynn, pt. III, 144–149; Rees and Rees, 91, 120, 161, 186, 192, 282, 284, 287, 296, 349; Robert Bevan-Jones, *The Ancient Yew* (Macclesfield: Windgather Press, 2002). See also Ross, *Pagan Celtic Britain*; Calder; McManus; and Newton, *Warriors of the Word*, pages cited above.

Chapter 14

1. Megaw and Megaw, 20–22, 51–68, 76–88, 115–121, 135–145; G. Frank Mitchell, ed., *Treasures of Early Irish Art—1500 B.C. to 1500 A.D.* (New York: Metropolitan Museum of Art, 1978), 10–17, 54–60.

2. Megaw and Megaw, 143–145, 160–163, 171, 174–182; Cunliffe, *The Celtic World*, 73–81.

3. Lloyd Laing and Jenny Laing, *The Picts and the Scots* (Stroud: Wren Park, 1993); Graham Ritchie and Anna Ritchie, *Scotland: Archaeology and Early History* (Edinburgh: Edinburgh University Press, 1991), 160–167.

4. Green, *Animals in Celtic Life*, 196–238.

5. Ibid., 162–164.

6. Ibid., 148–149, 164–168, 230–238; Ross, *Pagan Celtic Britain*, 66, 175–201, 208–212, 277, 286, 295, 303, 410, 417–423; Megaw and Megaw, 32–33, 46, 94, 144, 163; Cunliffe, *The Celtic World*, 18.

7. Green, *Animals in Celtic Life*, 135, 153–156, 187–190, 204–210; Ross, *Pagan Celtic Britain*, 56, 69, 99–100, 104, 189, 213–214, 255, 257, 263, 267–268, 286–288, 290, 296, 316, 342, 344, 351, 393, 404–417, 429, 438–439, 457, 460–461; Megaw and Megaw, 28, 32, 82–83, 133, 168, 176, 179–181; Cunliffe, *The Celtic World*, 18, 50–55, 76, 122.

8. Green, *Animals in Celtic Life*, 143, 146, 183–185, 220–224; Ross, *Pagan Celtic Britain*, 83, 129, 174–175, 179–180, 184, 190, 198, 201–202, 214–215, 289, 311, 351, 361–362, 380, 385–386, 388, 420, 441, 450; Megaw and Megaw, 143, 174, 182, 223; Cunliffe, *The Celtic World*, 80.

9. Green, *Animals in Celtic Life*, 158–159, 164–166, 169–171, 218–219; Ross, *Pagan Celtic Britain*, 175, 208, 387, 390–404, 420, 430, 438–440, 470, 479; Megaw and Megaw, 94, 161, 171, 220; Cunliffe, *The Celtic World*, 142, 158, 18, 25, 53, 56, 76, 81.

10. Green, *Animals in Celtic Life*, 53, 55–57, 64, 128, 133, 147, 150–151, 159–160, 170, 185–187, 192–193, 197–203; Ross, *Pagan Celtic Britain*, 186–189, 426–427; Ó Cathasaigh, *Cormac mac Airt*, 26–38: Megaw and Megaw, 35, 94, 170–171, 175; Cunliffe, *The Celtic World*, 80, 92, 109.

11. Green, *Animals in Celtic Life*, 217–218; Ross, *Pagan Celtic Britain*, 433–435, 471, 477; Ó Cathasaigh, *Cormac mac Airt*, 38–41; Cunliffe, *The Ancient Celts*, 80.

12. Green, *Animals in Celtic Life*, 148, 192, 222, 237; Ross, *Pagan Celtic Britain*, 102, 119, 174–177, 181–187, 198–203, 212–213, 234–244, 249, 382, 427–430, 438–439; Megaw and Megaw, 52; Cunliffe, *The Celtic World*, 18, 73.

13. Green, *Animals in Celtic Life*, 48–51, 58–60; Ross, *Pagan Celtic Britain*, 343, 435–436; Ireland, 94–95.

14. Green, *Animals in Celtic Life*, 142, 164, 170, 241; Ross, *Pagan Celtic Britain*, 135–136, 383; Megaw and Megaw, 86.

15. Green, *Animals in Celtic Life*, 190–192, 195, 234; Ross, *Pagan Celtic Britain*, 52, 126, 232, 343, 436–437, 440; Logan, 121–126; Megaw and Megaw, 220.

16. Green, *Animals in Celtic Life*, 182–183, 190–194, 224–234; Ross, *Pagan Celtic Britain*, 174–187, 196–201, 212–213, 243, 247, 295, 393, 431–433, 438–439, 470, 478; McNeill, vol. 2, 27–28; Danaher, 14.

17. Bruford and MacDonald, 365–368; Laing and

Laing, 103 (second row from the top, third figure from the left).

18. Green, *Animals in Celtic Life*, 147, 222; Ross, *Pagan Celtic Britain*, 254, 437; Megaw and Megaw, 175. See also Laing and Laing, 103 (third row from the top, third figure from the left). Previously described in the scholarship as a "swimming elephant," the figure clearly represents a dolphin with its beaked nose, flippers, and water plume emerging from the head.

19. Green, *Animals in Celtic Life*, 133–134, 143, 160–161, 172, 177–181, 183, 195, 198, 211–212, 215, 242; Ross, *Pagan Celtic Britain*, 77, 131, 243, 302, 318–331, 336, 344, 366–368, 393, 424, 430–431; Koch and Carey, 19.

20. Green, *Animals in Celtic Life*, 174–176, 178, 181, 193; Ross, *Pagan Celtic Britain*, 176, 200, 302–311, 321, 332–336, 417; Megaw and Megaw, 87, 114.

21. Green, *Animals in Celtic Life*, 133, 159–160, 163, 172, 176–178, 181, 184, 193–194, 214–215, 223; Ross, *Pagan Celtic Britain*, 111, 253, 278, 302–303, 330, 337, 342, 357–359, 351–365, 369, 389; Fergus Kelly, *A Guide to Early Irish Law*, 60; Cunliffe, *The Celtic World*, 117.

22. Green, *Animals in Celtic Life*, 142, 144, 149, 159, 170–173, 192, 195, 222; Ross, *Pagan Celtic Britain*, 60, 72, 103, 129, 230, 302, 342, 346–351, 369, 393; Ford, *The Mabinogi*, 106–107; Megaw and Megaw, 145; Cunliffe, *The Celtic World*, 53.

23. Green, *Animals in Celtic Life*, 173, 192; Ross, *Pagan Celtic Britain*, 278, 302, 344–346, 369; Ford, *The Mabinogi*, 108; Megaw and Megaw, 143, 145.

24. Green, *Animals in Celtic Life*, 87–88, 150, 214; Ross, *Pagan Celtic Britain*, 69, 99, 111–112, 130–131, 247, 287, 302–303, 320, 336–337, 342–344, 368–369, 406, 435–436; Megaw and Megaw, 94–95, 177; Cunliffe, *The Celtic World*, 59.

25. Ford, *The Mabinogi*, 100–101; Danaher, 243–250; Ross, *Pagan Celtic Britain*, 330–331, 368.

26. Green, *Animals in Celtic Life*, 130, 136–138, 143–144, 212–213; Megaw and Megaw, 27, 77; Cunliffe, *The Celtic World*, 119.

27. Green, *Animals in Celtic Life*, 181; Ross, *Pagan Celtic Britain*, 156, 288, 296, 339–340.

Chapter 15

1. Caerwyn Williams and Ford, 20–25, 30–31, 34, 38, 40–41; Jarman and Hughes, *Welsh Literature: Volume One*, 17–18, 142; Knott and Murphy, 13, 21–22; Newton, *Warriors of the Word*, 55–59.

2. Rankin,, 68, 70–71, 278; Koch and Carey, 10, 12, 31.

3. Ross, *Pagan Celtic Britain*, 251, 289, 452–453.

4. Rivet and Smith, 324–325.

5. Ibid., 267.

6. Ireland, 183.

7. NicMhacha, *Queen of the Night*, 15–16, 137–141.

8. Ross, *Pagan Celtic Britain*, 182–184, 196, 200, 212.

9. Ibid., 194–195.

10. Ibid., 184, 194–201, 431, 433; Mallory, "The Career of Conall Cernach," 22–28.

11. O'Brien, *Corpus Genealogiarum Hiberniae*; Thomas O'Rahilly, 467.

12. Thomas O'Rahilly, 288–289, 528.

13. Ibid., 210.

14. Ross, *Pagan Celtic Britain*, 92; Green, *Celtic Goddesses*, 30–31.

15. Ross, *Pagan Celtic Britain*, 425.

16. Scowcroft, "*Leabhar Gabhála* — Part II," 1–64; Carey, "Introduction to *Lebor Gabála Érenn*," 1–21.

17. Scowcroft, "*Leabhar Gabhála* — Part II"; Koch and

Carey, 226–271.

18. John Carey, "The Origin and Development of the Cessair Legend," *Éigse* XXII (1987), 37–48.

19. Thomas O'Rahilly, 484, 492; Muller-Lisowski, "Contributions to a Study in Irish Folklore: Traditions About Donn" and "Donn Firinne, Tech Duinn, An Tarbh."

20. John Carey, "Native Elements in Irish Pseudohistory," in *Medieval Studies: Cultural Identity and Cultural Integration: Ireland and Europe in the Middle Ages* (Dublin: Four Courts Press, 1995), 54.

21. Sharon Paice MacLeod, "The Descent of the Gods: Creation, Cosmogony and Divine Order in *Lebor Gabála*," *Proceedings of the Harvard Celtic Colloquium*, XXI, 2001, 312, 322–329.

22. Koch and Carey, 226–271.

23. Paice MacLeod, "The Descent of the Gods," 322–323, 327–328; Rees and Rees, 104–105.

24. Ireland, 187.

25. Hull, 53–58.

26. Carey, "Native Elements in Irish Pseudohistory."

27. Caerwyn Williams and Ford, 20–25, 30–31, 34, 38, 40–41; Rees and Rees, 11–25.

28. Paice MacLeod, "The Descent of the Gods," 328–329.

29. Ibid., 361–365.

30. Ibid., 334–361.

31. Koch and Carey, 35; Rankin, 233, 235; Freeman, 50–51.

32. Ó Duinn; Thomas O'Rahilly, 466, 490–492, 519–521.

33. Ó Cathasaigh, *Cormac mac Airt*; Edward Gwynn, pt. I, 14–15.

34. Koch and Carey, 354–358.

35. P. C. Bartrum, *Early Welsh Genealogical Tracts* (Cardiff: University of Wales Press, 1996).

36. Robin Gwyndaf, *Welsh Folk Tales* (Cardiff: National Museums and Galleries of Wales, 1999), 78.

37. Hillers.

38. Patricia Lysaght, *The Banshee* (Boulder: Roberts Rinehart, 1986).

39. Bruford and MacDonald; Gregory.

40. Swire, 104–122; MacLeod Estate Office, *Dunvegan Castle* (Isle of Skye, 2003), 34–42.

41. Swire, 108; MacLeod Estate Office, 42.

Chapter 16

1. Charles Thomas, *Celtic Britain* (London: Thames and Hudson, 1986), 37–52, 69–76; Barry Cunliffe, *Iron Age Britain* (London: Batsford, 1997), 59–70, 76–80, 115–118; Nora Chadwick, *Celtic Britain* (North Hollywood: Newcastle, 1989), 35–51; Ireland, 158–172; Thomas Charles-Edwards, "The Arthur of History," in *The Arthur of the Welsh* (Cardiff: University of Wales Press, 2008), 15–32 (see also 1–14); Kenneth H. Jackson, "The Arthur of History," in *Arthurian Literature in the Middle Ages* (Oxford: Oxford University Press, 2001), 1–11.

2. Oliver J. Padel, *Arthur in Medieval Welsh Literature* (Cardiff: University of Wales Press, 2000), 3–13; James J. Wilhelm, "Arthur in the Latin Chronicles," in *The Romance of Arthur: An Anthology of Medieval Texts in Translation* (New York: Garland Publishing, 1994), 1–10; Charles-Edwards, "The Arthur of History," 15–32; Jon B. Coe and Simon Young, eds., *The Celtic Sources for the Arthurian Legend* (Felinfach: Llanerch, 1995), 2–5.

3. Charles-Edwards, "The Arthur of History," 15–32; Jackson, "The Arthur of History," 1–11; Wilhelm, *The Romance of Arthur*, 1–10.

4. Charles-Edwards, "The Arthur of History," 15–

32; Jackson, "The Arthur of History," 1–11; Wilhelm, *The Romance of Arthur*, 3–10; Padel, 3–13; Coe and Young, 6–11.

5. Charles-Edwards, "The Arthur of History," 15–32; Jackson, "The Arthur of History," 1–11; Wilhelm, *The Romance of Arthur*, 1–10; Padel, 3–13; Coe and Young, 12–13.

6. Brynley F. Roberts, "*Culhwch ac Olwen,* The Triads, Saints' Lives," in *The Arthur of the Welsh: The Arthurian Legend in Medieval Welsh Literature* (Cardiff: University of Wales Press, 2008), 73–96; Roger S. Loomis, "The Oral Diffusion of the Arthurian Legend," in *Arthurian Literature in the Middle Ages.* (Oxford: Oxford University Press, 2001), 52–63; Wilhelm, *The Romance of Arthur*, 6; Padel, 38–45; Coe and Young, 14–47.

7. Roger S. Loomis, "The Legend of Arthur's Survival," in *Arthurian Literature in the Middle Ages* (Oxford: Oxford University Press, 2001), 64–71; Patrick Sims-Williams, "The Early Welsh Arthurian Poems," in *The Arthur of the Welsh: The Arthurian Legend in Medieval Welsh Literature* (Cardiff: University of Wales Press, 2008), 49–50; Wilhelm, *The Romance of Arthur*, 6–7.

8. Rachel Bromwich, A. O. H. Jarman, and Brynley F. Roberts. *The Arthur of the Welsh: The Arthurian Legend in Medieval Welsh Literature* (Cardiff: University of Wales Press, 2008), 3–6; Jackson, "The Arthur of History," 3; John K. Bollard, "Arthur in the Early Welsh Tradition," in *The Romance of Arthur: An Anthology of Medieval Texts in Translation* (New York: Garland Publishing, 1994), 11–24; Padel, 6–10; Coe and Young, 156–159; Jarman and Hughes, *Welsh Literature: Volume One*, 68–80.

9. Sims-Williams, "The Early Welsh Arthurian Poems," 33–72; Jackson, "The Arthur of History," 12–19; Bollard, "Arthur in the Early Welsh Tradition," 11–24; Jarman and Hughes, *Welsh Literature: Volume One*, 11–40; Padel, 47–50; Coe and Young, 99–101.

10. Sims-Williams, "The Early Welsh Arthurian Poems," 33–72; Jackson, "The Arthur of History," 12–19; Bollard, "Arthur in the Early Welsh Tradition," 11–24; Padel, 17–33; Coe and Young, 127–133.

11. Bromwich, *Trioedd Ynys Prydain*; Rachel Bromwich, "The Welsh Triads," in *Arthurian Literature in the Middle Ages* (Oxford: Oxford University Press, 2001), 44–51; Roberts, "*Culhwch ac Olwen,*" 80–88; Sharon Paice MacLeod, "Abduction, Swordplay, Monsters and Mistrust: Findabair, Gwenhwyfar and the Restoration of Honour," *Proceedings of the Harvard Celtic Colloquium*, Vol. XXVIII, 2008, 185–199.

12. Roberts, "*Culhwch ac Olwen,*" 73–96; Idris Foster, "*Culhwch and Olwen* and *Rhonabwy's Dream*," in *Arthurian Literature in the Middle Ages* (Oxford: Oxford University Press, 2001), 31–43; Richard M. Loomis, "Arthur in Geoffrey of Monmouth," in *The Romance of Arthur: An Anthology of Medieval Texts in Translation* (New York: Garland Publishing, 1994), 25–58; Jarman and Hughes, *Welsh Literature: Volume One*, 214–223, 231–232, 240–241; Coe and Young, 56–73.

13. Haycock, *Legendary Poems*, 433–451; Sims-Williams, "The Early Welsh Arthurian Poems," 54–57; Jackson, "The Arthur of History," 15–18; Bollard, "Arthur in the Early Welsh Tradition," 19–21; Ireland, 23.

14. Middle Welsh translation by the author.

15. Sims-Williams, "The Early Welsh Arthurian Poems," 54–57; Jackson, "The Arthur of History," 15–18; Wilhelm, *The Romance of Arthur*, 7–9; Loomis, *Arthurian Literature in the Middle Ages*, 64–71.

16. Brynley F. Roberts, "Geoffrey of Monmouth, *Historia Brittaniae* and *Brut y Brenhinedd*," in *The Arthur of*

the Welsh: *The Arthurian Legend in Medieval Welsh Literature* (Cardiff: University of Wales Press, 2008), 97–116; John Parry and Robert Caldwell, "Geoffrey of Monmouth," in *Arthurian Literature in the Middle Ages* (Oxford: Oxford University Press, 2001), 72–93; Loomis, "Arthur in Geoffrey of Monmouth," 59–94; Padel, 72–77, 83–85.

17. A. O. H. Jarman, "The Merlin Legend and the Welsh Tradition of Prophecy," in *The Arthur of the Welsh: The Arthurian Legend in Medieval Welsh Literature* (Cardiff: University of Wales Press, 2008), 117–146; Parry and Caldwell, 72–93; Loomis, "Arthur in Geoffrey of Monmouth," 59–94. It is interesting to note a shadowy late fifth-century figure by the name of *Riothamus* (a word which may be a title, rather than a proper name) who was said to have been a "king" of the Britons and who was involved in a number of military campaigns. Betrayed by the Gaulish prefect Arvandus, he was defeated near Bourges in 469–470 C.E. The Burgundian town of Avallon (from the Gaulish *Aballone*, "the place of apples") has been proposed as a site which may commemorate his demise.

18. Roger S. Loomis, "Layamon's *Brut*," in *Arthurian Literature in the Middle Ages* (Oxford: Oxford University Press, 2001), 104–111; James J. Wilhelm, "Layamon: *Brut* (The Death of Arthur)," in *The Arthur of the Welsh: The Arthurian Legend in Medieval Welsh Literature* (Cardiff: University of Wales Press, 2008), 109–120.

19. Transliteration from the Middle English by the author.

Chapter 17

1. Proinsias Mac Cana, *The Mabinogi* (Cardiff: University of Wales Press, 1996); Eric P. Hamp, "Mabinogi," *THSC* (1974/1975): 243–249; Eric P. Hamp, "Mabinogi and Archaism," *Celtica* XXIII (1999); Ford, *The Mabinogi*, 1–30; Sioned Davies, *The Mabinogion* (Oxford: Oxford University Press, 2007), i–xxxiii; John K. Bollard, trans., *The Mabinogi: Legend and Landscape of Wales* (Llandysul: Gomer, 2006), 9–17, 110–122; Jarman and Hughes, *A Guide to Welsh Literature: Volume 1*, 189–202.

2. Ford, *The Mabinogi*, 35–56; Sioned Davies, *The Mabinogion*, 1–21; Bollard, *Landscape of Wales*, 19–41.

3. Ford, *The Mabinogi*, 4–12, 22–27; Sioned Davies, *The Mabinogion*, 227–232; Mac Cana, *The Mabinogi*, 38, 46, 51, 55–56; Juliette Wood, "The Horse in Welsh Folklore: A Boundary Image in Custom and Narrative," in *The Horse in Celtic Culture* (Cardiff: University of Wales Press, 1997), 162–177; Miranda Green, "The Symbolic Horse in Pagan Celtic Europe: An Archaeological Perspective," in *The Horse in Celtic Culture* (Cardiff: University of Wales Press, 1997), 1–19; Ross, *Pagan Celtic Britain*, 156, 288, 290, 313, 316, 338–340, 406–407, 410, 414, 416, 439, 449.

4. Ford, *The Mabinogi*, 57–72; Sioned Davies, *The Mabinogion*, 22–34; Bollard, *Landscape of Wales*,, 42–61.

5. Ford, *The Mabinogi*, 27, 57–59; Sioned Davies, *The Mabinogion*, 232–237; Mac Cana, *The Mabinogi*, 29, 40–41, 45–46, 50, 53, 55–56; Ross, *Pagan Celtic Britain*, 94–171, 322, 324, 326–331, 338, 367; Bromwich, "The Welsh Triads," 44–51.

6. Ford, *The Mabinogi*, 73–87; Sioned Davies, *The Mabinogion*, 35–46; Bollard, *Landscape of Wales*, 62–77.

7. Ford, *The Mabinogi*, 27–28, 73–75; Sioned Davies, *The Mabinogion*, 237–239; Mac Cana, *The Mabinogi*, 46–48, 54–58.

8. Ford, *The Mabinogi*, 89–109; Sioned Davies, *The Mabinogion*, 47–64; Bollard, *Landscape of Wales*, 78–109.

9. Ford, *The Mabinogi*, 13, 16, 27–29, 89–91; Sioned

Davies, *The Mabinogion*, 239–244; Mac Cana, *The Mabinogi*, 56–57; John Carey, "A British Myth of Origins?" *History of Religions*, vol. 31, no. 1 (Chicago: University of Chicago Press, 1991), 25–38; Sarah L. Keefer, "The Lost Tale of Dylan in the Fourth Branch of *The Mabinogi*," *Studia Celtica* XXIV–XXV (1989–1990): 26–37; Ross, *Pagan Celtic Britain*, 59–64, 82, 234, 290, 346–351, 369, 404, 426, 457.

10. Ford, *The Mabinogi*, 16–21, 159–187; Haycock, *Legendary Poems*.

Chapter 18

1. Ó Dónaill, *síog*; Dwelly, *sìth, sìtheach*.
2. Ross, *Folklore of Wales*, 133–135.
3. Yeats, 1–49.
4. Ronald Black, ed., *The Gaelic Otherworld: John Gregorson Campbell's Superstitions of the Highlands and Islands of Scotland* and *Witchcraft and Second Sight in the Highlands and Islands* (Edinburgh: Birlinn, 2005), 1–81; Gregory, 104–147, 162–184, 202–247, 255–273; Henderson and Cowan, 8–105; Katherine Briggs, *The Fairies in Tradition and Literature* (London: Routledge and Kegan Paul, 1968), 12–24, 71–139; Evans-Wentz, only pages 23–225 should be consulted; Peter Narváez, ed., *The Good People: New Fairylore Essays* (Lexington: University of Kentucky, 1997), 22–115, 155–214; Briggs, *Encyclopedia of Fairies*, 134–139, 143–145, 148–151, 153–160.
5. Black, 240–270, Henderson and Cowan, 74–93; Briggs, *Fairies in Tradition*, 191, 327.
6. Briggs, *Fairies in Tradition*, 71–86.
7. Black, 1–43; Henderson and Cowan, 47–73; Briggs, *Fairies in Tradition*, 143–145, 153–158.
8. Black, 11, 24–26; Briggs, *Fairies in Tradition*, 350–353, 376–378.
9. Gregory, 31–79, 148–161; Black, 199–233; Henderson and Cowan, 74–105; Yeats, 219–274.
10. Gregory, 50–79.
11. Ibid., 31–50; Edmund Lenihan, *In Search of Biddy Early* (Cork: Mercier Press, 1987).
12. Gregory, 71.
13. Ibid., 62.
14. Ibid., 61.
15. Ibid., 68.
16. Black, 199–233, 448–499; Carmichael, 48, 81, 86, 94, 108, 117, 134, 125–170, 173, 238, 267–270, 280–281, 365–374, 377–426.
17. Black, 200–201, 205–206; Carmichael, 397–398, 647.
18. Carmichael, 416–417, 653.
19. Ibid., 403–406, 648–650; Black, 225, 487–488.
20. Carmichael, 138, 267–269.
21. Ibid., 384–392, 644. For traditions concerning the evil eye in Ireland, see Gregory, 80–103.
22. Carmichael, 529–532, 642–643.
23. Ibid., 673; Ross, *Scottish Highlands*, 33–63; Gregory, 31–79, 148–161.
24. Gregory, 31–79, 148–161; Black, 199–233; Carmichael, 148–158, 377–426.
25. Gregory, 148–161; Mac Coitir.
26. Gregory, 148–161; Mac Coitir, 11–12, 240–243.
27. Gregory, 71–73.
28. Ibid., 151.
29. Carmichael, 148–158, 365–372; McNeill, Vol. 1, 77–84; Black, 199–200, 229–232.
30. Carmichael, 150, 152, 159; Black, 219, 230–231.
31. Carmichael, 156–157, 370–371, 641–642; Black, 232.

32. Carmichael, 151, 157–158, 366.
33. Ibid., 148–151, 608–611; McNeill, Vol. 1, 82.
34. Carmichael, 369; McNeill, Vol. 1, 80–81; Newton, *Warriors of the Word,* 199.
35. Black, 232; McNeill, Vol. 1, 83.
36. Black, 230–231; Carmichael, 152–154, 365–366, 611.
37. Carmichael, 155–156, 612.
38. Black, 231; Carmichael, 152–153, 611.
39. McNeill, Vol. 1, 82.
40. Ibid., 84; Briggs, *Fairies in Tradition*, 82–86. For the symbolism of trees in traditional Gaelic society and poetry, see Newton, *Warriors of the Word,* 291.
41. Carmichael, 360.
42. McNeill, Vol. 1, 78–79.
43. Ibid., 79.
44. McNeill, Vol. 1, 79; Newton, *A Handbook of the Scottish Gaelic World*, 214; Bevan-Jones, 125–149.
45. Black, 219–224; McNeill, Vol. 1, 90–96; Ross, *Folklore of Wales*, 88–93.
46. Black, 228–229; McNeill, Vol. 1, 65–74; Ross, *Folklore of Wales*, 78–86; Logan.

Chapter 19

1. Patterson, 135–140.
2. Stokes, *Sanas Chormaic*, 23; Gray, 119; Eric P. Hamp, "*imbolc, óimelc*," *Studia Celtica* 14–15 (1979–1980): 107–113; *DIL*, s.vv. "*imm-*," "*bolg*."
3. Ó hAodha, *Bethu Brigte*; John J. O'Meara, ed., *Gerald of Wales: The History and Topography of Ireland* (London: Penguin, 1982), 83; Lisa M. Bitel, "Ekphrasis at Kildare: The Imaginative Architecture of a Seventh-Century Hagiographer," *Speculum* 79, no. 3 (2004): 605–627; Katherine McKenna, "Between Two Worlds: Saint Brigit and Pre-Christian Religion in the *Vita Prima*," in "Identifying the 'Celtic,'" CSANA Yearbook 2 (2002): 66–74.
4. O'Meara, 81–84, 88.
5. Ó hAodha.
6. Carmichael, 189–196, 237–239, 259–264; McNeill, vol. 2, 19–29.
7. Carmichael, 148–151, 237–239.
8. Translation from Scottish Gaelic by the author.
9. Danaher, 13–37; McNeill, vol. 2, 19–30; Ó Catháin, 12–34.
10. Owen, 70–71; Ross, *Folklore of Wales*, 37–38.
11. Patterson, 135–140.
12. Ibid.; McNeill, vol. 2, 55–73; Carmichael, 83–85, 586–587.
13. Danaher, 86–127.
14. Owen, 95–110; Ross, *Folklore of Wales*, 39–42.

Chapter 20

1. Watkins, *Dictionary of Indo-European Roots*, 49.
2. Gray, 126–127.
3. Rivet and Smith, 267.
4. Patterson, 141; Edward Gwynn, pt. IV, 146–147.
5. Edward Gwynn, pt. IV, 146–163.
6. Ibid., pt. III, 1–25.
7. Ibid., 10–11.
8. Old Irish translation by the author.
9. Danaher, 167–177; Máire MacNeill, *passim*.
10. McNeill, vol. 2, 94–101, 116–132.
11. Carmichael, 98–99, 596–597.
12. Scottish Gaelic translation by the author.
13. Ibid.
14. McNeill, vol. 2, 116–132.

15. Owen, 113–121; Ross, *Folklore of Wales*, 26–29.
16. Patterson, 121–129; Green, *Animals in Celtic Life*, 164–165, 169–171.
17. Patterson, 119–120, 126; Rees and Rees, 83–94.
18. Patterson, 119–120, 126; Rees and Rees, 83–94; Marie-Louise Sjoestedt, *Gods and Heroes of the Celts* (Berkeley: Turtle Island Foundation, 1982), 62–72; Eliade, *The Myth of the Eternal Return*, 51–92.
19. Danaher, 200, 228–229; Owen, 122–123, 135–136.
20. Danaher, 200–227; Green, *Animals in Celtic Life*, 187–190, 204–207.
21. Owen, 27, 40–41, 49–56, 135–136.
22. Ibid., 53–54.
23. Welsh translation by the author.
24. Owen, 121–141; Danaher, 218–227; McNeill, vol. 3, 29–39.
25. McNeill, vol. 3, 11–41.
26. Charles W. J. Withers and R. W. Munro, eds., *A Description of the Western Islands of Scotland Circa 1695* (Edinburgh: Birlinn, 1995): 29; McNeill, vol. 3, 20–21; Dwelly, 809.
27. McNeill, vol. 3, 21–22, 147.
28. Ibid., 24–29.
29. Ibid., 39, 149.
30. Scottish Gaelic translation by the author.
31. McNeill, vol. 3, 99–116; Carmichael, 76–79, 579.
32. Scottish Gaelic translation by the author.
33. Ibid.

Chapter 21

1. Koch and Carey, 6–23, 30–36.
2. John Carey, "Symbol and Mystery in Irish Religious Thoughts," *Temenos* 13 (1992): 101–111.
3. Ibid., 102.
4. Ibid., 103.
5. Caerwyn Williams and Ford, 193–202, 208–215; A. O. H. Jarman and Gwilym Rees Hughes, *A Guide to Welsh Literature: Volume 2* (Llandybie: Christopher Davies, 1984), 95, 98–101, 103–106, 108–110.
6. Anthony Conran, *Welsh Verse* (Bridgend: Seren, 1993), 220–222, 224–225.
7. Welsh translation by the author.
8. Caerwyn Williams and Ford, 309.
9. Derick Thomson, *An Introduction to Gaelic Poetry* (Edinburgh: Edinburgh University Press, 1990), 221.
10. Translation from Scottish Gaelic by the author.
11. Barry Cunliffe, *The Celts: A Very Short Introduction* (Oxford: Oxford University Press, 2003), 111–132; Barry Cunliffe, *Druids: A Very Short Introduction* (Oxford: Oxford University Press, 2010), 100–130; Newton, *Warriors of the Word*, 44–79, 327–332. Some interesting essays on Celtic identity and nationalism may also be found in Robert O'Driscoll, *The Celtic Consciousness* (New York: George Braziller, 1982).

Appendix A

1. Rankin, 245–258; Koch and Carey, 6, 8–9, 14, 18–19, 23–24, 34–35, 37–46.
2. Fergus Kelly, *A Guide to Early Irish Law*, 45, 49–50, 68–79, 95–97, 104–105, 112–113, 121, 123, 133–134, 187–188, 202, 207–208, 220, 349, 351; Charlene M. Eska, *Cáin Lánamna: An Old Irish Tract on Marriage and Divorce Laws* (Leidon and Boston: Brill, 2010), 3–34, 303–341.
3. Lisa M. Bitel, *Land of Women: Tales of Sex and Gender from Early Ireland* (Ithaca: Cornell University

Press, 1996); Joanne Findon, *A Woman's Words: Emer and Female Speech in the Ulster Cycle* (Toronto: University of Toronto Press, 1997).
4. Koch and Carey, 42–46; Rankin, 245–258.
5. Bitel, *Land of Women*; Findon; Ross, *Pagan Celtic Britain*, 48, 61, 235, 252–253, 279–293, 296–297, 313, 316, 400, 406–407, 410, 416, 439, 449, 452, 454, 456; Edyta Lehman, "'And Thus I Will It': Queen Medb and the Will to Power," *Proceedings of the Harvard Celtic Colloquium*, Vol. XXVIII, 2008, 142–151.
6. Meyer, *The Triads of Ireland*, 1–55.
7. Fergus Kelly, *A Guide to Early Irish Law*, 43–51, 55, 59, 68–69, 75–78, 91.
8. Ibid., 70–73; Charlene Eska, 13–18.
9. Fergus Kelly, *A Guide to Early Irish Law*, 70–72, 81–90; Charlene Eska, 8–9, 13–20.
10. Fergus Kelly, *A Guide to Early Irish Law*, 73–75; Charlene Eska, 20–24.
11. Fergus Kelly, *A Guide to Early Irish Law*; Charlene Eska, 9–12.
12. Fergus Kelly, *A Guide to Early Irish Law*, 76–78, 104–105, 120–121; Charlene Eska, 9–11.
13. Fergus Kelly, *A Guide to Early Irish Law*, 43–51, 55, 59, 68–69, 75–78, 91.
14. Ibid., 78–79, 134.
15. Ibid., 79, 134.
16. Ibid., 202, 207–208.
17. Ibid., 95–98.
18. Ibid., 186–188.
19. Ibid., 130–133.
20. Ibid., 43–49.

Appendix B

1. Alan Bruford, "Song and Recitation in Early Ireland," 61–74; Noel Hamilton, "'Ancient' Irish Music," *Proceedings of the First North American Congress of Celtic Studies*, Ottawa, 1986, 283–291; Purser; Newton, *Warriors of the Word*, 243–254.
2. The Celtic language lyrics presented in this appendix are from the oral tradition (and thus in the public domain). Translations into English from the original Scottish Gaelic, Modern Irish, Welsh, Cornish, Breton and Manx are by the author.
3. Graham Aubrey, "The Influences of Nineteenth Century Anthologies of Celtic Music in Redefining Celtic Nationalism," *Proceedings of the Harvard Celtic Colloquium*, Vol. XXVIII, 2008, 1–8.
4. For more information on this and other Irish Beltaine customs, see Danaher, 127.
5. Owen, 51–57.
6. I would like to thank Dr. Benjamin Bruch for teaching me this song.
7. An example of the juxtaposition of fair hair with dark brows (possibly referring to eyebrows which are enhanced with cosmetics) is seen in the description of Étain in "The Wooing of Étain," Cross and Slover, 83.
8. Thomas Wentworth Higginson, *Tales of the Enchanted Isles* (New York: Chelsea House, 1983), 55–56 (an edited reprint of the 1898 edition); Lewis Thorpe, trans., *Geoffrey of Monmouth: The History of the Kings of Britain* (Hammondsworth: Penguin, 1982), 171.
9. Newton, *Warriors of the Word*, 252.
10. This song may be a development of an early chant, and thus one of the oldest Irish airs. See Hamilton, 288.
11. Paul-André Bempéchat, "Rekindling Celtic Solidarity: The Abergavenny Eisteddfod of 1838 and the Birth of the *Barzaz Breiz*," *Ars Lyrica Celtica* 17 (2008): 97–130.

Bibliography

Alcock, Leslie. *Arthur's Britain.* Harmondsworth: Penguin, 1983.

Allen, Stephen. *Lords of Battle.* Oxford: Osprey, 2007.

Arbuthnot, Sharon, ed. *Cóir Anmann.* Part 1. Dublin: Irish Texts Society, 2005.

Armit, Ian. *Celtic Scotland.* London: Batsford, 1997.

Arnold, Bettina, and D. Blair Gibson. *Celtic Chiefdom, Celtic State.* Cambridge: Cambridge University Press, 1995.

Aubrey, Graham. "The Influences of Nineteenth Century Anthologies of Celtic Music in Redefining Celtic Nationalism." *Proceedings of the Harvard Celtic Colloquium,* Vol. XXVIII, 2008.

Ayto, John. *Dictionary of Word Origins.* New York: Little, Brown, 1990.

Ball, Martin J., ed. *The Celtic Languages.* London and New York: Routledge, 2002.

Barclay, Gordon, ed. *The Peoples of Scotland: Picts, Vikings, Angles and Scots.* Edinburgh: Canongate, 1999.

Bartrum, P. C. *Early Welsh Genealogical Tracts.* Cardiff: University of Wales Press, 1996.

Beith, Mary. *Healing Threads: Traditional Medicines of the Highlands and Islands.* Edinburgh: Polygon, 1995.

Bell, Martin. "People and Nature in the Celtic World." In *The Celtic World,* Miranda Green, ed. New York: Routledge, 1995.

Bempéchat, Paul-André. "Rekindling Celtic Solidarity: The Abergavenny Eisteddfod of 1893 and the Birth of the *Barzaz Breiz.*" *Ars Lyrica Celtica* 17 (2008).

Benard, Elisabeth, and Beverly Moon, eds. *Goddesses Who Rule.* Oxford: Oxford University Press, 2000.

Bergin, Osborn. *Irish Bardic Poetry.* Dublin: Dublin Institute for Advanced Studies, 1984.

Berlin, Brent, and Paul Kay. *Basic Color Terms: Their Universality and Evolution.* Berkeley: University of California Press, 1969.

Best, R. I. "The Settling of the Manor of Tara." *Ériu* IV (1910).

_____, and Osborn Bergin. *Lebor na hUidre.* Dublin: Dublin Institute for Advanced Studies, 1992.

_____, _____, and M. A. O'Brien, eds. *The Book of Leinster.* Dublin: Dublin Institute for Advanced Studied, 1954.

Bevan-Jones, Robert. *The Ancient Yew.* Macclesfield: Windgather Press, 2002.

Billington, Sandra, and Miranda Green. *The Concept of the Goddess.* London: Routledge, 1996.

Bitel, Lisa M. "Ekphrasis at Kildare: The Imaginative Architecture of a Seventh-Century Hagiographer." *Speculum* 79, no. 3 (2004).

_____. *Land of Women: Tales of Sex and Gender from Early Ireland.* Ithaca: Cornell University, 1996.

Black, Ronald, ed. *The Gaelic Otherworld: John Gregorson Campbell's Superstitions of the Highlands and Islands of Scotland and Witchcraft and Second Sight in the Highlands and Islands.* Edinburgh: Birlinn, 2005.

Bollard, John K. "Arthur in the Early Welsh Tradition." In *The Romance of Arthur: An Anthology of Medieval Texts in Translation,* James J. Wilhelm. New York: Garland, 1994.

_____, trans. *Companion Tales to the Mabinogi.* Llandysul: Gomer, 2007.

_____, trans. *The Mabinogi: Legend and Landscape of Wales.* Llandysul: Gomer, 2006.

Breatnach, Liam. "The Caldron of Poesy." *Ériu* 32 (1981).

_____. "The Chief's Poet." *Proceedings of the Royal Irish Academy,* Vol. 83c, 1983.

_____. ed. *Uraicecht na Ríar.* Dublin: Dublin Institute for Advanced Studies, 1987.

Bridgman, Timothy P. "*Keltoi, Galatai, Galli*: Were They All One People?" *Proceedings of the Harvard Celtic Colloquium,* Vol. XXV, 2005.

_____. "Names and Naming Conventions Concerning Celtic Peoples in Some Early Ancient Greek Authors." *CSANA Yearbook* 7.

Briggs, Katherine. *An Encyclopedia of Fairies.* New York: Pantheon, 1976.

_____. *The Fairies in Tradition and Literature.* London: Routledge and Kegan Paul, 1968.

Bromwich, Rachel, "The Welsh Triads." In *Arthurian Literature in the Middle Ages,* Roger S. Loomis, ed. Oxford: Oxford University Press, 2001.

_____, ed. and trans. *Trioedd Ynys Prydein: The Welsh Triads*. Cardiff: Cardiff University Press, 1978.

_____, A. O. H. Jarman, and Brynley F. Roberts. *The Arthur of the Welsh: The Arthurian Legend in Medieval Welsh Literature*. Cardiff: University of Wales Press, 2008.

Brooke, Daphne. *Saints and Goddesses: The Interface with Celtic Paganism*. Mansefield: Whithorn Trust, 1999.

Bruford, Alan. "Song and Recitation in Early Ireland." *Celtica* XXI (1990).

_____. "The Twins of Macha." *Cosmos* 5 (1989).

Bruford, A. J., and D. A. MacDonald. *Scottish Traditional Tales*. Edinburgh: Polygon, 1994.

Brunaux, Jean Louis. *The Celtic Gauls: Gods, Rites and Sanctuaries*. London: Seaby, 1987.

Buck, Carl D. *A Dictionary of Selected Synonyms in the Principal Indo-European Languages*. Chicago: University of Chicago Press, 1988.

Byrne, Cyril J., Margaret Harry, and Pádraig Ó Siadhail, eds. *Proceedings of the Second North American Congress of Celtic Studies*. Halifax: 1989.

Caerwyn Williams, J. E. "The Celtic Bard." In *A Celtic Florigelium*, Kathryn A. Klar, Eve E. Sweetser, and Claire Thomas, eds. Lawrence: Celtic Studies Publications, 1996.

_____. "The Court Poet in Medieval Ireland." Sir John Rhys Memorial Lecture, British Academy, 1972.

Caerwyn Williams, J. E., and Patrick K. Ford. *The Irish Literary Tradition*. Cardiff: University of Wales Press, 1992.

Caesar, Julius. *De Gallico Bello*: *Classic Interlinear Translations*. New York: David McKay, 1959.

Calder, George. *Auraceipt na n-Éces*. Dublin: Four Courts Press, 1995.

Campbell, Bruce. *The Oxford Book of Birds*. Oxford: Oxford University Press, 1977.

Campbell, J. F. *Popular Tales of the West Highlands*. Edinburgh: Birlinn, 1994.

Carey, John. "A British Myth of Origins?" *History of Religions*, Vol. 31, No. 1. Chicago: University of Chicago Press, 1991.

_____. "Cosmology in *Saltair na Rann*." *Celtica* XVII (1985).

_____. *Ireland and the Grail*. Aberystwyth: Celtic Studies Publications, 2007.

_____. "The Irish Otherworld: Hiberno-Latin Perspectives." *Éigse* XXV (1991).

_____. "The Location of the Otherworld in Irish Tradition." *Éigse* XIX (1982).

_____. "The Name 'Tuatha Dé Danann.'" *Éigse* XVIII.

_____. "Native Elements in Irish Pseudohistory." Doris Edel, ed. *Cultural Identity and Cultural Integration: Ireland and Europe in the Middle Ages*. Dublin: Four Courts Press, 1995.

_____. *A New Introduction to Lebor Gabála Érenn*. London: Irish Texts Society, 1993.

_____. "Nodons in Britain and Ireland." *Zeitschrift fur Celtische Philologie* 40 (1984).

_____. "Notes on the Irish War Goddess." *Éigse* XIV, pt. II (1983).

_____. "The Origin and Development of the Cesair Legend." *Éigse* XXII (1987).

_____. "Suibne Geilt and Tuán mac Cairill." *Éigse* XX (1984).

_____. "Symbol and Mystery in Irish Religious Thought." *Temenos* 13 (1992).

_____. "The Three Things Required of a Poet." *Ériu* 48 (1997).

_____. "Time, Memory and the Boyne Necropolis." *Proceedings of the Harvard Celtic Colloquium*, Vol. X, 1990.

_____. "Time, Space and the Otherworld." *Proceedings of the Harvard Celtic Colloquium*, Vol. VII, 1987.

_____. "A Tract on the Creation." *Éigse*, XXI (1986).

_____. "A *Tuath Dé* Miscellany." Bulletin of the Board of Celtic Studies 39, 1992.

_____. "Vernacular Irish Learning: Three Notes." *Éigse* XXIV (1990).

Carey, John, John Koch, and Pierre-Yves Lambert, eds. *Ildánach Ildírech*: *A Festshrift for Proinsias MacCana*. Andover and Aberystwytha; Celtic Studies Publications, 1999.

Carmichael, Alexander. *Carmina Gadelica*. Hudson: Lindisfarne, 1992.

Carney, James, ed. *Early Irish Poetry*. Cork: Mercier, 1965.

Chadbourne, Kathryn. "The Celtic Otherworld." *Cosmos* 14, no. 2 (1988).

_____. "Giant Women and Flying Machines." *Proceedings of the Harvard Celtic Colloquium,* Vol. XIV, 1994.

Chadwick, H. M., and N. K. Chadwick. *The Growth of Literature, Volume 1.* Cambridge: Cambridge University Press, 1986.

Chadwick, Nora. *Celtic Britain*. North Hollywood: Newcastle, 1989.

_____. "Dreams in Early European Literature." In *Celtic Studies Essays in Memory of Angus Matheson*, James Carney and David Greene, eds. New York: Barnes and Noble, 1968.

_____. "Geilt." *Scottish Gaelic Studies* V, pt. 1 (1942).

_____. "Imbas Forosnai." *Scottish Gaelic Studies* IV, pt. II (1935).

_____. *Poetry and Prophesy*. Cambridge: Cambridge University Press, 1952.

Champion, Timothy. "Power, Politics and Status." In *The Celtic World*, Miranda Green, ed. London: Routledge, 1995.

Charles-Edwards, Thomas. "The Arthur of History." In *The Arthur of the Welsh*, Rachel Bromwich, A. O. H. Jarman, and Brynley Roberts, eds. Cardiff: University of Wales Press, 2008.

_____. *The Early Medieval Gaelic Lawyer*. Cambridge: University of Cambridge Press, 1999.

Clarke, Basil, trans. *Life of Merlin*: *Vita Merlini by*

Geoffrey of Monmouth. Cardiff: University of Wales Press, 1973.

Coe, Jon B., and Simon Young. *The Celtic Sources for the Arthurian Legend.* Felinfach: Llanerch, 1995.

Conner, Nancy. *Shamans of the World.* Boulder: Sounds True, 2008.

Conran, Anthony. *Welsh Verse.* Bridgend: Seren, 1993.

Cross, Tom P., and Clark H. Slover. *Ancient Irish Tales.* New Jersey: Barnes and Noble, 1981.

Cunliffe, Barry. *The Ancient Celts.* Oxford: Oxford University Press, 1997.

_____. *The Celtic World.* New York: McGraw Hill, 1979.

_____. *The Celts — A Very Short Introduction.* Oxford: Oxford University Press, 2003.

_____. *Druids — A Very Short Introduction.* Oxford: Oxford University Press, 2010.

_____. *Iron Age Britain.* London: Batsford, 1997.

_____. *The Oxford Illustrated History of Prehistoric Europe.* Oxford: Oxford University Press, 2001.

Curtin, Jeremiah. *Hero-Tales of Ireland.* Boston: Little, Brown, 1894.

Danaher, Kevin. *The Year in Ireland: Irish Calendar Customs.* Cork: Mercier, 1972.

Darling, F. Fraser, and J. Morton Boyd. *The Highlands and Islands.* London: Fontana, 1969.

Darwin, Tess. *The Scots Herbal: The Plant Lore of Scotland.* Edinburgh: Mercat Press, 1996.

Darvill, Timothy. *Prehistoric Britain.* London: Routledge, 1996.

Davidson, Hilda Ellis. *Gods and Myths of Northern Europe.* London: Penguin, 1964.

_____. *Myths and Symbols in Pagan Europe.* Syracuse: Syracuse University Press, 1988.

Davies, Owen. *Popular Magic: Cunning-folk in English History.* London: Hambledon Continuum, 2007.

Davies, Sioned. *The Mabinogion.* Oxford: Oxford University Press, 2007.

_____, and Nerys Ann Jones, eds. *The Horse in Celtic Culture.* Cardiff: University of Wales Press, 1997.

Demakopoulou, Katie, Christiane Eluère, Jorgen Jensen, Albrecht Jockenhovel, and Jean-Pierre Mohen. *Gods and Heroes of the European Bronze Age.* New York: Thames and Hudson, 1999.

Dillon, Myles. "The Archaism of Irish Tradition." *Proceedings of the British Academy*, Vol. XXXIII, 1947.

_____. "The Consecration of Irish Kings." *Celtica* X, 1973.

_____. *The Cycles of the Kings.* Dublin: Four Courts Press, 1994.

_____. *Early Irish Literature.* Dublin: Four Courts Press, 1997.

_____, ed. *Serglige Con Culainn.* Dublin: Dublin Institute for Advanced Studies, 1975.

_____. "Wasting Sickness of Cú Chulainn." *Scottish Gaelic Studies*, Vol. 7.

Dillon, Myles, and Nora Chadwick. *The Celtic Realms.* London: Phoenix Press, 2000.

Dinneen, Patrick. *Foclóir Gaedilge agus Béarla.* Dublin: Irish Texts Society, 1996.

Dinneen, P. S., ed. *The History of Ireland: Forus Feasa ar Eirenn, by Geoffrey Keating.* London: 1908–1914.

Dooley, Ann, and Harry Roe. *Tales of the Elders of Ireland.* Oxford: Oxford University Press, 1999.

Dumézil, Georges. *The Destiny of a King.* Chicago: University of Chicago Press, 1988.

_____. "*Le Puits de Nechtan.*" *Celtica* VI (1963).

Dumville, David. "*Echtrae* and *Immram*: Some Problems of Definition." *Ériu* XVIII (1976).

Duval, Paul-Marie, and Georges Pinault. XLViéme supplément á *Gallia, Recueil des inscriptions gauloises*, vol. III *Les Calendriers: Coligny, Villards d'Héria.* Paris: 1986.

Dwelly, Edward. *Faclair Gaidhlig gu Beurla.* Glasgow: Gairm, 1994.

Edel, Doris, ed. *Cultural Identity and Cultural Integration: Ireland and Europe in the Middle Ages.* Dublin: Four Courts Press, 1995.

Eliade, Mircea. *The Myth of the Eternal Return.* 1954; Rprt., Princeton: Princeton University Press, 1971.

_____. *Rites and Symbols of Initiation.* Woodstock: Spring Publications, 1995.

_____. *The Sacred and the Profane: The Nature of Religion.* San Diego: Harcourt Brace, 1957.

_____. *Shamanism: Archaic Techniques of Ecstasy.* Princeton: Princeton University Press, 1974.

Enright, Michael J. *Lady with a Mead Cup: Ritual, Prophecy and Lordship in the European Warband from La Tène to the Viking Age.* Dublin: Four Courts Press, 1996.

Eogan, George. *Knowth and the Passage-Tombs of Ireland.* London: Thames and Hudson, 1986.

Eska, Charlene M. *Cáin Lánamna: An Old Irish Tract on Marriage and Divorce Law.* Leidon and Boston: Brill, 2010.

Eska, Joseph P. "Remarks on Linguistic Structures in a Gaulish Ritual Text." In "Indo-European Perspectives," R. V. South, ed. *Journal of Indo-European Studies*, Monograph 43 (2002).

Evans, E. Estyn. *Irish Folk Ways.* London: Routledge, 1976.

Evans, H. M., and W. O. Thomas. *Y Geiriadur Mawr.* Llandybie: Gomer, 2001.

Evans-Wentz, W. Y. *The Fairy Faith in Celtic Countries.* New York: Citadel, 1990.

Fenster, Thelma S., ed. *Arthurian Women.* New York: Routledge, 2000.

Findon, Joanne. *A Woman's Words: Emer and Female Speech in the Ulster Cycle.* Toronto: University of Toronto Press, 1997.

Fitter, Richard, Alasdair Fitter, and Marjorie Blamey. *The Wild Flowers of Britain and Northern Europe.* London: William Collins, 1974.

Flanagan, Deirdre, and Laurence Flanagan. *Irish Place Names.* Dublin: Gill and Macmillan, 2002.

Flower, Robin. *The Irish Tradition*. Oxford: Oxford University Press, 1947.

Ford, Patrick K., ed. *Celtic Folklore and Christianity*. Los Angeles: University of California Press, 1983.

_____. *The Celtic Poets*. Belmont: Ford and Bailie, 1999.

_____. "Celtic Women: The Opposing Sex." *Viator* 19 (1988).

_____. "A Fragment of the Hanes Taliesin by Llywellyn Siôn." *Revue Celtique* XIV (1975).

_____. *The Mabinogi and Other Medieval Welsh Tales*. Berkeley: University of California Press, 1977.

_____. "The Well of Nechtan and '*La Gloire Lumineuse*.'" In *Myth in Indo-European Antiquity*, Gerald J. Larson, ed. Los Angeles: University of California, 1974.

Foster, Idris. "Culhwch and Olwen." In *The Romance of Arthur: An Anthology of Medieval Texts in Translation,* James J. Wilhelm. New York: Garland, 1994.

_____. "Culhwch and Olwen and Rhonabwy's Dream," in *Arthurian Literature in the Middle Ages*, Roger Loomis, ed. Oxford: Oxford University Press, 2001.

Freeman, Philip. *War, Women and Druids: Eyewitness Reports and Early Accounts of the Ancient Celts*. Austin: University of Texas Press, 2002.

Friel, Brian. *The Last of the Name*. Nashville: J. S. Sanders, 1999.

Gantz, Jeffrey. *Early Irish Myths and Sagas*. London and New York: Penguin, 1981.

Gillies, William. "The Classical Irish Poetic Tradition." *Proceedings of the Seventh International Congress of Celtic Studies*, Oxford, July 1983.

Gourvest, Jacques. "*Le Culte de Belenos*." *Ogam* VI (1954).

Grant, I. F. *Highland Folk Ways*. London: Routledge, 1989.

_____, and Hugh Cheape. *Periods in Highland History*. London: Shepheard-Walwyn, 1997.

Gray, Elizabeth. *Cath Maige Tuired*. Naas: Irish Texts Society, 1982.

Green, Miranda. *Animals in Celtic Life and Myth*. New York: Routledge, 1992.

_____. *Celtic Goddesses*. New York: George Braziller, 1996.

_____, ed. *The Celtic World*. London: Routledge, 1995.

_____. "The Gods and the Supernatural." *The Celtic World*. London: Routledge, 1995.

_____. "The Symbolic Horse in Pagan Celtic Europe: An Archaeological Perspective." In *The Horse in Celtic Culture*, Sioned Davies and Nerys Ann Jones, eds. Cardiff: University of Wales Press, 1997.

Gregory, Lady. *Visions and Belief in the West of Ireland*. Gerrards Cross: Colin Smythe, 1992.

Gricourt, Jean. "Epona-Rhiannon-Macha." *Ogam* VI (1954).

Gwyndaf, Robin. "Fairylore: Memorates and Legends from Welsh Oral Tradition." In *The Good People: New Fairylore Essays*, Peter Narváez, ed. Lexington: University of Kentucky Press, 1997.

_____. *Welsh Folk Tales*. Cardiff: Amgueddfeydd Ac Orielau Cenedlaethol Cymru, 1999.

Gwynn, Edward. *The Metrical Dindsenchas*. 5 Vol. Dublin: Royal Irish Academy, 1991.

Gwynn, E. J. "An Old-Irish Tract on the Privileges and Responsibilities of Poets." *Ériu* 13, Pt. 1 (1940).

Halifax, Joan. *The Fruitful Darkness*. San Francisco: Harper, 1993.

_____. *Shamanic Voices*. London: Penguin, 1992.

Hamilton, Noel. "Ancient Irish Music." *Proceedings of the 1st North American Congress of Celtic Studies*, Gordon W. MacLennan, ed., Ottawa, 1986.

Hamp, Eric P. "British Celtic *Brige* and Morphology." *Studia Celtica* XXVI–XXVII (1991–1992).

_____. "*imbolc, óimelc*." *Studia Celtica* 14–15 (1979–1980).

_____. "Mabinogi." *THSC* (1974–1975).

_____. "Mabinogi and Archaism." *Celtica* XXIII (1999).

Handford, S. A., ed. *Caesar: The Conquest of Gaul*. London: Penguin, 1982.

Harbison, Peter. *Pre-Christian Ireland*. London: Thames and Hudson, 1988.

Haycock, Marged. *The Legendary Poems from the Book of Taliesin*. Aberystwyth: CMCS Publications, 2007.

_____. "'Preiddeu Annwn' and the Figure of Taliesin." *Studia Celtica* XVIII–XIX (1983–1984).

Henderson, Lizanne, and Edward J. Cowan. *Scottish Fairy Belief*. East Linton: Tuckwell, 2001.

Henry, P. L. "The Caldron of Poesy." *Studia Celtica* 14–15 (1979–1980).

Herbert, Maire. "Goddess and King: The Sacred Marriage in Early Ireland." *Cosmos* 7 (1992).

_____. "Some Irish Prognostications." *Éigse* XIV, Pt. IV (1972).

Herity, Michael, and George Eogan. *Ireland in Prehistory*. New York: Routledge, 1996.

Higginson, Thomas Wentworth. *Tales of the Enchanted Isles*. New York: Chelsea House, 1983.

Hillers, Barbara, "Music from the Otherworld: Modern Gaelic Legends About Fairy Music." *Proceedings of the Harvard Celtic Colloquium,* Vol. XIV, 1994.

Hull, Vernum, "De Gabáil in t-Sída." *Zeitschrift fur Celtische Philologie* XIX (1933).

Hyde, Douglas, *The Stone of Truth and Other Irish Folktales*. Dublin: Irish Academic Press, 1979.

Ireland, Stanley. *Roman Britain: A Sourcebook*. London: Routledge, 1986.

Jackson, Kenneth. "The Arthur of History." In *Arthurian Literature in the Middle Ages*, Roger S. Loomis, ed. Oxford: Oxford University Press, 2001.

_____. *A Celtic Miscellany*. New York: Dorset Press, 1986.

_____. *Studies in Early Celtic Nature Poetry*. Cambridge: Cambridge University Press, 1935.

Jarman, A. O. H. "The Merlin Legend and the Welsh Tradition of Prophecy." In *The Arthur of the Welsh: The Arthurian Legend in Medieval Welsh Literature*. Cardiff: University of Wales Press, 2008.

_____. "The Welsh Myrddin Poems." In *Arthurian Literature in the Middle Ages*, Roger S. Loomis, ed. Oxford: Oxford University Press, 2001.

_____, and Gwilym Rees Hughes. *A Guide to Welsh Literature, Volume 1*. Cardiff: University of Wales Press, 1992.

_____. *A Guide to Welsh Literature, Volume 2*. Llandybie: Christopher Davies, 1984.

Jones, Gwyn, and Thomas Jones. *The Mabinogion*. London: John Dent, 1993.

Kalweit, Holger. *Dreamtime and Inner Space*. Boston: Shambhala, 1988.

_____. *Shamans, Healers and Medicine Men*. Boston: Shambala Press, 2000.

Keefer, Sarah L. "The Lost Tale of Dylan in the Fourth Branch of the *Mabinogi*." *Studia Celtica* XXIV–XXV (1989–1990).

Kelekna, Pita. *The Horse in Human History*. Cambridge: Cambridge University Press, 2009.

Kelly, Eamonn P. *Early Celtic Art in Ireland*. Dublin: National Museum of Ireland, 1993.

Kelly, Fergus. *Audacht Morainn*. Dublin: Dublin Institute for Advanced Studies, 1976.

_____. *A Guide to Early Irish Law*. Dublin: Dublin Institute for Advanced Studies, 1998.

_____. "The Old Irish Tree List." *Celtica* XI (1976).

Kinsella, Thomas. *The New Oxford Book of Irish Verse*. Oxford: Oxford University Press, 1979.

_____. *The Táin*. Oxford: Oxford University Press, 1969.

Klar, Kathryn A., Eve E. Sweetser, and Claire Thomas, eds. *A Celtic Florigelium*. Lawrence: Celtic Studies Publications, 1996.

Knott, Eleanor. *Irish Classical Poetry*. Dublin: Coman Cultúra Éireann, 1960.

_____, and Gerard Murphy. *Early Irish Literature*. New York: Barnes and Noble, 1966.

Koch, John. "New Thoughts on *Albion, Ierne* and the Pretanic Isles (Part One)." *Proceedings of the Harvard Celtic Colloquium*, Vol. VI, 1986.

_____. "Some Suggestions and Etymologies Reflecting on the Mythology of the Four Branches." *Proceedings of the Harvard Celtic Colloquium*, Vol. IX, 1989.

_____, and John Carey. *Celtic Heroic Age*. Oakville and Aberystwyth: Celtic Studies Publications, 2000.

Kruta, Venceslas. "Celtic Religion." *The Celts*. New York: Rizzoli, 1997.

_____, ed., *The Celts*. New York: Rizzoli, 1997.

_____. *The Celts: History and Civilization*. London: Hachette, 2004.

Laing, Lloyd, and Jenny Laing. *The Picts and the Scots*. Stroud: Wrens Park, 1993.

Lang, David C. *The Complete Book of British Berries*. London: Threshold, 1987.

Larner, Christina. *Enemies of God: The Witch-hunt in Scotland*. Baltimore: Johns Hopkins University Press, 1981.

Larson, Gerald J., ed. *Myth in Indo-European Antiquity*. Los Angeles: University of California, 1974.

Lazar-Meyn, Heidi Ann. "Colour Terms in *Táin Bó Cuailgne*." *Ulidia* (1994).

Lehmacher, Gustav. "The Ancient Celtic Year." *The Journal of Celtic Studies*, Vol. One (1949–1950).

Lehman, Edyta. "'And thus I will it': Queen Medb and the Will to Power." *Proceedings of the Harvard Celtic Colloquium*, Vol. XXVIII, 2008.

Lenihan, Edmund. *In Search of Biddy Early*. Cork: Mercier, 1987.

Le Roux, Francoise M. "Les Îles au Nord du Monde." In *Hommages à Albert Grenier*, Marcel Renard, ed. Brussels: Latomus, 1962.

Levin, Theodore. *Where Rivers and Mountains Sing: Music and Nomadism in Tuva and Beyond*. Bloomington: Indiana University Press, 1996.

Lincoln, Bruce. *Myth, Cosmos and Society*. Cambridge: Harvard University Press, 1986.

Lindahl, Carl, John McNamara, and John Lindow. *Medieval Folklore*. Oxford: Oxford University Press, 2002.

Lindow, John. *Norse Mythology*. Oxford: Oxford University Press, 2001.

Livingstone, Sheila. *Scottish Customs*. New York: Barnes and Noble, 1997.

Lloyd-Morgan, Glenys. "Appearance, Life and Leisure." In *The Celtic World*, Miranda Green, ed. London: Routledge, 1995.

Logan, Patrick. *The Holy Wells of Ireland*. Gerrards Cross: Colin Smythe, 1980.

Loomis, Roger S. "Arthur in Geoffrey of Monmouth." In *The Romance of Arthur: An Anthology of Medieval Texts in Translation*, James J. Wilhelm. New York: Garland, 1994.

_____, ed. *Arthurian Literature in the Middle Ages*. Oxford: Oxford University Press, 2001.

_____. *The Development of Arthurian Romance*. New York: Norton, 1963.

_____. "Layamon's *Brut*." *Arthurian Literature in the Middle Ages*. Oxford: Oxford University Press, 2001.

_____. "The Legend of Arthur's Survival." In *Arthurian Literature in the Middle Ages*. Oxford: Oxford University Press, 2001.

_____. "The Oral Diffusion of the Arthurian Legend." In *Arthurian Literature in the Middle Ages*. Oxford: Oxford University Press, 2001.

Lucas, A. T. "The Sacred Trees of Ireland." *Journal of the Cork Historical and Archaeological Society* LXVIII (1963).

Lyle, Emily. *Archaic Cosmos.* Edinburgh: University of Edinburgh Press, 1997.

_____. "Old Myth and New Morality: A Theogonic Interpretation of the Fourth Branch of the *Mabinogi.*" *Cosmos* 5, 1989.

_____. *Scottish Ballads.* New York: Barnes and Noble, 1994.

Lynn, Chris. "That Mound Again: The Navan Excavations Revisited." *Emania* 15 (1996).

Lysaght, Patricia. *The Banshee: The Irish Death Messenger.* Boulder: Roberts Rinehart, 1986.

MacAlister, R. A. S. *Lebor Gábala Érenn.* London: Irish Texts Society, 1997.

_____. *The Secret Languages of Ireland.* Cambridge: Cambridge University Press, 1937.

Mac Cana, Proinsias. "Aspects of the Theme of King and Goddess in Irish Literature." *Études Celtiques* VII (1995).

_____. "Celtic Goddesses of Sovereignty." In *Goddesses Who Rule*, Elisabeth Bernard and Beverly Moon, eds. Oxford: Oxford University Press, 2000.

_____. *Celtic Mythology.* New York: Peter Bedrick, 1987.

_____. *The Mabinogi.* Cardiff: University of Wales Press, 1992.

_____. "Placenames and Mythology in Irish Tradition: Places, Pilgrimages and Things." *Proceedings of the First North American Congress of Celtic Studies*, 1986.

Mac Coitir, Niall. *Irish Wild Plants: Myths, Legends and Folklore.* Wilton: Collins Press, 2008.

MacLeod Estate Office. *Dunvegan Castle.* Isle of Skye: 2003.

MacLeod, Sharon Paice. "Abduction, Swordplay, Monsters and Mistrust: Findabair, Gwenhywfar and the Restoration of Honour." *Proceedings of the Harvard Celtic Colloquium*, Vol. XXVIII, 2008.

_____. "A Confluence of Wisdom: The Symbolism of Wells, Whirlpools, Waterfalls and Rivers in Early Celtic Sources." *Proceedings of the Harvard Celtic Colloquium*, Vol. XXVII, 2007.

_____. "The Descent of the Gods: Creation, Cosmogony and Divine Order in *Lebor Gabála.*" *Proceedings of the Harvard Celtic Colloquium*, Vol. XXI, 2001.

_____. "*Éicse, Gáeth ocus Muir*: Three Notes on Archaic Celtic Cosmology." *Cosmos: A Journal of the Traditional Cosmology Society* 18 (2002).

_____. *The Hazel of Immortality*, Lecture notes (unpublished) for GSAS Research Lecture, Harvard University, Department of Celtic Languages and Literatures, December 2000.

_____. "*Mater Deorum Hibernensium*: Identity and Cross-Correlation in Early Irish Myth." *Proceedings of the Harvard Celtic Colloquium*, Vol. XIX, 1999.

_____. "*Oenach Aimsire na mBán*: Early Irish Seasonal Celebrations, Gender Roles and Seasonal Cycles." *Proceedings of the Harvard Celtic Colloquium*, Vol. XXIII, 2003.

Mac Mathúna, Liam. "The Christianization of the Early Irish Cosmos?" *Zeitschrift fur Celtische Philologie* 45–50 (1997).

_____. "Irish Perceptions of the Cosmos." *Celtica* XXIII (1999).

Mac Mathúna, Séamus. *Immram Brain: Bran's Journey to the Land of the Women.* Tubingen: Niemeyer, 1985.

MacNally, L. *Highland Year.* London: Pan Books, 1972.

MacNeill, Eóin. "On the Notation and Chronography of the Calendar of Coligny." *Ériu* X (1926–1928).

MacNeill, Máire. *The Festival of Lughnasa.* Oxford: Oxford University Press, 2008.

Mallory, J. P. "The Archaeology of the Irish Dreamtime." *Proceedings of the Harvard Celtic Colloquium,* Vol. XIII, 1993.

_____. ed. *Aspects of the Táin.* Belfast: December Publications, 1992.

_____. "The Career of Conall Cernach." *Emania* 6 (1989).

_____. "Excavations at Haughey's Fort: 1989–1990." *Emania* 8 (1991).

_____. *In Search of the Indo-Europeans.* London: Thames and Hudson, 1989.

Martin, Martin. *A Description of the Western Islands of Scotland — Circa 1695.* Edinburgh: Birlinn, 1999.

Matonis, A. T. E., and Daniel F. Melia. *Celtic Language, Celtic Culture: A Festschrift for Eric P. Hamp.* Van Nuys: Ford and Bailie, 1990.

Mattingly, H., and S. A. Handford, eds. *Tacitus: The Agricola and the Germania.* London: Penguin, 1970.

McCone, Kim. *The Celtic Question: Modern Constructs and Ancient Realities.* Dublin: Myles Dillon Memorial Lecture, 2008.

McKenna, Katherine. "Between Two Worlds: Saint Brigit and Pre-Christian Religion in the *Prima Vita.*" In *Identifying the "Celtic,"* Joseph Falaky Nagy, ed. CSANA Yearbook 2 (2002).

McKenna, Lambert, ed. *Bardic Syntactical Tracts.* Dublin: Dublin Institute for Advanced Studies, 1979.

McLaughlin, Roisin. *Early Irish Satire.* Dublin: Dublin Institute for Advanced Studies, 2008.

McManus, Damian. *A Guide to Ogam.* Maynooth: An Sagart, 1997.

McNeill, F. Marian. *The Silver Bough: A Four Volume Study of the National and Local Festivals of Scotland.* 1959. Reprint, Glasgow: Maclellan, 1971.

Megaw, Ruth, and Vincent Megaw. *Celtic Art: From its Beginnings to the Book of Kells.* London: Thames and Hudson, 1989.

Melia, Daniel F. "Law and the Shaman Saint." In *Celtic Folklore and Christianity*, Patrick K. Ford, ed. Los Angeles: University of California Press, 1983.

Meyer, Kuno. *Fianaighecht: Irish Poems and Tales Relating to Finn and His Fiana.* Dublin: Dublin Institute for Advanced Studies, 1993.

_____. *Selections from Ancient Irish Poetry.* London: 1911.

_____. *Tecosca Cormaic: The Instructions of King Cormac mac Airt.* Dublin: Todd Lecture Series 15, 1909.

_____. *The Triads of Ireland.* Dublin: Todd Lecture Series 13, 1906.

Mitchell, G. Frank, ed., *Treasures of Early Irish Art—1500 B.C. to 1500 A.D.* New York: Metropolitan Museum of Art, 1978.

Morford, Mark P. O., and Robert J. Lenardon. *Classical Mythology.* New York: Longman, 1991.

Muller-Lisowski, Kate. "Contributions to a Study of Irish Folklore: Traditions about Donn." *Béaloideas* 18, 1945.

_____. "Donn Firinne, *Tech Duin, An Tarbh.*" *Études Celtiques* VI (1953–1954).

Murphy, Gerard, ed. *Duanaire Finn.* Dublin: Irish Texts Society, 1953.

_____. *Early Irish Lyrics.* Oxford: Oxford University Press, 1956.

_____. *Early Irish Metrics.* Dublin: Royal Irish Academy, 1961.

Murray, Kevin, ed. *Baile in Scáil.* London: Irish Texts Society, 2004.

Nagy, Joseph Falaky. "The Herons of Druim Ceat Revisiting, and Revisited." *Celtica* XXI (1990).

_____, ed. *Identifying the "Celtic."* CSANA Yearbook 2 (2002).

_____. "Intervention and Disruption in the Myths of Finn and Sigurd." *Ériu* 31 (1980).

_____. "Liminality and Knowledge in Irish Tradition." *Studia Celtica* XVI–XVII (1981–1982).

_____. "The Wisdom of the Geilt." *Éigse* XIX (1982).

Narby, Jeremy, and Francis Huxley. *Shamans Through Time: 500 Years on the Path to Knowledge.* New York: Penguin, 2004.

Narváez, Peter, ed. *The Good People: New Fairylore Essays.* Lexington: University of Kentucky Press, 1997.

Néill, Uilleam. *Buile Shuibhne.* Inbhirnis: Club Leabhar, 1974.

Newall, Venetia. *The Witch in History.* New York: Barnes and Noble, 1996.

Newton, Michael. *A Handbook of the Scottish Gaelic World.* Dublin: Four Courts Press, 2000.

_____. *Warriors of the Word: The World of the Scottish Highlanders.* Edinburgh: Birlinn, 2009.

NicMhacha, Sharynne MacLeod. *Queen of the Night.* Boston: Weiser, 2005.

_____. "Second Sight and Healing Charms: Cultural Transmission and Survivals of Celtic Shamanism." In *Shamanism: Journal of the Foundation for Shamanic Studies.* Mill Valley: Foundation for Shamanic Studies, 2007.

Nicolaisen, W. F. H. *The Picts and Their Place-Names.* Rosemarkie: Groam House Museum Trust, 1996.

Nicolson, Alexander, ed. *Gaelic Proverbs.* Edinburgh: Birlinn, 1996.

Ní Shéaghda, Nessa. *Tóruigheacht Dhiarmada agus Ghráinne.* Dublin: Irish Texts Society, 1967.

Normand, Lawrence, and Gareth Roberts. *Witchcraft in Early Modern Scotland.* Exeter: University of Exeter Press, 2000.

O'Brien, M. A., ed. *Corpus Genealogiarum Hiberniae.* Dublin: Dublin Institute for Advanced Studies, 1976.

Ó Broin, Tomás. "*Lia Fáil*: Fact and Fiction in the Tradition." *Celtica* XXI (1990)

Ó Catháin, Seamas. "Hearth-Prayers and Other Traditions of Brigit: Celtic Goddess and Holy Woman." *JRSAI* 22 (1982).

Ó Cathasaigh, Tomás. "The Eponym of Cnogba." *Éigse* XXIII (1989).

_____. *The Heroic Biography of Cormac mac Airt.* Dublin: Dublin Institute for Advanced Studies, 1977.

_____. "The Semantics of *Síd.*" *Éigse* XVII, Pt. II.

Ó Crualaoich, Gearóid. *The Book of the Cailleach.* Cork: Cork University Press, 2003.

_____. "Continuity and Adaptation in Legends of Cailleach Bheara." *Béaloideas* 56 (1988).

_____. "Non-Sovereignty Queen Aspects of the Otherworld Female in Irish Hag Legends: The Case of the Cailleach Bhéarra." *Béaloideas* 62–63 (1994–1995).

Ó Cuív, Brian. "The Romance of Mis and Dubh Ruis." *Celtica* 2, Pt. 2 (1954).

Ó Dónaill, Niall. *Foclóir Gaeilge-Béarla.* Baile Átha Cliath: An Gúm, 1992.

O'Driscoll, Robert, ed. *The Celtic Consciousness.* New York: George Braziller, 1982.

Ó Duinn, Séan. *Forbhais Droma Damhghaire.* Dublin: Mercier Press, 1992.

O'Dwyer, Simon. *Prehistoric Music of Ireland.* Stroud: Tempus, 2004.

O'Grady, Standish H., ed. and trans. *Silva Gadelica.* New York: Lemma, 1970.

Ó hAodha, Donncha, ed. *Bethu Brigte.* Dublin: Dublin Institute for Advanced Studies, 1978.

O'Kelly, Michael J. *Newgrange: Archaeology, Art and Legend.* London: Thames and Hudson, 1982.

Oliver, Lisi, ed. *Watkins, Calvert: Selected Writings,* Vol. II. Innsbruck: 1994.

Ó Madagáin, Breandáin. "Echoes of Magic in the Gaelic Song Tradition." *Proceedings of the Second North American Congress of Celtic Studies,* Cyril J. Byrne, Margaret Harry, and Pádraig Ó Siadhail, eds., Halifax, 1989.

O'Meara, John J., ed. *Gerald of Wales: The History and Topography of Ireland.* London: Penguin, 1982.

O'Rahilly, Cecile. *Táin Bó Cúailgne,* Rescension I. Dublin: Dublin Institute for Advanced Studies, 1976.

O'Rahilly, Thomas F. *Early Irish History and Mythology*. Dublin: Dublin Institute for Advanced Studies, 1984.

Ó Riain, Pádraig. "A Study of the Irish Legend of the Wild Man." *Éigse* XIV (1972).

Osbon, Diane K., ed. *A Joseph Campbell Companion*. New York: Harper Collins, 1991.

O'Sullivan, Sean. *Folktales of Ireland*. Chicago: University of Chicago Press, 1966.

Owen, Trefor M. *Welsh Folk Customs*. Llandysul: Gomer, 1987.

Padel, Oliver J. *Arthur in Medieval Welsh Literature*. Cardiff: University of Wales Press, 2000.

Parry, John, and Robert Caldwell. "Geoffrey of Monmouth." In *Arthurian Literature in the Middle Ages*, Roger S. Loomis, ed. Oxford: Oxford University Press, 2001.

Partridge, Angela. "Wild Men and Wailing Women." *Éigse* XVIII, Pt. 1.

Patterson, Nerys. *Cattle Lords and Clansmen*. Notre Dame: University of Notre Dame Press, 1994.

Philip, Neil, ed. *The Penguin Book of Scottish Folktales*. London: Penguin, 1995.

Piggott, Stuart. *The Druids*. New York: Thames and Hudson, 1975.

Pokorny, J. ed. "On the Briatharthecosc Conculaind." *Zeitschrift fur Celtische Philologie* XV (1925).

Powell, T. G. E. *The Celts*. New York: Thames and Hudson, 1980.

Pughe John, ed. *The Physicians of Myddfai*. Felinfach: Llanerch, 1993.

Puhvel, Jaan. *Comparative Mythology*. Baltimore: Johns Hopkins University Press, 1987.

Purser, John. *Scotland's Music*. Edinburgh: Mainstream Publications, 1992.

Quin, E. G., ed. *Dictionary of the Irish Language: Based Mainly on Old and Middle Irish Materials. (DIL)*. Dublin: Royal Irish Academy, 1983.

Raftery, Barry. *Pagan Celtic Ireland*. London: Thames and Hudson, 1994.

Rankin, David. *Celts and the Classical World*. London: Routledge, 1987.

Rees, Alwyn, and Brinley Rees. *Celtic Heritage*. New York: Thames and Hudson, 1961.

Renard, Marcel, ed. *Hommages à Albert Grenier*. Brussels: Latomus, 1962.

Renfrew, Jane. *Food and Cooking in Prehistoric Britain*. English Heritage, 1985.

Ritchie, Graham, and Anna Ritchie. *Scotland: Archaeology and Early History*. Edinburgh: Edinburgh University Press, 1991.

Rivet, A. L.F., and Colin Smith. *The Place-Names of Roman Britain*. London: Batsford, 1981.

Roberts, Brynley F. "*Culhwch ac Olwen,* The Triads, Saints' Lives." *The Arthur of the Welsh: The Arthurian Legend in Medieval Welsh Literature*. Cardiff: University of Wales Press, 2008.

_____. "Geoffrey of Monmouth, *Historia Brittaniae* and *Brut y Brenhinedd.*" *The Arthur of the Welsh: The Arthurian Legend in Medieval Welsh Literature*. Cardiff: University of Wales Press, 2008.

Romer, F. E. *Pomponius Mela's Description of the World*. Ann Arbor: University of Michigan Press, 1998.

Ross, Anne. "The Divine Hag of the Pagan Celts." in *The Witch Figure*, Venetia Newall, ed. New York: Barnes and Noble, 1996.

_____. *The Folklore of the Scottish Highlands*. New York: Barnes and Noble, 1993.

_____. *Folklore of Wales*. Stroud: Tempest, 2001.

_____. *Pagan Celtic Britain*. Chicago: Academy, 1996.

_____. *The Pagan Celts*. Ruthin: John Jones, 1998.

Rowlands, E. I. "Bardic Lore and Education." *Bulletin of the Board of Celtic Studies*, Vol. XXXII (1985).

Rowlett, Ralph M. "North Gaulish Forms on the Gundestrup Cauldron." *Proceedings of the Harvard Celtic Colloquium,* Vol. XXIII, 1993.

Ryan, Michael, ed. *The Illustrated Archaeology of Ireland*. Dublin: Country House, 1991.

Sailer, Susan Shaw. "Leaps, Curses and Flight: Suibne Geilt and the Roots of Early Irish Culture." *Études Celtiques* XXIII (1997).

Seymour, St. John D. *Irish Witchcraft and Demonology*. New York: Dorset, 1992.

Scowcroft, R. Mark. "*Leabhar Gabhála*— Part I: The Growth of the Text." *Ériu* 38 (1987).

_____. "*Leabhar Gabhála*— Part II: The Growth of the Tradition, *Ériu* 39 (1988).

Shaw, Margaret Fay. *Folksongs and Folklore of South Uist*. Aberdeen: Aberdeen University Press, 1986.

Shaw-Smith, David. *Ireland's Traditional Crafts*. London: Thames and Hudson, 1986.

Sims-Williams, Patrick. *The Celtic Inscriptions of Britain: Phonology and Chronology, c. 400–1200*. Oxford and Boston: Publications of the Philological Society, 2003.

_____. "The Early Welsh Arthurian Poems." In *The Arthur of the Welsh: The Arthurian Legend in Medieval Welsh Literature*, Rachel Bromwich, A. O. H. Jarman, and Brynley F. Roberts. Cardiff: University of Wales Press, 2008.

_____. "Some Celtic Otherworld Terms." In *Celtic Language, Celtic Culture: A Festschrift for Eric P. Hamp*, A. T. E. Matonis and Daniel F. Melia, eds. Van Nuys: Ford and Bailie, 1990.

Sjoestedt, Marie-Louise. *Gods and Heroes of the Celts*. Berkeley: Turtle Island, 1982.

Smyth, Marina. *Understanding the Universe in Seventh-Century Ireland*. Woodbridge: Boydell Press, 1996.

South, R. V., ed. *Indo-European Perspectives. Journal of Indo-European Studies*, Monograph 43 (2002).

Stacey, Robin Chapman. *Dark Speech: The Performance of Law in Early Ireland*. Philadelphia: University of Pennsylvania Press, 2007.

_____. *The Road to Judgment: From Custom to Court in Medieval Ireland and Wales.* Philadelphia: University of Pennsylvania Press, 1994.

Stead, Ian. *Celtic Art.* Cambridge: Harvard University Press, 1996.

Stokes, Whitley. "*Immacalam in Dá Thuarad.*" *Revue Celtique* 26 (1905).

_____. "*Immram curaig Maíle Dúin.*" *Revue Celtique* 9 (1888–1889).

_____. "The Prose Tales in the *Rennes Dindsenchas.*" *Revue Celtique* 15–16 (1894–1895).

_____. *Sanas Chormaic.* Calcutta: Irish Archaeological and Celtic Society, 1868.

Sutherland, Elizabeth. *A Guide to the Pictish Stones.* Edinburgh: Birlinn, 1997.

Swire, Otta F. *Skye: The Island and Its Legends.* London: Blackie and Son, 1961.

Ternes, Charles Marie, and Hartmut Zinser, eds. *Dieux des Celts.* Luxembourg: Eurassoc, 2002.

Thomas, Charles. *Celtic Britain.* London: Thames and Hudson, 1986.

Thomson, Derick. *An Introduction to Gaelic Poetry.* Edinburgh: Edinburgh University Press, 1990.

Thomson, R. L. *Pwyll Pendeuic Dyuet.* Dublin: Dublin Institute for Advanced Studies, 2003.

Thorpe, Lewis, trans. *Geoffrey of Monmouth: The History of the Kings of Britain.* Hammondsworth: Penguin, 1982.

_____, ed. *Gerald of Wales: The Journey Through Wales and the Description of Wales.* London: Penguin, 1978.

Torrance, Robert M. *The Spiritual Quest: Transcendence in Myth, Religion and Science.* Berkeley: University of California Press, 1994.

Tymoczko, Maria. "Knowledge and Vision in Early Welsh Gnomic Poetry." *Proceedings of the Harvard Celtic Colloquium,* Vol. III, 1983.

_____. "Unity and Duality: A Theoretical Perspective on the Ambivalence of Celtic Goddesses." *Proceedings of the Harvard Celtic Colloquium,* Vol. V, 1985.

Uí Ógáin, Ríonach. "Music Learned from the Fairies." *Béaloideas* 60–61 (1992–1993).

Verling, Martin, ed. *Beara Woman Talking: Folklore from the Beara Peninsula.* Collected by Tadgh Ó Murchú. Cork: Mercier Press, 2003.

Wagner, H. "Origins of Pagan Irish Religion." *Zeitschrift fur Celtische Philologie* 38 (1981).

Watkins, Calvert. *Dictionary of Indo-European Roots.* New York: Houghton Mifflin, 2000.

_____. "Indo-European Metrics and Archaic Irish Verse." *Celtica* VI (1963).

Watson, Alden. "The King, the Poet and the Sacred Tree," *Études Celtiques* XVIII (1981).

Watson, W. J. *The Celtic Placenames of Scotland.* Edinburgh: Birlinn, 1993.

Webster, Jane. "Sanctuaries and Sacred Places." In *The Celtic World,* Miranda Green, ed. London: Routledge, 1995.

West, M. L. *Indo-European Poetry and Myth.* Oxford: Oxford University Press, 2007.

White, John. *Forest and Woodland Trees in Britain.* Oxford: Oxford University Press, 1995.

Wilde, Lady. *Irish Cures, Mystic Charms and Superstitions.* New York: Sterling, 1991.

Wilhelm, James J. "Arthur in the Latin Chronicles." *The Romance of Arthur: An Anthology of Medieval Texts in Translation.* New York: Garland, 1994.

_____. "Layamon: *Brut* (The Death of Arthur)." *The Romance of Arthur: An Anthology of Medieval Texts in Translation.* New York: Garland, 1994.

_____. *The Romance of Arthur: An Anthology of Medieval Texts in Translation.* New York: Garland, 1994.

Williams, Ifor. *Lectures on Early Welsh Poetry.* Dublin: Dublin Institute for Advanced Studies, 1954.

Williamson, Henry, ed. *Nature in Britain.* London: Batsford, 1936.

Withers, Charles W. J., and R. W. Munro, eds. *A Description of the Western Islands of Scotland Circa 1695.* Edinburgh: Birlinn, 1995.

Wood, J. "The Folklore Background of the Gwion Bach Section of *Hanes Taliesin.*" *The Bulletin of the Board of Celtic Studies* 19 (1980–1982).

_____. "The Horse in Welsh Folklore: A Boundary Image in Custom and Narrative." In *The Horse in Celtic Culture,* Sioned Davies and Nerys Ann Jones, eds. Cardiff: University of Wales Press, 1997.

Yeats, W. B. *Fairy and Folk Tales of Ireland.* New York: Collier, 1983.

_____. *Writings on Irish Folklore, Legend and Myth.* Edited by Robert Welch. London: Penguin, 1993.

Youngs, Susan, ed. *The Work of Angels: Masterpieces of Celtic Metalwork, 6th–9th Centuries ad.* Austin: University of Texas Press, 1989.

Index